T0369627

International Cooperation Against All Odds

Mai'a K. Davis Cross is the Dean's Professor of Political Science, International Affairs and Diplomacy and Director of the Center for International Affairs and World Cultures at Northeastern University. She is the author of four books, including *The Politics of Crisis in Europe* (Cambridge University Press, 2017) and *Security Integration in Europe: How Knowledge-Based Networks are Transforming the European Union* (University of Michigan Press, 2011), which is the 2012 winner of the Best Book Prize from the University Association of Contemporary European Studies. She holds a PhD in Politics from Princeton University and an AB in Government from Harvard University. She is also a member of the Council on Foreign Relations.

International Cooperation Against All Odds

The Ultrasocial World

MAI'A K. DAVIS CROSS

OXFORD
UNIVERSITY PRESS

OXFORD
UNIVERSITY PRESS

Great Clarendon Street, Oxford, OX2 6DP,
United Kingdom

Oxford University Press is a department of the University of Oxford.
It furthers the University's objective of excellence in research, scholarship,
and education by publishing worldwide. Oxford is a registered trade mark of
Oxford University Press in the UK and in certain other countries

© Mai'a K. Davis Cross 2024

The moral rights of the author have been asserted

All rights reserved. No part of this publication may be reproduced, stored in
a retrieval system, or transmitted, in any form or by any means, without the
prior permission in writing of Oxford University Press, or as expressly permitted
by law, by licence or under terms agreed with the appropriate reprographics
rights organization. Enquiries concerning reproduction outside the scope of the
above should be sent to the Rights Department, Oxford University Press, at the
address above

You must not circulate this work in any other form
and you must impose this same condition on any acquirer

Published in the United States of America by Oxford University Press
198 Madison Avenue, New York, NY 10016, United States of America

British Library Cataloguing in Publication Data

Data available

Library of Congress Control Number: 2023938533

ISBN 9780192873903
ISBN 9780198894995 (pbk.)

DOI: 10.1093/oso/9780192873903.001.0001

Printed and bound by
CPI Group (UK) Ltd, Croydon, CR0 4YY

Links to third party websites are provided by Oxford in good faith and
for information only. Oxford disclaims any responsibility for the materials
contained in any third party website referenced in this work.

For Bailey and Finley

Acknowledgments

The research for this book, which began in 2016, took me in many new directions and down many new avenues of interdisciplinary research. It has truly been a challenging and rewarding adventure. I am so grateful to the people who helped me and supported me along the way. Northeastern University awarded me the Edward W. Brooke Chair from 2016 to 2022, which enabled me to travel to and consult archives in Lausanne (the Jean Monnet Foundation), Washington DC (the National Archives and the National Aeronautics and Space Administration (NASA) Headquarters Library), Fiesole, Italy (the European University Institute Historical Archives), Oslo (the Nobel Peace Institute Library), Pittsburgh (Archive of European Integration), Boston (John F. Kennedy Presidential Library and Radcliffe Institute Archives), Paris (Bibliotheque Nationale de France), Bellevue, Washington (Boeing Archives), and Vienna (UN Office for Outer Space Affairs). The archivists and librarians in each of these locations were incredibly helpful. I am especially grateful to the archivist at NASA Headquarters, Elizabeth Sukow.

My research assistants, Giuliano Espino, Justin Haner, Christopher LaGrutta, Jennifer Ostojski, and Taylor Valley were excellent contributors to this project, doing everything from archival research to final copy-editing. I am also indebted to my friend and colleague Denise Garcia, who enabled me to gain access to the United Nations COP21 in Paris as an official observer and connected me to those working on space at the United Nations in Geneva. I also received valuable feedback from a number of scholars on various sections of the book, including Thomas Christiansen, Ana Juncos, Jan Melissen, Mitchell Orenstein, Marianne Riddervold, Holbrook Robinson, Ezra Suleiman, and Asle Toje, who selected me for the Nobel Peace Institute fellowship in 2016. I am additionally grateful to Simon Duke, Teresa La Porte, and John Peterson for their strong encouragement at the earliest stages of my work.

My husband, Robert Cross, discussed so many aspects of this book with me from start to finish, and was the first to read it from cover to cover. His expansive expertise in history and political philosophy was incredibly valuable as he encouraged me to keep my analysis focused on the big picture and what I really wanted to say. My parents, Pamela J. Davis-Lee and Michael Davis, each loved the idea of the ultrasocial world from the moment I described it to them. I'm sure my own worldview was in some way instilled in me by them from an early age—the spirit of adventure, the power of possibility, the importance of ideas, and the global perspective.

As I completed the final chapter of this book, our magnificent golden retriever, Bailey, also known as Siatham Bernard, Sir Bales of Hay, passed away at the age of thirteen. Born in England, he traveled to nine countries and all forty-eight mainland US states. He also spent nearly every summer of his life in Yosemite, where many pages of this book were written. With his big smile and unabashed affection, he brought out the ultrasociality in everyone he encountered, oftentimes drawing crowds of people together. He is deeply missed. During his last two years, he instilled his ultrasocial spirit in his little brother Finley, and so this book is dedicated to them.

Contents

List of Figures

List of Tables

Introduction

The reasons to be pessimistic about the prospects for a stable, peaceful world order are all around us. From Russian aggression, to China's military build-up, to intractable conflicts in the Middle East and strained international alliances, there is much to be concerned about. Beyond the realm of high politics, regular citizens across the world suffer in many ways—climate change, terrorism, mass migration, brutal dictatorships, ethnic cleansing, and global health pandemics, just to name a few. Even in the more developed parts of the world, such as in North America and Europe, there are reasons to question whether democracy really has the longevity it was assumed to have, how economic prosperity will ever spread beyond the "one percent," and if nationalistic extremism can really be kept at bay. Indeed, many foreign policy experts and pundits have concluded that the liberal world order is likely coming to an end.[1] Capturing the climate of the times, the Bulletin of the Atomic Scientists moved the doomsday clock just ninety seconds to midnight in January 2023, the closest it has ever been.[2]

Beyond the events themselves, pessimism about the human capacity to navigate toward a brighter future on this planet is no coincidence. The scholarly study of international relations, whose theories and prescriptions regularly filter into popular discourse—from media punditry to the actions of world leaders—has largely focused on explaining why we cannot trust each other, how self-interest dominates the system of states, and why the miscalculation and fear of leaders regularly triggers brinksmanship, oftentimes spiraling to the precipice of war. One of the most fundamental mainstream assumptions in international relations, both in the

---

[1] See, e.g., Stephen M. Walt, "The Collapse of the Liberal World Order," *Foreign Policy*, June 26, 2016, https://foreignpolicy.com/2016/06/26/the-collapse-of-the-liberal-world-order-european-union-brexit-donald-trump (accessed May 22, 2023); Emile Simpson, "This Is How the Liberal World Order Ends," *Foreign Policy*, February 19, 2016, https://foreignpolicy.com/2016/02/19/this-is-how-the-liberal-world-order-ends (accessed May 22, 2023); Amitav Acharya, "After Liberal Hegemony: The Advent of a Multiplex World Order," *Ethics & International Affairs* 31, 3 (2017): 271–285, https://doi.org/10.1017/S089267941700020X; Robert Kagan, "The Twilight of the Liberal World Order," The Brookings Institution, January 24, 2017, https://www.brookings.edu/research/the-twilight-of-the-liberal-world-order (accessed May 21, 2023).

[2] In 1947, Manhattan Project scientists who deeply regretted their role in developing atomic weapons technology created the symbolic Doomsday Clock to indicate how close the world was to total destruction during any given year. They originally focused on the likelihood of fallout from nuclear war but, more recently, have included other factors in their estimates such as climate change, fake news, and drones. See Bulletin of the Atomic Scientists, "The Doomsday Clock: A Timeline of Conflict, Culture, and Change," *Bulletin of the Atomic Scientists*, n.d., http://thebulletin.org/timeline (accessed May 22, 2023).

International Cooperation Against All Odds. Mai'a K. Davis Cross, Oxford University Press. © Mai'a K. Davis Cross (2024).
DOI: 10.1093/oso/9780192873903.003.0001

scholarly and policy worlds, is that human beings maximize material self-interest in their preferences, actions, and behavior and that the international system is one of anarchy and violence. As Hans Morgenthau puts it, "All states are either preparing for, recovering from, or engaged in war."[3] In many ways, this so-called "classical realist" approach has set the parameters for how we understand world order today. Other approaches, which have less influence on foreign policy, try to avoid making any assumptions at all about human nature and, in so doing, continually cede the default high ground to realism.

The problem with allowing such pessimism to become common wisdom is that it is based on a starting point about human motivations that is, quite simply, entirely wrong.[4] As a species, we are actually *not* self-interested and power maximizing by nature. A recent groundswell of findings from a range of different fields—including neuroscience, anthropology, evolutionary biology, psychology, and ecology, among others—provides overwhelming evidence that we are actually pre-wired (enabled), hard-wired (compelled), and soft-wired (pre-disposed) to be empathic, cooperative, and socially oriented.[5] As Jeremy Rifkin writes,

> A radical new view of human nature is emerging in the biological and cognitive sciences and creating a controversy in intellectual circles, the business community, and government. Recent discoveries in brain science and child development are forcing us to rethink the long-held belief that human beings are, by nature, aggressive, materialistic, utilitarian, and self-interested. The dawning realization that we are a fundamentally empathic species has profound and far-reaching consequences for society.[6]

In other words, we are a fundamentally *ultrasocial* species. This knowledge should have a vital bearing on how we understand international relations and the potential futures we can create for ourselves and future generations.

Ultrasociality is a human predisposition to be other-regarding, empathic, and inclined to seek wide-scale cooperation, even among strangers.[7] Across the natural and social sciences, a broad array of empirical findings strongly supports the notion that we are far more prone to wide-scale cooperation than to the pursuit of

---

[3] Hans Morgenthau, *Politics among Nations: The Struggle for Power and Peace* (New York: McGraw Hill, 1985).

[4] In future chapters, I show how there have actually been many periods in which it was popular to be optimistic and forward thinking. Perhaps unlike today, cynics were considered to be more counterproductive in the quest to devise policies.

[5] For more on "pre-wired," see Nicholas Christakis, *Blueprint: The Evolutionary Origins of a Good Society* (New York: Little Brown, 2019). For more on "soft-wired," see Jeremy Rifkin, *The Empathic Civilization: The Race to Global Consciousness in a World in Crisis* (New York: TarcherPerigee, 2009).

[6] Rifkin, *The Empathic Civilization*, p. 1.

[7] The use of the term "ultrasociality" mainly appears in the field of anthropology, also in Peter Turchin, *Ultra-Society: How 10,000 Years of War Made Humans the Greatest Cooperators on Earth* (Chaplin, CT: Beresta Books, 2016).

individual self-interest. Research into the nature of human cooperation using lab experiments, big data analyses, neuro-imaging, and extensive field observations consistently reveals that we are remarkably oriented toward our fellow humans, and not just in a tit-for-tat, transactional way. Evolutionary biologists actually define a cooperator as "someone who pays a cost for another to receive a benefit."[8] For them, cooperation truly entails altruism and "restraint from competition."[9] As human evolution scholar Sarah Mathew explains,

> Humans cooperate with strangers, and cooperate in groups comprising millions of genetically unrelated individuals [. . .] Even without coercion from the state, people voluntarily cooperate: they donate blood, contribute to charity, assist in disaster relief, organize community events, protest unjust laws, give up their seat on a bus for an elderly person, return items to lost-and-found locations, give directions to travelers, etc. Even politically uncentralized societies can organize cooperation at an impressively large scale.[10]

Indeed, a team of evolutionary scientists recently found that human morality itself is universally based on cooperation and promotes cooperation.[11]

On a physical level, neuroscientists, biologists, and cognitive psychologists have discovered that the brain's default mode is to think socially, whether we intend it to or not. On a psychological level, individual humans fail to thrive if they do not have social interaction, the absence of which leads to documented illness, and even death, in infants. It has been established that the need to be social is a stronger requirement for human flourishment than even food and water.[12] Even babies as young as three months old understand fairness, cooperation, and morality. Before any significant exposure to society, infants can identify an actor (such as a puppet or a shape) as "good" if it cooperates and "bad" if it prevents cooperation.[13] Ethnographers and anthropologists have documented this in terms of identifying common human behaviors and ways of communicating across the world. These characteristics are so clearly evident that scholars have compiled a list of thousands of *human universals*, defined as, "those features of culture, society, language,

---

[8] Martin A. Nowak, "Five Rules for the Evolution of Cooperation," *Science* 314, 5805 (2006): 1560–1563, 1560, https://doi.org/10.1126/science.1133755.

[9] Robert Axelrod and William D. Hamilton, "The Evolution of Cooperation," *Science* 211, 4489 (1981): 1390–1396, https://doi.org/10.1126/science.7466396.

[10] Sarah Mathew, "Evolution of Human Cooperation," in *International Encyclopedia of the Social & Behavioral Sciences*, 2nd edn, Vol 11, ed. James D. Wright (Oxford: Elsevier, 2015), pp. 259–266.

[11] University of Oxford News, "Seven Moral Rules Found All Around the World," February 11, 2019, https://www.ox.ac.uk/news/2019-02-11-seven-moral-rules-found-all-around-world#:~:text=The %20rules%3A%20help%20your%20family,from%20all%20around%20the%20world (accessed May 20, 2023).

[12] Matthew Lieberman, *Social: Why Our Brains Are Wired to Connect* (New York: Crown Publishing Group), p. 43.

[13] Paul Bloom psychology experiments on infants in Christakis, *Blueprint*, p. 5.

behavior, and psyche for which there are no known exception."[14] Putting all of this together, there is *consilience* across multiple disciplines—independent studies of various phenomena are all reaching the same conclusion about the nature of human inclinations.[15]

While most international relations experts have long assumed, and continue to believe, that the achievement of international cooperation is the product of persuasion, bargaining, or simply happenstance of the balance of power in the international system, they do not take into account that practically from birth, humans have a basic sense of right and wrong. Every society across the planet regards cooperation—with kindness, empathy, and altruism—as virtues and cruelty toward others as immoral. Every human grouping around the world displays empathy. And yet, even the most socially oriented of international relations approaches only considers the possibility that we may be *moved* toward empathic cooperative behavior away from what they still consider to be our default of self-interest. But this has it exactly backwards. In actuality, we are *anchored* in cooperative behavior. And this is not just *any* cooperation but empathic cooperation.

This book argues that ultrasociality must be our starting point in understanding international relations. In so doing, it recasts how we understand processes and events through an examination of how the human evolutionary predisposition to be ultrasocial impacts which political ideas succeed, transform, manipulate, and inspire on a global scale. New discoveries about the human propensity to be empathically cooperative show that at a broad, species level, we are pulled toward certain tendencies more than others, and this is true regardless of the culture into which we are born. This means that within the broad parameters of our ultrasociality (what I call the ultrasocial landscape), certain types of ideas about how to build our global future resonate better with our nature than others. Those ideas that clash with our innate inclinations, and fall outside of these parameters, ultimately prove to be self-destructive. Indeed, to be accepted and acted upon, ideas that rail against our ultrasocial tendencies are nearly always manipulative.

At the same time, it is very clear that biology does not *cause* outcomes of human behavior. Our brains are also malleable to some degree, with the capacity to create new neural networks; that is, we learn from our environment, and it changes our brains in tangible ways throughout our lives, especially before we reach adulthood. Thus, it is important to steer well clear of biological determinism when exploring our ultrasocial world.[16] Rather, this book takes the approach that the innate qualities of our species play an important role in setting the parameters around what we are able, willing, and aspire to do, but they do not control it.

---

[14] Donald E. Brown, *Human Universals* (New York: McGraw Hill, 1991).

[15] Edward O. Wilson, *Consilience: The Unity of Knowledge* (New York: Vintage, 1998).

[16] Steven Pinker, *The Blank Slate: The Modern Denial of Human Nature* (New York: Penguin Books, 2002), pp. 112–113, 122.

Even though our history books have largely focused on bloodshed, battles, and societal struggle,[17] through the lens of ultrasociality it becomes clear that the human story has also been one of amazing breakthroughs and cooperative successes that often seem to defy the odds. *This* story deserves far more attention. Advancements in norms to promote such things as good governance, human rights, international law, global regimes, transparent institutions, and scientific breakthroughs are actually far more numerous than the wars, ideological crusades, and various plagues on society. In just the past few years, the strength of the Black Lives Matter movement, the growth of the Women's March into a worldwide phenomenon, widespread support for Ukraine in the face of Russian aggression, among many other examples, showcase the ways in which we come together across borders, even in support of faraway causes.

Time and time again, at critical junctures, we, as a global society, choose to take the paths that improve our international system in some way. For instance, the number of people on Earth living in poverty has gone down by more than 50% in just the period since 1990.[18] And much evidence suggests that the world is actually getting *less* violent and more secure.[19] When considered on a grand scale, we are actually in the midst of a long period of unprecedented peace not seen since the days of the Roman Empire.[20] Great powers have not gone to war with each other since the Second World War, and the numbers of military and civilian deaths since then have been strikingly low in historical terms.[21] We can now safely say that this *long peace* is not simply the product of the Cold War[22] but of something more fundamental to human motivations. Humankind is on a trajectory toward increasing progress, gradually turning away from past mistakes that often clashed with ultrasociality.

---

[17] Even in this realm of violence and conflict among humans, it is worth noting that war is, at the same time, one of the strongest manifestations of altruistic selflessness at the individual level as soldiers are willing to make the ultimate sacrifice in the name of the society or group from which they come. See John R. Alford and John R. Hibbing, "The Origin of Politics: An Evolutionary Theory of Political Behavior," *Perspectives on Politics* 2, 4 (2004): 712, https://www.jstor.org/stable/3688539 (accessed May 22, 2023). They write, "While the importance of cooperation for peace may seem self-evident, cooperation is no less critical to war."

[18] World Bank, "Poverty Headcount Ratio at $2.15 a Day (2017 PPP) (% of Population)," n.d., https://data.worldbank.org/indicator/SI.POV.DDAY? end=2018&start=1960&view=map&year=2018 (accessed May 20, 2023).

[19] Steven Pinker, *The Better Angels of Our Nature: Why Violence has Declined* (New York: Penguin Books, 2011).

[20] Neil Halloran, "The Fallen of WWII," documentary, 2015, http://www.fallen.io/ww2 (accessed May 20, 2023); Pinker, *The Better Angels of Our Nature.*

[21] Indeed, the countries with the forty-four largest economies in the world have not gone to war with each other at all since the Second World War. There has been violence of various kinds as well as civil wars, but the number of deaths has been dramatically smaller since the Second World War, especially when one takes into account the percentage of the population globally that has been affected.

[22] In 1989, John Gaddis termed the period since the Cold War the "long peace" because nuclear powers had not gone to war since the Second World War. This definition of peace has, of course, extended far beyond 1989.

To examine how ultrasociality works in practice, this book looks at four crucially important cases of international cooperation: (1) the European integration project, (2) the international relations of space exploration, (3) the global nuclear weapons taboo, and (4) the worldwide climate change regime. The story of how each of these issues emerged as unexpected examples of widespread, international cooperation is central to showing why an ultrasocial lens is so valuable. The launch of the early European Union rested on a public outpouring of support—the European Federalist Movement—for the idea that a United States of Europe could be the means to end the possibility of war on the continent, for which nationalism was to blame. In the 1920s and 1930s, the idea of human beings reaching toward the stars gathered steam and spread across the world through a transnational spaceflight movement. The global nuclear weapons taboo grew out of the world peace movement, successfully championing the non-use idea. And more recently, the efforts of the climate change movement have led to 136 countries and thousands of major companies pledging to bring their carbon emissions down to net zero by the middle of the twenty-first century.

I will show how, in each of these cases, groundbreaking cooperation became possible because of an ultrasocial landscape that enabled these ideas to emerge and eventually win the day. These are each pivotal examples of major turning points in how we have tackled global security problems: centuries of war in Europe, the space race, the advent of nuclear weapons, and catastrophic levels of global warming. Each of these cases is typically considered to be in the realm of high politics, controlled by state interest or elite decision makers. But rather than just focusing on great power competition or the ins and outs of diplomatic summits, I will show how the impetus first comes from global society. Strong social support for eradicating previous policies of national self-interest—even rising to the level of a social movement—is noticeably present in the lead-up to significant and lasting policy change.[23]

With only a conventional understanding of international relations, it would seem that in each case, international cooperation happened against all odds. Indeed, most accounts of these cases still depict outcomes of failure and conflict far more than they recognize success. In an attempt to uphold their theories, international relations scholars and the policymakers influenced by them tend to fit the evidence to their expectations as it is hard to make sense of cooperative breakthroughs with only the tools of mainstream approaches. But if we first become aware of the ultrasocial landscape, it becomes clear that certain ideas matter much more than others. Learning how to recognize this is the first step in developing

---

[23] Unlike the literature on protest social movements that is focused on making the powerful give rights to the non-powerful (i.e. human rights, women rights, LGBTQ rights, etc.), I am instead focused on *transcendent social movements*, which are focused on changing our world and the appropriate behavior of actors in our world.

awareness of what works in our efforts to create a more peaceful, stable world order.

All four issues—European integration, space exploration, nuclear weapons, and climate change—are ongoing and have undergone important developments in the twenty-first century,[24] but their ideational origins can be traced back much earlier (see Table 1). Indeed, these transformational ideas were, at various points, nurtured, diffused, challenged, and condemned before they were ultimately embraced. In following the path of these ideas and the people who championed them, I explain why ultrasocial outcomes tend to prevail over tribalistic alternatives. Our ultrasocial predisposition is visible through the narratives within these societal movements, the reasons given for choosing some ideas over others, the common passion they incite across borders, and the grip they gain on society's collective imagination, that is, *the power of possibility*. In each case, change was not inevitable, and it took human agency, at a highly collective level, for these ideas to take hold.

Not only do these cases represent key transformational ideas central to international cooperation in the twentieth and twenty-first centuries, but also their diversity sheds light on major types of revolutionary change that have relevance for other instances of international cooperation.[25] In the first case, the European Union (EU) integration project represents fundamental change in the Westphalian state system. As our global political landscape incorporates increasing numbers of non-state actors with power to change the international system, the historical trajectory of the EU through the lens of ultrasociality is valuable as an example of how sovereignty has the potential to transform, a kind of *sovereignty revolution*. As for the second case, the origins of the international social movement that led to outer space exploration are an example of socially driven scientific or technological change, a *technological revolution*. The lessons from this case can shed light on other technological leaps, such as the advent of cyberspace, robotics, or artificial intelligence. Similarly, in my third case, the evolution of the strong norm against the use of weapons of mass destruction is an example of restraint in military competition and violence or what might be thought of as a *peace revolution*. Given that, prior to 1928, all countries generally viewed war as a legitimate means of resolving differences or misunderstandings,[26] in the context of the conquest taboo, the nuclear weapons taboo was the next major step and has been followed by many cases of increased restraint in the use of weapons. Finally, the emergence

---

[24] The creation and growth of the United Nations could have been one of the cases as well, but since it is an overarching example of ultrasociality that, in many ways, ties together all four cases, it will have a presence across all four of these cases.

[25] Although these cases are not your typical *revolutions*, in the sense of violent upheaval, I nonetheless use the term to denote the relative suddenness of the transformation they brought about, largely through the emergence and subsequent diffusion of a transformational idea at the societal level.

[26] Oona Hathaway and Scott Shapiro, *The Internationalists: How a Radical Plan to Outlaw War Remade the World* (New York: Simon & Schuster, 2017).

Table 1 The power of possibility

	Ideational origins	Transformational idea	Transformational social movements	Transformational policy-change leaders (examples)
European integration and *sovereignty revolution*	Seventeenth–nineteenth centuries	Federalism *Giving up national sovereignty*	European federalist movement; Atlantic federalist movement; world federalist movement	Immanuel Kant, Richard von Koudenhove-Calergi, Jean Monnet, Altiero Spinelli
Space exploration and *technological revolution*	1920s	Preservation of space as a peaceful domain for all humankind *Expanding the boundaries of human existence*	Spaceflight movement	Robert H. Goddard, Hermann Oberth, Konstantin Tsiolkovsky, John F. Kennedy
Nuclear weapons taboo and *peace revolution*	Nineteenth–twentieth centuries	Non-use of nuclear weapons *Restraining the conduct of war to achieve world peace*	Anti-nuclear movement; peace movement	Bertrand Russell, Albert Einstein, Dagmar Wilson, Bella Abzug, Jane Addams, Emily Balch, Margaret Dungan, Mikhail Gorbachev
Climate change regime and *Earth revolution*	Eighteenth century	Net zero *Co-existing with and protecting nature*	Climate change and climate justice movement; environmental movement	Al Gore, Naomi Klein, Bill McKibbens, Greta Thunberg, Vanessa Nakate

of a strong, transnational climate change regime is a case of empathy extending beyond the present and beyond humans, toward a kind of *Earth revolution*.

This book highlights the stories of hope for what we can accomplish as a species. With an ultrasocial lens, the traditional explanations of great power politics or an emphasis on strategic bargaining fade into the background, providing only a superficial foil for what is actually a very *human* struggle, over the triumph of good ideas. While there will always be skeptics and those more easily drawn into tribalism, it is only when humans actually believe in the power of possibility that breakthroughs in cooperation are achieved. We are hard-wired to want to explore, discover, and satisfy our curiosity. It is in human nature to have a collective optimism and to yearn for ways in which to express empathy, altruism, and a common sense of morality. The good news is that over time, ultrasociality has increasingly had boundary-setting power, reigning in our worst impulses and setting the stage for our best.

The bad news is that this trajectory is not inevitable, and it remains at risk today. There are many factors in our environment that can work against, and even derail, this ultrasocial urge. Indeed, the very way we talk about and conceive of things can have real, influential power. In particular, if our narratives about international politics are imbued with the language of threat, competition, and distrust, cooperation becomes all the more difficult. For some time, it has been popular to focus on the drama of crisis and demise and not the numerous successes and day-to-day achievements made possible because of human empathy, altruism, and sociality. After all, bad news sells. And the impact of this is far more embedded in our governance structures and institutions than we realize. As Matthew Lieberman observes, the scientific innovations that have enabled us to understand the social nature of our brains have only occurred in the past few decades, but our societal institutions were designed well before this and were largely based on erroneous foundations.[27] This book does not strive to be an optimistic antidote to the pessimism of the day but rather a corrective. Ultimately, if our theories continue to over-determine conflict, despite everything we now know about the fundamentals of human nature, we risk creating a self-fulfilling prophecy.[28] But if we can fundamentally change the way we look at international relations to take into account these new discoveries and developments, the possibilities for improving international cooperation become much more promising.

***

---

[27] Lieberman, *Social*, p. 10.

[28] Robert Merton first described a self-fulfilling prophecy as: "a *false* definition of the situation evoking a new behavior which makes the originally false conception come *true*. The specious validity of the self-fulfilling prophecy perpetuates a reign of error. For the prophet will cite the actual course of events as proof that he was right from the very beginning." Merton, as quoted in Tali Sharot, *The Optimism Bias: A Tour of the Irrationally Positive Brain* (New York: Vintage, 2012), p. 44.

The book proceeds as follows. Part I surveys the literature from a range of disciplines—neuroscience, evolutionary biology, anthropology, psychology, and ecology, among others—to establish the empirical reality that humans are more prone to empathic cooperation than to self-interested materialism. Its purpose is also to convince any skeptics that ultrasociality does, indeed, have a strong scientific basis, with implications for how we understand international relations. In so doing, it explains how the ubiquity of ultrasociality has shaped our world, providing insights into many trends, transformations in governance, political innovations, narratives, and institutions. The four major case studies of this book comprise Parts II–V. Rather than comprising complete, definitive accounts of every time period, they are intended to illustrate the value of an ultrasocial approach and the dynamics that become visible when starting with this key dimension of human nature.

Part II examines the origins and development of the European integration project, which has resulted in the EU. Using ultrasociality as my point of departure, I offer a novel explanation of the drivers behind EU integration. Rather than the story of elites deciding the fate of Europe behind closed doors, fresh archival research traces just how widespread social support for the idea of a United States of Europe was right from the beginning, in the 1940s and 1950s. I argue that without the strength of the societal-level European Movement, which rallied around the idea of federalism for Europe, leaders like Jean Monnet, Altiero Spinelli, Richard von Koudenhove-Calergi, Robert Schuman, and others may not have emerged as the founders of the European experiment. While this pro-European societal movement continues to this day, it has ebbed and flowed in strength. This analysis proceeds through the pessimism of the 1970s and 1980s and the optimism of the 1990s and early 2000s and continues up through to today, drawing connections between the inspirational ideas that have captured the imagination of many Europeans and the evolution of integration at the European level.

Part III examines the international relations of space from the inception of the idea some hundred years ago, on through to the Space Race, the International Space Station, and the goal to send humans to Mars in the 2030s. The International Space Station—recognized as one of the most ambitious examples of international scientific collaboration today, involving twenty-six countries, with astronauts from seventeen of them—has provided us with a permanent international presence in space for over two decades. Drawing upon archival documents and extensive participant observation of space actors today, this case provides a fresh understanding of how societies grew to support the idea of space exploration as a cooperative endeavor and collaborative opportunity. Rather than standard accounts about the twentieth century's Space Race as a nationalist fight to the finish line and more recent assumptions about the twenty-first century's so-called Space Race 2.0, I show how ultrasocial cooperation has been stronger than conflict when it comes to space. In bringing the analysis up to the present, I also assess the role of international networks, such as the International Astronautical Federation, and private companies, such as SpaceX, in adding to or detracting from the context of ultrasociality as the number of space actors rapidly grows.

Part IV focuses on the rise of the societal-level norm against the use of nuclear weapons and how this has ultimately manifested in worldwide policies restricting these deadly weapons. Most analyses of nuclear weapons invoke the balance of power, deterrence, and mutually assured destruction to explain their non-use. By contrast, I trace the process by which what started out as a dangerous game of nuclear one-upmanship, including the actual use of nuclear weapons in Hiroshima and Nagasaki, quickly developed into the widely held belief that these weapons should not be used despite their overwhelming power. Unlike other accounts of the nuclear taboo, an ultrasocial approach reveals the power of possibility that underpinned the anti-nuclear movement. The public was not only focused on banning the bomb but also on ensuring a peaceful future for all humankind. Even though the international community today struggles to prevent countries like North Korea and Iran from developing their own nuclear weapons, and there have been a few nuclear close-calls, I show how the power of the ultrasocial world is strongly felt in this regard. While the memories of the Second World War and the collective revulsion may no longer be as visceral as they once were, the nuclear taboo persists, anchored in its contribution to peace and the ultrasocial landscape.

Part V turns to the emergence of the global climate change regime over the past thirty years and the idea of net zero—the scientific finding that net carbon emissions must reach zero by the mid-twenty-first century to keep Earth's temperature rise to manageable levels. I explain why early environmental leadership decisions initially worked against ultrasocial cooperation but then how various sectors of civil society came together to achieve an ultrasocial breakthrough in the lead-up to the 2015 Paris climate change agreement. Society was galvanized behind the idea of net zero in large part because the climate movement amplified the positive, transformational narrative that it was achievable alongside economic growth and climate justice goals. This eventually translated into watershed advancements in climate technology and the participation of many cities, localities, and regions, as well as significant transformations in the private sector. While it is important to acknowledge that emerging solutions to climate change may still be too little too late, ultrasociality provides a context for understanding the extent to which and why there might be light at the end of the tunnel.

Looking ahead, the book concludes with an acknowledgement of future challenges. After all, the ultrasocial landscape can be overwhelmed, exerting less of a pull on society, when good ideas are not forthcoming and leadership is lacking. In today's world, we are missing much-needed new ideas on how to stop radicalization, global inequality, and failed states. And formerly strong ideas, such as democracy, liberalism, and free trade, are starting to lose ground. We are particularly vulnerable in the face of unprecedented crises. However, we do not need to simply ride the tide of ultrasociality. We can capitalize on it and use its logic to make empathic cooperation and new forms of global governance more likely. Thus, the final chapter of the book looks to the future and translates the findings of the book into a road map for how we might cultivate ultrasociality.

PART I
HUMANS ARE ULTRASOCIAL
BEINGS

Over the past two decades, there has emerged a strong consensus in nearly every area of expertise devoted to understanding human behavior that, on a broad scale, humans cooperate altruistically and have empathy. And even when we are not engaged in this behavior, we are still pre-wired, hard-wired, and soft-wired to think socially more than competitively.[1] Whether we look at evolutionary biology, neuroscience, genetics, psychology, or anthropology, scholars from a range of disciplines have moved far past the kinds of erroneous assumptions that are central to basic international relations "rationalism." This approach, often adapted from economics, argues that humans seek to maximize material self-interest in the name of survival.[2]

International relations scholars scale up rationalism to support the realist school of thought, which, on a broad level, assumes that states as unitary actors in the international system—like individuals or firms in a market—act only to maximize national power.[3] They believe human nature is to pursue power and to be untrusting of others, and so when humans organize themselves into states, the former infuses the latter with these properties.[4] As such, they argue that the very survival of a state is predicated on how much power it has relative to other states because they exist in a competitive, anarchic environment where survival is difficult. There are a whole host of theories within realism that build on this assumption and claim to be timeless, such as the causes and outcomes of the balance of power, bandwagoning, balance of threat, use of force, and war, among others.[5] With the widespread

---

[1] Nicholas Christakis, *Blueprint: The Evolutionary Origins of a Good Society* (New York: Little Brown, 2019); Jeremy Rifkin, *The Empathic Civilization: The Race to Global Consciousness in a World in Crisis* (New York: TarcherPerigee, 2009).

[2] Herbert Spencer actually coined the phrase, "survival of the fittest" upon reading Charles Darwin and noticing similarities between natural selection and his own economic theories.

[3] Kenneth Waltz, *Theory of International Politics* (Long Grove, IL: Waveland Press, 1979).

[4] Hans Morgenthau, *Politics among Nations: The Struggle for Power and Peace* (New York: McGraw Hill, 1985).

[5] Stephen Walt, *The Origins of Alliances* (Ithaca, NY: Cornell University Press, 1990); John Mearsheimer, *The Tragedy of Great Power Politics* (New York: W. W. Norton & Company, 2001); Robert Jervis, "Cooperation under the Security Dilemma," *World Politics* 30,. 2 (1978): 167–214.

diffusion of these assumptions, everyone from pundits, to politicians, to the regular public tend to talk about international relations using the language of threat, rising powers, and a world divided between allies and adversaries.

Indeed, international relations is a field that has built so much of its foundations on rationalism that even realism's biggest competitor, neoliberal institutionalism, uses the same language, despite arguing that cooperation is widespread in the international system.[6] States (and non-state actors) are assumed to be utility maximizing whether they are deciding to wage war, negotiating the terms of trade treaties, participating in international organizations, or forming alliances.[7] Even the more recent theories that seek to debunk this approach, such as social constructivism or critical theory, are often compelled to use this material-maximizing assumption or "null hypothesis" as their default in order to be in dialogue with the rest of the field.[8] As a result, nearly all understandings of international relations today in some way rest on the apparent default for human beings to prioritize power and wealth above all other motivations.

There are a few approaches that have attempted to go in a different direction. The first is classical liberalism, which builds upon Immanuel Kant's eighteenth-century idea that "perpetual peace" can be achieved with the creation of a federation of free states. However, this argument, known now as democratic peace theory (i.e., democracies almost never go to war with other democracies), only anticipates peaceful interactions, cooperation, and empathy among *democracies*, leaving out interactions of democracies with non-democracies or non-democracies with each other. In so doing, democratic peace theory essentially adheres to rationalist or realist arguments when examining interactions outside of the zone of peace.

A second approach that challenges the material self-interest assumption is feminist international relations theory. This school of thought generally argues for the necessity of "making women visible" and shining light on what has been traditionally ignored because it has been viewed as a "feminine" space (regardless

---

[6] International relations neoliberalism is distinct from common understandings of neoliberalism, which tend to emphasize free market capitalism and laissez-faire economics. In international relations, it refers to the pursuit of both relative and absolute gains in the international political system of states. International institutions are assumed to facilitate states in maximizing profit and power and also allowing them to cooperate by reducing transaction costs, increasing transparency, and solidifying long-term interactions.

[7] Robert Axelrod, *The Evolution of Cooperation*, 2nd edn (New York: Basic Books, 2006); Mancur Olsen, *The Logic of Collective Action: Public Goods and the Theory of Groups* (Cambridge, MA: Harvard University Press, 1971); David Lake and Robert Powell (eds), *Strategic Choice and International Relations* (Princeton, NJ: Princeton University Press, 1999); Thomas C. Schelling, *The Strategy of Conflict* (Cambridge, MA: Harvard University Press, 1981).

[8] Lisa Martin and Beth A. Simmons, "Theories and Empirical Studies of International Institutions," *International Organization* 52, 4 (1998): 729–757, https://doi.org/10.1162/002081898550734; Oran R. Young, "International Regimes: Problems of Concept Formation," *World Politics* 32, 3 (1980): 331–356; Robert O. Keohane, "International Institutions: Two Approaches," *International Studies Quarterly* 32, 4 (December 1988): 379–396.

of the gender identity of the actors involved).[9] For example, many international relations studies focus on male soldiers in wars and do not consider the role or victimization of women or non-fighting men during war. Moreover, they tend to focus on male leaders because they are assumed to be the source of aggression, while ignoring the role of aggressive female leaders or peace-seeking male leaders. Through creating an opening to not only regard women as key actors in international relations but also examine different forms of power, this approach has the potential to shift the analysis toward seeing cooperation as just as important as conflict. Unfortunately, however, feminist international relations has, so far, been almost entirely marginalized in the field.[10]

Similarly sidelined in the field are approaches known as critical theory, such as post-structuralism, postmodernism, and queer theory, which exist purely to position themselves in contrast to mainstream, rationalist assumptions in international relations. Post-structuralism, and its counterpart postmodernism, argue critically that dominant framings in the field of international relations itself create and recreate the power relationships we observe in the world.[11] To break this cycle, post-structuralists question many concepts inherent in the field, from claims of objectivity to use of language, to assumptions about the role of militarism and sovereignty. Queer theory, which builds on feminist theory, points out that the binary language in international relations—structure versus agency, state versus system, North versus South—neglects the space in between.[12] Again, it calls for us to question the epistemologies, ontologies, and methods of mainstream international relations without offering a concrete alternative. These approaches play a useful role in casting doubt on knowledge production itself, but they almost never inform or filter into actual policy debates. Their role is relegated to standing in opposition to rationalism.

Such is the hold that mainstream, rationalist assumptions have in international relations. This takes on a great deal of meaning when we consider how leaders and decision makers translate the most visible international relations arguments into the policymaking realm. Of course, if there is a dominant belief that the international system really boils down to competition, conflict, anarchy, and material self-interest, then our politicians will also act on that. Any security dilemma we face in the real world is, in fact, a manifestation of our belief in the existence of

---

[9] Sarah Smith, "Feminism," in *International Relations Theory*, ed. Stephen McGlinchey, Rosie Walters, and Christian Scheinpflug (Bristol: E-International Relations Publishing, 2017), pp. 62–68.

[10] J. Ann Tickner, "You May Never Understand: Prospects for Feminist Futures in International Relations," *Australian Feminist Law Journal* 32, 1 (2010): 9–20.

[11] For a good overview of the approach, see: Aslı Çalkıvik, "Poststructuralism and Postmodernism in International Relations," in *Oxford Research Encyclopedia of International Studies*, ed. Nukhet A Sandal (Oxford: Oxford University Press, 2017). https://global.oup.com/academic/product/oxford-research-encyclopedias-international-studies-9780190846626?cc=us&lang=en&#

[12] Markus Theil, "LGBT Politics, Queer Theory, and International Relations," *E-International Relations*, October 31, 2014, https://www.e-ir.info/2014/10/31/lgbt-politics-queer-theory-and-international-relations (accessed May 20, 2023).

a security dilemma. In this sense, the post-structuralists are right. The power of perception is a very important thing.

In contrast, I argue that we can no longer afford to ignore the latest findings on human nature—universal qualities of human beings—in the study of international relations or, even worse, continue to make so many wrong assumptions about it. Scaling up research from the biological and natural sciences to the level of international relations is challenging in that it represents an entirely new starting point, but it is worthwhile for the reasons discussed so far. The debate between rationalists and so-called idealists—those who believe in humankind's peaceful potential—is, of course, not new, although our ability to settle the debate scientifically is.

An Old Debate

Are humans naturally predisposed to be social, empathic, and cooperative, or are we actually selfish, violent, and materialistic? Philosophers have grappled with this question across millennia.[13] In Ancient Greece, Plato recognized that humans are fundamentally social beings, mainly because we cannot be self-sufficient. For him, it is actually the "prison" of the physical body that forces humans into groups or cities. While he argued that humans should strive to be governed by reason, he also believed that it is in our nature to satisfy biological drives, which could only be fulfilled as members of society. Plato's overall judgment was that a "good" person is one who could overcome physical desires and operate purely according to reason. This kind of utilitarian argument about human sociality was fundamentally pessimistic and also refuted by others. One of the key implications of Plato's philosophical approach was a kind of authoritarian, or top-down, political order.

Aristotle, Plato's student, argued that man by nature is social, and to be without society is such a state of deprivation that he considered it a kind of punishment. He wrote, "Man is a social animal. He who lives without society is either a beast or God."[14] He argued that the creation of the *polis* is natural and inevitable because it associates people together and allows for more virtuous behavior. If left on our own, we would have a passion for war and live without justice. He predicted that the creation of a *polis* would happen organically, with various roles for different people. Deviating from Plato, he emphasized the diversity of individuals within the polity, who, in their natural cooperation and drive to live with one another, ultimately provide the sense of harmony that helps lift the society and its individual members to a happier, more fulfilling existence greater than the mere sum

---

[13] See Rifkin, *The Empathetic Civilization*, pp. 315–316.
[14] Aristotle, *Politics*, Book I, trans. Carnes Lord, (Chicago: University of Chicago Press, 1984).

of its parts.[15] Many other philosophers and social thinkers that followed agreed with Aristotle in this regard, focusing on the importance of the common good and arguing that man is fundamentally cooperative, although many of them, such as Aquinas, sought to adapt Aristotle's philosophy for religious purposes as much as political ones.[16]

The debate among Ancient Greek philosophers helped provide the foundation for another one that occurred much later during the lead-up to the European Enlightenment, in the crucial years for the creation of modern states and the international system. Building upon the work of the influential Renaissance thinker Niccolò Machiavelli, Thomas Hobbes argued that human beings are, by nature, selfish and predisposed toward ambition and trying to dominate others. However, rather than seeing this (as Machiavelli did) as part of an ultimately healthy drive that tended to encourage progress and maintain liberty within the context of otherwise Aristotelian communitarian human impulses, Hobbes was truly horrified, seeing this as an overriding corrosive flaw that needed to be tamed at all costs. In the state of nature, before the social contract, Hobbes argued that life is so awful that people just take each other's things and kill one other at the drop of the hat. Human beings are constantly in a state of war, of all against all, each against each. In his famous line, human life in its natural state is "solitary, poor, nasty, brutish, and short."[17] To get out of this situation, people give up everything except for their theoretical right to self-preservation when they agree to the social contract.

By contrast, John Locke agreed with Aristotle in terms of the notion that man is social and strives to achieve social harmony as part of a larger community.[18] He based this argument on the belief that people are born as a *tabula rasa* (blank slate), and then strive to achieve reason and moderation as they grow and learn.[19] He believed this to be true even before agreement on a social contract takes place. In other words, for Locke, humans in a state of nature behave in a way that seeks social harmony, and they generally obey the tenets of natural law within which this is embedded. However, as no world is absolutely perfect and differing individual perspectives could muddy the waters and lead to competition, retaliation, and violence, they enter into the social contract, forming governments in order to establish a neutral judge, who will ensure protection of their three inalienable rights: to life, liberty, and property. Since Locke's view of the state of nature was

[15] Aristotle, *Politics*, Book II, trans. Carnes Lord, (Chicago: University of Chicago Press, 1984).

[16] Aquinas, St Thomas, *Aquinas on Politics and Ethics: A New Translation, Backgrounds, Interpretations*, ed. Paul E. Sigmund (New York: Norton, 1988).

[17] Thomas Hobbes, *Leviathan* (Glasgow: Oxford University Press, 1929 [1651]).

[18] John Locke, "Second Treatise of Government, Chapter 2," in *The Project Gutenberg eBook of Second Treatise of Government*, April 22, 2003, https://www.gutenberg.org/files/7370/7370-h/7370-h.htm (accessed May 20, 2023).

[19] John Locke, "An Essay Concerning Human Understanding," Liberty Fund, 1689, https://oll.libertyfund.org/title/locke-the-works-vol-1-an-essay-concerning-human-understanding-part-1 (accessed July 3, 2023).

significantly more optimistic than Hobbes's, the people were justified in returning to it and starting anew if their government failed to protect these rights as humanity's fundamentally social nature gave them less to fear outside the bounds of the state.

Later, in the eighteenth century, Jean-Jacques Rousseau had an even more positive view of the innate qualities of man. In the state of nature, he argued that groups of people are actually peaceful and cooperative because they have empathy and repulsion toward human suffering. In this way, his philosophical approach builds on the conclusions of Aristotle and Locke and is based on his belief in an innate sense of compassion. In fact, his view of human nature was so positive that it actually brought him to distrust structures that might be brought in to restrain it. Ultimately, Rousseau believed that human nature is good and peaceful and that, to reach true fulfillment, humans needed to come together in society but that, in doing so, the social contract tends to corrupt this nature, socializing people into a range of selfish and unproductive behaviors. So, for Rousseau, the answer had to be found in a proper form of democratic governance that would aim to restrain these tendencies toward egoism and work toward what he called the "general will."[20]

Locke's and Rousseau's ideas helped lay the foundation for the rise of modern democratic societies beginning toward the end of the eighteenth century. Here, they were merged with the classical republican tradition that stretched from Cicero in ancient Rome, to Machiavelli in Renaissance Italy, to Montesquieu in Enlightenment France, which emphasized the need for cooperation from all sectors of society. This tradition ultimately went one step further, stressing the ways in which humans' secondary tendencies toward rivalry, competition, and ambition could actually be put to good social use, channeled to help serve their greater communitarian impulse.[21]

In short, many of the most influential philosophers in history have long suspected that there exists an innate human sociality, so much so that they built their entire analysis of politics and ethics on this assumption, and this, in turn, has helped provide the foundation for much of the modern world.[22] But only relatively recently have scientists discovered the ways that the human brain responds to the contexts in which we find ourselves, providing the micro-foundations of ultrasociality. Using a building-blocks approach, Part I of the book surveys areas of recent

[20] Jean-Jacques Rousseau, *The Social Contract*, trans. with an historical and critical introduction and notes by Henry John Tozer (London: Swan Sonnenschein & Co., 1895).

[21] Cicero, *The Republic and the Laws*, trans. Niall Rudd (Oxford: Oxford University Press, 2009); Niccolo Machiavelli, *The Discourses*, trans. Leslie Walker (New York: Penguin Classics, 1983); Charles de Montesquieu, *Spirit of the Laws* (New York: Prometheus Books, 2002 [1748]); Thomas Jefferson, "The Declaration of Independence," Miscellaneous Papers of the Continental Congress, 1774–1789; Records of the Continental and Confederation Congresses and the Constitutional Convention, 1774–1789, Record Group 360; National Archives; James Madison, *Federalist Papers* No. 51 in ed. Clinton Rossiter, *The Federalist Papers* (New York: Penguin, 1961).

[22] I am grateful to Robert Cross for filling in the details behind this philosophical and historical discussion.

scientific consensus that help us to actually answer some of these long-standing philosophical questions with scientific evidence. It should serve to overcome any skepticism readers might have about the scientific basis of human ultrasociality and its connections to international relations.

The first chapter looks at this micro level of analysis (the biology of the brain, cognition, and genetics), which provides an important basis for understanding how humans are, in some ways, hard-wired to be natural cooperators. The second chapter considers findings from the field of human evolution and brings culture—defined as our common human mentality and behavior—into the mix. Where biology meets culture, it becomes clear that evolution is more than just survival of the fittest. The co-evolution of human inventions and genes means that social relationships are firmly intertwined with natural selection, defined as the increase in certain genetic traits across a population as a result of the advantages those genes provide. Humans have evolved in such a way that we cannot actually survive, let alone thrive, without empathy and a web of social relationships. On a broader, more holistic level, the third chapter explores the *social* in the social sciences. Cognitive and social psychology, anthropology, sociology, and ecology have much to say about the human drive to cooperate in terms of learning, teaching, norms, and perceptions. Finally, the fourth chapter turns to international relations, and builds a bridge from these other disciplines to a new understanding of how our species behaves on a global, political scale.

1

The Micro Level

For centuries, stretching back to the earliest writings that exist (the Epic of Gilgamesh written on clay tablets dates back to 1,800 BCE), philosophers and theorists have separated humans from the natural world. We have been assumed to have some kind of prioritized position compared to nature, in a position to conquer nature rather than exist as part of it. It was only in the nineteenth century that some thinkers began to question this approach, not least of which was Charles Darwin. But the divide between the study of human biology and the social sciences remains strong even today. As sociologist Nicholas Christakis points out, there are still only a few exceptions—such as evolutionary psychology, social neuroscience, and behavioral genetics—that actively seek to bridge the divide.[23] These fields are remarkably useful for understanding the building blocks of ultrasociality, which inform a new understanding of international relations that accounts for our inclination toward empathic cooperation.

At the smallest, or most micro level, social neuroscientists have made some exciting discoveries in support of the notion that humans are fundamentally motivated by our sociality. On a species level, we are hard-wired, or biologically predisposed, to be empathic, and even altruistic, toward our fellow humans, even if we do not always behave that way.

Some scientists, especially behavioral psychologists, would dispute the value of going so deep into our biological make-up to find the origins of behavior. Cognitive psychologists, for example, argue that there is no need to look inside the brain or the mechanics of the mind because, ultimately, the only thing that truly matters is the external manifestation of these internal drives or behavior itself. If we can easily *see* behavior, why even consider what the brain is doing? And since scientific conclusions about the brain are simply averages and not consistencies across individuals, can we really even pinpoint some kind of fundamental human nature that applies to our whole species?[24] Clearly, looking at the brain is not enough. The biological underpinnings of behavior are *suggestive* but not conclusive. Nonetheless, in a building-blocks approach, it is a reasonable place to start. If, generally, across a range of fields and findings, there is sufficient consensus or consilience that we are an ultrasocial species, then that is enough to push toward a fundamental rethink of international relations.

---

[23] Nicholas Christakis, *Blueprint: The Evolutionary Origins of a Good Society* (New York: Little Brown, 2019), pp. 396–397.
[24] I am grateful to Ajay Satpute for this point.

International Cooperation Against All Odds. Mai'a K. Davis Cross, Oxford University Press. © Mai'a K. Davis Cross (2024).
DOI: 10.1093/oso/9780192873903.003.0002

As we move from biology to culture to politics, layering these findings is useful in demonstrating why we are anchored in an ultrasocial landscape. It is worth noting that humans across the world, from a vast range of different cultures and languages, have very similar mental processes. Human emotion, language, candid facial expressions—mental computations in general—are likely universal across the globe.[25] If we only pay attention to behavior, which is learned and changeable, among other things, we might miss a significant part of human *similarity* across cultures. And this is one of the key building blocks to our understanding of so-called *human universals* discussed in Chapter 3.

The Brain

The advent of functional magnetic resonance imaging (fMRI) in the 1990s has been crucial for seeing how neural activity in the brain changes in reaction to basic experiments. The standard MRI can only give a static view of the brain. Without the need to have surgery or other invasive measures, the fMRI measures and maps blood flow to certain regions of the brain, indicating the presence of neural activity. Scientists have learned, in particular, that several regions of the brain are actually dedicated to sociality. Through a range of new experiments using the fMRI, neuroscientists and psychologists have been able to gain new insights into how the brain reacts to various situations that we perceive.

In one experiment, for instance, when American participants were asked to perform a risk-taking task, their brain activity was relatively accurate in predicting whether they were republicans or democrats. Those that had more activation in the right amygdala, where emotion and fear originates, were likely to be republicans, and those with activation in the left posterior insula, where the brain processes social and self-awareness, were more likely to be democrats.[26] Adding to this, scientists found, in genetic studies of fear and political persuasion, that being politically conservative does not come before being a fearful person but rather the other way around: fearful people are more likely to be conservative.[27]

Of more relevance to empathy specifically, in 1996, brain scans revealed the existence of *mirror neurons*.[28] Significantly, mirror neurons were shown to fire *both* when primates take an action as well as when they observe someone else taking

[25] Steven Pinker, *The Blank Slate: The Modern Denial of Human Nature* (New York: Penguin Books, 2002), p. 39.

[26] Darren Schreiber, "Red Brain, Blue Brain: Republicans and Democrats Process Risk Differently, Research Finds," *Science Daily*, February 13, 2013, https://www.sciencedaily.com/releases/2013/02/130213173131.htm (accessed May 20, 2023); and see Chris Mooney, *The Republican Brain: The Science of Why They Deny Science—and Reality* (New York: Wiley, 2012).

[27] Peter Hatemi and Rose McDermott (eds), *Man Is by Nature a Political Animal: Evolution, Biology, and Politics* (Chicago, IL: University of Chicago Press, 2011).

[28] Matthew Lieberman, *Social: Why Our Brains Are Wired to Connect* (New York: Crown Publishing Group), p. 135.

THE MICRO LEVEL 23

that action. Mirror neurons are crucial for empathy, and by extension, ultrasociality. According to Matthew D. Lieberman, whose work is at the intersection of social neuroscience and psychology, "the mirror system is constantly doing the work of preparing the brain for mindreading," which he defines as the human capacity to anticipate and infer the emotions of others.[29]

Of course, while mirror neurons are likely an important prerequisite in the story of human sociality, empathy goes beyond the existence of mirror neurons. As Jeremy Rifkin argues, "Unlike sympathy, which is more passive, empathy conjures up active engagement—the willingness of an observer to become part of another's experience, to share the feeling of that experience."[30] He writes that, "The recognition of another's finite existence is what connects empathic consciousness to entropic awareness. When we identify with another's plight, it's their will to live that we empathize with and seek to support."[31] Emotions, like empathy, are also constructed and complex, not just automatically given to us when one part of the brain fires.[32]

The so-called *theory of mind* is closely related to understandings of empathy and the awareness of others. It refers to the ability of humans to know that others have certain beliefs, emotions, aspirations, motivations, and perspectives that are distinct from our own. It takes time for each person to develop a theory of mind, and some have it to a greater or lesser extent. Those with brain damage, autism, or other mental impairments, for instance, may not have a theory of mind at all. However, such general awareness of one's own mind as well as others' across the species facilitates many other mental processes relevant to ultrasociality and, by extension, international relations. Our propensity to be highly vulnerable to social rejection is a key example of this, and numerous experiments have tested this aspect of human mentality.

For example, Kip Williams was the first to develop an experiment that revealed how the brain responds to social rejection using the cyber-ball game.[33] Participants in the experiment play an internet game (previously, this was done in a room with real people) that involves throwing a ball back and forth with two other people who are presumably also online playing the game from different locations. Test subjects are informed that the point of the game is to understand how humans work together to do basic tasks. However, unbeknownst to the subjects, the other players in the game are actually just computer-generated (in the non-computer version, the other players are secretly part of the scientific team). At a certain point in the

[29] Lieberman, *Social*, p. 150.
[30] Jeremy Rifkin, *The Empathic Civilization: The Race to Global Consciousness in a World in Crisis* (New York: TarcherPerigee, 2009), p. 12.
[31] Rifkin, *The Empathic Civilization*, pp. 40–41.
[32] Lisa Feldman Barrett, *How Emotions Are Made: The Secret Life of the Brain* (New York: Mariner Books, 2017).
[33] Lieberman, *Social*, pp. 56–60.

game, the other two "participants" stop throwing the ball to the subjects and just throw the ball to each other. Subjects are then interviewed to understand how they felt under circumstances of social rejection. The result is invariably some sense of sadness or anger, demonstrating how sensitive people are to social inclusion or exclusion.

But why would we really care if people who we do not know and cannot see exclude us from a digital game of catch? In 2001, Lieberman and Naomi Eisenberger took this experiment a step further and performed it with test subjects in an fMRI scanner. While confirming Williams's findings, they also made an unexpected breakthrough. They discovered that brain data for physical pain was the same as for social pain. In other words, they found that we experience *social pain* in reaction to being socially excluded, and this actually activates the same part of the brain as physical pain does. Thus, even prior to psychological reactions to social rejection, evolution has apparently given priority to social pain even though it does not seemingly threaten immediate survival in the same way that a physical injury or illness does.

Even the relatively large size of the human brain, compared to that of other species, reflects our capacity for social pain and, by extension, ultrasociality. We have big brains because social thinking happens in a different part of the brain than non-social thinking and has a big task.[34] Social thinking allows our species uniquely to maintain *social information*—the identity, relationships, and personal contact—of 150 others, known as "Dunbar's number." In order to exist cohesively in these very large groups,[35] we need our big brains to keep track and store social information on all of those other people.[36]

Thus, social intelligence is not just a subset of regular intelligence. It is a product of evolution, which gradually worked toward giving us the ability to remember and know many others at the same time, ultimately feeding back into our sociality.[37] A case in point is the fact that human fetuses have evolved to have as large brains as possible while still being able to make it through the birth canal. And then, even after birth, the capacity of human brains continues to grow and mature for a relatively long period of time compared to other species—approximately until the age of twenty-seven. As Lieberman concludes, "Our social nature is not an accident of having a larger brain. Rather, the value of increasing our sociality is a major reason for why we evolved to have a larger brain."[38]

---

[34] Lieberman, *Social*, p. 32.
[35] So-called "Dunbar's number" is 150—humans are able to maintain social information of 150 others, which is much larger than other species.
[36] Lieberman, *Social*, p. 34.
[37] Lieberman, *Social*, pp. 27–28.
[38] Lieberman, *Social*, p. 33.

In addition to contributing to human ultrasociality, social pain and social intelligence suggest implications for international relations that are worth further exploration. Mirror neurons and theory of the mind give us empathy for and understanding of others, even those far away. For example, tapping into this could enable support for humanitarian aid and operations as well as a willingness to help out in unexpected crises, such as in the aftermath of hurricanes or floods. A biological desire not to experience social rejection suggests that those engaged in diplomacy, for example, might typically seek inclusion in international agreements, even if it means compromise.

The Brain and Cognition

The cognitive dimension of the brain is just as important, if not more so, as the brain itself in understanding the nature of ultrasociality and, ultimately, its relevance for international relations. While, in the past, it had been a common assumption that the mind was somehow separate from human biology (i.e., from the brain), several newer fields now serve as bridges in the study of mind and matter.

First, a revolution in *cognitive science* (the study of the mind) has shown that humans must have an innate mental system for learning certain behaviors and that the learning system does not come from culture but is likely universal across humans. Second, *cognitive neuroscience* (the study of the brain) has found that the size and arrangement of brain matter is very similar across humans (those with differences in behavior, such as psychopaths or geniuses, seem to also have physical differences in the brain) and that the process of learning or practicing new skills can change the brain.[39] Third, *behavioral genetics* (the study of the environment and genes) has found that genes impact the mind and behavior even if only in a probabilistic way. (Since genetic variation across humans is very individualized, however, it does not tell us much about universal qualities of humans.)[40] Finally, the relatively new field of *evolutionary psychology* (the study of psychological adaptation in the process of evolution) finds that various emotions that have evolved over time have tended to favor survival and the thriving of the species.[41] In light of all of this, as cognitive psychologist Steven Pinker puts it, "the mind no longer looks like a formless lump pounded into shape by culture."[42]

[39] Pinker, *The Blank Slate*, p. 45.
[40] Pinker, *The Blank Slate*, p. 50.
[41] Pinker, *The Blank Slate*, p. 54.
[42] Pinker, *The Blank Slate*, p. 55. However, also in *The Blank Slate*, Pinker does not accept the ultrasocial nature of the brain that many other scientists have identified. He writes, "many intellectuals have embraced the image of peaceable, egalitarian, and ecology-loving natives [. . .] In a nutshell: Hobbes was right, Rousseau was wrong." Pinker, *The Blank Slate*, p. 56 and, for justifications, see p. 294, also,

Besides the discovery of how our brains process *social pain*, in looking more at cognition, Lieberman also finds that the human brain actually has a default mode. His research shows that when we are not engaged in any specific activity, our brains come back to what he calls *social cognition*; that is, our brains tend to gravitate back toward thinking about others—our relationships, interactions, and dreams about other humans—when we are not doing anything else. He writes,

> What the brain does when we stop doing a motor task does not sound like the kind of thing a social neuroscientist would usually care about. But as it happens, the network in the brain that reliably shows up during social cognition studies is virtually identical to the default network. In other words, the default network supports social cognition—making sense of other people and ourselves.[43]

He points out that while most people assume that abstract thinking, language, reason, and opposable thumbs explain how humans are different from other animals on this planet, it is actually the ability of humans to think socially that distinguishes us.[44] Indeed, we even tend to remember social facts more easily than non-social facts, especially social facts that involve a person who does not act in accordance with our social norms.[45] This default mode is behind the *mindreading* or *mentalizing*, the "ability to understand that other people have thoughts that drive their behavior."[46] As the human brain developed over time, Lieberman writes, "evolution made this 'choice'—for the brain to reset to thinking socially, and to mute the impact of nonsocial thinking, every chance it gets."[47]

In line with this, Robert Kurzban and Athena Aktipis argue that, sometimes, the fact that we are aware that those around us engage in mentalizing behavior can also be used unconsciously but strategically to make ourselves as desirable as possible in our social world. They hypothesize that the brain has a *social cognitive interface* (SCI), which they liken to "a Machiavellian spin doctor," seeking to make others overestimate how desirable and valuable we each are.[48] Since humans can detect when they are being misled through the mindreading process, the SCI

chapter 17. Research on the brain and cognition that has emerged since the 2002 publication of this book casts quite a lot of doubt on this particular conclusion.

[43] Lieberman, *Social*, p. 19.

[44] Lieberman, *Social*, p. 7.

[45] Dan Chiappe, Adam Brown, and Marisela Rodriquez, "Remembering the Faces of Potential Cheaters and Cooperators in Social Contract Situations," paper presented at the annual meeting of the Human Behavior and Evolution Society, June 8, 2002, New Brunswick, NJ, as cited in John R. Alford and John R. Hibbing, "The Origin of Politics: An Evolutionary Theory of Political Behavior," *Perspectives on Politics* 2, 4 (2004): 711, https://www.jstor.org/stable/3688539 (accessed May 22, 2023).

[46] Lieberman, *Social*, p. 108. This is done in the dorsomedial prefrontal cortex (DMPFC) and the temporal-parietal junction (TPJ).

[47] Lieberman, *Social*, p. 120.

[48] Robert Kurzban and X. Athena Aktipis, "Modularity and the Social Mind: Are Psychologists Too Self-ish?" *Personality and Social Psychology Review* 11, 2 (May 2007): 131–149, https://doi.org/10.1177/1088868306294906.

strikes a balance between being convincing while not exaggerating. This is also suggestive in terms of what might go into effective international interactions, such as multinational negotiations, social movement cohesion, public diplomacy outreach, and transnational network communication. Not only does social exclusion cause us real pain, but we also strive for others to see us as highly valued.

One might be inclined to counter these findings, arguing that human empathy and social thinking must be learned and that there is no way to differentiate between automatic neuro-functions and socialized empathy. Here, research into the default network is again illustrative.[49] Two-month-old babies have active brain regions where social cognition takes place (even two-day-old infants have this but not premature babies, whose brains have not yet reached the size where this capability is possible). Lieberman writes, "default network activity precedes any conscious interest in the social world [...] it's the brain's preferred state of being."[50] We can learn to be more or less socially oriented after infancy, but baseline inclinations toward social thinking are our default.

From these various findings, among others, Lieberman observes that Abraham Maslow's famous hierarchy of needs is, in fact, upside down. Our most basic need is actually to be social, and this takes precedence over food, water, warmth, and rest—and we share this with various of our primate cousins. For example, in Harry Harlow's experiments involving baby Rhesus monkeys, when given a choice between a wire mannequin that had fur over it but no milk and another wire mannequin that had no fur but did offer milk, the monkeys consistently chose the former because the fur more closely approximated social contact with a real mother.

Observational findings about human babies in orphanages in the 1930s and 1940s resulted in a similar conclusion. For a while, caregivers in certain nurseries received instructions to avoid touching or holding new infants in order to avoid exposing them to germs and illnesses, while still providing for their needs. As a result, the death rate in these orphanages turned out to be unusually high. This tragedy promoted René Spitz to make the 1947 film, *Grief: A Peril in Infancy*, showing how healthy babies quickly degenerated into a catatonic state in the absence of human contact. The babies had all of the nutrients they needed and virtually no exposure to disease but, at the same time, received no social interaction. As a result, two weeks after arriving at the orphanage, perfectly healthy and happy infants would exhibit severe psychological degradation. These studies support the argument that social connection with others is even more primary than food and water.[51]

---

[49] Lieberman, *Social*, p. 20.
[50] Lieberman, *Social*, pp. 20–21.
[51] Lieberman, *Social*, p. 43.

Looking at the adult population, Dirk Helbing found that people living in cities, highly social environments, gain a 10–15% health advantage because of the social forces present there.[52] Moreover, if, beyond just a physical crowd (e.g., a crowded subway), there is also a *psychological crowd* with a strong sense of shared identity, there are additional health benefits. India's annual Maha Kumbh Mela pilgrimage, during which around 120 million Hindus gather to bathe in a sacred river, is a case in point. Even though the water they bathe in and drink is highly polluted, participants in this ritual actually stay relatively healthy.[53] This can be attributed in part to the benefit that comes from being in a group in which a powerful "we" feeling emerges, something sociologist Emile Durkheim calls "collective effervescence"—the overwhelming awe that emerges when individuality becomes subsumed within a collective. Even people with a network of *casual* acquaintances—so-called weak-tie relationships—have been shown to experience more happiness, more information, and a feeling of belonging than those who do not.[54] On the opposite end of the spectrum, another study shows how chronic loneliness is just as detrimental to human health as smoking fifteen cigarettes per day.[55] During the COVID-19 pandemic, for example, one of the chief drawbacks to long-term social distancing and lockdowns was the isolation and subsequent increase in mental illness within the public.[56]

Beyond our overwhelming and primary need for social contact, many studies have explored the nuances of how our social cognition works in light of human sociality. One of the most distinctive dimensions of human cognition is our ability to imagine what the future will be like for each of us. Since international relations requires the generation and diffusion of ideas, opinion-shaping, selection of leaders, governance, and planning, it is fundamentally about imagining the future. The hippocampus, the part of the brain that stores past memories, also enables us to imagine future scenarios. This opens the door to cognitive biases or mental shortcuts that the brain provides, which could result in distortions of thinking

---

[52] Dirk Helbing, as quoted in Laura Spinney, "Karma of the Crowd," *National Geographic*, February 2014, pp. 123–135.

[53] Spinney, "Karma of the Crowd," pp. 123–135.

[54] Ian Leslie, "Why Your 'Weak-Tie' Friendships May Mean More Than You Think," *The Life Project*, July 2, 2020; Mark Granovetter, "The Strength of Weak Ties," *American Journal of Sociology* 78, 6 (May 1973): 1360–1380, https://www.jstor.org/stable/2776392 (accessed May 20, 2023).

[55] Julianne, Holt-Lunstad, Timothy B. Smith, Mark Baker, Tyler Harris, and David Stephenson, "Loneliness and Social Isolation as Risk Factors for Mortality: A Meta-analytic Review," *Perspectives on Psychological Science* 10, 2 (2015): 227–237, https://doi.org/10.1177/1745691614568352, as cited in Jamil Zaki, "We Volunteer to Help Others, But Research Shows How Much it Helps Us, Too," *Washington Post*, January 13, 2020, https://www.washingtonpost.com/health/we-volunteer-to-help-others-but-research-shows-how-much-it-helps-us-too/2020/01/10/7b365ee2-331b-11ea-9313-6cba89b1b9fb_story.html?utm_campaign=wp_main&utm_medium=social&utm_source=facebook (accessed May 21, 2023).

[56] Sujata Gupta, "Social Distancing Comes with Psychological Fallout," *Science News*, March 29, 2020, https://www.sciencenews.org/article/coronavirus-covid-19-social-distancing-psychological-fallout (accessed May 20, 2023).

when considering the future. It turns out that these distortions, however, are also indispensable to fulfilling our ultrasocial drive.

Cognitive Bias

In *Thinking Fast and Slow*, psychologist and behavioral economist Daniel Kahneman famously argues that our minds have two main systems of thinking.[57] System 1 tends to feed into biases as the generator of quick thinking or gut responses, while system 2 is a slower and more deliberate style of assessment and judgment. Especially in light of the power of System 1, there are literally hundreds of documented cognitive biases that scientists have exposed. For example, the availability bias is the tendency to rely much more heavily on recent exposure to information or impressions.[58] The anchoring bias is an unwillingness to update one's beliefs when new evidence is presented. The egocentric bias is the propensity to believe that your own perspective is superior to that of others. The list goes on and on. There is much debate in the field of psychology about where these biases come from and whether they are helpful to us or not.

Since I am most concerned with the relevance of species-level ultrasociality to international relations, much of the individual-based research on cognitive biases is not directly relevant here. However, I would like to zoom in on one type of cognitive bias that does have particular relevance on a broader scale: the optimism bias. This bias, in particular, is valuable to understanding how we collectively think about and imagine the future and ultimately why we decide to cooperate internationally. Rather than being a purely learned cognitive bias, the optimism bias is distinctly related to how we have evolved and survived.

What is the optimism bias? It is important to first understand it at the individual level. Tali Sharot conducted a series of experiments to show the optimism bias at work.[59] She asked participants how likely it was that something negative would befall them in the future. For example, one experiment asked participants how likely they thought it was that they would get cancer.[60] Sharot observed that when a respondent gave himself a 10% chance of getting cancer and then was told that the actual average probability was 30%, he would then only slightly increase his odds when asked the question a second time. Interestingly, respondents repeatedly did *not* adjust their odds up to match the actual average. They would, for instance,

---

[57] Daniel Kahneman, *Thinking Fast and Slow* (New York: Farrar, Straus and Giroux, 2013).

[58] Amos Tversky and Daniel Kahneman, "Availability: A Heuristic for Judging Frequency and Probability," as cited in Steven Pinker, *Enlightenment Now: The Case for Reason, Science, Humanism, and Progress* (New York: Viking Press, 2018), pp. 41–42.

[59] Tali Sharot, *The Optimism Bias: A Tour of the Irrationally Positive Brain* (New York: Vintage, 2012).

[60] Tali Sharot, "The Optimism Bias," TED conference, 2012, https://www.ted.com/talks/tali_sharot_the_optimism_bias#t-648688 (accessed May 20, 2023).

increase their odds to 11%, even while knowing that the actual odds were 30%. The same was true in experiments asking participants about their odds of getting divorced, which is, in reality, around 40%. Perhaps unsurprisingly, newlyweds, would almost always put their odds of divorce at 0%, but even non-newlywed participants continually answered this question with far lower odds, even when told the actual average. From these experiments and others, Sharot concluded that humans have a striking inclination toward personal optimism.

Why? Sharot accounts for this personal optimism through the concept of *mental time travel*—the capacity to imagine the future—which evolved over the course of human history. She writes,

> Mental time travel—going back and forth through time and space in one's mind—may be the most extraordinary of human talents. It is also one that seems necessary for optimism. If we are unable to imagine ourselves in the future, we may not be able to be positive about our prospects, either.[61]

While being able to envision the future means that we are also aware of our ultimate death, we have also evolved as a species to think optimistically about the future. This is potentially a necessary protection mechanism and could have a bearing on what we do on the international level. Without this ability, awareness of death would have resulted in total despair in humans, possibly even leading to the demise of the species. As Sharot explains, "The only way conscious mental time travel could have been selected over the course of evolution is if it had emerged at the same time as false beliefs. In other words, an ability to imagine the future had to develop side by side with positive biases."[62] Thus, the human inclination to be optimistic is, in part, a necessary coping mechanism. When it comes to international relations, this suggests that ideational leaders, whose narratives provide reason to be optimistic and help others envision a better world, may be able to attract more people to the cause on a cognitive level. Those who rely on fear and doom-and-gloom scenarios may draw in followers, but mainly for the short run.

Naturally, as with everything, there is variation—some people are more optimistic than others, and we are also each impacted by our environment. As Sharot writes, "Humans are largely affected by the expectations placed upon them."[63] People who are mildly depressed are actually the most realistic about their future prospects. But studies show that real optimists live longer and make more money because their expectations are higher, and so they act to achieve them.[64] There is an actual biological process that happens merely at the thought of imagining a positive future scenario: the amygdala and rostral anterior cingulate cortex (rACC),

---

[61] Sharot, *The Optimism Bias*, p. 27.
[62] Sharot, *The Optimism Bias*, p. 39.
[63] Sharot, *The Optimism Bias*, p. 48
[64] Sharot, *The Optimism Bias*, pp. 57–58.

a region in the frontal cortex, are activated.[65] Even though optimism is a kind of false belief, as Sharot describes it, it can also create a self-fulfilling prophecy.

Crucially, individual optimism also has a bearing on *public* or communal optimism. Sharot finds that public optimism spiked worldwide in 2008, with 80% of the public in the United States reporting a sense of optimism that year. This spike in the United States encouraged optimism around the world too.[66] Much of this could be attributed to the election of Barack Obama because there was such a strong need for good news after the failures and crises of the George W. Bush presidency that positive expectations were much higher. As Sharot writes, "It is during hard times that people rely on optimism the most."[67] Again, this not only contributes to an understanding of ultrasociality, but it is also suggestive of what might work in galvanizing the public around transformational ideas.

The course of events in people's brains that lead to high levels of global optimism is illustrative of one dimension of how ultrasociality works. When Obama gave his election acceptance speech, people listening felt "elevation," which happens when the vagus nerve is stimulated to release oxytocin, produced in the hypothalamus. When oxytocin levels are high, we feel less uncertainty about "social stimuli" of various types.[68] We are usually more optimistic when we feel we have more control, even if this is just an imagined belief in control.[69] Optimism and a sense of control, in turn, lead to a sense of increased trust among people.[70] It would not be a stretch to suggest that a similar spike in oxytocin, elevation, public optimism, and sense of control occurred on November 7, 2020, when Joe Biden was declared the winner of the presidential election against Donald Trump.

Ultimately, Sharot concludes that episodes of widescale public optimism are few and far between, while private optimism is far more common.[71] And when public optimism surfaces, it does not usually last long.[72] The irony about private optimism is that in order to be confident in one's own great future, one also must be pessimistic about the future of others; that is, if you are better than average, others must be worse. So, general public optimism is difficult to achieve and sustain, but it is more likely to happen during very low points or crises in human history. Perhaps this provides the cognitive underpinnings for why, after each major existential crisis for the European Union, there is a surge in pro-integration sentiment and optimism about the future of Europe, for example.[73] Sharot writes that

[65] Sharot, *The Optimism Bias*, p. 88.
[66] Sharot, *The Optimism Bias*, p. 60.
[67] Sharot, *The Optimism Bias*, p. 62.
[68] Sharot, *The Optimism Bias*, p. 63.
[69] Sharot, *The Optimism Bias*, p. 69.
[70] Sharot, *The Optimism Bias*, p. 64.
[71] Sharot, *The Optimism Bias*, p. 70.
[72] Sharot, *The Optimism Bias*, p. 66.
[73] Maïa K. Davis Cross, *The Politics of Crisis in Europe* (New York: Cambridge University Press, 2017).

when society reaches unprecedented lows that affect our personal lives directly, the only way for our situation to improve is to take the rest of the world upward with us [. . .] That is the time when people turn to bearers of good news such as Barack Obama and Shirley Temple. That is when optimism sweeps the world. Or at least it does until the economy stabilizes, at which point we are quite happy to go back to public pessimism.[74]

Thus, our biology and cognition can provide important insights into why we succeed in achieving cooperative breakthroughs at some points in time and not others. As I mention in my return to this topic in Chapter 4, major crises may be valuable in encouraging ultrasocial outcomes in international relations specifically because they prime us for periods of public optimism, and subsequently, increased trust.

But to stay at the level of building blocks for now, a relevant finding in all of this is that optimism indicates a capacity *to imagine a bright future*, which can be a self-fulfilling prophecy. And when this happens on a collective level, especially in the midst of international crises, there is a kind of collective elevation which, in turn, leads to more certainty about how things will play out, a sense of control, and more trust amongst people. In sum, optimism is not the only reason why individuals would choose to cooperate, but it is a crucial element.

Genes

Our genetic composition is the most fundamental part of human evolution. While genes mainly point to a high level of similarity as a species (we are all 99.9% identical to one another in our genetic make-up), genes also indicate differences. Although I am mainly interested in species-level qualities as this is where the building blocks of ultrasociality can be found, there is one dimension of genetic variation that has a bearing on ultrasocial behavior: the difference between liberals and conservatives.

To be sure, much of the research into genes is focused on isolating individual-level variation. Scientists have found, for example, that the presence of certain genes may indicate probabilities toward being liberal or conservative, aggressive or passive, intelligent or less intelligent, and so on.[75] On an individual level, it seems that genes do matter in at least partially explaining political attitudes. Of course, the environment in which a person grows up and is socialized also matters. As political scientist Rose McDermott writes, "social scientists tend to describe the environment as broadly defined social forces that may limit or enable particular

---

[74] Sharot, *The Optimism Bias*, p. 71.
[75] Hatemi and McDermott, *Man Is by Nature*.

attitudes or behaviors."[76] In some instances, genes and environment may have relatively more or less impact. For instance, a person with a politically active genetic predisposition who lives in a repressive country may not ever demonstrate political behavior because the environment prevents them from doing so. Or, a person's genes may lead them to choose environments to work, live, and socialize where others are similarly politically inclined.

Despite the importance of environment, there is still significant evidence that genes contain political information for each of us. Thousands of studies of monozygotic twins—those with the same genetic code—show that even when twins are separated at birth and raised in very different environments, they share numerous types of behavior, such as being politically conservative or not.[77] These twin studies are almost unanimous in their agreement that separated twins end up with very similar, if not the *same*, political views, even though their ultimate political identification is strongly dictated by their upbringing and socialization. So, even if one twin votes for liberal politicians and the other supports conservative ones, they would still espouse very similar political views based on the same personality traits.[78]

Biology and genes influence our personality traits, which scientists have boiled down to five major qualities: (1) openness, (2) conscientiousness/orderliness, (3) extraversion, (4) agreeableness, and (5) neuroticism. These qualities are stronger or weaker in each of us. In terms of political beliefs (i.e., whether one is liberal or conservative), the personality traits of orderliness and openness are the most important. A team of researchers at the University of Toronto found that "Conservatives tend to be higher in a personality trait called orderliness and lower in openness. This means that they're more concerned about a sense of order and tradition, expressing a deep psychological motive to preserve the current social structure," while, "liberalism is more often associated with the underlying motives for compassion, empathy and equality," which come from high openness and low orderliness.[79]

What about the role of socialization in changing these personality traits? As C. J. Soto and his team of social psychologists found in 2011, these traits are extremely stable through adulthood, and it is exceedingly rare to see any significant change.[80] Indeed, one of the few studies that has actually been able to identify changes to

[76] Jason D. Boardman, "Gene–Environment Interplay for the Study of Political Behaviors," in *Man Is by Nature*, ed. Hatemi and McDermott, p. 187.
[77] Alford and Hibbing, "The Origin of Politics," p. 714.
[78] For a review of this literature, see Bryan Caplan, *Selfish Reasons to Have More Kids: Why Being a Great Parent is Less Work and More Fun Than You Think* (New York: Basic Books, 2012).
[79] University of Toronto, "Personality Predicts Political Preferences," *ScienceDaily*, June 10, 2012, https://www.sciencedaily.com/releases/2010/06/100609111312.htm (accessed May 20, 2023).
[80] Christopher J. Soto, Oliver P. John, Samuel D. Gosling, and Jeff Potter, "Age Differences in Personality Traits from 10 to 65: Big Five Domains and Facets in a Large Cross-Sectional Sample," *Journal of Personality and Social Psychology* 100, 2 (2011): 330–348, https://doi.org/10.1037/a0021717.

major personality traits in adults has been through the use of psychedelic drugs.[81] These drugs were shown to increase openness in a way that would seem highly unlikely without drug use. Interestingly, before this could be shown scientifically, the Nixon administration classified psychedelic drugs as a controlled substance precisely because Nixon worried that their widespread use was actually creating hippies—it turns out that this wasn't such a far-fetched idea.

But how does an understanding of human nature at the individual level inform societal level outcomes and behaviors? Does this mean that liberals are more likely to uphold and pursue ultrasocial ideas? In a word: yes. Indeed, psychologists have shown, through a range of studies, that liberals have more empathy than conservatives.[82] This could play some role in explaining why some people are more likely to be captured by tribalism and others are not. However, it is still important to emphasize that, on the whole, whether liberal or conservative, our species is remarkably empathic.

Indeed, this chapter has shown how, at a micro level, we are predisposed to be highly socially oriented. It is literally painful for us to experience social rejection, and we recognize pain in others, even suffering that as our own. Our brains and minds are constantly processing what others are doing and thinking, whether consciously or not, and we seek to shape those impressions in a favorable direction. We want others to value us. From birth, we seek to be surrounded by a rich social environment. Humans are literally healthier together than alone. We seek to empathically cooperate with each other and define ourselves in the context of our societies. Our brains have given us the capacity to imagine and plan for the future and we do so with optimism. All of this contributes to the building blocks of ultrasociality, which, in turn, underpin international relations—the ideas that inspire us to work together, the motivations that allow cooperative breakthroughs, and the agreements that enable us to include each other in our imagined future.

[81] David Erritzoe, Leor Roseman, Matthew M. Nour, Katherine MacLean, Mendel Kaelen, David J. Nutt, and Robin L. Carhart-Harris, "Effects of Psilocybin Therapy on Personality Structure," *Acta Psychiatrica Scandinavica* 138, 5 (November 2018): 368–378, https://doi.org/10.1111/acps.12904.
[82] Paul Bloom, *Against Empathy: The Case for Rational Compassion* (New York: Harper Collins, 2016), pp. 177–212.

2
Biology Meets Culture

The physical brain has its automatic and default modes, and the mind that inhabits it goes beyond this, infusing these responses with conscious and unconscious meaning. However, the mind does not develop in isolation, with each individual nurturing his or her own mind independently. The brain and mind are intrinsically connected to our *social* world, our culture. As psychologist and neuroscientist Lisa Feldman Barrett writes, "culture is not some gauzy, amorphous vapor that surrounds you. It helped to wire your brain, and you behave in certain ways that wire the brains of the next generation [. . .] it takes more than one brain to create a mind."[83]

Evolution

Adding another layer to the building blocks of ultrasociality is the field of evolutionary biology. Many evolutionary biologists focus on the intersection between biology and culture to understand our evolution as a species. These scientists explain why humans developed a strong desire to cooperate over millions of years, making us one of the most social species on the planet. We know that even prehuman societies were highly social and that other primates engage in cooperation. However, as evolution proceeded, *homo sapiens*, more than other species, developed the capacity to form much larger groups. Survival itself became contingent upon this. In other words, evolution has favored those who are socially oriented. The creation of much larger groups required a distinct and complex language, the ability to give speeches to large crowds of people, and eventually, remote communication.[84] Humans alone developed this capacity, and in obvious ways, it has made the international relations we see today possible.

However, much of the basis for modern-day thinking about evolution uses the concept of "survival of the fittest" as a shorthand, which emphasizes individuals over societies. Because of this, the concept has had long-standing ramifications for what non-experts assume to be true. In terms of human behavior, "survival

[83] Lisa Feldman Barrett, *How Emotions Are Made: The Secret Life of the Brain* (New York: Mariner Books, 2017), pp. 153–154.

[84] Darby Proctor and Sarah Brosnan, "Political Primates: What Other Primates Can Tell Us About the Evolutionary Roots of Our Own Political Behavior," in *Man Is by Nature a Political Animal*, ed. Peter K. Hatemi and Rose McDermott (Chicago, IL: University of Chicago Press, 2011), pp. 47–71.

International Cooperation Against All Odds. Mai'a K. Davis Cross, Oxford University Press. © Mai'a K. Davis Cross (2024).
DOI: 10.1093/oso/9780192873903.003.0003

of the fittest" is typically thought to mean that we are hard-wired to compete at the expense of our fellow man. Thomas Hobbes, for example, is often associated today with this approach, with his power-driven, competitive view of the world (of course, he wrote *Leviathan* some 200 years before Darwin). However, this common catchphrase does not really capture the full complexity of human evolution from a more biological or anthropological standpoint.

Indeed, Charles Darwin himself did not actually take such an individualized, harsh view of human behavior and natural selection. It is a common misconception that he coined the phrase, "survival of the fittest." This dubious credit actually goes to Herbert Spencer, who saw similarities between Darwin's argument and his own economic theories. Thomas Huxley subsequently popularized the theory but, in the process, boiled evolution down to a matter of violent self-interest. In contrast, Darwin himself recognized the importance of sociality, even in a theory built on natural selection. Unlike his occasional co-author, Alfred Russel Wallace, who actually came up with the theory of evolution based on natural selection before Darwin wrote *On the Origin of Species*, Darwin believed natural selection was *both* behavioral and physical.[85]

Since Darwin, a debate has raged among scientists over the specific nature of evolution. This has included the extent to which natural selection is purely genetic or both genetic and cultural, as well as whether its impetus comes from the individual versus group levels or both. So-called *multilevel selection*, defined as natural selection at both the individual and the group level, like other contemporary approaches, explicitly denies that evolution is just about individual survival or survival of the fittest. Working at the intersection of neuroscience and cultural evolution, E. O. Wilson writes that, "an iron rule exists in genetic social evolution. It is that selfish individuals beat altruistic individuals, while groups of altruists beat groups of selfish individuals. The victory can never be complete; the balance of selection pressures cannot move to either extreme."[86] Known for his controversial sociobiology argument, Wilson argues that evolution gives us not only our biological and genetic make-up but also, to some degree, our *social* behavior.

As theoretical biologist Samuel Bowles describes it, early humans' need for food naturally led to a need for territory, and this prompted them to begin conquering and then protecting that territory.[87] The only way to really hold on to their territory was to form cooperative groups that transcended simply kin-based relationships. As these cooperative groups competed with one another, they developed prejudices against other groups, tightening their in-group bonds. Ultimately, those groups that were better at competition with others became dominant in social evolution. Over time, *homo sapiens* did not just display strong empathy for each other,

[85] John R. Alford and John R. Hibbing, "The Origin of Politics: An Evolutionary Theory of Political Behavior," *Perspectives on Politics* 2, 4 (2004): 714, https://doi.org/10.1017/S1537592704040460.
[86] Edward O. Wilson, *The Social Conquest of Earth* (New York: Liveright, 2013), p. 243.
[87] As cited in Wilson, *The Social Conquest of Earth*, p. 72.

they displayed *kindness*.[88] Critics of sociobiology counter that genes play some role in how we behave but that group dynamics and episodes of violence stem more from nurture than nature.[89] This debate notwithstanding, there is still general agreement that evolution—for whatever reason—has featured stronger and stronger *social* ties, with *social* behavior being passed down from generation to generation. In this sense, it is not surprising that the culmination of all of this has been the capacity and desire to engage with each other socially on a global scale.

Another major debate in evolutionary scholarship is the extent to which the urge to cooperate in groups is stronger among genetically related individuals or not. Past research has relied on a kind of "selfish-gene approach," not unlike inclusive fitness or kin selection theory, meaning that the more people are genetically similar, the more they display altruism toward each other. This has been firmly debunked in more recent research.[90] For example, in a rare collaboration between a scientist and a political scientist, Robert Axelrod and William D. Hamilton find that both altruism and "restraint in competition" are manifested in in-group behavior but that altruism and reciprocity are *not* stronger for those who are in the same kinship group.[91] Similarly, Adrian V. Bell, Peter J. Richerson, and Richard McElreath find that large societies are strongly altruistic and that this is not about just reciprocity because the "altruism is directed at strangers."[92]

E. O. Wilson, Martin Nowak, and Corina Tarnita also argue that the assumption of individual or kin-based selfishness is both mathematically and biologically wrong. They base this on their study of highly cooperative, ultrasocial insects. It is not about cooperation or defection, with workers in a colony seen as individual actors, but rather about *group* selection.[93] Moreover, while ultrasocial insect species are either genetically identical or closely related (e.g., they often share a single reproductive queen), this is not the case for humans. Nonetheless, as Wilson writes, "Human beings are prone to be moral—do the right thing, hold back, give aid to others, sometimes even at personal risk—because natural selection has favored those interactions of group members benefitting the group as a whole."[94] Importantly, especially in terms of relevance for international relations, the more

[88] Jamil Zaki, *The War for Kindness: Building Empathy in Fractured World* (New York: Broadway Books, 2019), p. 6.

[89] Steven Pinker, "The False Allure of Group Selection," *The Edge*, June 18, 2012, https://www.edge.org/conversation/steven_pinker-the-false-allure-of-group-selection (accessed May 20, 2023); Steven Pinker, *The Blank Slate: The Modern Denial of Human Nature* (New York: Penguin Books, 2011), p. 442.

[90] Richard Dawkins, *The Selfish Gene* (Oxford: Oxford University Press, 1976).

[91] Robert Axelrod and William D. Hamilton, "The Evolution of Cooperation," *Science* 211, 4489: 1390–1396, https://doi.org/10.1126/science.7466396.

[92] Adrian V. Bell, Peter J. Richerson, and Richard McElreath, "Culture Rather Than Genes Provides Greater Scope for the Evolution of Large-Scale Human Prosociality," *Proceedings of the National Academy of Sciences of the United States of America* 106, 42: 17671–17674, https://www.jstor.org/stable/i25592873 (accessed May 20, 2023).

[93] As cited in Wilson, *The Social Conquest of Earth*, p. 143.

[94] Wilson, *The Social Conquest of Earth*, p. 247.

complex the society, whether in the animal or human kingdom, the more altruism it displays.[95]

Altruism not only extends beyond related individuals but also transcends reciprocity. A number of scholars, such as John Maynard Smith and Adrian Bell and colleagues, among others, rely on mathematical game theory to study what they see as *reciprocal cooperation*; that is, you might act for the good of others now, but that's only because you expect to be paid back in some way later. However, scholars across a range of disciplines have argued that the use of game theory is actually counterproductive because it still ultimately assumes that cooperation involves tit-for-tat maneuvering as opposed to true self-sacrifice. Altruism is actually about more than just simply being socially inclined.[96] *Reciprocal* altruism—which is what game theory tries to track[97]—is not the same as *authentic* altruism. As Wilson explains, authentic altruism can only be explained by "instinctive empathy" or "a biological instinct for the common good of the tribe, put in place by group selection, wherein groups of altruists in prehistoric times prevailed over groups of individuals in selfish disarray."[98]

Thus, multilevel selection acknowledges that an integral part of human survival has involved living and working together in groups, a key quality that eventually makes large-scale national and international organization of humans possible. While earlier evolution scholars like Richard Dawkins, known for his 1976 book *The Selfish Gene*, have assumed that each individual only works for himself, later scholars have recognized that the chances of survival are much higher if humans find ways to divide labor, specialize in certain tasks, and cooperate in an effort to compete with other groups.[99] These are not unlike the qualities that have enabled economic, political, and social globalization to take place in the modern world. So, evolution does not necessarily predispose humans toward genes that are best at selfish competition, as international relations rationalists would assume. There are competing pressures: individually selfish humans will ultimately gravitate toward cooperation because that is often the only path to survival.

Taking this knowledge into account, evolutionary biologists ultimately define a cooperator differently than we might normally think of one, especially in the realm of international relations. While international relations experts would most typically define cooperation as when two or more actors—be they states or individuals—both see it in their self-interest to work together and gain together

---

[95] Wilson, *The Social Conquest of Earth*, p. 109.

[96] Alford and Hibbing "The Origin of Politics," p. 710.

[97] See, e.g., Michael Gurven, "Reciprocal Altruism and Food Sharing Decisions among Hiki and Ache Hunter-Gatherers," *Behavioral Ecology and Sociobiology* 56, 4 (2004): 366–380, https://doi.org/10.1007/s00265-004-0793-6.

[98] Wilson, *The Social Conquest of Earth*, p. 251.

[99] Alford and Hibbing, "The Origin of Politics," pp. 708–709.

(preferably gaining more than the others), many evolutionary biologists see cooperation more in terms of altruism and a willingness for self-sacrifice. Martin A. Nowak emphasizes this surprising understanding of cooperation in evolutionary terms:

> Every gene, every cell, and every organism should be designed to promote its own evolutionary success at the expense of its competitors. Yet we observe cooperation at many levels of biological organization [. . .] Humans are champions of cooperation. From hunter-gatherer societies to nation-states, cooperation is the decisive organizing principle of human society.[100]

We tend to think of cooperation as making a choice based on our preferences and whether we see it in our interests. This is the definition of "rationalism" in international relations. However, cooperation is far more intrinsic to the evolution of our species than simply a choice in a given moment. It is also far more than just which genes win out in the evolutionary process.

In another universe, we might have evolved to be more individualistic or cutthroat competitors. The stark differences between the bonobos and chimpanzees illustrates this.[101] The two were originally the same species, living in the tropical forests of the Zaire River, but 2.5 million years ago, there was an evolutionary split, seemingly as a result of a drought south of the river, which reduced competition for food. Those apes south of the river evolved to become bonobos, a peaceful and easy-going society of great apes that practices sexual equality, holds strong social bonds, and engages in almost constant recreational sex (which blurs paternity and thus reduces the potential for conflict). By contrast, those north of the Zaire River, where there was no drought, faced ongoing competition for food. They evolved to become chimpanzees, a male-dominated society that resolves disputes through fighting and practices infanticide as a competitive tactic.

In short, while, in another universe, things might have turned out differently, we instead evolved to be fundamentally *social*. As Christakis argues,

> Natural selection has shaped a kind of fundamental way in which we go about living socially [. . .] most people nowadays are familiar with the idea that natural selection in genes guides the structure and function of our bodies. And people are also increasingly aware that national selection in genes can guide the structure

---

[100] Martin A. Nowak, "Five Rules for the Evolution of Cooperation," *Science* 314, 5805 (December 2006): 1560, https://doi.org/10.1126/science.1133755.
[101] Richard Wrangham and Amy Parish, "Evolution: Why Sex?," WGBH Educational Foundation, Clear Blue Skies Productions (video), 2001, https://www.pbs.org/wgbh/evolution/library/01/5/quicktime/l_015_01.html (accessed May 21, 2023).

and function of our minds [. . .] Natural selection and our genes also play a role
[. . .] in the structure and function of our societies.[102]

Evolution and natural selection of our genes has led to a fundamental capacity for
love, friendship, cooperation, teaching, and learning from each other, what Christakis calls a *social suite* of predispositions—a blueprint—or "pre-wiring" to be
socially oriented and good. This social suite is a key building block of ultrasociality
and suggests that we would gravitate toward international interactions that allow
us to express these qualities collectively. Again, genes do not determine behavior,
but they do mean that we have much more in common as a species than we have
that separates us. As I describe in Chapter 4, on a species level, we are anchored
in an ultrasocial landscape.

Cultural Evolution

An everyday understanding of culture is usually associated with regional- or
national-level practices . . . Andalusian cuisine, Brazilian music, or Japanese tea
ceremonies, for example. In the context of evolution, culture takes on a significantly broader meaning. As psychologist Richard W. Robins puts it, "There is a
core human mentality and social behavior that cuts across nations, cultures, and
ethnic groups. Even such profoundly different countries as Burkina Faso and the
United States do not differ substantially in the average personality tendencies of
their people."[103]

Beyond biological or genetic evolution, cultural adaptation and learning play a
significant role in explaining widescale human cooperation too. Evolution led to
collective learning, making humans distinct from other animals, with the ability to
pass learning from one to another and to subsequent generations. At the heart of
this is the essential notion that "self-interest" is not fixed or pre-determined. It is
entirely open-ended.[104] Donald T. Campbell writes that

> From the standpoint of evolutionary biology, our innate pleasures, hungers, lusts,
> fears, and pains are subgoals, selected as mediating inclusive fitness. Learning
> takes place in the mediating of such goals. The message of cybernetics and pur-
> pose behaviorism is that learning itself is a chaining not of muscle contractions
> but rather of "acts" organized around the achievement of subgoals.[105]

---

[102] Nicholas Christakis, "Blueprint: Evolutionary Origins of a Good Society," lecture delivered for
the Beckman Institute, October 7, 2021.

[103] Richard W. Robins, "The Nature of Personality: Genes, Culture, and National Character," as cited
in Wilson, *The Social Conquest of Earth*, p. 100.

[104] Donald T. Campbell, "Rationality and Utility from the Standpoint of Evolutionary Biology,"
Journal of Business 59, 4 (1986): S355–S364, https://www.jstor.org/stable/2352766.

[105] Campbell, "Rationality and Utility," p. S357.

Through a process of *learning*, humans infuse their self-interest with meaning and morality.

Moreover, cultural evolution can happen much more quickly than genetic evolution, with cultural evolution at many points even leading the way. For example, when humans invented fire, it led to biological and genetic changes. Because fire makes digesting food much easier, it allowed pre-humans to consume more nutrients and spend less time hunting for food. Humans' intestines then evolved to become shorter. This led to increased efficiency, enabling the size of the human brain to grow. As the human brain got bigger, childbirth became more difficult. This meant that it was necessary for humans to cooperate to enable childbirth to happen successfully. As these processes played out, competitive social environments led to the spread of increasingly socially oriented behavior.[106]

The specific nature of human aggression and how it evolved is an important and relevant example of this. In general, scientists have identified two main forms of aggression: reactive and proactive. As a species, *reactive aggression*—the kind that involves lashing out without thinking—is remarkably rare, while *proactive aggression*—pre-meditated and thought out—is more common.[107] Reactive aggression involves instances of hot-headed responses, such as bar brawls or road rage. By contrast, proactive aggression involves planning and strategy, such as war. Biological anthropologist Richard Wrangham argues that, starting from around 200,000–300,000 years ago, as our species emerged, reactive aggression began to be suppressed through a process of self-domestication; that is, humans began to punish members of their tribe or community who displayed reactive aggressive tendencies—the so-called execution hypothesis. Violent men who were bullies and did not care about their reputations were executed. With antisocial individuals got rid of, those with more docile behavior, self-restraint, and tolerance were favored over time.[108] Ironically, Wrangham argues that groups needed to use proactive aggression to stop reactive aggression.[109] While this argument is somewhat controversial, it grapples with the seeming evolutionary contradiction of simultaneous cooperation and competition. Many millennia ago, the latter played a role in encouraging and diffusing the former, and as a result, *homo sapiens* emerged as a much more peaceful and docile species than other, closely related species, such as chimpanzees.[110]

---

[106] Robert Boyd and Peter J. Richerson, "Culture and the Evolution of Human Cooperation," *Philosophical Transactions of the Royal Society* B364 (2009): 3281–3288, https://doi.org/10.1098/rstb.2009.0134.

[107] Richard Wrangham, *The Goodness Paradox: The Strange Relationship between Virtue and Violence in Human Evolution* (New York: Vintage Books, 2019), p. 9.

[108] Wrangham, *The Goodness Paradox,* pp. 128–129.

[109] Wrangham, *The Goodness Paradox,* pp. 248–249.

[110] It is controversial because it potentially leaves open the possibility that humans are biologically predisposed to engage in other forms of proactive aggression, such as collective acts of violence, war, and conflict. However, as Wrangham points out, war and other forms of violence do not just "naturally" emerge out of our genetic code; they are in reaction to social circumstances and human decisions.

Continuing with the story of cultural evolution, eventually, as brain power increased, humans gained the ability to think symbolically, which led to the creation of language. The use of language changed the human brain further, making collective learning possible as early as 100,000 years ago. Collective learning became a distinct feature of human life. Among other things, this enabled gossiping, a sense of morality, caring what others think, avoiding rule breaking, striving to conform, and forming reputations.[111] No other animal can pass on learning from one generation to the next. Other species communicate only in the present. Collective learning meant that cooperation could occur in a cross-generational way. Then, about 70,000 years ago, *homo sapiens* likely underwent a cognitive revolution in which they started to become markedly more intelligent and able to invent a range of new tools, create art, and develop more sophisticated language.[112]

The rise of agriculture in the Neolithic period, beginning around 12,000 years ago, enabled humans to settle in a single place over their lifetimes, thus enhancing community and social bonds, more firmly extending empathy beyond the immediate family or tribe. Instead of just dozens of people working together, the bonds of cooperation could be extended to thousands, and ultimately millions, of people as specialization became more widespread.[113]

The invention of writing enabled communication over longer periods of time but also led to a stronger sense of self, a prerequisite for empathy.[114] At some point between the twelfth and eighth centuries BCE, the international trading system started to emerge, and from there, we can see an acceleration in the importance of ideas. Ultimately, the flourishing of discoveries in the sixteenth through to the eighteenth centuries, thanks to the Renaissance, the development of printing and the scientific method, and the spread of the Enlightenment, paved the way to the modern era and eventually the Industrial Revolution.

Since the Second World War, cooperation has become truly global. In modern times, as humans had begun to live in cities, certain types of people had become more adapted to city life, and future generations have evolved to have genes better suited for life there. Cultural evolution shows that human-made innovations have the capacity to change our genes down the road. Indeed, at some point thousands of years from now, the rise of the internet will likely have some kind of similar

---

Proactive aggression is not automatic, and it is also preventable. Wrangham, *The Goodness Paradox*, pp. 252–254.

[111] Wrangham, *The Goodness Paradox*, pp. 274–275.

[112] Yuval Noah Harari, *Sapiens: A Brief History of Humankind* (New York: Harper Collins Books, 2015), pp. 20–22.

[113] Toby Ord, *Precipice: Existential Risk and the Future of Humanity* (New York: Hachette Books, 2020).

[114] Jeremy Rifkin, *The Empathic Civilization: The Race to Global Consciousness in a World in Crisis* (New York: Tarcher/Penguin, 2009), p. 1.

effect on the human genetic code. As Christakis states, "Cultural inventions of our making are re-shaping evolution in historical time."[115]

Cultural evolution shows that human evolution more generally is intimately connected to societal developments in addition to biology. As Robert Boyd and Peter Richerson put it, "Scraps of individual insight and luck are spread widely to others, recombined with other scraps, and form the basis for additional innovations, all rather quickly."[116] They reject the evolutionary argument of some that cooperation results from reputation, reciprocation, and retribution (the so-called three Rs) because "repeated interactions can stabilize a vast range of alternative behaviours in different groups. A variety of other mechanisms also can lead to multiple stable equilibria."[117] Given the rapid cultural adaptation and evolution that occurs in humans, we have

> new social instincts suited to life in such groups including a psychology which "expects" life to be structured by moral norms, and that is designed to learn and internalize such norms. New emotions evolved, like shame and guilt, which increase the chance the norms are followed. Individuals lacking the new social instincts more often violated prevailing norms and experienced adverse selection.[118]

Thus, alongside evolution, culture is passed from one generation to the next through social processes—learning, teaching, imitation, socialization, and so on. Cultural transmission, in other words, is key to understanding evolution itself.[119] It has played an important role in building our species' ultrasocial nature.

But why are we so culturally adaptable in the first place, and what does this mean for our ultrasocial anchoring? It turns out that humans are "credulous"— our minds are open to believing various ideas, even if sometimes the beliefs we acquire are "bad."[120] As Robert Sapolsky explains, the development of the frontal cortex and genetics going back centuries gives us particular propensities to act, but we can also change our neuro-driven behavior in seconds because we understand the importance of "good" ideas.[121] However, this does not mean that the sky's the limit in terms of where we go with these ideas.

---

[115] Reason Podcast, "The Reason Interview with Nicholas Christakis," April 2019, https://reason.com/podcast/2019/04/05/the-yale-professor-attacked-by-angry-stu (accessed May 23, 2023).
[116] Boyd and Richerson, "Culture and the Evolution of Human Cooperation," p. 3282.
[117] Boyd and Richerson, "Culture and the Evolution of Human Cooperation," p. 3282.
[118] Boyd and Richerson, "Culture and the Evolution of Human Cooperation."
[119] Robert Boyd and Peter Richerson, *Culture and the Evolutionary Process* (Chicago, IL: University of Chicago Press, 1985).
[120] Boyd and Richerson, "Culture and the Evolution of Human Cooperation," p. 3286.
[121] Robert Sapolsky, *Behave: The Biology of Humans at Our Best and Worst* (New York: Penguin Press, 2017); also see: Robert Sapolsky, "The Biology of Our Best and Worst Selves," Ted conference, 2017, https://www.ted.com/talks/robert_sapolsky_the_biology_of_our_best_and_worst_selves?utm_source=newsletter_weekly_2017-05-14&utm_campaign=newsletter_weekly&utm_medium=email&utm_content=talk_of_the_week_image#t-913951 (accessed May 20, 2023).

Our societies, and the stability of them, strongly depend on a common set of norms and a shared view of morality. It is perhaps this quality that underpins present-day innovations like treaties to protect human rights, ensures peace between countries, and enables international trade. David Lahti and Bret Weinstein advance an understanding of evolution that connects the adoption and diffusion of ideas and norms in society to what they call stability-dependent cooperation.[122] They argue that shared norms—that is, standards of appropriate behavior, for example, helping the elderly or not stealing other people's belongings—help to solidify and stabilize groups of people, but the extent to which these norms are shared and followed can vary depending on the specific societal group. They find that *less* stable groups have weaker shared norms, and *more* stable groups have distinct advantages in group evolution.

Relatedly, Jordan Theriault, Liane Young, and Lisa Feldman Barrett find that as evolution has proceeded, humans have learned that the more they break recognized group norms, the more the brain's natural ability to predict and anticipate the behavior of others—like mindreading—is undermined.[123] For example, if the norm of not stealing your neighbor's belongings erodes, it becomes increasingly difficult to live your daily life in a whole host of different ways. Should you leave your home to go to work? Should you attempt to get your belongings back? Would this involve violence? Is it necessary to buy a gun? The consequences of breaking recognized norms can be pretty dire. With less of an ability to predict the behavior of others, humans become far less certain about the actual parameters of behavior. Then, for example, erroneous expectations lead to food shortages, lack of trust, less chance for survival. Crucially, therefore, evolution itself has pushed people toward following the norms of the group. And if new ideas are embraced, they typically have to spread through the larger community to be effective.

We can readily draw an analogy of this to the international level. When Russia invaded Ukraine in 2022, it violated Ukraine's sovereignty as well as international law, which also made it very difficult for the international community to anticipate what Russian President Vladimir Putin was willing to do next. The world also became far less stable when US President Donald Trump was in office as his norm-breaking actions and rhetoric made international relations far less predictable. In light of this, various members of the Council on Foreign Relations—the United States' premier international affairs thinktank—emphasized growing hostility to

[122] David C. Lahti and Bret S. Weinstein, "The Better Angels of Our Nature: Group Stability and the Evolution of Moral Tension," *Evolution and Human Behavior* 26, 1 (2005): 47–63, https://doi.org/10.1016/j.evolhumbehav.2004.09.004.

[123] Jordan E. Theriault, Liane Young, and Lisa Feldman Barrett, "The Sense of Should: A Biologically-Based Framework for Modeling Social Pressure," *Physics of Life Reviews* 36 (2021), https://doi.org/10.1016/j.plrev.2020.01.004.

multilateralism, a broken global economic system, and decaying trust around the world.[124]

As we can see, evolution and cultural evolution both demonstrate the various ways in which, over hundreds of thousands of years, human existence has steadily followed a path toward cooperation, altruism, empathy, and common norms. Alongside evolution's contribution to ultrasociality, it sets the stage for international relations itself to gravitate toward the establishment of common, empathic norms. While there will likely always be some debate about the specific origins of our species, it is clear that scientists have now significantly refined our understanding away from simplistic notions of survival of the fittest and toward some form of *social* evolution. Our individual minds only make sense in the context of the group. Indeed, it certainly does "[take] more than one brain to create a mind."[125]

[124] Terrence Mullan, "The Corrosion of World Order in the Age of Donald Trump," Council on Foreign Relations, February 13, 2020, https://www.cfr.org/blog/corrosion-world-order-age-donald-trump (accessed May 20, 2023); Council on Foreign Relations, "Council of Councils Twelfth Regional Conference Report," January 30, 2020, https://www.cfr.org/report/council-councils-twelfth-regional-conference (accessed May 20, 2023).
[125] Barrett, *How Emotions Are Made*, pp. 153–154.

3

The *Social* in Social Science

From psychology to anthropology, and from philosophy to sociology, the social sciences have contributed much to the building blocks that comprise our understanding of human ultrasociality. Some take into account the biological basis of our social predisposition, while others do not. But the most exciting work in this area, and arguably the most important, crosses disciplinary boundaries. Much of this research converges on recognition of the human capacity to cooperate, empathize, communicate, and improve our collective lives on Earth. At the same time, some of this work also identifies the antisocial qualities of which we are capable and, specifically, how our ultrasocial nature can also be lured into tribalism. The social sciences bring us closest to an understanding of the politics of international relations as they shed light on human behavior and social interaction on a broader scale.

Human Universals

Beyond the common mental processes that we possess, there are at least hundreds of qualities of human behavior that answer the question of what is universal in human nature. Several anthropologists, such as Clark Wissler, Bronislaw Malinowski, George Murdock, and Donald Brown, have tried to capture these universal qualities through meticulously finding and documenting the behavior that is found across diverse societies everywhere on the planet.

Brown compiled a list of so-called human universals—several hundred qualities of behavior and language that ethnographers have directly observed across all human cultures.[126] For example, when very young children play without adult supervision, their practices look similar all around the world: children at play cooperate. Our species also, without exception, engages in social teaching and social learning, passing knowledge and practice from one to another and to subsequent generations. The list goes on.[127]

---

[126] Donald Brown, *Human Universals* (New York: McGraw, 1991), as cited in Steven Pinker, *The Blank Slate: The Modern Denial of Human Nature* (New York: Penguin Books, 2002) pp. 435–439.

[127] Other examples include beliefs about fortune and misfortune, classification of inner states, collective identities, division of labor, facial expressions, the ability to manipulate social relations, myths, narratives, planning for the future, rites of passage, ritual, socialization expected from senior kin, tabooed utterances, turn taking, some forms of proscribed violence, fear of death, and so on.

International Cooperation Against All Odds. Mai'a K. Davis Cross, Oxford University Press. © Mai'a K. Davis Cross (2024).
DOI: 10.1093/oso/9780192873903.003.0004

Bringing together his work on evolution and sociology, Christakis puts forward a more streamlined version of the universal list, focusing on universals that have evolutionary origins rather than ecological or environmental causes.[128] He emphasizes that, "the human ability to construct societies has become an instinct. It is not just something we *can* do—it is something we *must* do."[129] Christakis's so-called "social suite"—genes that create a blueprint for human society—is the following:

(1) The capacity to have and recognize individual identity
(2) Love for partners and offspring
(3) Friendship
(4) Social networks
(5) Cooperation
(6) Preference for one's own group (that is, "in-group bias")
(7) Mild hierarchy (that is, relative egalitarianism)
(8) Social learning and teaching.[130]

While acknowledging that there is always room for individual deviation, Christakis's main argument is that genes tend to encourage *similarity* across humans rather than differences.[131] Indeed, if deviation from our universal blueprint occurred at a societal level, rather than at an individual level, the result could be devastating (see Chapter 2). Instead, Christakis finds that humans together form a fundamentally "good" society that is based on mutual respect, cooperation, and learning from each other. Rifkin boils this down even further to say that, to the extent that there is a common human culture, it gravitates toward empathy.

More traditional philosopher-sociologists, such as Jürgen Habermas, agree with this vision of human society, although they put the emphasis more on the communicative capacity of humans than our biology. Habermas's *social theory* is that through language, speech, and our inherent sense of purpose, we pursue mutual understanding and a shared sense of universal morality.[132] While we may not always be successful at finding common ground, our drive to communicate with each other, from the high politics of diplomatic negotiations to the low politics of transnational networks, means that we have the potential to continually improve our society. Through communicative action, Habermas argues, we produce our sense of reason and rationality and ultimately seek more inclusiveness, democracy, and equality.[133] Altogether, this suggests that cooperation in international relations may not always be as elusive as it sometimes seems.

[128] Nicholas Christakis, *Blueprint: The Evolutionary Origins of a Good Society* (New York: Little Brown, 2019), pp. 12–13.
[129] Christakis, *Blueprint,* p. 13.
[130] Christakis, *Blueprint,* p. 13.
[131] Christakis, *Blueprint,* p. 16.
[132] Jürgen Habermas, *Communication and the Evolution of Society* (Toronto: Beacon Press, 1979).
[133] Jürgen Habermas, *The Theory of Communicative Action* (Toronto: Beacon Press, 1981).

Bringing in a different dimension, anthropologists often focus on food and agriculture to understand the origins of certain human universals and the nature of human society over time. For them, the agricultural revolution, some 10–12,000 years ago, was a major critical juncture. It ushered in the geological epoch known as the Anthropocene, the period in which humans began to have a tangible impact on the Earth and its ecosystems.[134] Although human prosociality—behaviors that benefit others or the community at large—existed before then,[135] agriculture enabled altruism, selflessness, and empathy to rise to a new order of magnitude.

From an ecological perspective, economists John Gody and Lisi Krall write, "We are one of a handful of species that became ultrasocial, a broad term including humans as well as other species that have achieved higher level social organization."[136] They argue that ultrasociality characterizes

> the most social of animal organizations, with full time division of labor, specialists who gather no food but are fed by others, effective sharing of information about sources of food and danger, self-sacrificial efforts in collective defense. This level has been achieved by ants, termites, and humans in several scattered archaic city-states.[137]

At the same time, according to them, ultrasociality also became a key *constraint* on what was possible. As humans increasingly started to behave as a single, ultrasocial organism, the species also became bent on producing a surplus of goods, a development that continues to this day to negative effect.[138] They write that

> Ultrasociality has given human society features that make it extremely difficult to change course even in the face of impending disaster [. . .] the role of human agency is much less powerful than we think. *Individual intentionality* is not the same as *societal intentionality* and it is the latter that we call into question.[139]

Thus, the agricultural revolution and subsequent ultrasociality in humans was, for them, an "evolutionary leap," but it also brought a significantly negative dimension of human cooperation.[140] Once we humans became an agricultural society, division of labor and specialization ensued, giving each individual more specifically

---

[134] There is some debate amongst anthropologists and others about when to date the beginning of the Anthropocene.

[135] John Gowdy and Lisi Krall, "The Ultrasocial Origin of the Anthropocene," *Ecological Economics* 95 (November 2013), https://doi.org/10.1016/j.ecolecon.2013.08.006.

[136] Gowdy and Krall, "The Ultrasocial Origin of the Anthropocene," p. 137.

[137] Donald T. Campbell, "Legal and Primary-Group Social Controls," in *Law, Biology and Culture: The Evolution of Law*, eds. Margeret Gruter and Paul Bohannan (Santa Barbara, CA: Ross Erikson, 1982).

[138] Gowdy and Krall, "The Ultrasocial Origin of the Anthropocene," p. 138.

[139] Gowdy and Krall, "The Ultrasocial Origin of the Anthropocene," p. 138.

[140] Gowdy and Krall, "The Ultrasocial Origin of the Anthropocene," p. 138.

defined roles in the name of material production. Now, we are a human superorganism with a single production system that has become so efficient that it needs to be restrained and transformed if the planet itself is to survive (see Part V on climate change).[141] This illustrates that ultrasociality may have unintended consequences. Our tendency to work together for the common good may sometimes require even more empathic cooperation to ensure beneficial outcomes for humanity. We may pursue good outcomes, but we are still human and can make mistakes in these efforts.

Psychologists, particularly evolutionary psychologists, also observe ultrasociality in their work. They find that individual acts that benefit society can stem from either altruism and empathy or from self-interest (anticipation of future reciprocity) and practicality. There is consensus in this field that being highly connected to others through networks, marriage, friendships, neighbors, clubs, civic engagement, and work relationships (collectively known as social capital) leads to more happiness and well-being.[142] In particular, the field of psychology delves into how we not only embrace cooperation and crave social ties as an intimate part of our identities but also restrain our behavior in order to fulfill these needs.

Discipline and Judgment

We are not just pulled toward ultrasociality, we are also pushed into it. As Lieberman writes,

> We imagine the self—our sense of who we are—to be a hermetically sealed treasure chest, an impenetrable fortress, that only we have access to [. . .] the self is actually a secret agent working for them more than for us.[143]

Through socialization and upbringing, many of us believe that our lives are about navigating through the world as separate, private individuals, seeking to stand out in some ways while conforming to society in other ways. Many people feel a tension between these two pulls, as if they are in opposition. However, we do not usually realize that the pull of societal conformation is actually already intimately engrained in our sense of self.[144]

For the most part, in order to succeed as individuals, humans need to fit into society at large. Like when early humans punished reactive aggressors (see Chapter 2), our society values and trusts people who have self-control and

---

[141] Gowdy and Krall, "The Ultrasocial Origin of the Anthropocene," p. 139.

[142] John F. Helliwell and Robert D. Putnam, "The Social Context of Well-Being," *Philosophical Transactions Biological Sciences* 359, 1449 (2004): 1435–1446, https://doi.org/10.1098/rstb.2004.1522.

[143] Matthew Lieberman, *Social: Why Our Brains Are Wired to Connect* (New York: Crown Publishing Group, 2013), p. 189–190.

[144] Lieberman, *Social*, p. 202.

discipline rather than those who act in whatever way strikes them. We sort out who excels and who is given opportunities through judging a person's ability to exercise self-control. It is no coincidence that university admissions exams in the United States, SATs or ACTs, are not about how advanced a student's intelligence is but rather how well they have devoted themselves to studying basic-level information.[145] Even as American universities slowly do away with the standardized exam requirement in light of criticisms that they are unfair to under-represented groups, the value of discipline will not go away. A different proxy will have to emerge to discern which students have the discipline to get through a university education and excel at it. The profile of an average Harvard freshman, for example, includes not only a near-perfect grade point average but also having performed Prokofiev Sinfonie Concertante at Carnegie Hall, or starred in a Broadway show, or launched a successful non-governmental organization (NGO) in Africa . . . all strong indicators of sustained discipline.

This desire to restrain our own pleasures in order to be accepted or valued by society, in spite of any pain that might cause, is so hard-wired into our psyches that we tend to take it for granted. Lieberman refers to this constant focus on what others believe and value as *harmonizing*.[146] In experiments involving tempting participants with rewards and pleasures, individuals are more likely to violate social norms if no one is watching. In a Halloween experiment, for example, children are told to go up to a house to ask for candy. The adult who answers the door then leaves the candy bowl with the child while he answers a phone call, instructing the child to take one piece of candy. If there is a mirror facing the door such that the kid can see herself, she is far more likely to take just the one piece of candy. But if there is no mirror, the kid is much more likely to take more than one piece of candy. Lieberman explains, "only humans are built such that seeing themselves, a reminder of their potential visibility to others, is sufficient to trigger self-restraint."[147]

Numerous other experiments confirm this. If a poster reads "No littering allowed" and features an image of eyes, individuals are far less likely to litter than if the poster had no eyes but the same words. The same is true even if the "eyes" are portrayed in a very abstract way, such as three dots placed in a triangle, reminiscent of eyes and a nose. This is played out in a more all-encompassing way in Jeremy Bentham's idea of the panopticon, an ideal-type prison designed to make those inside feel watched at all times.[148] Prisoners are never sure whether they are being watched but will behave as if they are.

[145] Lieberman, *Social*, p. 225.
[146] Lieberman, *Social*, p. 11.
[147] Lieberman, *Social*, p. 232.
[148] Harry Strub, "The Theory of Panoptical Control: Bentham's Panopticon and Orwell's Nineteen Eighty-Four," *Journal of the History of the Behavioral Sciences* 25, 1 (1989): 40–59, https://doi.org/10.1002/1520-6696(198901)25:1<40::AID-JHBS2300250104>3.0.CO;2-W.

The weakness of studies based on focus groups is another example of harmonizing. Using focus groups to anticipate public reactions is rarely that useful because public perception actually depends on how *the public* reacts. Lieberman writes, "As it turns out, the way our [medial prefrontal cortex] responds to an advertisement not only predicts how we will change but also how entire populations will change."[149] People regularly and subtly shift their preferences together, but mainly with others en masse.

So, we have a keen awareness of whether we are being watched, even if only by strangers. The fact that we care about being judged makes self-restraint easier and ultimately contributes to socially oriented behavior.[150] And because this has been going on for so long through the course of human existence, we are arguably increasingly in tune with one another, unconsciously harmonizing at every turn. Ultimately, the push and pull of ultrasociality mean that humans both *want* to think and act socially and also *must* do so. Constraint, self-control, conformity, empathy, and selflessness all operate in tandem.

These findings from ecology, psychology, anthropology, sociology, and psychology add a further layer onto the structure of the ultrasocial world. As a whole, we are attuned toward the public, how others see us, and a desire to be accepted. The existence of human universals means that we often share universal views of what this entails, from recognizing each other's individual identity to forming social networks. These additional building blocks provide a solid starting point for understanding the conduct of international relations.

Human Initiative

Even though we face constraints that are built into our sense of identity, humans also have agency, an important dimension of how international relations plays out. We are not simply cogs in a societal machine or products of the structural forces around us. Studying this aspect of human behavior is, of course, a particular specialty of the social sciences. While our ultrasocial nature has the power to restrict our behavior within society, change is also far more possible within this landscape of behavior than many recognize. And while we may be more constrained as a result of the agricultural revolution and material production, as anthropologists argue, we are not necessarily constrained in other ways.

Indeed, it is in the interplay of individual and societal intentions that we can find hope for our ecological future. While we are unlikely ever to depart from the need for food, agriculture, and specialization of labor, we still have a strong capacity to find solutions to our environmental damage. In particular, the optimism bias, our ability to experience awe, our innate curiosity, and our capacity to believe must

---

[149] Lieberman, *Social*, p. 198.
[150] Lieberman, *Social*, p. 232.

all be taken into account. The impulse to explore, even at high personal risk, as well as our willingness to embrace transcendence stem from human initiative and ingenuity. In the context of ultrasociality, optimism, awe, curiosity, and beliefs are stepping stones on the path to new ideas and transformational change, even at the international level.

Curiosity is not included in the list of human universals—it is even more fundamental than behavior. Many psychologists and neuroscientists have examined the curiosity impulse, both in animals and humans. At its most basic level, curiosity is necessary for learning and plays an important role in how we make decisions. Nearly everything we do on an average day involves satisfying our curiosity. Surfing the web, reading, catching up on the news, watching a murder mystery on TV, playing a musical instrument, hiking, playing sports . . . unless we are doing activities required to survive (going to the bathroom, eating food, drinking water), we are actually doing something that relies on curiosity.[151] Philosopher-psychologist William James defines curiosity basically as "the impulse towards better cognition."[152]

At the same time, curiosity is more than just information seeking. We are not only curious in terms of wanting to discover novel things (perceptual curiosity) (i.e., new ideas, new places, new experiences, and so on) but also in terms of wanting to increase the knowledge that we already have (epistemic curiosity). Indeed, psychologists have found that we are more likely to be curious if we have been exposed to bits of information than none at all. Like an appetizer before the main course, new knowledge appeals to our curiosity if we've had a taste of it first.[153]

I argue that curiosity directly ties into our ultrasocial character and explains why it is that, over time, as a species, we have become increasingly able to express this character. It is our curiosity for novel things that paves the way for change and provides the allure of new, transformational ideas. Perceptual curiosity is so intrinsic to our species that hundreds of developmental psychology studies show that infants as young as between two and six months have a preference for novelty—after engaging with a toy or looking at a particular visual design, they crave something new.[154] With more complex language capacity and adulthood, the craving for new knowledge feeds directly into developing epistemic curiosity. The combination of the two forms of curiosity, among others, have pushed humans to sail the oceans, find new lands, and launch into outer space. Collective curiosity leads to creativity, sparks of ingenuity, and fundamental change.

---

[151] Celeste Kidd and Benjamin Hayden, "The Psychology and Neuroscience of Curiosity," *Neuron* 88 (November 2015): 449–460, https://doi.org/10.1016/j.neuron.2015.09.010.

[152] As cited in Kidd and Hayden, "The Psychology and Neuroscience of Curiosity," p. 449.

[153] Kidd and Hayden, "The Psychology and Neuroscience of Curiosity."

[154] Grant Currin, "Why Are Humans So Curious?," *LiveScience*, July 19, 2020, https://www.livescience.com/why-are-humans-curious.html (accessed May 20, 2023).

In other words, curiosity underpins our capacity to believe. In *Why We Believe*, anthropologist Augustín Fuentes draws the specific connection between our social roots as a species, our cognitive and social abilities, and our capacity to believe.[155] Indeed, in evolutionary terms, as Fuentes argues, our capacity to believe is one of the most important reasons why humans came to dominate the Earth. Primates display "strong and diverse personalities" as well as "certain possibilities for seeing the world, for complex behavior, for an intense inquisitiveness, and an ability to manipulate objects and other group members in fascinating ways."[156] Thousands of scientists have engaged in countless hours of observations to establish this understanding of primate abilities, as well as their ability to innovate and behave flexibly. But humans in particular, of all the primates, uniquely translate these capacities into *beliefs*. Most animals have a kind of transactional sociality. By contrast, humans evolved to be transcendental, possessing the ability to imagine what is possible beyond the boundaries of known experience and comprehension.[157]

For example, around 12,000 years ago, one important belief system emerged that continues to this day: the dog–human relationship. As dogs became domesticated from their wolf origins, humans began to structure their daily lives and routines differently in order to encompass another species in an unprecedented way. The experience of love, friendship, and loyalty with dogs changed the way many humans defined these emotions more generally. Billions of people on Earth have been significantly impacted by having dogs in their lives, and all of this stemmed from a capacity to believe in dogs as man's best friend.[158]

For anthropologists, we do not form our beliefs alone but as part of our experience in human culture, which they define as a "world of social and physical ecologies, patterns, institutions, and ideologies that become inextricably entangled with our biological structures and processes before we even leave the womb."[159] In other words, culture is not simply relegated to the agency side of human existence but is intimately intertwined with our very biological existence. As Fuentes argues, there is no such thing as "nature versus nurture" because the two cannot be separated. We constitute, and are constituted by, human culture. Because we have the higher-order ability to imagine, which is just as intrinsic to being human as having hands and arms, we can also be influenced by transformational ideas. These ideas or beliefs lead to new skills, actions, and creations.[160] Since we exist in human culture in the first place, our ideas are also embedded in community.

[155] Agustín Fuentes, *Why We Believe: Evolution and the Human Way of Being* (New Haven, CT: Yale University Press, 2019).
[156] Fuentes, *Why We Believe*, p. 7.
[157] Fuentes, *Why We Believe*, p. 95.
[158] Fuentes, *Why We Believe*, pp. 54–57.
[159] Fuentes, *Why We Believe*, p. 80.
[160] Fuentes, *Why We Believe*, pp. 109–110.

Paradoxically, the cultural and cognitive complexity that give us the capacity for transcendent ultrasociality also rests on individuality. One of the most important, and indeed ironic, aspects of empathy is that individualism—the opposite of ultrasociality—makes it possible in the first place. In evolutionary terms, humans had to develop a sense of self before they could have empathic consciousness. The invention of writing was one of the most important steps in the development of empathy as it allowed humans to experience a sense of privacy and individual self-consciousness, just as reading brings with it a sense of self-reflection.[161] This type of higher, abstract thinking requires going beyond expressing oneself orally. According to Rifkin, in writing *The Confessions*, Saint Augustine might very well be the first human to have produced an "in-depth narrative about his own awakening self-consciousness."[162] By writing and becoming self-aware, we are then capable of recognizing the individuality of others and empathizing with their struggles. Even in the modern world, we still have to be able to experience and explore the depths of our own selves before being able to recognize this in others.

Individualism has been crucial for human flourishing, but, of course, in its extreme form, it has diminishing returns. Indeed, it has the potential to reverse ultrasociality. In *Bowling Alone*, political scientist Robert Putnam documents how society in the United States has become increasingly individualized and atomized, threatening the social fabric of a country that Alexis de Tocqueville had praised for its rich associational life in the nineteenth century. Depending on time and place, certain communities around the world may lean more toward community or more toward individuality—many Asian and European communities are thought to be closer to the former while Americans are closer to the latter—albeit still within the overall context of our ultrasocial species. At the same time, a high level of individualism is only one way in which ultrasociality might be challenged. Another is tribalism.

Tribalism

Ultrasociality has a dark side. Humans have engaged in catastrophically horrific treatment of each other for as long as our species has existed. Slavery, genocide, conquests, misogyny, and holocausts have occurred repeatedly in human history—the very opposite of what we might expect in an ultrasocial world. Instances of intra- and inter-state war are numerous, as well as societal rejection of peaceful alternatives. Tribalism exists all over the world. It can be as innocuous as a strong sense of group identity, but it can also escalate into racism, xenophobia, extremism, terrorism, sexism, and other forms of intolerance.

---

[161] Jeremy Rifkin, *The Empathic Civilization: The Race to Global Consciousness in a World in Crisis* (New York: TarcherPerigee, 2009), pp. 172, 206–209.
[162] Rifkin, *The Empathic Civilization*, p. 247.

To be clear, I do not mean tribalism in the sense of the early human tribes of hunter-gatherers or the present-day indigenous peoples of New Guinea, sub-Saharan Africa, or the South American rainforests. Here, I mean tribalism as the more subjective phenomenon of belonging to, or joining, a group whose members specifically seek to identify more closely with each other than with outsiders. Moreover, I am specifically looking at this phenomenon in its more derogatory incarnation, that is, in the ways in which it promotes antisocial, as opposed to ultrasocial, behavior. The question is: how can such antisocial tribalism happen within a species that is evolutionarily, genetically, psychologically, and sociologically predisposed to cooperate and behave with altruism?

The answer is that tribalism takes advantage of human ultrasociality but in a very different way than individualism. Indeed, the reason why tribalism is so insidious is that it actually comes out of our ultrasocial inclinations. Psychologist Paul Bloom finds that devious political leaders manipulate empathy to cultivate feelings of us-versus-them. By playing groups off against one another and showing empathy only to some groups, power-hungry leaders use it to try to lure in more followers. Bloom argues, "empathy can be weaponized by unscrupulous leaders to get us to support things that ultimately make the world worse [. . .] there are many instances in which empathy is tweaked to motivate us to support aggression and violence against a group."[163] In other words, empathy can be directed at antisocial ends, even while the weight of the majority remains anchored in ultrasociality.

In the United States, for example, Donald Trump capitalized on selective manipulation of empathy in his presidential campaigns. Breaking from the norm in US politics, instead of running on a message of bringing Americans together, Trump cultivated specific empathy for "rust belt" factory workers who felt that their jobs had gone overseas through previous administrations' unfavorable trade policies. Once in power, the Trump administration then used this cache of support to put in place protectionist trade policies.

Similarly, when García Zárate, an immigrant, apparently killed thirty-two-year old Kate Steinle by accident (he found a gun that went off) on Pier 14 in San Francisco, Trump capitalized on empathy with the parents' loss to push for what he called Kate's Law (the parents' lack of support for this notwithstanding). Zárate had five times re-entered the United States after being deported for non-violent felonies, and Kate's Law would have defunded sanctuary cities and imposed a zero-tolerance policy on re-entry. Kate's Law was ultimately never voted upon in Congress, but Trump had already regularly used Kate Steinle's death to stoke anti-immigrant sentiment amongst his base.[164]

[163] Econlib (Library of Economics and Liberty), "Paul Bloom on Empathy," February 27, 2017, https://www.econtalk.org/paul-bloom-on-empathy (accessed May 20, 2023).
[164] Paul Bloom, *Against Empathy: The Case for Rational Compassion* (New York: HarperCollins, 2016), p. 192.

Rather than an emphasis on mirror neurons, or our genetic pre-wiring as a species, Bloom argues that empathy is a form of individual bias. In particular, psychologists have found that on an individual level, our empathy is stronger toward people more similar to ourselves and for people who are more attractive and friendly. Consequently, he finds that collective empathy can regularly lead to violence in situations where strong empathy for those in the tribe leads them to lash out at those outside of the tribe.[165] This is especially true if the tribe has succeeded in dehumanizing their groups' perceptions of others, such as in the case of Nazis dehumanizing the Jews, the African slave trade, or any sort of racism or sexism today.

While most empathy scholars argue that prevention of dehumanization is precisely the value of empathy, Bloom contends that empathy is not necessarily directed at everybody equally. He argues that people with higher levels of empathy do not necessarily behave with more altruism. Instead, they might try to remove themselves from situations where their empathy would make them feel bad. For example, nurses who test high for empathy actually spend less time with their patients. Bloom ultimately comes to the negative conclusion that empathy may actually make the world worse, and so we should rely on other dimensions of our prosociality to achieve good, such as rational compassion. This is, of course, debatable. Most others firmly believe in the capacity of empathy to make the world better.[166]

Bloom's ultimate conclusion notwithstanding, in the process, he does make an interestingly counter-intuitive point about the place of empathy, among other possible actions, in our ultrasocial world. Obviously, at times, our immediate empathic reaction to something may be more or less effective, but in reality, we do not typically just act the second that our mirror neurons fire. We process information, we deliberate, we listen to new ideas, we cooperate to make policies, and we modify institutions. This is all part of our ultrasocial way of life. However, sometimes, the pursuit of cooperation, belonging, and society is perverted. And this usually requires deceitful leaders who find ways to cloak selfishness and tribalism with empathy. These deceitful leaders are often themselves entirely lacking in empathy, which, as psychopathologist Simon Baron-Cohen argues, is a pathway to cruelty.[167]

Again, Donald Trump provides an illustrative example of this. In *The Dangerous Case of Donald Trump*, a group of thirty-seven psychiatrists warn that Trump poses a significant threat to the world because of his mental instability, narcissism, and capacity to indoctrinate his followers. Based on their shared medical expertise, the psychiatrists argue that Trump is a classic narcissistic psychopath and,

[165] Bloom, *Against Empathy*, pp. 177–212.
[166] Simon Baron-Cohen, *The Science of Evil: On Empathy and the Origins of Cruelty* (New York: Basic Books, 2011); Rifkin, *The Empathic Civilization*.
[167] Baron-Cohen, *The Science of Evil*.

from a position of leadership, has the capacity to infect others with the same mental condition. As Elizabeth Mika writes in this volume, "Our human propensity to submit to inhumane rules established by pathological authority cannot be overestimated."[168] Comparing the indoctrination of a swath of American society under Trump to Germany on the eve of the Second World War, she writes that "the process the Nazis themselves had not understood is the very narcissistic collusion, a near-psychotic infection with this virus of grandiosity and rage on a mass scale."[169]

Indeed, observers of Hitler's rallies described a similar dynamic: Hitler would whip the crowd into a trance, and in the glow of their admiration, Hitler himself would become enraptured.[170] An obsessive, mutual dependence would intensify. This psychological pattern is also repeated in radical church indoctrinations, cults of personality, and other dictatorial regimes around the world. The psychologically vulnerable, in particular, but even the otherwise psychologically healthy, succumb to the spread of what amounts to a contagious mental illness.

Of course, sometimes, the dynamics of tribalism are not as clear-cut as Trump and his base or Hitler and the Nazis. There have also been inspirational and popular leaders like Charles Lindbergh, John Glenn, and Henry Ford, among others, who captured the public's imagination, on the one hand, while, at the same time, holding close-minded and xenophobic beliefs on the other. Even while sparking the public's hopes and dreams with their achievements, Lindbergh held Nazi sympathies, Glenn said female pilots should have no role in space, and Ford sponsored a weekly antisemitic newspaper. In the context of our ultrasocial world, there is a clear contradiction in what these individuals stood for. But most prominently, they elevated national self-esteem through their displays of "American exceptionalism," and the dark side of their beliefs was largely overlooked.

Henri Tajfel was one of the first psychologists to examine the contradiction between in-group and out-group preferences and pioneered social identity theory, which argues that people are driven by a desire to maximize positive distinctiveness;[171] that is, we seek a sense of identity and high self-esteem, and we often achieve that through belonging to a group. In this sense, an "America first" message can be alluring for some in the United States. But on the flip side, if the chosen group does not allow them to maintain positive distinction, then they are likely to either change the group or leave it.[172]

In tribalistic groups, the us-versus-them dynamic often becomes even stronger than the we-feeling upon which it was supposedly based. As the tribe evolves, if

[168] Elizabeth Mika, "Who Goes Trump: Tyranny as a Triumph of Narcissism," in *The Dangerous Case of Donald Trump*, ed. Bandy Lee (New York: St Martin's Press, 2019), p. 305.
[169] Mika, "Who Goes Trump," p. 302.
[170] Jerrold Post, "The Charismatic Leader–Follower Relationship," in Lee, *The Dangerous Case of Donald Trump*, pp. 389–390.
[171] Henri Tajfel and John C. Turner, "The Social Identity Theory of Intergroup Behavior," *Psychology of Intergroup Relations* 2 (1986): 7–24, https://doi.org/10.4324/9780203505984-16.
[172] Tajfel and Turner, "The Social Identity Theory."

the competitive, exclusive nature of its collective identity shifts into a more open, inclusive mindset, it can easily chart a course toward ultrasociality—progressive tribalism, so to speak, on an increasingly global scale. But if those who have been lured into tribalism become increasingly radicalized by their leaders, the overtones of exclusion and xenophobia instead become more dominant over time. In this exclusionary tribalism, leaders focus so much on dehumanizing "the other"—those outside of the tribe—that followers become blind to just how far from their original intentions they have traveled and the extent to which the promises made to them have been broken.

Ultimately, tribalism and ultrasociality are based on fundamentally different—indeed, opposing—ideational grounds. This divergence is easily visible through observing social narratives, media rhetoric, government policies, and leadership platforms. Far-right movements are clear examples of this. Staking a position against immigration, religious diversity, gender equality, LGBTQ rights, human rights . . . these movements are the very definition of tribalism: separating out those who are different from their own group. Supporters of tribalism have no qualms about arguing for their own tribes' interests exclusively, especially to the detriment of those who do not share the same identity. They also often speak in terms of individual self-interest, as long as that individual is part of the tribe.

Tribalism's Downfall

Ultimately, the battle between ultrasociality and tribalism, when it occurs, is highly uneven. Tribalism rarely lasts. At the height of far-right populist movements, for example, members of the tribe lose all capacity to express what they are fighting for and can only say what they are against. Tribalism contains the seeds of its own destruction. If its extremism intensifies, at some point it can go too far, and eventually there is a day of reckoning.

Indeed, futurist Alvin Toffler argued with remarkable prescience in 1970 that "tribal turnover" would accelerate in our world:

> And so, even when he seemingly adopts a subcult or style, he withholds some part of himself. He conforms to the group's demands and revels in the belongingness it gives him. But this belongingness is never the same as it once was, and secretly he remains ready to defect at a moment's notice. What this means is that even when he seems most firmly plugged in to his group or tribe, he listens, in the dark of night, to the short-wave signals of competing tribes.[173]

---

[173] Alvin Toffler, *Future Shock* (New York: Bantam, 1984), p. 296.

There will always be some segment of society that is prone toward tribalism, but ultimately, it is a fluid segment, and it still has to come up against the push and pull of ultrasociality and the inherent failures of tribalism.

Moreover, given human agency, we have the capacity to steer the course of history toward the good, especially on a societal level. Bad leaders who seek power are usually the ones who exploit in-group feelings to turn them into hatred, but collective-oriented societies are more likely to be tolerant and reject such leaders. Societies with a history and culture of strong societal bonds, egalitarianism, democracy, and community, naturally quell the potential emergence of tribal leaders.[174] They provide a buffer of protection against this kind of corruption.

To be sure, evolution has given humans a natural sense of affinity with whoever they define as part of their in-group. And this loyalty to the in-group is often strengthened in reaction to out-groups. Like identity more generally, people tend to define themselves against an "other." However, as Christakis argues, there is much variation in terms of how those feelings of us versus them are expressed. At its most extreme, hatred, and even violence, can result against the out-group. Xenophobia, ethnocentrism, a sense of superiority, and prejudice can all emerge on one end of the spectrum. But on the other, people can belong to a group without any negative feelings toward those who are outside of it. In our globalized world, with more and more people having cross-cutting identities, many of us switch our membership between in-group and out-group quite fluidly, strengthening the pull of ultrasociality.[175]

In short, not only does tribalism contain the seeds of its own destruction, but also over time as a species, we are getting more efficient and effective at letting ultrasociality prevail. With the strong synergies between human universals and human initiative, there is much to buttress our evolutionary inclinations as well as our progress toward peaceful, cooperative, and creative ways forward.

---

[174] Christakis, *Blueprint*, pp. 276–277.
[175] Christakis, *Blueprint*, p. 275.

4

In an Ultrasocial World, Certain Ideas Matter More

In the past few years, evidence from biology, evolution, neuroscience, cognitive science, anthropology, sociology, and psychology has emerged, documenting various dimensions of the surprising human propensity to be "good" and to strive to create good societies. Some of the work done in this area briefly alludes to the important bearing this has on the nature of our political world today, how we live in it, and our potential, at least, to respect and work with others, no matter how different we might seem to each other. However, this literature is still more focused on establishing this scientific reality, grounding it in evidence from its respective fields, and correcting common assumptions that humans are mainly conflictual, competitive, and self-interested.

I use this groundbreaking work from these other fields as my point of departure into international relations. I pick up where these other scholars left off to focus on how this can change our understanding of world politics. In doing so, I am cutting against the grain of mainstream international relations. Despite paying some lip service to interdisciplinarity, the field of international relations is still surprisingly closed off from the work of other fields, especially from the biological sciences. Indeed, strong consideration of any element of human nature in the study of politics is more or less taboo, and there is a long history of this (see the book's conclusion). Nonetheless, given the magnitude of what I have discussed until this point, I believe it is important and necessary to build bridges from these other fields to international relations. Doing so fundamentally changes how we approach, study, and plan international relations.

How can we understand world politics differently with the knowledge that we are an ultrasocial species? How can we scale up these new insights about human nature to the level of the international system? I argue here that ultrasociality provides us with both an ontology—a clear starting point for the assumptions we should have about our social reality—and a structure—a landscape within which political transformations are most likely to occur. This provides fertile ground for gaining better insights into the nature and potential of international cooperation. In particular, I argue broadly that the more that new political ideas and worldviews resonate with ultrasociality, the more likely they are to be successful at capturing the public imagination and eventually precipitating change.

International Cooperation Against All Odds. Mai'a K. Davis Cross, Oxford University Press. © Mai'a K. Davis Cross (2024).
DOI: 10.1093/oso/9780192873903.003.0005

A New Starting Point

All of us live by an ontology, a so-called theory of being, the basis of what we assume is our social reality. There are countless ontologies out there in the world, some unexamined and some arrived at more consciously. The *ultrasocial ontology*, as I call it, means that we understand our social reality to be one based on our species' evolutionary predisposition to be other-regarding, empathic, cooperative, and altruistic whenever possible. In contrast, the dominant ontology in the field of international relations to date, and by extension the policy world, centers on assumptions that humans are rationally self-interested, seek more power than others, and willingly engage in conflict to get it. The ultrasocial ontology flies in the face of this. Other approaches tend to remain silent when it comes to human nature and yield the default high ground to rationalism, even while disagreeing with it.

Self-professed "realist" scholars and politicians constantly reveal their underlying ontology in their choice of language about international relations. There are countless examples, but to name just a few:

"International politics, like all politics, is a struggle for power"—Hans Morgenthau.[176]

"War made the state, and the state made war"—Charles Tilly.[177]

"America has no permanent friends or enemies, only interests"—Henry Kissinger.[178]

"It was the rise of Athens and the fear that this instilled in Sparta that made war inevitable"—Thucydides.[179]

"As long as we have faith in our own cause and an unconquerable will, victory will not be denied us"—Winston Churchill.[180]

"Wars end when nations agree that war is an unsatisfactory instrument for solving their dispute; wars begin when nations agree that peaceful diplomacy is an unsatisfactory instrument for solving their dispute. Agreement is the essence of the transition from peace to war and from war to peace, for those are merely alternating phases of a relationship between nations"—Geoffrey Blainey.[181]

---

[176] Hans Morgenthau, *Politics among Nations: The Struggle for Power and Peace*, 2nd edn (New York: Alfred A. Knopf, 1954).

[177] Charles Tilly, "Reflections on the History of European State-Making," in *The Formation of National States in Western Europe*, ed. Charles Tilly (Princeton, NJ: Princeton University Press, 1975), p. 45.

[178] Henry Kissinger, *The White House Years* (Boston, MA: Little, Brown and Company, 1979).

[179] Thucydides, *The Peloponnesian War*, trans by Martin Hammond (Oxford: Oxford World's Classics, 2009).

[180] Winston Churchill, "Masters of Our Fate," speech to Joint Session of the US Congress delivered on December 26, 1941.

[181] Geoffrey Blainey, *Causes of War*, 3rd edn (New York: Free Press, 1988), p. 161.

"A great deal of world politics is a fundamental struggle, but it is also a struggle that has to be waged intelligently"—Zbigniew Brzezinski.[182]

"Peace for us means the destruction of Israel. We are preparing for an all-out war, a war which will last for generations"—Yasser Arafat.[183]

Even those thinkers and leaders steeped in a more liberal approach, meaning that they believe in the possibility of cooperation and peaceful interaction, still imbue their own thinking in similar terms:

"[F]oreign policy is a matter of costs and benefits, not theology"—Fareed Zakaria.[184]

"The United States and China are the two largest consumers of energy in the world. We are also the two largest emitters of greenhouse gases in the world. Let's be frank: Neither of us profits from a growing dependence on foreign oil, nor can we spare our people from the ravages of climate change unless we cooperate. Common sense calls upon us to act in concert"—Barack Obama.[185]

"If we have to use force, it is because we are America. We are the indispensable nation. We stand tall. We see further into the future"—Madeleine Albright.[186]

"What governments and people don't realize is that sometimes the collective interest—the international interest—is also the national interest"—Kofi Annan.[187]

Statements that talk about the world as if the only actors of consequences are unitary states (i.e., China wants X or Russia will retaliate with Y) and as if these states only have strategic goals and interests are still implicitly stuck in an asocial ontology of competition, power, and self-interest.

When President Obama spoke about the need for the United States and China to cooperate on climate change, for example, he justified this in the name of the risk of depending on other countries for oil and the need for common sense. This assumes that the United States and China are unitary actors with a singular, rational interest and that other countries cannot be trusted. Underlying assumptions about threat

---

[182] As quoted in "Discussing Democracy," *The Hill*, March 4, 2021, https://thehill.news/opinion/the-eu-cant-stand-for-democracy-until-it-stops-sitting-for-china-and-russia (accessed May 23, 2023).

[183] Yasser Arafat, *The Times* (UK), August 5, 1980.

[184] Fareed Zakaria, *The Post-American World* (New York: W. W. Norton & Company, 2008), p. 224.

[185] Barack Obama, "Remarks by the President at the U.S./China Strategic and Economic Dialogue," The White House: Office of the Press Secretary, July 7, 2009, https://obamawhitehouse.archives.gov/realitycheck/the-press-office/remarks-president-uschina-strategic-and-economic-dialogue (accessed May 23, 2023).

[186] Madeleine K. Albright, "Interview on NBC-TV 'The Today Show' with Matt Lauer," Columbus, OH, February 19, 1998, as released by the Office of the Spokesman, US Department of State, https://1997-2001.state.gov/statements/1998/980219a.html#:~:text=It%20is%20the%20threat%20of,here%20to%20all%20of%20us (accessed May 23, 2023).

[187] Kofi Annan, "Interview Kofi Annan: 'Sometimes You Don't Have to Pick a Fight to Get Your Way'," *The Guardian*, September 30, 2012, https://www.theguardian.com/world/2012/sep/30/kofi-annan-dont-pick-fight#:~:text=But%20what%20governments%20and%20people,country%20won%20independence%20from%20Britain (accessed May 23, 2023).

and power serve to uphold a view of international relations that is not necessarily reflective of human behavior as a species.

Even though human nature is almost never mentioned in typical statements about the international system, as illustrated above, these statements are still permeated with assumptions not made explicit. Power, rivalry, inherent threat, and so on are taken to be the default of what we expect of our fellow humans on the international stage. Any alternative ontology, such as those of liberalism, constructivism, post-structuralism, feminism, and critical theory, is immediately cast into a weaker position because it must prove the default wrong.

To be sure, examples of thinkers and leaders who express themselves with a seemingly more ultrasocial ontology behind their statements are also plentiful. For example:

"Peace is not a relationship of nations. It is a condition of mind brought about by a serenity of soul. Peace is not merely the absence of war. It is also a state of mind. Lasting peace can come only to peaceful people"—Jawaharlal Nehru.[188]

"We may have different religions, different languages, different colored skin, but we all belong to one human race"—Kofi Annan.[189]

"We all share one planet and are one humanity; there is no escaping this reality"—Wangari Maathai.[190]

"Free expression is the base of human rights, the root of human nature and the mother of truth. To kill free speech is to insult human rights, to stifle human nature and to suppress truth"—Liu Xiaobo.[191]

Language like this is associated with leaders we tend to admire, and who widely inspire others, but is also often derided as being not very "realistic." Their words are almost always taken to be too naïve or idealistic, especially during periods of cynicism about the nature of the international order. This bias is not only unjustified but also often leads to misunderstandings or neglect of past breakthroughs and achievements. For example, in revisiting the historical record, international law scholars Oona Hathaway and Scott Shapiro find that the 1928 Paris Peace Pact (also known as the Kellogg–Briand Pact), ratified by nearly every country in the world at the time, "was among the most transformative events of human

---

[188] As quoted in Ruth Fishel, *Peace in Our Hearts, Peace in the World: Meditations of Hope and Healing* (New York: Sterling Publishing Co. Inc., 2008), p. 318.

[189] As quoted in *Simply Living: The Spirit of the Indigenous People*, ed. Shirley A. Jones (Novato: New World Library, 1999).

[190] Wangari Maathai, *The Challenge for Africa* (New York: Pantheon, 2009).

[191] As quoted in NPR (National Public Radio), "Liu Xiaobo: 'No Enemies, No Hatred,' Only Courage," *NPR*, February 16, 2012, https://www.npr.org/2012/02/16/146988012/liu-xiaobo-no-enemies-no-hatred-only-courage (accessed May 23, 2023).

history, one that has, ultimately, made our world far more peaceful."[192] Yet, historians have repeatedly undermined our understanding of it with their cynical take. For example, the highly influential Cold War historian George Kennan called the Paris Peace Pact "childish, just childish."[193] Indeed, idealism today is almost synonymous with naiveté and inexperience in the foreign policy establishment, even though idealism's underlying assumptions are actually far more grounded in the science of human behavior.

In short, my first entry point into international relations is this need for a more examined and updated ontology based on the latest scientific findings that I have outlined in Chapters 1–3. The current default is based on a faulty fundamental premise, and yet its assumptions have permeated deeply into the policy world. And this matters as the very language used to discuss international relations has connotations that undermine our collective goals for a peaceful, more effective international order.

The Ultrasocial Landscape

In the context of international relations, ultrasociality is not only an ontology but also a structure. Just as the system of nation states, international organizations, international law, and international norms structure what is possible in international relations, so does what I call the *ultrasocial landscape*. As with any structure, the ultrasocial landscape does not give us any specific outcomes in international relations.[194] Rather, it sets certain parameters within which the most important ideas about international relations are likely to flourish. The ultrasocial landscape anchors us. Ideas that *enable* ultrasocial behavior and transform our institutions to achieve ultrasociality are more likely to be accepted and championed in society. Ideas that *constrain* or go against ultrasocial inclinations are less likely to be accepted.

The idea of establishing resident diplomatic embassies during the Renaissance or the 1967 Outer Space Treaty are examples of transformational ideas that sit squarely within the ultrasocial landscape. By contrast, ideas centered on abandoning allies, such as the British move to leave the European Union (Brexit) or adopting an isolationist foreign policy, are examples that lie outside of the ultrasocial

---

[192] Oona Hathaway and Scott Shapiro, *The Internationalists: How a Radical Plan to Outlaw War Remade the World* (New York: Simon & Shuster, 2017), p. xiii

[193] Hathaway and Shapiro, *The Internationalists*, p. xii.

[194] Although the aim of this chapter is to expose a dimension of human nature that has relevance to international relations, I do not claim that human nature somehow *determines* human behavior, preferences, and actions. To the contrary, no true scientist anywhere believes in "biological determinism," and there is no evidence that any aspect of human biology fully determines human behavior. At the same time, science does tell us that not *everything* is socialized; human beings are not completely malleable.

landscape. Many kinds of developments in our world are clearly anchored in the ultrasocial landscape—peace treaties, trade agreements, scientific discoveries, globally oriented leaders—and others are not—unjust war, genocide, environmental degradation, fascist political parties, and so on. We consistently celebrate the former and denounce the latter. Whether we engage in the former or the latter rests first on the ideas we choose, then on the actions we take.

Just like with other structures in the international system (United Nations human rights charters, international norms on the conduct of maritime operations, the Geneva conventions on the conduct of war, and so on), the structure of the ultrasocial landscape is not absolute in its push and pull. Just because human rights charters make torture illegal does not mean that torture never happens. Just because there are laws against piracy on the open seas or against the use of chemical weapons does not mean that violations never occur. However, when these types of violations are discovered, they are widely condemned, demonstrating the influence of the ultrasocial landscape. In addition, it is not that every person contributes to ultrasociality but that our species *on the whole* tends to gravitate toward it.

Finally, the ecosystem of the ultrasocial landscape is not uniform. The center of it is robust. If it were a forest, it would be filled with centuries-old trees, a thick canopy, and healthy undergrowth. This is where ideas that foster large-scale cooperation, a focus on the well-being of others, and inclusivity emerge and a sense of shared, universal human morality is strong. At the edges of the landscape, the ecosystem becomes thinner, and these qualities start to diminish. Thus, even within the ultrasocial landscape, human agency, ingenuity, and creativity matter greatly. And many things influence our choices as a collective: education, politics, propaganda, cults of personalities, elite narratives, media spin, crises, traumas, thought leaders, expert opinion, and so on. The cognitive sciences and neurobiology find that our minds only make sense of the world in the context of society and that our minds and society are mutually constitutive. In other words, they construct each other at the same time. Human ultrasociality indicates that we are not born blank slates—there is a pre-existing, species-level structure—but neither is biology deterministic of behavior.[195]

From Our Ultrasocial Species to Our Ultrasocial Ideas

The existence of the ultrasocial landscape as an ontological starting point for international relations can underpin the full range of research questions, theories, and policy prescriptions. It should open up our inquiry rather than restrict it. In this

[195] Steven Pinker, *The Blank Slate: The Modern Denial of Human Nature* (New York: Penguin Books, 2002).

book, I focus on the role of ideas as the bridge between our nature as a species and our actual behavior on the world stage. Ideas are particularly revealing because they signal the prelude to action and capture the goals and reasons behind change. In other words, I argue that to understand the root causes of cooperative break-throughs on a global scale, it is necessary to first decipher their ideational origins. Current and future problems cannot be solved without understanding why other attempts succeeded or failed, and this comes from examining debates over ideas.

Ideas can be defined as "the substantive content of discourse."[196] More specifi-cally, political preferences and choices, which rely on underlying political beliefs, are expressed as ideas. They can be anything from flashes of inspiration to concrete technical road maps, but they require some kind of mechanism to matter;[197] that is, once an idea becomes accepted, a social and political process must translate an idea from words to action.

Ideas are also of different types[198] and different strengths.[199] From an inter-national relations perspective, Judith Goldstein and Robert Keohane argue that "ideas define the universe of possibilities for action"[200] and that there are generally three types: worldviews, principled beliefs, and causal beliefs.

Worldviews are the broadest level of ideas in that they are derived from the ontology underlying human thinking, which can include religion, culture, and science.[201] An example of a worldview is the idea that science matters in under-standing life or that the primary organization of humans on the planet is the system of nation states.

Principled beliefs are less expansive than worldviews, referring more specifi-cally to the norms we hold about what is right and what is wrong. The belief that the pursuit of scientific knowledge is necessary, and that anything learned from this should be shared with all people, is an example of a principled belief. Changes in principled beliefs can lead to transformational change in the international system itself.

Causal beliefs are ideas about the relationship between a cause and its effect. They typically come from elites, leaders, scientists, and experts.[202] As the nar-rowest of the three, causal beliefs are more precisely ideas about how to achieve

---

[196] Vivien Schmidt, "Discursive Institutionalism: The Explanatory Power of Ideas and Discourse," *Annual Review of Political Science* 11 (2008): 303–326, https://doi.org/10.1146/annurev.polisci.11.060606.135342.

[197] Nina Tannenwald, "Ideas and Explanation: Advancing the Theoretical Agenda," *Journal of Cold War Studies* 7, 2 (Spring 2005): 13–42, https://www.jstor.org/stable/26925808.

[198] Tannenwald, "Ideas and Explanations."

[199] Jeffrey Legro, "The Transformation of Policy Ideas," *American Journal of Political Science*, 44 3 (2002): 419–432, https://doi.org/10.2307/2669256.

[200] Judith Goldstein and Robert Keohane (eds), *Ideas and Foreign Policy: Beliefs, Institutions, and Political Change* (New York: Cornell University Press, 1993), pp. 7–8.

[201] Goldstein and Keohane, *Ideas and Foreign Policy*, pp. 8–9.

[202] Goldstein and Keohane, *Ideas and Foreign Policy*, p. 10.

certain policy goals. The causal belief that we need to reduce carbon emissions to stop climate change is an example.[203]

At the intersection of worldviews and principled beliefs are ideas about the way the world should work and what humans should do on a scale that goes beyond national borders. These ideas can be related to pursuing new human scientific achievement, political organization, acceptable or unacceptable behavior, economic relationships, institutions, and so on. The cases in this book are key examples: pooling national sovereignty, exploring space for peaceful purposes, avoiding use of the most powerful weapons on Earth, or reducing carbon emissions to net zero. Ideas can envision cooperation, conflict, or neither. Transformational ideas such as these can lead to critical junctures in international relations. Over time, I argue that a single idea can evolve and move among these categories, essentially lying somewhere on the spectrum between transformational (i.e., philosophical and normative) or transactional (i.e., policy-oriented and cognitive) in nature.

To really understand which ideas matter, it is necessary to go beyond the push and pull of the ultrasocial ontology and landscape. As I have emphasized repeatedly, biology is not deterministic of outcomes, and structures alone only provide some likely parameters. Human agency, creativity, imagination, beliefs, myths, and curiosity all combine to create the power of possibility—the ideas that matter.

International relations experts rarely investigate the independent impact of ideas. If they do, most are focused on day-to-day decision making on specific foreign policy issues (causal beliefs), such as ideas on how to regulate trade, police human trafficking, or plan a humanitarian operation. Moreover, the emphasis is on the extent to which ideas influence choices more than the default of rational, cost–benefit calculations. In other words, ideas are only "residual variables," explaining what other assumptions *cannot* explain.[204] Craig Parsons, for example, compares "close organizational peers" with policymaking authority, which faced comparable challenges in the development of the early European Union.[205] He contends that if these similarly positioned policymakers advance a range of ideas on what should be done, debate the ideas in a foreign policy setting, and adopt behavior that aligns with one of the ideas, then there is clear evidence that ideas matter. However, if we want to also understand major transformations in our world and take the power of ideas seriously, then the actual *qualities* of successful ideas and how they are championed takes on great importance.

---

[203] Similarly, Vivien Schmidt argues that ideas "exist at three levels—policies, programs, and philosophies—and can be categorized into two types, cognitive and normative." Cognitive ideas are essentially causal beliefs, whereas normative ideas refer more to the principles and underlying worldviews society holds. Schmidt, "Discursive Institutionalism," pp. 303–326.

[204] Tannenwald, "Ideas and Explanation," pp. 13–42, p. 18.

[205] Craig Parsons, "Showing Ideas as Causes: The Origins of the European Union," *International Organization* 56 1 (2002): 47–84, p. 51, https://www.jstor.org/stable/3078670 (accessed May 20, 2023).

Even within the ultrasocial landscape, some ideas are clearly more important than others when it comes to precipitating major junctures of change. As Lieberman writes, "The greatest ideas almost always require teamwork to bring them to fruition; social reasoning is what allows us to build and maintain the social relationships and infrastructure needed for teams to thrive."[206] Thus, I argue that there are *at least three* specific qualities of ideas that make their success more likely:

   (i)   transcendent impact,
   (ii) optimism,
   (iii) a new narrative.

First, large-scale ideas that lead to what William Bainbridge calls, "competing ideologies of transcendence"[207] are more likely to gain the attention of society, engage regular people, and capture their imagination (see Chapter 3). Ideas with potential transcendent impact are, by definition, aspirational. They clearly go beyond what is immediately possible, such as simply crafting new regulations or negotiating the terms of a peace treaty. Transcendent ideas have the capacity to spark the power of possibility in people and spread to wider and wider circles of society. Think of ideas that have radically changed systems of governance, revolutionized travel, cured diseases, and so on.[208] Ideas that do not imagine transcendent impact are unlikely to build social passion or momentum behind them. While these ideas—precisely *because* of their ambitious and aspirational nature—are not usually achieved in full (at least at first), the power behind them allows more transformation toward the goal than would have otherwise been possible and opens a path to getting there over time.

Second, since, as we have seen, humans are drawn more to optimistic worldviews than pessimistic ones, ideas that rest on a sense of optimism in what is possible are more likely to succeed (see Chapter 1).[209] During times of societal optimism, often triggered in the wake of existential crises, we can observe a veritable landslide of ideational acceptance and transformation, a forward-looking sense of achieving the "impossible," whether it is landing on the Moon or saving the planet. During times of general pessimism, progressive ideas often emerge, but

---

[206] Matthew Lieberman, *Social: Why Our Brains are Wired to Connect* (New York: Crown Publishing Group, 2013), pp. 7–8.

[207] William Sims Bainbridge, *The Spaceflight Revolution: A Sociological Study* (Malabar, FL: Krieger Publishing Co., 1983), Preface.

[208] Some refer to ideas of this caliber as "Moonshots" after JFK's 1962 challenge of landing humans on the Moon before the end of the decade. From a more technological perspective, Google actually created an entire company, known as X—the Moonshot Factory, to support Moonshot ideas. Google defines Moonshot thinking this way: "Throughout the course of history, we've seen that when people set their minds to wildly ambitious goals, the seemingly impossible starts to become possible. Moonshot thinking is about just that—pursuing things that sound undoable, but if done, could redefine humanity," https://x.company/moonshot (accessed May 23, 2023).

[209] Tali Sharot, *The Optimism Bias: A Tour of the Irrationally Positive Brain* (New York: Vintage, 2012).

instead of gaining traction through action, they often end up being dismissed in favor of a more cynical, transactional view. The power of possibility is quashed, and many people look to the past for solutions to problems: why embrace the demands of the anti-capitalist Occupy Movement when one could simply pass a few policies that pay lip service to unemployment and fair wages?

Third, ideas that put forward a new narrative, myth, or origin story about how the world works tend to appeal more than those that only work within existing understandings. As Harari writes,

> The ability to create an imagined reality out of words enabled large numbers of strangers to cooperate effectively. But it also did something more. Since large-scale human cooperation is based on myths, the way people cooperate can be altered by changing the myths—by telling different stories. Under the right circumstances, myths can change rapidly.[210]

These are not myths in the sense of fantasy but rather the underlying stories we tell each other to explain why we want to act in new ways. Indeed, we have a unique capacity to recognize good ideas and can even change long-standing behavior within seconds,[211] especially when new myths emerge to support this, but particularly when these myths support ideas that are optimistic and transformational. For example, the origin story behind the European Union is that in order to put a stop to wars driven by nationalism, European nation states needed to voluntarily pool their sovereignty in a new supranational order. New narratives explain why the past necessitates a change to a new future.

Thus, while the ultrasocial landscape provides the context, ideas emerge out of this, making change and progress possible. Ideas are not all created equal: those that engage our capacity for transcendence, provide an optimistic vision, and tap into our imagined reality tend to be more appealing. These ideas are more likely to resonate with ultrasocial inclinations, to captivate, and to spur to action a sufficient swath of society to effect change. Since new, transformational ideas require a societal following or movement, as well as the emergence of ideational leaders, to succeed, the specific qualities of ideas and how they engage with ultrasociality are key.

When Do Ultrasocial Ideas Matter?

Why, in some instances, are we, as humans, able to pull off major feats of international cooperation, while at other points not? Certain periods in human history

---

[210] Yuval Noah Harari, *Sapiens: A Brief History of Humankind* (New York: HarperCollins Books, 2015), p. 32.
[211] Robert Sapolsky, *Behave: The Biology of Humans at Our Best and Worst* (New York: Penguin Press, 2017).

have been more conducive to ideational emergence and transformation than others. I argue that these come from two primary drivers. First, when we perceive we are in an existential crisis, we are more likely to seek out new ideas, consider them as possibilities, and clear away the hurdles to achieving them. Ironically, it is when crises have taken their deepest toll that periods of optimism kick in. When disasters happen, the norms of civilization break down, but they also tend to trigger the acceptance of new norms.[212]

International crises may create the impression of cyclical global change that alternates between periods of transformational ideas and transactional ideas or societal optimism versus pessimism. However, I argue that international crises have their own origins and dynamics.[213] Although there are periods more conducive to ultrasocial breakthroughs and those that are not, this is not a "pendulum swings" kind of argument. There are no automatic cycles of change. Rather, international crises may be long-standing or short-lived, and many factors related to natural disasters or human agency may trigger them. Nonetheless, the longer and deeper the crises, the more there is an opening for transformational change and the more likely societal optimism will enable this.

The second primary driver in making a period conducive to ideational emergence and transformation is the necessary emergence or presence of leaders who can advocate for these ideas. These leaders must be transformational instead of transactional, as well as eager to work with others in order to pursue peace, increase transparency, initiate diplomacy, and strengthen multilateralism. In other words, they must be leaders who are well grounded in the ultrasocial landscape. It is no coincidence that the most influential leaders in the world are honored every year with Nobel Peace Prizes for embodying precisely these qualities. We respect leaders that propose ultrasocial solutions. Even on a global level, our society clearly values this.

A case in point is US President John F. Kennedy during the Cuban Missile Crisis. He is celebrated for preventing nuclear annihilation, not criticized for missing an opportunity to go to war with an adversary. Think about King Juan Carlos I of Spain, who is remembered as the leader who transformed his country's fascist dictatorship into a constitutional monarchy in the 1970s. Or take Mikhail Gorbachev, the last leader of the Soviet Union, who is praised for moving his country from communism to social democracy and pursuing a range of reforms in the early 1990s. If Kim Jong-un were to suddenly open up North Korea, normalize relations, and pursue peaceful, empathic cooperation with other countries, he would undoubtedly be considered one of the most visionary leaders of the

---

[212] Rutger Bregman, "People are Basically Good," Youtube, 2020, https://www.youtube.com/watch?v=tZ_unq8rDzU&feature=share&fbclid=IwAR0ZHeqdNfpSzBdV0oVpExbzwR2h-N32bqv0CatkCu5NO0nkZ-q3Svx_Uaw (accessed May 20, 2023).

[213] Mai'a K. Davis Cross, *The Politics of Crisis in Europe* (New York: Cambridge University Press, 2017).

post-Cold War era. This is not just about *any* international cooperation (after all, authoritarians could pursue tribalistic cooperation with other authoritarians), this is about cooperation anchored in the ultrasocial landscape—empathic, altruistic, and inclusive forms of cooperation. Intrinsically, viscerally, structurally, the world honors leadership behavior that reflects ultrasociality.

At any given time and in any given place, there are always people with the potential to be leaders, but the opportunity for them to rise requires a society that empowers them. As I will show in the following chapters, many breakthroughs in international cooperation that scholars usually credit to elite designs were actually preceded by strong calls from the public to embrace certain ideas well before the leaders typically associated with those ideas arrived on the scene. Leaders do not act alone and cannot achieve their aims unless they have followers.[214] And if they seek to be transformational, they need masses of enthusiastic followers, typically rising to the level of a social movement. Leaders cannot even emerge in the first place without such societal support. This is why it is so fundamentally important to change our starting point when it comes to understanding international relations. Change starts at the intersection of powerful, new ideas and our ultrasocial predisposition as a species. Starting with the expectation that the driving force of international outcomes is conflict and competition primes us to miss the major, defining events and processes of our lives and our history.

Of course, this dynamic is not just positive. Leaders are not always cut from ultrasocial cloth. There are many instances in which seemingly transformational leaders cloak tribalism in ultrasocial discourse to devastating effect, such as the cultural revolution in China, the Holocaust, and authoritarian populist leaders today. Just because humans tend to prefer transformational, ultrasocial policy does not mean they will always choose this or that these policies will always be good for society overall. There are mitigating factors. For example, leaders who are already in power may pursue policies without public support. Or leaders may choose coercive policies, such as sanctions, in retaliation against others for not being cooperative in their own actions. Ultimately, tribal ideas may still sometimes prevail.

Tribal Ideas in International Relations

Some ideas are a double-edged sword, promoting cooperation, on the one hand, but also providing the very seeds for violence on the other. These ideas exist outside of the ultrasocial landscape but often, at first, appear to be within it. For example, twentieth-century fascism was often sold as the only way to achieve true national unity and greatness. This notion, especially if promoted with skillful use

---

[214] Joseph S. Nye Jr, *Powers to Lead* (Oxford: Oxford University Press, 2010).

of propaganda and a cult of personality surrounding a fascist leader, attracted many people to the cause. But after a while, it became clear that the ideology was less about belonging to a great nation and more about suppressing domestic opposition and using violence to achieve objectives. In other words, as discussed in Chapter 3, one of the main reasons why ideas that fall outside of the ultrasocial landscape succeed is that corrupt leaders are able to manipulate followers into accepting them precisely because they appeal to the followers' ultrasocial wiring, a desire to belong to something bigger.

At any given time, there are always some segments of society that are more vulnerable to tribal manipulation and xenophobic politics than others. Even if our species as a whole is empathic, not all individuals are necessarily like this. Some of us have more empathy for people outside of our immediate circle, supporting policies that redistribute wealth, uphold a social safety net, and provide for the least fortunate among us. But for others, empathy fades quickly the further from their own circle they go, as depicted in Figure 1—out of sight, out of mind. Empathy can be an instinctual reaction to those closest to us. It is relatively easy to have empathy for family members and friends, and even strangers in distress when they are right in front of us. However, empathy can become somewhat more difficult when we broaden the circle to members of our local community, then to the level of our nation, and then to the level of the international community.

Unfortunately, this means that elite manipulation of the public is somewhat easier when it comes to international politics. Given that the further our gaze gets from those closest to us the more difficult it is to sustain empathy, leaders can

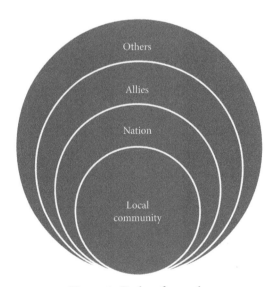

Figure 1 Circles of empathy

essentially draw lines in the sand. Using the power of language, they can try to convince the public that we should empathize with some people and not others.

Indeed, since tribalism is nearly always manufactured by unscrupulous or corrupt leaders, at its most extreme, it relies on dehumanizing those not in the tribe. In effect, the main method of undermining ultrasocial alternatives is to argue that certain others are not part of our shared ultrasocial landscape. For example, Hitler dehumanized anyone that was not part of what he defined as the "master" or "Aryan" race. Many leaders of far-right parties explicitly dehumanize those that are not considered part of the "tribe"—women, people of color, Muslims, and immigrants, among others.

To be sure, corrupt tribalist leaders cannot act without those around them being complicit with the manipulation. Here again, the cadre surrounding a tribalist leader can be drawn into a warped desire to belong to a group. As Anne Applebaum writes about the inner circle of people who colluded with Trump, there is a "pleasure of conformity."[215] Citing Czesław Miłosz, a Nobel Prize-winning poet, Applebaum refers to the pattern by which some people succumb to a desire to belong to the collective, even if they initially felt deeply uncomfortable with the beliefs it espoused, because it is easier than experiencing the isolation that comes from railing against it.[216]

Upon exposure to corrupt leaders, followers have to be primed to accept such manipulations. This can stem from, for example, a widespread feeling of "aggrieved entitlement."[217] If followers feel they have been left behind and no longer have the status they once had, this can create a context conducive to tribalism. Related to this is the growing fear, prompted by a corrupt leader, that the manufactured "other" poses an existential threat, triggering so-called "extinction anxiety";[218] that is, a leader may persuade followers to believe that if they do not act to prevent it, their very identity as a group could be erased.

Futurists, as modern philosophers of a sort, place the emphasis not only on the dangers of human corruption but also on the impact of a rapidly changing world.[219] They often consider what it would take for dystopian societies to emerge, usually in terms of how totalitarianism gains a grip on people. Alvin Toffler, in his classic 1970 book *Future Shock*, argues that many people, even experts, tend to

[215] Anne Applebaum, "History Will Judge the Complicit," *The Atlantic*, June 1, 2020, https://www.anneapplebaum.com/2020/06/01/history-will-judge-the-complicit (accessed May 23, 2023).

[216] Czesław Miłosz, "The Captive Mind," 1951, as cited in Applebaum, "History Will Judge the Complicit," https://www.anneapplebaum.com/2020/06/01/history-will-judge-the-complicit (accessed May 23, 2023).

[217] Michael Kimmel, *Angry White Men: American Masculinity at the End of an Era* (New York: Nation Books, 2013), as cited in Elizabeth Mika, "Who Goes Trump?: Tyranny as a Triumph of Narcissism," in The Dangerous Case of Donald Trump, ed. Bandy Lee (New York: St Martin's Press, 2019), p. 297.

[218] Thomas Singer, "Trump and the American Psyche," in Mika, *The Dangerous Case of Donald Trump*, p. 278.

[219] Alvin Toffler, *Future Shock* (New York: Bantam, 1984), p. 318.

ignore the possibility of accelerated change in our world and how this triggers a need to identify with something.[220] He argues that as change and diversity increase at a more alarming rate, it surpasses the ability of people to adapt.[221] He writes that there are "greater opportunities for self-realization than any previous group in history,"[222] but while this brings newfound freedom, it also subjects people to what he calls "over-choice."[223] He writes:

> When diversity, however, converges with transience and novelty, we rocket the society toward an historical crisis of adaptation. We create an environment so ephemeral, unfamiliar and complex as to threaten millions with adaptive breakdown. This breakdown is future shock.[224]

Tribalism can step in during a crisis of adaptation because tribes or subcultures provide prepackaged choices—"styles"—in an age of being able to choose anything. Psychologist Barry Schwartz finds that to be happy, we need autonomy and freedom; however, if we have too much choice, it can lead to anxiety.[225] Such exclusionary beliefs as "the pleasure of conformity," "aggrieved entitlement," and "extinction anxiety" then become more likely. Tribalistic ideas can lure in followers when old systems of conformity and common values become difficult to discern in a rapidly changing world.

Thus, within a context of new and changing ideas, many bad ideas have also been adopted and implemented. Ideas that seem at first to resonate with our ultrasocial drives have, instead, turned out to be dark manipulations of them. However, it is important to recognize that even terrible periods of democratic backsliding, genocides, wars, and fascism have nearly always been overcome. Rather than taking on a life of their own, these episodes are used as lessons for what never to repeat. The struggles of the day continue, but over time, the good ideas that reflect our ultrasocial nature have gradually prevailed.

Ideas Are Making the World a Better Place

Ideas may simply be one-off policy decisions or take us on an entirely new path, but it is clear that over the course of human history, we have become increasingly able to act on our innate ultrasociality. What is driving this? There is a pattern in which the most successful ideas, those with staying power, are firmly anchored in the ultrasocial landscape. Steven Pinker's wide-ranging study across millennia

---

[220] Toffler, *Future Shock*, p. 216.
[221] Toffler, *Future Shock*, p. 296.
[222] Toffler, *Future Shock*, p. 320
[223] Toffler, *Future Shock*, pp. 310–312.
[224] Toffler, *Future Shock*, p. 322.
[225] Barry Schwartz, *The Paradox of Choice: Why More is Less* (New York: Ecco, 2004).

of human history, for example, points to the decline of violence.[226] Starting from 8,000 BCE, and working his way up to the present, Pinker shows how violence amongst humans—everything from human sacrifice to capital punishment to slavery to murder, rape, and punishment—have steadily and dramatically declined. As Pinker writes, "No aspect of life is untouched by the retreat from violence."[227] He brings to bear an impressive range of statistics and examples which all support the notion that, at many levels of analysis (families, social groups, neighborhoods, tribes, states, etc.), the trend lines in the decline of violence are the same. He also finds that a kind of virtuous circle takes on a life of its own: "Across time and space, the more peaceable societies also tend to be richer, healthier, better educated, better governed, more respectful of their women, and more likely to engage in trade."[228]

His findings lend support to the notion that our ultrasocial inclination is getting stronger over time. The ultrasocial landscape resonates with our innate inclination to be empathic and to work with others, but it is also an edifice that is constructed and improved by us over time. Our ideas infuse the landscape with meaning, making it increasingly tangible.

Indeed, examples of ideational change in human history are numerous and are, at times, even intertwined with human evolution itself. When our species experienced a cognitive revolution some 70,000 years ago, the capacity to hold onto complex and intangible ideas was born. As Harari writes,

> fiction has enabled us not merely to imagine things, but to do so *collectively* [. . .] Such myths give Sapiens the unprecedented ability to cooperate flexibly in large numbers [. . .] with countless numbers of strangers. That's why Sapiens rule the world.[229]

Thus, ideas have driven progress, whether it is the advent of the bow and arrow, the rise of the nation state, or the drive to go further into outer space. Our ultrasocial wiring has manifested itself in increasingly larger-scale cooperative behaviors through new, shared myths and transformational ideas.[230] This has impacted how we have organized ourselves across and within societies. From tribes, to city states, to empires, to nation states, the politics of global interactions has been diverse and fluid through much of human history—even while maintaining the same fundamental socially oriented and cooperative elements. Over time, this

---

[226] Steven Pinker, *The Better Angels of Our Nature: Why Violence Has Declined* (New York: Penguin Books, 2011).
[227] Pinker, *Better Angels*, p. xxi.
[228] Pinker, *Better Angels*, p. xxiii.
[229] Harari, *Sapiens*, pp. 24–25.
[230] Harari, *Sapiens*, p. 27.

has come to encompass clearer hierarchies, networks, bureaucracies, and other institutions—all driven initially by ideas.

Since the advent of democracy, participatory governance has become increasingly common. Even during periods of democratic erosion in some countries, demand for democracy at the popular level grows in direct response, and democratization in other countries continues.[231] Violence has declined. War for conquest has been outlawed.[232] Colonialism has ended. The number of international norms and laws that protect human dignity have grown exponentially. In the twentieth and early twenty-first centuries, human rights, civil rights, and women's rights have been established and widely accepted as goals for nearly all states and societies. Especially since the Second World War, the number of international and transnational organizations has flourished.[233] In the process, it has become easier, over time, to recognize in other societies similar political structures (bureaucracies, courts, constitutions), modes of cross-border interaction (diplomacy, information sharing, summitry, negotiation), and methods of solidifying international agreements (treaties, laws, secretariats).

These international inventions were all products of ideas. As ideas crystallize, garner widespread support, and get implemented, the contours and borders of the ultrasocial landscape are thrown into sharper relief. There is a kind of stickiness as it becomes increasingly difficult to deviate from the progressively established rules of the ultrasocial landscape, that is, the institutions, norms, constructs, and practices that allow the expression of human ultrasociality. Then, when tribal ideas or corrupt leaders seek to erode what has been established, the countervailing forces happen almost automatically: popular protests, court cases, and the emergence of new leaders, new ideas, and new voices. From an international law perspective, Hathaway and Shapiro describe one key countervailing force as *outcasting*. They write:

> Outcasting occurs when a group denies those who break its rules the benefits available to the rest of the group. Outcasting is nonviolent: instead of doing something *to* the rule breakers, outcasters refuse to do something *with* the rule breakers.[234]

They argue specifically that the institutions that ensure peace and respect for international law require outcasting. Many ideas come and go with little attention, but certain ideas are more likely to succeed than others because of their location

[231] V-Dem, "Autocratization Surges—Resistance Grows," Democracy Report 2020, University of Gothenburg, 2020: https://v-dem.net/documents/14/dr_2020_dqumD5e.pdf (accessed July 11, 2023).
[232] Hathaway and Shapiro, *The Internationalists*.
[233] Peter Turchin, *Ultrasociety: How 10,000 Years of War Made Humans the Greatest Cooperators on Earth* (Chaplin, CT: Beresta Books, 2015).
[234] Hathaway and Shapiro, *The Internationalists*, p. 375.

within the ultrasocial landscape, and once entrenched, they are hard to change. Even while ideas that rail against the development of a better world sometimes win the day, it has become increasingly easy to know "bad" ideas when we see them.

An Ultrasocial Approach to International Relations

Bringing everything together, I have argued that one way to build a bridge from ultrasocial research in a range of disciplines to international relations is to focus on the power of ideas. If humans are ultrasocial as a species, then certain political ideas that allow us to fulfill this ultrasocial drive are likely to be more attractive than others. Building on this, I have suggested that ideas that are transcendent, optimistic, and feature a new narrative are more likely to capture public attention. At the same time, major crises and effective leadership are likely to facilitate this. Ultimately, to really precipitate change on a global level, a societal movement of some kind in support of new ideas is usually necessary. Figure 2 illustrates the pattern, which is also visible in the four major case studies—European integration, space exploration, nuclear weapons, and climate change—examined in this book.

As this diagram shows, societal movements usually accompany the successful spread of ultrasocial ideas. (The social movements literature likely deserves much more attention from international relations scholars than has been the case so far.) However, it is important to note that the ultrasocial approach is distinct from the classic social movements literature that emerged in the field of sociology in the 1960s and then experienced a resurgence of attention in the 1990s.[235] This other

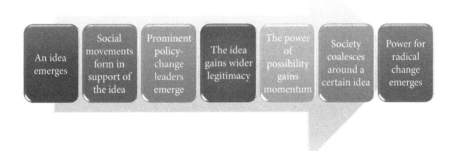

Figure 2 Pattern behind cooperative breakthroughs

[235] Alain Touraine, *Le Mouvement de Mai oule communism utopique* (Paris: Seuil, 1968), as cited in Charles Tilly and Lesley J. Wood, *Social Movements 1768–2012*, 3rd edn (London: Paradigm

research is focused on a specific kind of movement that is more protest oriented, identity based, and specifically targets what is seen as government-sanctioned oppression in one form or another. For example, Charles Tilly defines a social movement as "a sustained challenge to powerholders in the name of a population living under the jurisdiction of those powerholders by means of repeated public displays of that population's numbers, commitment, unity, and worthiness."[236] Similarly, Dieter von Rucht defines them as "an action system, formed for a certain period of time and based on collective identity, of mobilized networks of groups and organizations which aim to bring about, prevent, or reverse social change by means of protest—if necessary, violent protest."[237] For these scholars, social movements demand autonomy from the powers that be and often draw upon identity claims to justify their demands.[238] In these types of movements, the goal is usually framed in terms of the transactional and political interests of those engaged in protest.[239]

Instead, I am interested, here, in a broader phenomenon that is not so much about protesting to serve the benefit of a certain identity-based group but about examples of how social impetus envisions and then pushes for a better future for all.[240] This leads to somewhat different sorts of societal movements and issues than are usually found in the social movement literature. While there may be an element of political protest, particularly in examples like eradicating nuclear weapons and stopping climate change, I see protest and other tactics or strategies as a relatively narrow lens with which to understand these dynamics of change. From an ultrasocial perspective, the emphasis is more about how society crafts a new worldview rather than how it ends an old one. It is about understanding the forward-looking

---

Publishers, 2013), pp. 70–71; Alain Touraine, "An Introduction to the Study of Social Movements," *Social Research* 52, 4 (1985): 749–787, https://www.jstor.org/stable/40970397 (accessed May 21, 2023).

[236] Charles Tilly, "Social Movements as Historically Specific Clusters of Political Performances," *Berkeley Journal of Sociology*, 38 (1993): 1–30, 7, https://www.jstor.org/stable/41035464 (accessed May 20, 2023).; Tilly and Wood, *Social Movements 1768–2012*, 3rd edn (New York: Routledge, 2012), pp. 4–5.

[237] Dieter von Rucht, *Modernisierung und neue soziale Bewegungen* (Frankfurt: Campus, 1994), pp. 76–77, as cited and translated in *Routledge Handbook of the Climate Change Movement*, ed. Matthias Dietz and Heiko Garrelts (London and New York: Routledge, 2014), p. 6.

[238] Alain Touraine divides social movements into the older variety (pre-1968), which he describes as instrumental and mainly stemming from workers and groups that claimed exploitation, and the so-called "new social movement," which emphasizes efforts to expose and change entrenched power (i.e., upend the institutionalized ways of governments and bureaucracies) as well as claims to identity (women, homosexual, indigenous, and so on). Alain Touraine, *Le Mouvement de Mai ou le communism utopique*; Touraine "An Introduction to the Study of Social Movements," pp. 749–787.

[239] Jeff Goodwin and James Jasper (eds), *The Social Movements Reader: Cases and Concepts*, 3rd edn (Oxford: Wiley Blackwell, 2015). This literature also devotes much effort into investigating the structure, composition, tactics, and mobilization of the movement.

[240] The standard social movements literature tends to focus instead on cases of protest, such as the women's movement, civil rights movement, gay liberation movement, Occupy Wall Street, Egyptian revolution, democracy movements, and so on. There is some overlap with my approach, but this literature comes from an entirely different ontological starting point and is thus aimed at explaining different sorts of phenomenon.

nature of the idea championed by society and the ways in which this idea then transforms beliefs and behavior on a broad scale.

At the same time, an ultrasocial approach challenges some of the conclusions from research on social movements. This other work expects that movements addressing domestic issues that are lower profile will have more chance of success than those addressing international issues that are higher profile in nature. Thus, for example, environmental movements would have an easier time than movements related to peace.[241] As I find in comparing Parts IV (nuclear weapons) and V (climate change), the opposite has been true. It may often be the case, in light of ultrasociality, that the more far-reaching, aspirational ideas galvanize the public precisely because they are *harder* to achieve and thus capture the imagination in terms of the power of possibility.

From Society to Governments

Certain ideas tend to matter more, but they still usually require governments to translate them into policy. As will be described in the case studies to follow, when it comes to truly transformational ideas, governments are often *not* leading the way. Sometimes, ideational leaders even feel the need to leave official positions to be able to push boundaries more, as happened when Jean Monnet stepped down from his formal position at the helm of the fledgling European Union. At other times, governments need to be persuaded to move away from previously confrontational positions, such as in the development and growth of the non-use of nuclear weapons. And even when governments do agree to international cooperation, they are not necessarily signing agreements that reflect ultrasocial ideas. The *content* of international agreements matters. Not all forms of international cooperation are automatically rooted in the ultrasocial landscape.

Once ideas move from society to governments, a full range of theories and explanations is necessary to understand outcomes that emerge out of social ideas and enter into political processes. As Ben Rhodes argues in his analysis of the Obama administration,

Obama's view was that movements can provide the spark that initiates change and apply new forms of pressure on those in power; but he insisted that the moral vision and kinetic energy of movements ultimately has to be channeled into the accumulation of power and the reform of institutions—the business of political

---

[241] Marco Giugni, *Social Protest and Policy Change: Ecology, Antinuclear, and Peace Movements in Comparative Perspective* (Oxford, UK: Roman & Littlefield, 2004), pp. 8–9.

parties, laws, and programs. Movements that failed to do so risked chaos or the setbacks that come from the reprisals of those in power.[242]

Theories of political science are valuable in explaining how political parties, electoral processes, institutions, and rules ultimately solidify and translate ultrasocial ideas after they emerge from society and enable a breakthrough. Political science offers mid-range and micro-level theories that account for gradual shifts in political outcomes. As society pushes for transformation, leaders emerge amplifying these ideas, and eventually governments respond. This does not mean that governments always translate transformational ideas into full-blown policy change. There is usually a gap between aspiration and reality, but nonetheless, the big ultrasocial push from society often enables breakthroughs in the first place.

Post-breakthrough, the original societal movement may fade into the background, having achieved its objectives, as happened in the case of the anti-nuclear movement, for example. But as the following case studies illustrate, ultrasocial ideas tend to anchor the behavior and reign in the choices of governments even after they achieve cooperative breakthroughs.

[242] Ben Rhodes, *After the Fall: Being American in the World We've Made* (New York: Random House, 2021), p. 227.

Conclusion to Part I

Human beings have evolved to be ultrasocial and to have an empathic consciousness.[243] The preponderance of scientific evidence from a range of disciplines supports this. To the extent that there is a common *human culture*, it gravitates toward empathy. Ideas that express empathy, selflessness, and common values are more likely to matter than others because of their deep resonance with this ultrasocial landscape.

As a species, we might have instead created a world with thicker barriers between nations or one that permits more, rather than less, violence—or even one in which the weight of history restricts the definition of what it means to be human. Instead, the momentum has gone in the opposite direction, toward valuing empathy, mutual respect, selflessness, and the pursuit of peaceful interactions. Given a range of choices, humans as a superorganism will tend to gravitate toward *social* solutions that involve more, rather than less, cooperation. Our ultrasocial nature as a species does not directly cause these outcomes, but it has provided a social environment conducive to them.

Consequently, international actors have increasingly sought cooperative solutions, and the instances of acting in violent and conflictual ways are gradually decreasing in terms of quantity and intensity over time. At the same time, ultrasocial behavior is not always peaceful. Sometimes, it is necessary to temporarily consider violence in the name of upholding certain ultrasocial ideas, such as in response to Russia's war in Ukraine in 2022, which threatened democracy, sovereignty, and rules against the use of force. And often, reaching empathic cooperation can sometimes involve taking two steps forward and one step back. But as a species, we value progress, which we now overwhelmingly define as more inclusivity, more equality, more peace, less violence, and greater interaction with our fellow humans around the world. While we have not necessarily developed all of the institutions, norms, and rules that enable the expression of ultrasociality, we have been getting better at it over time. As Rifkin emphasizes, the drive for "the extension of empathy to broader and more inclusive domains of reality and the expansion of human consciousness, is the transcendent process by which we

---

[243] Jeremy Rifkin, *The Empathic Civilization: The Race to Global Consciousness in a World in Crisis* (New York: TarcherPerigee, 2009), p. 11.

explore the mystery of existence and discover new realms of meaning [. . .] Society requires being social and being social requires empathic extension."[244]

The study of international relations, however, has historically tended to focus on crises, conflict, violence, tribalism, and ruthless competition. Of course, the journey of a successful idea is not without many challenges and obstacles. To the extent that we do not find ways to cooperate as a species, other powerful dynamics get in the way, pulling us out of the ultrasocial landscape. Change, especially transformational change, is not easy. Just because we share an ultrasocial landscape does not mean that we are uniform as a species. We get socialized into different behaviors. We face manmade and natural catastrophes, psychopathic leaders, corrupt elites, and propaganda. However, if we do not simply cherry-pick these darker moments but, instead, examine human interaction on a broader scale, we begin to see that violent, conflictual crises quickly become the exception rather than the rule. They just happen to garner much more of our time and attention, especially because they cut against the grain of normal, everyday life.[245] While large-scale cooperation may sometimes be fragile,[246] it is also nevertheless innately likely.

By taking human nature seriously, I seek to consider the broader landscape in which we exist as a species and to recognize that we are fundamentally social beings. We are both pushed and pulled toward ultrasocial behavior. If we can integrate the most recent discoveries about the social brain into our approach to politics and international relations, not only will we gain crucial understanding about how things have happened and continue to happen, but also new possibilities for international cooperation will emerge. Simply put, the stakes are too high to ignore the underlying presence of ultrasociality. By choosing this new starting point, a new approach to international relations, infused with the power of possibility, can be revealed.

Parts II–V illustrate how the power of transformative ideas championed at the societal level can impact outcomes of international cooperation. It is beyond the scope of the book to provide a complete history of each of the four cases, but the purpose is to highlight how strong, ultrasocial ideas emerge in the wake of major crises, spark widespread societal-level movements, and shape debates at the elite, political level. In each case, the idea for change, whether it is to relegate national sovereignty to the past (Part II), become a multiplanetary species (Part III), prevent the use of the world's most powerful weapons (Part IV), or roll back the destructive nature of industrial output (Part V), is initially highly aspirational

---

[244] Rifkin, *The Empathic Civilization*, p. 42.

[245] Rifkin, *The Empathic Civilization*, p. 22.

[246] In *Ultrasociety: How 10,000 Years of War Made Humans the Greatest Cooperators on Earth* (Chaplin, CT: Beresta Books, 2015), Peter Turchin, argues, "military competition in history eliminated less cooperative societies" (p. 42), the end of a state or empire happens because of a "failure to sustain social cooperation" (p. 43), and cooperation within large-scale societies is "inherently fragile" (p. 43).

and forward-looking. Each idea's transcendent nature inspires optimism, creativity, new beliefs, and new narratives about how the world works or could work. As such, these ideas are not executed all at once but instead open up pathways for progressive change. Without the motor of this initial idealism, however, in each case, it would have been difficult to progress in the direction of change at all. Thus, each example is a story of the origins of the idea, the power of the society in advocating for it, the struggles to execute it at the political level, and the resulting path to transformation.

PART II

EUROPEAN INTEGRATION

The European Union (EU) is arguably the most successful example of international cooperation in existence today. Since its founding as the European Coal and Steel Community in 1952, the EU has enlarged its membership from six to twenty-seven at the same time as it has steadily and democratically deepened integration—that is, the voluntary transfer of sovereign decision-making power from the national to the supranational (or federal) level. These areas of so-called *pooled* sovereignty have grown to encompass everything from the common market to fundamental rights to internal security to some areas of defense.[1] Indeed, the founding idea behind the European project was to achieve some form of European federalism, and over the past seventy years, there has been undeniable momentum toward this goal.

Scholars have offered a range of explanations accounting for various aspects of European integration, but they have tended to focus on certain time periods and policy areas rather than the overarching trajectory. To name the most prominent approaches, the theory of *neo-functionalism*—spillover of integration from one policy area to another—was a reaction to the rapid integration that took place in the first decades of the European Economic Community.[2] In turn, *intergovernmentalism*, which re-emphasized the sovereignty of member states, was a reaction to the slowing of integration in the 1970s and early 1980s.[3] The rise in popularity of *supranationalism*, a form of institutionalism, clearly reflected an effort to explain the strengthening of EU institutions from the mid-1980s through the 1990s and

---

[1] At various junctures, usually with the signing of new EU treaties, member states decide which policy areas they would like to move to the supranational or federal level of governance. They are not required to do this but, with each successive treaty, have decided that more and more policy areas are better handled at this level. When issues of "vital" importance come up, member states can invoke a national veto over an issue that has already been deemed supranational, but this has very rarely happened.

[2] Ernst B. Haas, *Beyond the Nation State: Functionalism and International Organization* (Colchester: ECPR Press, 2008).

[3] Stanley Hoffmann, "Obstinate or Obsolete? The Fate of the Nation-State and the Case of Western Europe," *Daedalus* (1966): 862–915, https://www.jstor.org/stable/20027004 (accessed May 20, 2023); Andrew Moravcsik, "Preferences and Power in the European Community: A Liberal Intergovernmentalist Approach," *JCMS: Journal of Common Market Studies* 31, 4 (1993): 473–524, https://doi.org/10.1111/j.1468-5965.1993.tb00477.x.

emphasizes the impact of their particular internal characteristics.[4] *Multi-level governance* in the 2000s sought to put a range of previous theories together in a kind of "catch-all" explanation.[5] Subsequently, *constructivists* have sought to explain the fine-tuning of EU integration, which has often involved informal processes and norm diffusion.[6]

But again, scholars of EU integration have had the tendency to put forward explanations when events have called for them, while lacking an overarching perspective. In particular, most accounts have almost entirely neglected the nature and strength of the underlying societal drive to integrate further, under the assumption that the European project is primarily elite driven. The drawback of overlooking the root causes and driving forces of European integration over the longer term is the opening it creates for pundits and the international media to just focus on crises of the moment and virtually ignore the EU the rest of the time. Despite the EU's remarkable progress over a relatively short period of time, it is often portrayed as stumbling from crisis to crisis and even as being on the verge of dissolution.[7]

Given the nature of this groundbreaking experiment in international cooperation, it is natural that the EU should have faced many challenges along the way—the Eurozone crisis, the constitutional crisis, the migration crisis, and Brexit, to name but a few. But the common wisdom that the EU is fragile and lacks resilience is fundamentally wrong. This stems from strong misperceptions about the origins and purpose of the European project that have made their way into the public consciousness.[8] After all, it is easy for most people to conjure up associations of the EU with populist leaders, migrant flows, Brexit, and sovereign debt,

[4] George Tsebelis and Geoffrey Garrett, "The Institutional Foundations of Intergovernmentalism and Supranationalism in the European Union," *International Organization* 55, 2 (2001): 357–390, https://www.jstor.org/stable/3078635 (accessed May 21, 2023); Peter L. Lindseth, "Democratic Legitimacy and the Administrative Character of Supranationalism: The Example of the European Community," *Columbia Law Review* 99, 3 (1999): 628–738, https://doi.org/10.2307/1123519; Robert O. Keohane and Stanley Hoffmann, *Institutional Change in Europe in the 1980s* (London: Macmillan Education, 1994); Alec Stone Sweet and Wayne Sandholtz (eds), "Integration, Supranational Governance, and the Institutionalization of the European Polity," *European Integration and Supranational Governance* 1 (1998), https://doi.org/10.1093/0198294646.001.0001.

[5] Liesbet Hooghe and Gary Marks, *Multi-level Governance and European Integration* (Lanham, MD: Rowman & Littlefield, 2001); Liesbet Hooghe, *Cohesion Policy and European Integration: Building Multi-level Governance* (Oxford: Oxford University Press, 1996).

[6] Jeffrey T. Checkel, "Why Comply? Social Learning and European Identity Change," *International Organization* 55, 3 (2001): 553–588, https://www.jstor.org/stable/3078657; Jeffrey T. Checkel, "International Institutions and Socialization in Europe: Introduction and Framework," *International Organization* 59, 4 (2005): 801–826, https://www.jstor.org/stable/3877829 (accessed May 20, 2023); Kathleen R. McNamara, *The Currency of Ideas: Monetary Politics in the European Union* (Ithaca, NY: Cornell University Press, 1998); Nicolas Jabko, *Playing the Market: A Political Strategy for Uniting Europe, 1985–2005* (Ithaca, NY: Cornell University Press, 2006); Maïa, K. Davis Cross, *Security Integration in Europe: How Knowledge-Based Networks Are Transforming the European Union* (Ann Arbor, MI: University of Michigan Press, 2011).

[7] Maïa K. Davis Cross, *The Politics of Crisis in Europe* (New York: Cambridge University Press, 2017).

[8] Cross, *The Politics of Crisis in Europe.*

but who remembers when the EU launched the biggest diplomatic service in the world, added ten new member states from Central and Eastern Europe, or first sent troops under the EU flag to engage in humanitarian operations abroad? The media and most international relations scholars, especially realists, far too often portray the EU as simply a trading bloc to be discarded when member states cease to reap immediate economic benefit from it. However, the EU's roots run much deeper than this, and to ignore the ultrasocial underpinnings of it is to miss the entire point of its existence and evolution.

Using the lens of ultrasociality, I seek to uncover the overarching power of ideas, specifically what I call the European federalist idea, in providing the backbone of the European project since its inception. The federalist idea is the strongly held belief that Europeans should aspire to eradicate national boundaries and national self-interest in favor of a common approach, shared sovereignty, and permanent peace on the continent. As explained in Part I, we, as humans, are predisposed to embrace ideas that enable ultrasocial behavior unless other factors combine to distort this tendency. This does not necessarily mean that ultrasocial ideas will always win the day, but it does mean that they are more likely to be convincing in the absence of would-be spoilers. In other words, certain ideas tend to matter more, especially those with transcendent impact, optimism, and a new narrative, and the federalist idea in Europe has been a prominent example of this.

Even amongst those who actually understand the EU's origins, a common assumption is that the early years of European integration after the Second World War—when the federalist idea was undeniably strong—were an exceptional time, outside the norm. Since that time, many assume that the idealism of the early years quickly faded away to be replaced by various calculations about how powerful the institutions should be, how member states' national interests would be reflected in these institutions and subsequent treaties, and various ways to ensure democratic accountability. While all of these factors, among others, did gradually come to take on importance, I argue that they were and have always been, more by-products of the overarching integration process than driving forces.

By contrast, my starting point is that it is problematic to simply assume that the federalist idea failed. Certain policy proposals associated with it may not have always reached fruition, but the *idea*—the grand, philosophical vision—has strengthened and weakened in waves since the 1950s. There has been little scholarly attention to the "where, when, how, and why"[9] of this idea after the 1950s because of this tendency to assume that few were willing to champion federalism after it encountered its first major obstacles and once it was clear that European integration would proceed on a more gradualist, incremental path.

---

[9] Vivien Schmidt argues that in order to understand the power of ideas, we must look into how they are conveyed through discourse *and* the context in which they appear. Vivien A. Schmidt, "Discursive Institutionalism: The Explanatory Power of Ideas and Discourse," *Annual Review of Political Science* 11 (2008), dhttps://doi.org/10.1146/annurev.polisci.11.060606.135342.

But if we actually re-examine the historical and archival record, the story of European integration is very clearly a tale of the gradual achievement of federalism, not the failure of it. The centrality of the idea of federalism for Europe was crucial from the start, and it set the path for the future momentum of EU integration that continues today.[10] Acknowledging the importance of ultrasociality calls for an understanding of the significance of ultrasocial drives within society and the centrality of the ultrasocial landscape in Europe after the Second World War. Of course, the Second World War was a crisis of epic proportions, and as such, it provided an opening for new ideas to be accepted and a strong societal-level desire for something new. But without the strength of the societal-level *European Movement*, which rallied around the federalist idea, the influence of leaders like Jean Monnet, Altiero Spinelli, Richard von Koudenhove-Calergi, Robert Schuman, and others would not have taken hold. As Winston Churchill said in a speech at the Congress of Europe in May 1948, "This is not a movement of parties but a movement of peoples."[11]

Chapter 5 examines the development of the EU, with a focus on how and why, in the late 1940s and early 1950s, European leaders were finally able to make long-held ideas about uniting Europe a reality. Chapter 6 shows how from the mid-1950s to the mid-1980s, the formal European project became more transactional, while in more informal settings, the power of possibility continued to occupy people's imaginations and fuel change. There is a pattern in which the more transactional the European Economic Community became in its aims, the less the European public was inspired to push for change. However, as discussed in Chapter 7, during other periods, transformational ideas did take off, demonstrating the draw of the ultrasocial landscape. There may be an ebb and flow to such ideas, but ultimately, they tend to prevail.

The emergence and development of the EU is a revealing case of ultrasociality, given its pioneering progress in achieving peace. In an effort to shed light on the longevity of the European project, rather than a particular time period or policy area, my emphasis is on the ways in which the federalist idea drove the creation of the EU's early institutions and then continued to shape the EU into the actor that it is today. Of course, this cannot be a definitive account of every aspect of the history of EU integration. Instead, its value is spotlighting what we can learn through recognizing the ultrasocial context and using it as a starting point.

---

[10] Michael Burgess, *Federalism and European Union: The Building of Europe, 1950–2000* (Oxfordshire: Routledge, 2000).

[11] "Congress of Europe, "Message of Mr. Winston Churchill," May 1948, ME 424, Historical Archives of the European University Institute.

5

The Federalist Idea and the European Movement

The Federalist Idea Emerges

The idea of a united Europe has had a long history, stretching back to at least the philosophers of the seventeenth century. However, prior to the mid-twentieth century, it was more often than not considered a utopian ideal than an achievable goal. During the interwar period, this changed. Fresh ideas surrounding the establishment of a federal union flourished and subsequently re-emerged with greater strength in the wartime resistance movement on a new tide of optimism.[12] The very notion of voluntarily bringing sovereign nation states—many of which had been fighting gruesome battles for centuries—under a shared *supra*national governance system was wholly unprecedented, yet it had palpably galvanized the public. It would have transcendent impact. In line with ultrasociality, the new narrative of European federalism was that nationalism embodied selfishness and tribalism and thus had to be eradicated. The most influential written expressions of this were Richard Coudenhove-Kalergi's 1923 book *Pan-Europa* and Altiero Spinelli's 1941 *Ventotene Manifesto*, calling for an immediate federal constitution for Europe.[13]

During this time, it was actually not uncommon to go so far as to call for the establishment of a *world* government or a *world* federation (an idea that can be traced back to at least the Middle Ages). The main goal motivating proponents of this idea was the assurance of a permanent world peace, which would be built on a bulwark of international cooperation. To achieve this optimistic vision, they argued that they did not simply want another international institution like the League of Nations or United Nations (UN) but a central body to which countries would give up their sovereignty. This central body would be imbued with real power to enforce world law grounded in a world constitution. With the outbreak of war in 1939, and the devastating failure of the Versailles Treaty, it became clear that the existing system of diplomacy was profoundly insufficient. And after the

[12] Walter Lipgens (ed.), *Documents on the History of European Integration*, Series B, Vol. 1 (Berlin: Walter de Gruyter, 1985). As early as 1944, fifteen individuals met secretly in Geneva as the International Conference of Resistance Fighters to discuss and plan a European federation, complete with a common market. Martin Dedman, *The Origins and Development of the European Union: 1945–2008* (Oxfordshire: Routledge, 2009), p. 15.
[13] Desmond Dinan, *Ever Closer Union: An Introduction to European Integration* (Basingstoke: Palgrave MacMillan, 1999), p. 12.

International Cooperation Against All Odds. Mai'a K. Davis Cross, Oxford University Press. © Mai'a K. Davis Cross (2024).
DOI: 10.1093/oso/9780192873903.003.0006

Second World War, many worried that a Third World War was a distinct possibility. Fears also spread in reaction to the advent of nuclear weapons.[14] So-called one-worldism was thought to be the solution, bringing all people together under a system of deep international cooperation.[15] Such a system would have to rest on seeing each other as one people, with mutual empathy and a willingness to turn the corner from national competition and conflict—a clear manifestation of ultrasociality.

It is often forgotten in standard accounts of international relations that world or regional federalism was *widely* supported at the popular level, especially in Europe and the United States. As Thomas Weiss, former president of the International Studies Association, writes, "Throughout the 1940s, it was impossible in the United States to read periodicals, listen to the radio, or watch newsreels and not encounter the idea of world government."[16] A September 1947 Gallup Poll showed 56% of Americans in favor of turning the UN into a world government. There was even a hearing in the US Congress to consider the idea. In 1949, 111 congressmen, including John F. Kennedy and Gerald Ford, sponsored House Concurrent Resolution 64, which stipulated that it was "a fundamental objective of the foreign policy of the United States to support and strengthen the United Nations and to seek its development into a world federation."[17] There was even some discussion at the international level of abolishing the national veto at the UN so that it could effectively function as a world government.

Thus, in the mid-twentieth century, positive, far-reaching ideas about world government easily galvanized the public, demonstrating the draw of an ultrasocial solution to conflict. And in diplomatic summits, pessimistic naysayers were chastised for being counterproductive.[18] New leaders rose to prominence in the mid-twentieth century inspired to create an entirely different form of political organization for the achievement of peace. They translated popular ideas into action through the establishment of hundreds of international and regional institutions to foster cooperation among states in an emerging era of global governance.

While new forms of global governance flourished, the creation of *world* government ultimately proved to be too ambitious, especially given the fact that the Cold War was well underway by the mid-1950s, and Soviet leaders would never

---

[14] Mark Mazower, *Governing the World: The History of an Idea, 1815 to the Present* (London: Penguin, 2012).

[15] Wendell Willkie's book, *One World*, sold more than 2 million copies in the span of 2 years in the United States and Canada, and Emery Reves's book, *The Anatomy of Peace*, which also called for the establishment of world government was also a best-seller in 1945 and was translated into 20 languages. See Lawrence Wittner, *Confronting the Bomb: A Short History of the World Nuclear Disarmament Movement* (Stanford, CA: Stanford University Press, 2009), p. 10.

[16] Thomas G. Weiss, "What Happened to the Idea of World Government?," *International Studies Quarterly* 53, 2 (2009): 259.

[17] As cited in Weiss, "What Happened to the Idea of World Government?," p. 259.

[18] *Council of Europe documents*, Nobel Peace Institute Library and Archive, Oslo.

have accepted such a transformation of the UN. As is the case with truly transcendent ideas in general, world government was aspirational, not easily achievable in the moment. But that was precisely its strength. It forged a path to other ideas that would have otherwise been considered too far-reaching. Indeed, some considered the more limited possibility of transatlantic federalism or Atlantic Union, and still others were more focused on regional federation: the United Kingdom and France at the core of what would become a United States of Europe.[19] And it was world government that allowed these more circumscribed, but still bold, ideas to be taken more seriously.

Given the elite nature of EU policymaking today, it is often under-recognized that the inception of the European project would not have been possible without a widespread, popular movement in support of it at the outset—a European Movement—driven by the central idea of European federalism. As a more modest version of the world government movement, supporters of the idea thought it was highly desirable and achievable. This widespread societal support for the idea of a United States of Europe was indispensable to getting the project off the ground in the 1940s and 1950s.[20] And the early impetus from the European Movement would shape the future trajectory of the European project. The EU had its origin story.

The European Movement

As the European federalist movement blossomed,[21] in December 1947, several leaders of various social organizations in favor of a United Europe helped to bring people together under a common umbrella. This core group of new European leaders—later known as the EU's founding fathers—were determined to make regional *integration*, the pooling of sovereignty among European states, a reality. These leaders included Paul-Henri Spaak, Winston Churchill, Konrad Adenauer, Leon Blum, Alcide de Gasperi, Jean Drapier, Richard Coudenhove-Kalergi, and Robert Schuman. They were all highly politically prominent and had close ties to governments, which gave them access to decision makers.

The various chapters of the movement extended well beyond the original six members of what would become the fledgling EU (France, West Germany,

---

[19] Richard Mayne and John Pinder, *Federal Union: The Pioneers* (New York: St Martin's Press, 1990), chapter 1.
[20] Evidence for this empirical analysis is the result of archival research at the Jean Monnet Foundation, Lausanne, Switzerland; the John F. Kennedy Presidential Library, Boston, MA; the National Archives and Records Administration, College Park, MD; the Archive of European Integration, University of Pittsburgh; the EU Historical Archives, European University Institute, Fiesole, Italy; and the Nobel Peace Institute Library and Archive, Oslo, Norway.
[21] Jos Serrarens (Netherlands), "Official Report of the Fifth Sitting, 16th August 1949," Council of Europe Documents (Nobel Peace Archive), August 16, 1949, p. 103.

Italy, Belgium, the Netherlands, and Luxembourg) to include countries in Eastern Europe (Albania, Bulgaria, Estonia, Hungary, Latvia, Lithuania, Turkey, Yugoslavia, Czechoslovakia, Romania, Poland, and so on) as well as countries to the North (Great Britain, Ireland, Norway, Denmark, Sweden, and others).[22] Although the European Movement was a non-official organization, it had an international council of around 120 representatives from the various other organizations that together supported the goal of a united Europe. The people involved were clearly determined to make this a widely inclusive movement.

Young people, in particular, were a major force behind the European Movement, with organizations like *Jeune Europe* pushing for more vitality and action behind words. Countries that are considered Euroskeptic today at the time had significant numbers of federalists in universities and student organizations that regularly proclaimed their "militant" support for a united Europe. They created networks across Europe to bring people together for the cause and to push political leaders to take action. Their activities were diverse, everything from rallies, to publications (i.e., pamphlets, articles, and books), to speakers' series and conferences. Representative of these types of pro-Europe events at the time, students at the University of Manchester organized Europe Week, which took place January 28–February 4, 1955, "for the purpose of arousing interest and promoting discussion of the European Movement with its integral parts of political, economic, defense and cultural unity."[23]

It would be a mistake to think that the British were an exception to this pro-federal thinking and that they have always been skeptical of European federation. In fact, the idea of creating a federal Europe was part of the dominant discourse in Britain across all political parties. The *Federal Union*, an organization founded in 1939 that was comprised of the top political thinkers in the country, was particularly prominent in pushing for the idea. In just one year, the organization acquired 12,000 members and 225 branches.[24] However, there were many intellectuals and political leaders beyond this that were heavily involved in promoting the federalist idea in the United Kingdom. The Federal Union Research Institute, launched in 1939, also brought a range of prominent experts together to draw up detailed plans and a constitution for Europe.[25] That same year, 100,000 copies of W. B. Curry's *The Case for Federal Union* sold in just six months.[26] There was actually a

---

[22] Foreign Service, "Despatch No. 918 from Sheldon B. Vance, Second Secretary of Embassy, American Embassy in Brussels to the Department of State Washington," National Archives and Records Administration (NARA), RG 59, Box 3103, Folder 740.00/1–1056, February 21, 1956. These included prominent exiled representatives of the Soviet-occupied Baltic nations.

[23] Foreign Service, "Despatch No. 62 from William D. Wolle, American Consul in Manchester to the Department of State Washington," NARA, RG 59, Box 3101, Folder 740.00/2–855, February 8, 1955.

[24] Walter Lipgens (ed.) "General Introduction," in *Documents on the History of European Integration*, Series B, Vol. 2 (Berlin: Walter de Gruyter, 1985), p. 4.

[25] Dedman, *Origins and Development*, p. 17.

[26] Dedman, *Origins and Development*, pp. 16–17.

burgeoning literature on European federalism in the United Kingdom from 1939 to 1941, which not only gained a large readership in Britain but also influenced Altiero Spinelli as he wrote his federalist manifesto while imprisoned on Ventotene.[27]

There were, of course, many other organizations that were formed prior to the European Movement, and they also continued to push for federalism alongside this new and widespread impetus. Some were more ambitious than others. One such organization was the *Pan-European Union*, originally established in 1923, whose main goal at the time was the reunification of Germany and the creation of a federal Europe with a Franco-German union at its core. The founder of the Pan-European Union, Richard de Coudenhove-Kalergi, also saw the necessity of launching a broader Atlantic organization that would go beyond the military character of the North Atlantic Treaty Organization (NATO) and allow other countries to join.[28] The vision was to strengthen transatlantic ties by making NATO into "a political, economic, cultural, and social Union of the Atlantic Nations."[29] Thus, the Pan-European Union had many ideas that would push the boundaries of the post-Second World War window of opportunity. The ideas set forth were transformational but, again, sometimes went further than the main movement was prepared to pursue. For this reason, Robert Schuman, who was president of the European Movement at the time, actually wrote to Coudenhove-Kalergi saying that it was not possible for the European Movement to give any special consideration to the Pan-European Union. Again, even ideas that prove to be too aspirational—such as world government or Atlantic Union—still often play an important role in energizing society in that direction.

As the various branches of the movement came together, its members called for action to be taken. They found the goal of creating a new political organization for Europe, complete with a new set of governing institutions, to be both necessary and urgent. And they very much expected that the Council of Europe, founded in 1949 as the first European Assembly, would be the venue where European federalism would be achieved. The caliber and seriousness of the discussions in the Council of Europe about how to proceed with the creation of a United States of Europe is almost never mentioned in histories of the EU, but it is clear that the spirit and expression of the movement had spread from the streets, cafés, salons, and university campuses to the Council itself. Mutual empathy, a sense of common identity, and a strong desire to cooperate characterized this movement from the outset and clearly in a way that resonated with the ultrasocial drive that had strengthened in the wake of the horrors of the Second World War.

---

[27] Dedman, *Origins and Development*, p. 17.
[28] Count Coudenhove-Kalergi, speech given at the University of Heidelberg, NARA, January 26, 1956.
[29] Foreign Service, "Despatch No. 504 from Anthony Clinton Swezey, First Secretary of Embassy to the Department of State Washington," NARA, January 18, 1955.

The European Movement's widespread membership and momentum culminated first in the Congress of Europe in the Hague in May 1948, where the 800 in attendance (under Winston Churchill's chairmanship) established the Council of Europe. Dr. Henri Brugmans's speech, representative of much of the discussion at the congress, expressed the beliefs of the movement:

> The magic word "Europe" means not only a region of the globe; it means too a way of life for both groups and individuals. The European has never accepted for any length of time the supremacy of a master-group. He will never accept leaders unless they guarantee to him the rights of man. Europe has a feeling for liberty, of which the greater proportion of men who have lived on the earth have never dreamed either the excitements or the sweetness. Europe is Mozart; Europe is Charles Peguy; Shakespeare is their epitome. Europe is a civilization of non-conformists; it is the land of men continually at war with themselves. It is the place where no doctrine is accepted as the truth unless it is continually re-discovered. Other continents boast of their efficiency, but it is the European climate alone which makes life dangerous, adventurous, splendid and tragic—and, thus, worth living.[30]

The tone of the discussion was inspired, energetic, and forward-looking, with a strong mandate to achieve change. This included proposals for a common market, a European Assembly, a convention on human rights, and pooling of sovereignty.[31] And this was naturally carried over to the Council of Europe itself. On July 6, 1955, Harold Macmillan, at the time British Secretary of State for Foreign Affairs, reflecting on the earlier years, said:

> The Council of Europe and, especially, the Consultative Assembly were born out of the European Movement. This arose after the war by an almost spontaneous surge of emotion. I well remember the first gathering at The Hague in 1948. This meeting was organized by purely unofficial and voluntary efforts and yet it comprised the leading men and women of many countries [. . .] Those were the glorious, exciting, sometimes disorderly, but memorable days when our Movement began and the Council of Europe was founded. We had made it, not the Governments. Indeed, we had almost forced it upon the Governments. It was not just a political or a parliamentary phenomenon. It touched the imagination and raised the hopes of men and women in all walks of life, far transcending the normal confines of the political world.[32]

---

[30] Henri Brugmans, "The Vital Question," Congress of Europe speech, Folder ME 424, EUI Historical Archives, May 7, 1948.

[31] Dedman, *Origins and Development*, p. 23.

[32] Council of Europe Consultative Assembly, "Seventh Ordinary Session (First Part), Official Report, Third Sitting," NARA, Wednesday, July 6, 1955.

Indeed, in the wake of crisis, an opening had emerged for optimism, transformation, and the expression of ultrasociality.

Impetus from the United States

The United States, for the most part, welcomed all of these developments in Europe, especially encouraging moves toward supranationalism, the pooling of member-state sovereignty in central institutions.[33] The Marshall Plan was designed to encourage Europeans to set up their own system of multilateralism, but the support went well beyond this. The United States often framed other issues with Europe in terms of its support for the establishment of European federalism. For example, the United States was willing to help with the development of atomic energy in Europe through delivering atomic materials, with the stipulation that member states adopt a supranational approach. In other words, the United States was willing to provide these materials only to a supranational organization, otherwise agreements over atomic energy would have to be based upon bilateral stipulations. And in that case, the United States was unwilling to relinquish control over any atomic materials. In this way, and others, the United States essentially made the case that European countries would have *more* sovereignty through pursuing supranationalism as opposed to not.[34]

Beyond specific policy initiatives, American support for European federalism was also conveyed at the societal level. The enthusiasm for what could lead to an entirely new system of political organization in Europe, based on permanent and ever-closer cooperation, was clearly present. The European Movement had close ties to the *American Committee for a United Europe*, chaired by William A. Donovan, and received funding from the Ford Foundation, which sponsored a series of publications on European federalism.[35] Donovan and his followers were very active in writing letters to the White House to convince the US government to back this effort. They also engaged in frequent correspondences with their pro-federalist counterparts across the Atlantic to ensure the strength of their network and the exchange of ideas.

In response to the various letters from citizens, the US government certainly wanted to encourage European integration, but without being seen to interfere too much. For example, William T. Nunley of the Office of European Regional Affairs

---

[33] The difference between supranationalism and federalism is only a matter of emphasis. Both support shared sovereignty in common institutions, but while the former emphasizes pooled sovereignty above the state level, the latter emphasizes the division or balance of sovereignty between common institutions and the member states.

[34] Foreign Service, "Despatch No. 654 from J. Harold Shullaw, First Secretary of Embassy, American embassy in the Hague to the Department of State Washington," NARA, February 3, 1956.

[35] Foreign Service, "Despatch No. 918 from Sheldon B. Vance."

wrote to James Frederick Wiseman, a strong supporter of European federalism that

> There are, of course, various private organizations in Europe dedicated to the goal of European unity, of which the pan-European Union is only one. Taken altogether, it is clear that these private organizations have helped considerably to increase European understanding of the advantages of political economic and military integration. While the United States Government strongly encourages further progress toward closer European unity, I am sure you will appreciate the fact that it would be inappropriate for the Department of State to give an official endorsement to the activities of private organizations abroad.[36]

Thus, the encouragement for the establishment of European federalism came from both the US government and society, but there was also a kind of informal division of labor, with the former supporting such integration more at the political level and the latter doing so more at the public level.

Indeed, some US groups went beyond encouragement of European federalism to push for inclusion of the United States itself in such an arrangement, just as Coudenhove-Kalergi's Pan-European Movement was doing in Europe. Logistically, the idea of Atlantic Union involved deepening NATO to create a "European intellectual and cultural community" that would include the United States. This would mean a significant enhancement of NATO, going well beyond the promise of common defense. Many letters, articles, and pamphlets articulating this vision from individuals across the United States were sent directly to the president, outlining the justification for the creation of an Atlantic Union. As with the idea of world government, the level of ambition behind Atlantic federalism went too far for many, and Europeans were well aware that a transatlantic union would be unlikely.

As efforts solidified around regional—as opposed to world or Atlantic—federalism, the emphasis among European leaders of the movement was more on reassuring the US government that the fledgling union of European countries was not intended to overstep the power of the United States in any way. On January 23, 1961, Walter Hallstein, then President of the European Commission, said at a speech before the NATO's Defense College in Paris that

> If, as my friend Jean Monnet has put it, we are building in the European Community "a second America in the West," it is our intention that this "second America"

---

[36] "Letter to Mr. James Frederick Wiseman," in response to his letter in support of the work of Count Coudenhove-Kalergi's advocacy for European unity as chairman of the Pan-European Union, July 11, 1958.

shall be no "third force," no divisive factor in the Alliance, but a strong and valid partner for the "first America" and for all our other friends and allies.[37]

This statement clearly reflected the Atlanticization that had occurred within the first ten years of the establishment of NATO and the need to reassure partners that the European project in no way threatened the transatlantic one.

The Council of Europe

Back on the other side of the Atlantic, when the Council of Europe met for the first time, support for European federalism was so strong that the view shared among those gathered in Strasbourg was that there was *no choice* but to create a united Europe that would be federal in character. They met as "representatives of Europe trying to consider and solve problems in the interests of Europe as a whole."[38] The social movement had provided the legitimacy to bring them together in an unprecedented way, as a true European Assembly, representing the people directly. In effect, the central idea of the European Movement enabled ultrasocial behavior, and the Council of Europe called for the creation of institutions to achieve ultrasociality in the form of European federalism.

Not surprisingly then, on August 16, 1949, the first substantive topic discussed at the Council of Europe was the future political structure of Europe, reflecting the strong call of the European Movement. André Philip, a French representative, who was the first to address the Council in this first debate said:

What has brought us together at Strasbourg on this occasion is not merely the hope of achieving an ideal which dates back a long time in the traditions of our Continent, but also our consciousness of a situation of extreme urgency. It is the fact that public opinion in all our countries now realizes that the economic and political unification of Europe has become a matter of life and death for us all, and that unless we make rapid progress towards that unification we shall very soon find ourselves in what may become a tragic situation.[39]

He goes on to argue that the shared goal had to be a supranational Europe, a point of emphasis that all subsequent delegates present at the meeting echoed strongly.[40]

---

[37] Walter Hallstein, "The European Economic Community," speech, Jean Monnet Fondation, Lausanne, Paris, January 23, 1961.

[38] Council of Europe Secretariat-General, "European Unity: Achievement and Prospects," SG (58) I Part II (Nobel Peace Archive), Strasbourg, April 25, 1958, p. 7.

[39] André Philip (France), "Official Report of the Fifth Sitting," Council of Europe documents, August 16, 1949, p. 78.

[40] Philip, "Official Report of the Fifth Sitting," p. 80. Interestingly, countries that would not be part of the EU for several decades were just as fervent in their support of European unity and supranationalism as the others, including Turkey, Greece, the United Kingdom, and Ireland.

In essence, the first debate in the Council of Europe, which was later recognized as a "landmark" event,[41] featured unanimous support for a united Europe on a strong path to federalism.

Naturally, some views were more cautious, and others were more ambitious. Giuseppi Cappi, an Italian representative, expressing the more cautious side, pointed out the risks at stake on the first day of deliberations. As if foreshadowing the failure of the European Defence Community and European Political Community just five years later, he said:

> Wisdom teaches us that politics—and we are engaged in politics in the most sublime sense of the word—is the art of the possible. Indeed, if we wish great historical events to be abiding and fertile, they must ripen in spirit and in fact, that is to say, they should be justified by circumstances. If some attempts fail because they are too hasty, if they are followed by bitter disappointments, these disappointments might be used to our disadvantage by many sceptics and opponents to our idea of a united Europe.[42]

The risk was high because all present understood very clearly that they were *not* launching the Council of Europe merely to replicate a regional version of the League of Nations or United Nations. As British representative Macmillan put it,

> Neither the League of Nations nor the United Nations organization is in the least comparable. These were, and are, meetings of national delegations, on an official or governmental basis, with national loyalties. Ours is a very different body [. . .] We are all inspired by a higher responsibility and duty. Much perhaps divides us. One thing unites us. We meet as Europeans—free, unfettered, each responsible only to his own conscience and the over-riding conception of European unity which brings us all here.[43]

At the same time, there was recognition that this was not going to be the same as the establishment of the United States of America.[44] There were competing ideas (i.e., causal beliefs) of precisely how to accomplish the goal (unionists, functionalists, federalists, and so on), but it was also understood that these camps were not truly in opposition. The unionists, like Churchill, wanted to unite Europe in a broad sense, while the federalists, like Spinelli and the Union of European Federalists, also wanted the same but more specifically through the signing of a federal

[41] Council of Europe Secretariat-General, "European Unity: Achievement and Prospects," p. 7.

[42] Giuseppe Cappi (Italy), "Official Report of the Fifth Sitting," Council of Europe documents, August 19, 1949, p. 82.

[43] Harold Macmillan (UK), "Official Report of the Sixth Sitting," Council of Europe documents, August 17, 1949, p. 125.

[44] Feridun Düsünsel (Turkey), "Official Report of the Sixth Sitting," Council of Europe documents, August 17, 1949, p. 143.

constitution.[45] The functionalists too wanted federalism but thought that a grad-ualist approach to get there would be preferable. Thus, they all wanted to end up with a united Europe, firmly rooted in an ultrasocial landscape, but differed somewhat on the best path to get there. The British, Irish, and some Scandinavian representatives were more cautious, while most continental Europeans were more ambitious.[46]

In response to these variations in viewpoints, Jean Le Bail of France struck a strong chord at the end of the first day of debate in the Council of Europe:

> Those in favour of caution say we must beware of an Assembly which starts to look like a congress; beware of an enthusiasm which has no outcome, and we must not make a great deal of noise about nothing! But those in favour of bold-ness also call on us to beware! Beware of these legal quibbles which harden and paralyse the highest ideals! [. . .] I must say at once that I am on the side of the bold and opposed to the cautious. What is to become of us, in a few months or a few years time, if we are already timid? A great impulse has gone forth—a great creative impulse. It must be maintained at any price. How can we do this? By clearly perceiving the aim, which is very easy. Europe will not be created unless it is constantly allowed to outstrip its previous achievements.[47]

The representatives' strong mandate from the European Movement was tangible in the early sessions of the Council of Europe and showcased their passion for and power of possibility. They were clearly trying to find a concrete expression of the societal mandate that had brought them to Strasbourg. And they recognized the opportunity that lay before them as a result of these groundbreaking ideas.

As the first few days went by, however, the hope placed in achieving federalism as quickly as everyone wanted began to wane. The Assembly resolved to create a Committee on General Affairs, led by Bidault, to come up with a resolution on the political structure of Europe. Just twenty days after the start of discussions, the final report released was largely underwhelming and seemed to focus more on accounting for differences among viewpoints rather than consolidating a common goal. Italian representative Ferrucio Parri described the resolution as a "first-class funeral, especially when compared to the eloquent discussions which took place in this Assembly during the Debate."[48] He went on to say that he was "anxious that the Assembly of Europe should declare that it has not forgotten the reason for

---

[45] Dinan, *Ever-Closer* Union, p. 13.

[46] Éamon De Valera (Ireland), "Official Report of the Sixth Sitting," Council of Europe documents, August 17, 1949, p. 141.

[47] Jean Le Bail (France), "Official Report of the Sixth Sitting," Council of Europe documents, August 17, 1949, p. 119.

[48] Ferrucio Parri (Italy), "Official Report of the Fifteenth Sitting," Council of Europe documents, September 5, 1949, p. 481.

its existence."[49] Similarly, French representative Jacques Bardoux said, "this text is not only summary and cursory, but it is also thin and meagre; it lacks body; it is lifeless and it makes no appeal to the imagination. Yet Napoleon said: it is through imagination that people can be led."[50] In other words, he had invoked the notion that transcendent ideas, even if aspirational, is where the power for change resides.

The recognition of differences and national sovereignty had already become a matter of concern for Paul-Henri Spaak, president of the Council of Europe, who told *Le Monde* the day before the resolution was released that "Our task must surely be that of thinking and feeling as Europeans, in all the branches of the Assembly, whether in its Permanent Committee or on the floor of the house."[51] Those who were not fully in the federalist camp were satisfied with the resolution, particularly as it had unanimous approval by the committee. But the main reason these first steps were considered by most to have fallen short of aspirations was precisely because the power of possibility had grown to such a level that the ad hoc representatives at the Council of Europe risked disappointing the European Movement that brought them there.

Although the Council of Europe was not destined to be the venue for achieving the European Movement's demands, it did establish and legitimize a number of core principles born out of the federalist idea: (1) a reunified Germany was needed for peace in Europe, (2) those on the other side of the Iron curtain were considered part of Europe and of utmost concern to the Council even if they could not yet be part of the European project, (3) security through peace and disarmament must be achieved, and (4) engagement with the East to improve ties was necessary.[52]

Thus, the European Movement had high hopes that the Council of Europe would be the venue where federalism would be achieved. Participants in the debates within the Consultative Assembly earnestly sought to make the council the core organization for a peaceful, democratic, free, and united Europe. However, in light of different viewpoints that emerged on how to achieve this in more practical terms, a shift occurred. First, as described, some of those present had succeeded in downgrading initial ambitions.

Second, just a few months after the opening session of the Council of Europe, French Foreign Minister Robert Schuman announced Jean Monnet's plan (known as the Schuman Plan) for a far more limited European Coal and Steel Community (ECSC), with France and West Germany at its core. It would be focused much more narrowly on a common market in coal and steel, but it would still operate according to supranationalism. A smaller group of those present began to talk

---

[49] Ferrucio Parri (Italy), "Official Report of the Fifteenth Sitting," p. 482.

[50] Jacques Bardoux (France), "Official Report of the Fifteenth Sitting," Council of Europe documents, September 5, 1949, p. 483.

[51] As quoted by Édouard Bonnefous (France), "Official Report of the Fifteenth Sitting," Council of Europe documents, September 5th, 1949, p. 495.

[52] Council of Europe Secretariat-General, "European Unity: Achievement and Prospects," p. 45.

about achieving integration in this other venue and the ways in which this initial arrangement could allow the federalist idea to be brought to life. Despite the shift that took place in the Council of Europe, one that was very disappointing for many involved, there was a sense that by starting with the ECSC, there would then be room for the more gradual achievement of a fundamental European transformation. Indeed, they were not wrong, and it is clear that by embracing such an aspirational idea at the outset, an opening emerged for the European project to succeed over the longer term.

6

European Transformation

Most accounts of the origins of the European Union (EU) gloss over or ignore altogether the strength of the European Movement and the caliber of the ensuing deliberations at the Council of Europe, where the individuals gathered set the future trajectory of the European project. Indeed, a typical approach is to start with acknowledging the European Coal and Steel Community (ECSC) as a brief and disappointing precursor to the European Community and then jump ahead to the 1957 Treaties of Rome. An ultrasocial approach, however, requires going further back to examine the origins of ideas and why they gained traction. It also requires understanding where the power of an idea is manifested, whether in its people, new institutions, or new agreements.

An ultrasocial lens provides the all-important context and underlying meaning of what ensues in international relations. Something that may look small and incremental on the surface could actually be the first step in the drive toward transcendent impact. The ECSC was precisely this step for Europe. And the planning for the Treaties of Rome occurred in the Council of Europe, which is where the European Movement had found its expression. As this chapter shows, it takes human agency and continued passion for the power of possibility to maintain such momentum. In the case of the EU, key leaders were able to recall and re-energize the federalist idea and the federalist movement at various points in time. But in other periods, when governments have regarded the idea in a more transactional way (i.e., based on smaller concerns of efficient policymaking), it has lost inspiration and adherents. This dynamic has determined whether the European project has been closer to the core of the ultrasocial landscape or further away.

European Coal and Steel Community (ECSC)

With the European Movement's demands for a United States of Europe still very strong, the shift from the Council of Europe to the ECSC, formally established in 1951, was not a smooth path. At first, there was strong resistance to letting go of some of the initial lofty aspirations associated with the Council of Europe. Even as the European Defence Community (EDC) was proposed and failed, as the Western European Union was launched, and as the Organization for European Economic Cooperation (OEEC) took on responsibilities, representatives at the Council of Europe, which still embodied the European Movement, at first did not want to let go of their institution's core role in uniting

International Cooperation Against All Odds. Mai'a K. Davis Cross, Oxford University Press. © Mai'a K. Davis Cross (2024). DOI: 10.1093/oso/9780192873903.003.0007

Europe. They regarded other institutions, including the ECSC, and later, the European Atomic Energy Community (Euratom), as more specialist organizations that would work on certain issues in support of the Council of Europe's overall centrality.

However, from the very beginning, Jean Monnet, who became the architect of the EU, felt that the Council of Europe would go nowhere as long as it maintained the possibility of the national veto.[53] While he was, indeed, behind a more gradual, functionalist approach to European integration, he nonetheless held the spirit of the European Movement close to his heart. Monnet specifically designed the institutions of the ECSC to be free of a national veto, arguing that the ECSC would be "the first step towards European federation" with an "ultimate objective to contribute essentially to the creation of a United States of Europe."[54] Thus, as Jean Monnet advocated for the ECSC, he emphasized the importance of giving up some elements of national sovereignty to common institutions. He emphasized that, "Any of these institutions may be changed and improved in the light of experience. What cannot be challenged is the principle that they are supranational—in other words federal—institutions."[55]

The United States' support for the federalist idea continued to be important, especially in light of Monnet's strong ties to various political and business communities on the other side of the Atlantic. Conjuring up the selfless, ultrasocial spirit of the world government movement, Monnet said, "This is the first time in history that a great power [the United States], instead of basing its policy on the keeping-up of divisions, has continuously and resolutely supported the establishment of a great community founded on union between peoples hitherto living apart."[56] Along similar lines, the creation of this fledgling form of federalism in Europe was not simply a matter of balancing against the Soviet threat. In response to a US journalist, Monnet expressed the beliefs of the European Movement:

The Europe we are making is not born of fear. It is the result of the faith we have in ourselves and the certainty that if Europeans finally come to realize what qualities and abilities we have in common, we shall establish a Western world which will give to all civilization, to peace, to America, to Russia, a security which could not be achieved in any other way.[57]

[53] Jean Monnet, *Memoirs*, trans. Richard Mayne (Garden City: Doubleday & Company, Inc. 1978), pp. 273, 281.

[54] NARA (National Archives and Records Administration), "Statement before 'Randall Committee' Investigating United States Foreign Trade Policy," Paris, November 11, 1953.

[55] NARA, "Speech to the Council of Ministers," September 8, 1952.

[56] NARA, "Speech to the Common Assembly," Strasbourg, June 19, 1953.

[57] NARA, "Speech to the Common Assembly," June 16, 1953.

In other words, the fledgling EU, now under Monnet's leadership, was explicitly divorced from realist, national self-interest, and instead grounded in the notion of common humanity.

Despite the stronger, supranational structure of the ECSC, its membership was still far dwarfed by the Council of Europe, betraying the fact that not all governments were prepared to take such a transformational step toward regional federalism. In 1950, Monnet himself made a speech at the Council of Europe calling upon the others to join the Schuman Plan. Adhering to the inclusive nature of the movement, he believed that it was preferable at the beginning to avoid settling for only a "Little Europe," which was comprised of just the original Six. The movement, of course, was comprised of many people beyond France, Germany, Italy, and the Benelux countries. At the very least, many hoped that the community would also encompass Great Britain and Scandinavia. However, these countries were relatively more reluctant to embrace federalism at the state level; a Little Europe it was to be. As Carlo Schmid, a politician in the Social Democratic Party of West Germany said during a radio interview on January 25, 1956, "No politically responsible man dares to think of a freely elected All-European parliament today."[58]

So, the ECSC moved forward with the Six. It was smaller, to be sure, but it also carried forward the federalist idea. In a kind of last-ditch effort to associate the ECSC with the Council, conservative British PM Julien Amery put forward the Eden Plan, calling for the Council of Europe to take political control over both the ECSC and EDC. Not surprisingly, Monnet referred to this as an attempted "takeover."[59] Then, the early resignation of the Council of Europe's president, Spaak, in December 1951, contributed to a clear sign of the decline of the federalist idea in this setting.[60] As the Secretary General of the Council of Europe described it, the ECSC:

> was brought into being exclusively by the determined efforts of certain enlightened political circles. When the governments were found wanting, it was the European institutions themselves which took over. They would no doubt have been unable to survive a complete and final reversal of the European policy of the principal governments concerned, but the proof was given that they could at least survive the most serious jolts and jars of fluctuating national policy."[61]

[58] Foreign Service, "Despatch No. 1567 from Elim O'Shaughnessy, Counselor of Embassy, American embassy Bonn to the Department of State, Washington," NARA, RG 59, Box 3103, Folder 740.00/1–1056, January 30, 1956.
[59] Monnet, *Memoirs*, p. 380.
[60] Desmond Dinan, *Europe Recast: A History of European Union* (Basingstoke: Palgrave, 2004), p. 25.
[61] Council of Europe Secretariat-General, "European Unity: Achievement and Prospects," SG (58) I Part II (Nobel Peace Archive), Strasbourg, April 25, 1958, p. 13.

This was the final juncture in the separate paths that the ECSC and Council of Europe would take.

For its part, the Council of Europe remained important for a while even after the ECSC was launched, and the European Movement continued to exert pressure on it. From 1953 onward, the topics discussed in the Council of Europe had become ambitious and wide ranging, even if, ultimately, its hands were tied to act. Indeed, it was in the Council of Europe, rather than the ECSC, where the broad political debates took place on the future of the federalist idea, paving the way for the Treaties of Rome, which would launch the European Economic Community in 1957. While the Common Assembly of the ECSC focused on the practical economic matters at hand, the Consultative Assembly was free to discuss a much wider range of issues from European union to Europe's role in the world. It was also an arena in which those European representatives who were not part of the Six could still remain tied to them and could closely discuss the plans of the Six.[62]

Thus, even though federal efforts now fully lay with the ECSC, there was still recognition of the Council of Europe's role in facilitating this. A decade after the Congress of Europe met, the original impetus to create a United States of Europe through the Council of Europe had broken down into the ECSC, the Western European Union (WEU), and the OEEC. But the Secretary General of the Council of Europe still wanted the Council to have some credit. He wrote, in 1958, that a "European atmosphere" had been created, in which it became "embarrassing" for governments to use their veto power when most other countries favored a decision.[63] Without this atmosphere, he argued, the Council of Europe's Assembly may not have paved the way for the creation of the ECSC. As the Secretary General put it,

> It is a recognised fact that the Coal and Steel Community has found in the Council of Europe a political platform with access to a large international audience and that, without the Council, the European "new drive" would probably not have taken place so soon after 1954.[64]

The Secretary General effectively described the ECSC as the "concrete expression to the political decisions taken by the Assembly in favour of creating a European Authority."[65] However, in trying to define the ECSC as an offshoot of the Council of Europe, he had somewhat missed the point because, unlike the latter, the former involved true supranationalism from the start. It would be more accurate to say

---

[62] Council of Europe Secretariat-General, "European Unity: Achievement and Prospects," p. 28.

[63] Council of Europe Secretariat-General, "European Unity: Achievement and Prospects," p. 24.

[64] Council of Europe Secretariat-General, "European Unity: Achievement and Prospects," p. 27. This statement refers to cf. Resolution 64 (54), adopted on September 24, 1954, immediately after rejection of the EDC.

[65] Council of Europe Secretariat-General, "European Unity: Achievement and Prospects," p. 11.

that the early shortcomings of the Council of Europe inspired the launch of the ECSC and then the European Economic Community (EEC). And this occurred specifically because public opinion on both sides of the Atlantic was still in favor of European federalism. Again, even when actions fall short of ideas, the latter still shape the terms of the debate and extend the parameters of what is seen to be possible.

Indeed, undeterred by the early failure of the Council of Europe, the movement was still alive and well. The European Movement's Action Committee for the European Supranational Community (founded in 1952) aimed to take "militant action" to push for more integration through the ECSC. This group was a big proponent of the EDC (approved by all six governments but rejected in the French parliament).[66] The EDC and its political counterpart, the European Political Community, signaled the still highly ambitious thinking of the European Movement and the EU's founding fathers. Walter Hallstein said in 1961, "Both failed—not so much because of a general lack of the will to achieve them, as because of particular political circumstances, among others a virulent and largely Communist inspired propaganda campaign against them."[67] In spite of the setback, these ardent federalists continually lobbied for the ECSC to go further. In 1953, for example, they launched the Cahiers Européens "to inform parliamentarians, high officials and people influential in private life on problems concerning political integration of ECSC nations."[68] Now that Europeans had embarked upon a federalist trajectory, a core leadership group—to represent the ongoing interests of the movement and shape the institutions that arose from it—was emerging.

Once it was clear that the ECSC was going to be the venue where European countries could pursue federalism, the process of launching the early stages of the European Community began. However, moving from the relatively narrow structure of the ECSC to something far more expansive was challenging. The various aspirations for how to achieve this in practical terms were not necessarily aligned. Moreover, the ECSC was still generally seen as underwhelming in comparison to the federalist idea and the European Movement, despite being an important first step in a period of significant transformation for Europe. The ECSC certainly represented an accomplishment in line with the ultrasocial impulse, but as it got to work with the daily business of coal and steel, it slipped into transactionalism, that is, day-to-day concerns of carrying out policy. And with that, the ECSC began to lose its creative appeal in the movement.

[66] Foreign Service, "Despatch No. 918 from Sheldon B. Vance, Second Secretary of Embassy, American Embassy in Brussels to the Department of State Washington," NARA, RG 59, Box 3103, Folder 740.00/1-1056, February 21, 1956.
[67] Walter Hallstein, "Economic Integration and Political Unity in Europe," before the joint meeting of Harvard University and the Massachusetts Institute of Technology, Jean Monnet Fondation, Lausanne, Paris, May 23, 1961, p. 9.
[68] Foreign Service, "Despatch No. 918 from Sheldon B. Vance."

From Transformational to Transactional

In November 1954, against the wishes of many, Jean Monnet stepped down from his post at the helm of the ECSC. This was the first warning sign that the ECSC could be losing the momentum that had inspired the power of possibility in the minds of those in the movement. At first, those in the European federalist movement were alarmed by his departure from the High Authority (which would eventually become the European Commission) of the ECSC, and the press also speculated that Monnet had abandoned the project. However, Monnet did not leave because he had given up on the federalist idea. On the contrary, Monnet's aim was to help rejuvenate the European Movement because of its important role in providing the momentum and legitimacy for European integration, especially after the failed EDC. He actually felt that his influence would be much greater if he had a more informal role in promoting the European project. As he put it, "I think I can be of more use to you outside."[69]

By resigning from the High Authority, Monnet was free to become more active and did so through the creation of the Action Committee for the United States of Europe on October 13, 1955. Once outside of the ECSC, Monnet set about "re-launching" Europe. He spent months bringing together nearly all of the leaders of the Socialist, Christian Democrat, and Liberal political parties,[70] as well as trade unions across Europe to establish the Action Committee. He formed it as a private individual, using funding from his family's cognac business,[71] and its stated goal was "to arrive by concrete achievements at the United States of Europe."[72]

Significantly, membership in the committee rested with the organizations—political parties and trade unions—rather than the individuals who met on behalf of these organizations.[73] As with the Schuman Plan negotiations, Monnet adopted a particular kind of diplomatic approach that would favor some ideas over others. He kept the group small and focused on members of political parties and trade unions but purposefully excluded neo-fascists, communists, Gaullists, and other militant "European" groups. After all, the tribal nature of these groups would clearly detract from the ultrasocial aims of the movement.

Monnet knew he was up against a spreading malaise. The failure of the EDC had not only spurred him into action but also left general public opinion far less interested in the prospects for real integration. Thus, when the foreign ministers

---

[69] Monnet, *Memoirs*, p. 405.

[70] All non-Communist parties, representing around 60 million voters and 12 million trade unionists, equivalent to 67% of all citizens and 70% of organized labor.

[71] Colin Bingham, *Australian Financial Review*, February 2, 1961.

[72] Action Committee for the United States of Europe, "Note, 1970," accessible at Jean Monnet Fondation, Lausanne, Paris, record code AMK 1/2/11.

[73] Walter Yondorf, "Monnet and the Action Committee: The Formative Period of the European Communities," *International Organization* 19, 4 (1965): 885–912, https://www.jstor.org/stable/2705648 (accessed May 21, 2023).

of the Six spoke to the press after the Messina Conference in 1955, they had a formal agreement to relaunch the European project, but without much enthusiasm.[74] Many media reports noticed the emerging transactional nature of the ECSC. For example, a *Newsweek* article stated:

> When the French National Assembly seventeen months ago killed the idea of a European Defense Community, many Europeans gloomily wrote off the entire concept of European Union. But Jean Monnet, the indefatigable little Frenchman who is the principal apostle of a federal Europe, refused to concede defeat.[75]

In this context, Monnet saw the need to energize the European Movement once more. The sheer amount of work he put into this new push for a United States of Europe was an indication that the remaining societal energy for this goal had shifted from the Council of Europe and ECSC to Monnet's Action Committee. Strong support from US society and government continued, thanks in part to Monnet's strong reputation across the Atlantic. State Department summaries of meetings with Monnet clearly depicted the high level of trust and respect US officials had for him. In addition, he was regularly invited to give speeches explaining the European project to the US Congress and at American universities.

The Action Committee's work began in January 1956 and continued for two decades.[76] It met roughly once per year, holding fourteen meetings between 1956 and 1970. The first ten were in Paris, followed by a meeting in Bonn (1965), Berlin (1965), Brussels (1967), and London (1969). Each meeting was closed to the public, but upon its conclusion, a public announcement was made on the mutually agreed resolution. With all of the groundwork laid in advance of each meeting, most agreements were arrived at unanimously, but any abstentions or disagreements were noted in the public press conference. On occasion, national political parties also vetted some aspects of these agreements in advance, adding to their legitimacy.[77]

There emerged at least four key goals of the Action Committee, all designed to move the European project further down the road toward federalism. The first main task of the Action Committee was to expand the supranational precedent set by the ECSC to the 1957 creation of Euratom—a federal approach to nuclear energy. Indeed, the first few meetings were virtually exclusively devoted to this. And importantly, Monnet wanted to ensure that the institutional precedent set by the ECSC was the model for Euratom. The High Authority, in his view, needed to be endowed with significant federal power. The second main task was to ensure

---

[74] "Note sur l'histoire du comite," Jean Monnet Fondation, record code AMK 1/1/4.
[75] Newsweek, "Federated Europe: A Bold, New Plan," accessible at Jean Monnet Fondation, Lausanne, Paris, record code AMK 4–15, January 30, 1956.
[76] Monnet, *Memoirs*, pp. 405–417.
[77] Action Committee for the United States of Europe, "Note, 1970."

the establishment of the common market. Third, another key goal was the entry of Britain into this arrangement. Finally, Monnet's new proposals to launch a common foreign policy and defense—undoing the setback of the failed EDC—became a significant part of the Action Committee's work in the 1960s.

In some respects, even the ambitious proposal to transform the ECSC into a broader European common market was a reaction to the unsuccessful EDC. As Paul-Henri Spaak put it in a speech on October 21, 1955,

> We then considered that having failed on the political plane, we should take up the question of the economic plane and use the so-called functional method, availing ourselves to some extent [. . .] of the admittedly successful experiment already made with the European Coal and Steel Community.[78]

Spaak went on to lament that it is much more difficult to arouse the interest and passion of the European public in following a functionalist instead of federalist path. In his words, "The economic and functional method, therefore, is less likely to attract and retain the attention—let alone enthusiasm—of the masses that the constitutional method which is based on ideas of a more general nature and so easier to assimilate."[79] He appealed to decision makers not to focus primarily on technical details but instead on political resolve. He said, "The day that this political resolve gathers its full force there will be no technical problem that cannot be solved."[80] With this logic, he tried to make the case that big ideas matter more, and in this, he was correct. Ideas with transcendent impact are more likely to galvanize society, even if they start out as aspirational.

European Economic Community (EEC)

As Europe proceeded on the basis of a step-by-step approach to integration, the main idea driving these initiatives was still the creation of a federal United States of Europe. The difference was that the idea and the movement had begun to fade from prominence, just as Spaak had predicted.[81] Instead, the transactional focus on the direct economic benefits from integration took center stage. Once the EEC

---

[78] Council of Europe Consultative Assembly, "Seventh Ordinary Session, Speech Made by M. Paul-Henri Spaak, Minister for Foreign Affairs of Belgium at the Twenty-First Sitting of the Consultative Assembly," NARA, Friday, October 21, 1955. p. 3.

[79] Council of Europe Consultative Assembly, "Seventh Ordinary Session, Speech Made by M. Paul-Henri Spaak," p. 4.

[80] Council of Europe Consultative Assembly, "Seventh Ordinary Session, Speech Made by M. Paul-Henri Spaak," p. 6.

[81] Gilles Grin connects the decline of federalism with the development and growth of the EEC. See Gilles Grin, "The Community Method: From Jean Monnet to Current Challenges," *EuroAtlantic Union Review* 2, 2 (2015): 15–29, https://www.ecb.europa.eu/press/key/date/2017/html/ecb.sp170504.en.html (accessed May 20, 2023).

was launched, its striking success provided much momentum for the Six to surpass even their own goals. In 1960, trade among EEC member states was around 28% higher than the year before, and the Community's international trade increased by around 23%. Industrial production was 11% higher and gross national product (GNP) was 6.5% higher in 1960 compared to 1959. This economic success far exceeded initial projections about the impact of the common market.[82]

With the functional, economic logic as the focus, decision makers worked on policies that would make the common market as seamless as possible. They pursued free movement of persons, services, and capital and the prevention of discrimination across member states, such as financial penalties. These more specific, transactional rationales began to take over. In 1961, for example, European Commission President Walter Hallstein gave speeches in the United States that focused on the EEC, with only indirect mention of a United States of Europe. He instead emphasized that political integration must exist alongside economic integration, a far less ambitious framing than before. But he still noted that political integration would not be some kind of automatic process. A political choice had to be made. Moreover, he said, "There are two words by which I should like to characterize the development of the European Community in the past years and months: these words are success and recognition."[83]

In response to all of this, and the efforts of Monnet's Action Committee, there was clearly a sense of disappointment with the lack of true federalism among champions of the idea. Transactional ideas could not inspire the public in the same way as transformational ones. But at least, by this point, integration was infused into institutional life and continued its progress, nonetheless. Indeed, the principle and practice of free movement—especially that of people—was so fundamentally ultrasocial that there was no denying its strong contribution to the federalist idea.

Federalism is not a story of the rise and gradual decline of an idea, as is often assumed, neither is it the story of a failed idea. First, the idea has fundamentally shaped the nature of EU institutions all along and has ensured peace among European states. It has, at some points, been front and center and, at others, more in the background; at times, more of a public cause, and at others, more focused in specific networks of actors. Second, the idea has tended to galvanize more support when it is framed as transformational, bold, and visionary and less support when it is sold as more transactional, individualistic, and incremental. And third, opinion leaders who have been able to pursue transformational ideas *outside* of the EU's formal institutional structures have often been more effective in impacting institutions than those who have operated from the inside, highlighting the power of society to push for change, even in highly unanticipated ways. What is clear is that

---

[82] Walter Hallstein, "The European Economic Community," speech, Jean Monnet Fondation, Lausanne, Paris, January 23, 1961, p. 9.
[83] Walter Hallstein, "The EEC and the Community of the Free World," speech in Zurich to the Schweizerische Europa-Union, Jean Monnet Fondation, Lausanne, Paris, November 24, 1961, p. 2.

the early years of the European Movement opened up a path that would have not otherwise been there for transformation to occur over time. Although the path had twists and turns along the way, it is important not to lose sight that the key goal was nonetheless achieved (the pooling of national sovereignty in central institutions, a fundamentally ultrasocial goal), and this enabled transformation on the continent.

7

Optimism, Pessimism . . . and Repeat

Expanding Membership and Continued Integration

The achievement of federalism may not have happened all at once as the European Movement had hoped, but the idea had clearly put Europe's institutions on a strong trajectory toward actuating ultrasociality. Formal integration steadily proceeded, even alongside the challenge of expanding membership in the project. Of course, including countries beyond the original Six was always the goal—this was not a project based on us versus them, but one of inclusion. From the 1970s onward, the European Economic Community continued on a steady path of both enlargement of membership and deeper integration. With the United Kingdom, Denmark, and Ireland joining in 1973; then Greece, Spain, and Portugal in the 1980s; and Austria, Finland, and Sweden in 1995, the European Union (EU) quickly grew to fifteen member states.

Clearly, the narrative behind the origins and purpose of the EU proved to be attractive to those eligible to join, showing the magnetism of the European project and the transformational idea it represented. While potential member states, of course, stood to gain economically if they joined, membership required much more than conforming to economic standards. Each new member had to embrace democratic political norms and the values already established by the EU as a whole. In this sense, the enlargement process was not just about checking legalistic boxes but actually feeling that these new populations of Europeans were of the same mind. After all, new member states had to embrace the idea of pooling their own national sovereignty with that of the whole and to do this democratically, taking into account the preferences of their citizens. To do this, they could not see it as a sacrifice but as a desirable dimension of being part of a common, ultrasocial project.

In terms of integration itself, at times, such as during the 1970s and early 1980s, progress toward integration slowed, becoming transactional and outside of the public spotlight. At other times, such as during the late 1980s through to the early 2000s, with the signing of the 1986 Single European Act and the 1992 Maastricht Treaty, integration proceeded more rapidly, with more of a transformational energy. The ultrasocial lens points us toward the importance of enduring ideas, especially when bolstered with a strong, new narrative, the potential for transcendent impact, and optimism at the societal level.

International Cooperation Against All Odds. Mai'a K. Davis Cross, Oxford University Press. © Mai'a K. Davis Cross (2024). DOI: 10.1093/oso/9780192873903.003.0008

The relative speed of integration coincided with the rise and fall in popularity of the federalist idea, especially in the wake of major crisis periods and highlighting the ongoing centrality of the founding idea of European federalism. Importantly, federalism's popularity was *not* directly tied to increased economic gain as neoliberals might assume. For example, during the 1960s and 1970s, Europe fared better than the United States economically, and yet integration both accelerated (1960s) and slowed (1970s) during the same period. Instead, the driving force from societal level and informal federalist groups was key, and this changed in intensity over time, as summarized in Table 2.

As described in Chapter 5, the period from 1947 to 1954 was incredibly important to the success of the project at the outset. This was when the federalist idea was most transformational, and the momentum to achieve it was born out of the European Movement, which continued to loudly champion the cause. From 1954 to 1958, as the European project slipped into a more transactional approach, the original creativity, optimism, and energy at the popular level had faded somewhat. To be sure, the various federalist organizations, such as the Union of European Federalists, persisted, albeit with smaller membership numbers, but the main impetus had consolidated into certain key informal advocacy groups. Despite some periods of slower progress, the European project still chugged along for thirty years, from 1954 to 1984, taking a functionalist path to supranationalism. Integration proceeded even if it flew under the radar, and in fact, the creation of the common market, more or less completed in 1968, happened more quickly than anyone had anticipated, although primarily under elite initiative.

From 1968 to 1986, a time of relative Europessimism and Eurosclerosis ensued. This was not just the product of a decline in the European Movement but of a confluence of mostly external forces. Largely tribal in nature, these included (1) the 1973 and 1979 oil shocks as a result of war in the Middle East, (2) the Bretton Woods system on the verge of collapse, (3) the growing US trade deficit, (4) the failure of the European Community's early plans to launch a monetary union by 1980, and (5) anti-democratic regime change in several countries.[84] Such tribalistic developments clearly posed a challenge to the more ultrasocial nature of the European project, making it more difficult to focus on the power of possibility.

Despite this global context of multiple crises, the federalist movement in Europe nonetheless continued its advocacy in various forms, even if more behind the scenes. Indeed, informal pro-federalist organizations actually thrived in parallel to the formal evolution of EU institutions: the Crocodile Club, the Conference on European Federation, the Action Committee for the United States of Europe, the European Union of Federalists, Altiero Spinelli Action Committee for EU, and the Spinelli Group, among many others. Many of the most prominent EU leaders

---

[84] Desmond Dinan, *Ever Closer Union: An Introduction to European Integration* (London: Lynne Reiner, 2010).

Table 2 Tracing the federalist idea over time

Period	1947–1954	1954–1958	1958–1984	1986–1996	1997–2005	2006–2016	2016–
Nature of federalist idea	Transformational	Transactional	Transactional	Transformational	Transformational	Transactional	Transformational
Main insiders	Council of Europe	Council of Europe; ECSC	EEC/EC	EC/EU	EU	EU (including Spinelli Group)	EU (including Spinelli Group)
Main outsiders	European Movement; Union of European Federalists; Spinelli	Action Committee for the United States of Europe; Monnet	Action Committee for the United States of Europe; Crocodile Club; Spinelli, Monnet	Altiero Spinelli Action Committee for European Union	Union of European Federalists; European Movement International	Union of European Federalists; European Movement International; Spinelli Group	Union of European Federalists; European Movement International; Pulse of Europe

Source: author.

were also members of these pro-federalist groups, and this continues to be the case in the twenty-first century. The Spinelli Group, for example, founded in 2010, is where many ideas for advancing federalism are spawned and debated before being brought to the floor of the European Parliament. With the precedent Monnet set, pushing for federalism from outside of the formal institutions rather than from within them, the importance of these informal groups in nurturing the federalist idea should not be underestimated.

Ultimately, the institutions that Monnet had designed for the European Coal and Steel Community (ECSC) (i.e., the High Authority, the Court of Justice, the Common Assembly, and the Council) really mattered because the foundation of supranationalism had already been built. Pro-federalists only had to keep lobbying to go further down the same path. This supranational foundation served as a fulcrum for integration to continue, transforming the ECSC into the European Economic Community (EEC) and then the European Community (EC).

The formation of the common market was not just about economic prosperity but about European governance itself. To the satisfaction of the ongoing federalist movement, the EC was far more than a trading bloc or an intergovernmental organization. It increasingly encompassed environmental, social, and cohesion policies. In order to trade in goods and enable services to cross borders, creating standards was necessary, both for labor and for the products themselves. And with Europeans increasingly moving across borders to provide those services, among other reasons, it was natural that integration grew to include a broad range of things, such as health care, retirement protections, education, and mutual recognition. Cohesion policies promoted fairness and evenness in the integration process through a system of redistributing funds across the community.

This ever-emerging broader remit, all of which flowed naturally from the common market, would have made early federalists quite happy. However, I argue that these new common policy areas did not just automatically spill over from one area to another, as neo-functionalists like Ernst Haas have argued,[85] but rather that the pull of ultrasociality, the opportunity to show mutual empathy, the fulfillment that comes with working together on a range of issues that were better approached collectively than individually were all behind the success of this process.

Optimism Returns

With the 1986 Single European Act, the cloud had lifted, marking the end of the transactional period. With it, the launch of the *single* market went further than a common market because it explicitly worked to eliminate any remaining physical

---

[85] Ernst B. Haas, *Beyond the Nation State: Functionalism and International Organization* (Colchester: ECPR Press, 2008).

(borders) or technical (standards) and fiscal (taxes) barriers across the member states. The European Parliament, the main institution representing the people, became stronger, integration deepened, and political cooperation took on a more formal tenor.

Indeed, in the lead-up to the 1990s, ongoing support for federalism finally broke through the blockade that had separated foreign and security policy from the integration process since the early failure of the European Defense Community in the 1950s. The new Treaty on European Union, also known as the Maastricht Treaty, was actually drafted by prominent federalists in the Crocodile Club, an informal European parliamentary group that Spinelli had founded.[86] Reaching agreement on a political union for Europe that would include security was not only deeply political but also highly symbolic as security is typically thought to be at the very core of national sovereignty.[87] It is noteworthy that in the 1960s, Monnet's new proposals to launch a common foreign policy and defense were a significant part of the Action Committee's work. In 1970, the Six were able to put into place European Political Cooperation (EPC), but it was separated from European Community structures and not backed by treaty agreement until the Single European Act, when it was given legal status.

The end of the Cold War and the 1992 Maastricht Treaty finally enshrined the Common Foreign and Security Policy (CFSP) into a treaty. The EC was upgraded to the European Union (EU), now with both economic and political integration. Earlier drafts of the new treaty even included the word "federal," although it was ultimately taken out of the final text. Nonetheless, the fact that the federal idea was still part of formal discussion in the early 1990s shows its endurance and influence in framing what was possible. With the advent of the CFSP, the stage was set for more common external action. It called for the EU:

> to assert its identity on the international scene [...] including the eventual framing of a common defence policy, which might in time lead to a common defence [...] The Member States shall support the Union's external and security policy actively and unreservedly in a spirit of loyalty and mutual solidarity. They shall refrain from any action, which is contrary to the interests of the Union or likely to impair its effectiveness as a cohesive force in international relations.[88]

Then, in December 1998, during a summit in Saint-Malo, France, French President Jacques Chirac and British Prime Minister Tony Blair agreed that the EU

---

[86] William Wallace, "Europe as a Confederation: The Community and the Nation-State," *Journal of Common Market Studies* 21, 1 (1982): 57–68, 67, https://doi.org/10.1111/j.1468-5965.1982.tb00639.x.

[87] Maïa K. Davis Cross, *Security Integration in Europe: How Knowledge-Based Networks Have Transformed the European Union* (Ann Arbor, MI: University of Michigan Press, 2011).

[88] Treaty on European Union, Article J, 1992.

needed a true defense capability.[89] In other words, the two main security actors wanted the EU to "have the capacity for autonomous action, backed up by credible military forces."[90]

Blair and Chirac were both witnessing Europe's utter inability to act in the midst of the crisis in Kosovo and the collapse of Yugoslavia. The Saint-Malo Declaration represented a big shift in British policy, as the United Kingdom had resisted the idea for decades.[91] In 1999, member states approved the European Security and Defense Policy (ESDP), reflecting the goals of Saint-Malo. And in 2003, after decades of effort, the EU finally made ESDP (now, the Common Security and Defense Policy) operational, sending troops out to conduct humanitarian operations under the EU flag. For the first time, the EU had not only articulated a desire for a common foreign policy but had actually put concrete action behind these words, following this up with almost forty military operations and civilian missions across three continents. Even now, there is debate over how strong the EU is on the international stage, with some arguing that its power is rather limited,[92] while others describing the EU as an emerging superpower.[93]

Most international relations scholars and historians interpret the advent of the EU's common security and defense as a result of changes in the balance of power following the Second World War—for example, the bipolarity of the Cold War and subsequent unipolarity with the United States as guarantor of the liberal world order. Others emphasize the role of certain key individuals, like Jean Monnet, or the growing power of EU institutions as they took on a life of their own and sought to augment their own authority. However, these explanations entirely miss the far more fundamental pull of ultrasociality—a predisposition to want to cooperate peacefully—in the form of federalism that has been present since the founding of the project. The EU was balancing neither against the Soviet Union nor the United States when it expressed the desire to pursue a "spirit of loyalty and mutual solidarity" in the area of defense. Of course, other factors play into the specific form policy might take, but none of this would have been possible in the first place without those actually championing the federal idea and building the foundation

---

[89] The story behind how this agreement was reached is well told in Jolyon Howorth, "Discourse, Ideas, and Epistemic Communities in European Security and Defence Policy," *West European Politics*, 27, 2 (2004): 211–234; Frédéric Mérand, "Social Representations in the European Security and Defense Policy," *Cooperation and Conflict* 41, 2 (2006), pp. 131–152.

[90] Franco–British St. Malo Declaration (4 December 1998). https://www.cvce.eu/obj/franco_british_st_malo_declaration_4_december_1998-en-f3cd16fb-fc37-4d52-936f-c8e9bc80f24f.html (accessed July 3, 2023)

[91] Julian Lindley-French, *A Chronology of European Security and Defence Policy, 1945–2007* (New York: Oxford University Press, 2007), p. 247.

[92] Asle Toje, *The European Union as a Small Power: After the Post-Cold War* (Basingstoke: Palgrave Macmillan, 2011).

[93] John McCormick, *The European Superpower* (Basingstoke: Palgrave Macmillan, 2007); Andrew Moravcsik, "Europe: The Quiet Superpower," *French Politics* 7, 3 (2009): 403-422.

for it. Realist balance of power cannot explain the timing or nature of security integration in Europe, and ideas still underpin institutions.[94]

Pessimism Returns

In spite of the various existential crises of the twenty-first century, the federal idea endures. After a two-decade transformational period from the mid-1980s through to 2005, the process again became more transactional from 2005 to 2016. When the French and Dutch referenda rejected the 2005 Constitutional Treaty, the text of which invoked strong federalist symbolism, this signaled another turning point. There is clear evidence that the French and Dutch actually voted for reasons that had little to do with the actual content of the treaty or the direction of European integration, but nonetheless, the fact of the negative referenda did spark panic.[95]

The 2009 Lisbon Treaty, which had nearly all of the same components of the constitutional treaty, was ultimately approved, but the constitutional treaty crisis did mark a period of relative disillusionment, especially at the elite level. As Mark Mazower writes, "Integration has been driven by a bureaucratic elite that continues to see national sovereignty as an obstacle to be overcome, but this elite has largely lost sight of the principles of social solidarity and human dignity that Spinelli wished to resurrect."[96] At the same time, at least a significant portion of the negativity surrounding the EU during this period can be attributed to the media's tendency to exaggerate and sensationalize[97] (bad news sells), and some can be blamed on the dearth of inspirational leaders like Spinelli, Monnet, Spaak, and Jacques Delors to represent the interests of the people. During this same period, opinion polls consistently showed that Europeans trusted EU institutions more than their national institutions, and around 70% supported a stronger EU foreign and security policy.[98]

While it has become common for international observers to disparage the EU as stumbling from crisis to crisis, especially in the twenty-first century, it is clear that the EU is remarkably resilient and has actually been made stronger from each crisis.[99] The 1986 Single European Act, 2003 European Security Strategy, 2009 Lisbon Treaty, and 2011 Fiscal Compact, among many others, all followed seem-

---

[94] Cross, *Security Integration in Europe.*

[95] Maïa K. Davis Cross, *The Politics of Crisis in Europe* (New York: Cambridge University Press, 2017).

[96] Mark Mazower, *Governing the World: The History of an Idea, 1815 to the Present* (London: Penguin, 2012), p. 408.

[97] Maïa. K. Davis Cross and Xinru Ma, "EU Crises and Integrational Panic: The Role of the Media," *Journal of European Public Policy* 22, 8 (2015): 1053–1070, https://doi.org/10.1080/13501763.2014.984748.

[98] Eurobarometer, https://europa.eu/eurobarometer/screen/home (accessed May 24, 2023).

[99] Cross, *The Politics of Crisis in Europe.*

ingly serious existential crises. After each major crisis, opinion polls show a surge in pro-EU sentiment amongst the public across all member states.[100] The crises that seemingly threaten the very existence of the EU are only part of the story. And as I argue in Part I, ultrasocial ideas are more likely to emerge in the wake of crises, especially existential crises (think of the many times the media has declared "the end of Europe"). It is during these periods that we are more likely to seek out new ideas, believe them to be possible, and find ways to achieve them. Moreover, it is precisely when crises have harmed us most that collective optimism emerges. When we face disaster, standard norms may crumble, but they also create openings for the acceptance of new norms.[101]

What is ultimately most important is how Europeans grapple with and over-come crises. After these crises reach their height of intensity, seemingly bringing the EU to the brink of failure, they then dissipate and leave in their wake a renewed will to find consensus and move forward with integration. Even in its most trans-actional periods, the EU has often been compared to a bicycle. If it stops moving forward, it might fall over. In its more transformational periods, a European pub-lic sphere flourishes, leaders inspire, and the default is to speak with one voice. In times of crisis, especially, policy solutions consistently involve *more* integration, not less.

The EU's founding fathers thought that by forming institutions, the ideas of the European Movement would live on. They were concerned that future leaders in Europe would not have the same far-reaching, transformational ideas, and so if all else fails, institutions would solidify the process that they had started. The founders turned out to be right. EU institutions have helped to anchor what has already been agreed and advance integration further, even during transactional periods. The story of the European project shows that ideas reside in the people, but they also have a continual impact through institutions. Just because "federal" does not make it into a treaty text or other agreement does not mean it no longer influences insti-tutional processes. Indeed, strong and enduring ideas help to frame the parameters of what is possible, even if sometimes behind the scenes. And if these ideas have the advantage of being ultrasocial in nature, as is the case in the EU, there is always the possibility of renewed will to break more boundaries and go further down the path of integration. The flame of aspiration has been centrally important, and while naysayers see the EU as continually falling short of what it promises to do, they fail to see that these transformational ideas are actually setting the stage for the future.

[100] Cross, *The Politics of Crisis in Europe*.
[101] David Pakman Show, "Rutger Bregman: People Are Basically Good," Youtube, 2020, https://www.youtube.com/watch?v=tZ_unq8rDzU (accessed May 20, 2023).

Transformation Returns

In 2016, there was a return to the power of possibility in Europe, at least in part driven by a number of serious challenges to the integrity of the European project. Not unlike the period from the 1970s to mid-1980s, a number of crises emerged that have represented serious tests for European integration. This time, unlike the period of Eurosclerosis and Europessimism, on the whole, European leaders have continually responded with strong resolve to embrace many new and significant areas of integration.

Internally, the EU has had to grapple with a number of global trends that have also come to European shores. These have included the rise of extremist populism, the slide away from democracy in several countries, and a backlash against globalization, among others. In 2017, Hungary, Poland, Lithuania, and Slovakia regressed from liberal democracies to just electoral democracies.[102] Hungary and Poland then continued to present a challenge to European solidarity. The European Commission took Hungary to the European Court of Justice for cracking down on academic freedoms and the rights of civil society organizations to operate in the country.[103] Hungary's leader, Viktor Orban, declared that he had achieved "illiberal democracy" in his country. In 2018, the Commission also took Poland to the European Court of Justice for trying to erode the judicial independence of its Supreme Court.

Externally, the EU has struggled to have a tangible impact on stabilizing its southern neighborhood, as well as grappling with a trade war with China, hybrid attacks from Russia, and Russia's invasion of Ukraine. Added to this, the transatlantic relationship, which had been a bedrock of Europe's global role for seventy years, began to crack after the 2016 US election of Donald Trump to a degree that had been previously thought impossible. Trump administration officials openly questioned the value of the North Atlantic Treaty Organization (NATO) in unprecedented ways, and this seriously undermined trust in US global leadership over the longer term. Significant reversals in transatlantic agreements took place, such as the complete halt of negotiations to establish the Transatlantic Trade and Investment Partnership (TTIP) and US withdrawal from the landmark Paris climate change agreement. As the United States turned its back on the Iran nuclear deal, US extraterritorial legislation punished European firms for doing business with Iran, among other things.

---

[102] Gijs de Vries, "Cultural Freedom in European Foreign Policy," *Institut für Auslandsbeziehungen (IFA) Edition Culture and Foreign Policy*, 2019, p. 27, https://nbn-resolving.org/urn:nbn:de:0168-ssoar-62190-0 (accessed May 20, 2023).

[103] Jennifer Rankin, "EU Takes Hungary to ECJ Over Crackdown Aimed at George Soros," *The Guardian*, December 7, 2017, https://www.theguardian.com/world/2017/dec/07/eu-hungary-court-crackdown-george-soros (accessed May 20, 2023).

Anti-Europeanism not only happened at the governmental level but also within some sectors of US society. American entrepreneur Andrew Breitbart, the founder of Breitbart News (launched in 2012), said that he created this far-right news website, "to take back the culture," by which he meant to wage a "cultural and political war" against mainstream understandings of politics and values.[104] When Steven Bannon took over Breitbart, he also opened a UK website in 2014, and subsequently another one based in Rome. Although there were plans to have a French and German Breitbart service, these were ultimately unsuccessful. Carrying on the legacy of the website's founder, Bannon explicitly spoke about the spread of Breitbart as part of a cultural and political war. He invoked the notion of "weaponizing" the narrative. These arguments have since spread and intensified amongst right-wing media.

Other examples are the ongoing and concerted efforts to curtail abortion, women's rights, LGBTQ rights, and other key issues that the EU typically supports. A number of American billionaires have donated significant funds to anti-abortion lobbying groups, especially in Austria, Belgium, Poland, France, and Spain, with the aim of influencing EU policies in Brussels.[105] Michael Bird and Blaz Zgaga found that, from 2012 to 2017, six US conservative groups spent at least $19.4 million lobbying the EU. As the effort gets more organized, the threat has become significant enough for members of the European Parliament to be warned about what these lobbyists are trying to do: move European policy away from protecting rights to a far-right agenda of curtailing rights. The money behind this influence strikes at the heart of European culture, values, and way of life. It is tribalism in its purest form.

Significantly, the EU has not just been standing by while these threats to European priorities and values have taken place. Especially when it comes to tech companies and data privacy concerns, the EU has taken a notably strong stance in the context of growing public support for EU integration. The 2016 (implemented in 2018) EU General Data Protection Regulation (GDPR) was a major first step in protecting individual citizens' private data and extends well beyond EU citizens (EU Data Protection Rules). In addition, the EU has started to hold Facebook, Twitter, Google, and other tech giants to account in terms of following data protection rules. This has entailed investigations, fines, and content removal, among other things. The introduction of the GDPR is meaningful in terms of curtailing the most immediate and harmful abuses.

On the security side, spurred on by an unreliable EU–US relationship, also in light of Brexit and Russian aggression, the EU launched a defense union,

---

[104] Carole Cadwalladr, "Robert Mercer: The Big Data Billionaire Waging War on Mainstream Media," *The Guardian*, February 26, 2019, https://www.theguardian.com/politics/2017/feb/26/robert-mercer-breitbart-war-on-media-steve-bannon-donald-trump-nigel-farage (accessed May 20, 2023).
[105] Michael Bird and Blaz Zgaga, "US Billionaires Funding EU Culture War," *EUObserver*, August 22, 2019, https://euobserver.com/eu-political/145686 (accessed May 20, 2023).

which features Permanent Structured Cooperation (PESCO) as part of the Common Security and Defence Policy, among other initiatives. PESCO, for example, represents structural *integration* in defense, which is a major step toward formal supranationalism in the security arena. Forty-seven projects were launched between December 2017 and 2020 alone. The defense union also includes the European Defense Fund (as of 2017), which is designed to provide financial support to a range of defense companies across different member states that seek to cooperate, and the European Peace Facility (as of 2021), with a budget of almost €8 billion for 2021–2027 to finance EU military and defense actions. Ultimately, all of this enables EU militaries to develop weapons, deploy together, and streamline their systems in Europe.

Russia's war on Ukraine was a dramatic reminder not to take for granted the foundations of the European project. Indeed, the war demonstrated that Ukrainians were willing to die defending this idea. And Europeans reacted in a way that reflected the original purpose of the federal idea: the need to eradicate nationalism in favor of shared sovereignty and the maintenance of a permanent peace on the continent. In the name of this ultrasocial idea, EU citizens and governments rallied in support of Ukraine and quickly pursued further integration in previously difficult areas, including migration, energy, trade with Russia, military, defense, and foreign policy. The war also revealed that despite short-run differences in the transatlantic alliance, the United States and Europe were capable of rapidly fortifying their relationship when it really counts, creating fertile ground for a more transformational era in the achievement of closer European integration.

On the economic side, in reaction to the Coronavirus pandemic, the EU started acting much more like a federal state, with increased ability to borrow, tax, and spend. It took the important step of issuing common debt, fiscal burden sharing, and fiscal transfer, something that was difficult to agree to even during the Eurozone crisis. Of the €1.85 trillion common budget for 2021–2027, €750 billion is for Next Generation EU, the largest ever fund established at the supranational level. The European Commission also gained new powers to protect the rule of law through the capacity to suspend funding, including from the pandemic recovery fund, if countries fail to respect the values set out in Article 2 of the EU treaty. These new powers are highly popular at the societal level, with almost 80% of European citizens supporting the notion that funds should be tied to the rule of law—again, solidifying the now quasi-federal nature of the EU.

Indeed, during the period from 2016 to 2020, when Europeans were increasingly faced with the need to define themselves against the United States, opinion polls showed very high support for the European project. Trust in EU institutions has continued to be higher, on average, than trust in national institutions.[106] The

---

[106] European Commission, Directorate-General for Communication, "Standard Eurobarometer 93 Summer 2020 Report: European Citizenship, Fieldwork: July–August 2020," 2020, https://doi.org/10.2775/581547.

majority are "satisfied with the way democracy works in the EU," and a strong majority "feel that they are citizens of the EU."[107] Those that have a positive image of the EU are double those who have a negative view. Support for the euro is consistently high and, in recent years, in the mid-seventieth percentile. Optimism about the future of the EU has been around 60%.[108] Consistently, one of the reasons people support the EU is because the European project has brought peace to the continent.[109] This has even been true in the United Kingdom, where support for EU membership increased dramatically on the eve of the finalization of the Brexit negotiations. In June 2020, only 35% of British citizens supported Brexit, while 57% wanted to rejoin the EU.[110] These viewpoints show that the idea of a united Europe and an appreciation of the values this represents is widespread.

Alongside these general societal views, organized pro-federalist groups have continued to play an influential role, especially in reaction to some of the right-wing populist sentiment and far-right nationalist parties that have emerged in some member states. The Pulse of Europe, for example, is a grassroots organization launched in 2016 as a citizen's initiative. The various chapters have been active in 130 cities and 20 member states, pushing to uphold European values and unity. Since 2017, the Spinelli Group has had network membership of well over 7,000, bringing together members from the European Parliament but also academics, think tanks, non-governmental organizations (NGOs), and regular citizens who support the federal goal for Europe. Many of the most prominent leaders in Europe have comprised its steering board, including Jacques Delors, Joschka Fischer, Guy Verhofstadt, Kalypso Nicolaidis, and Sylvie Goulard, among many others. In 2020, seventy-four members of the European Parliament were also card-carrying members of the Spinelli Group,[111] effectively infusing the ideas of the European Movement directly into the EU's political process. Their 2018 manifesto, which closely echoes the Ventotene Manifesto, states that, "We believe that European disintegration would be a road to disaster, and that strong democratic government organised on federal lines is the best guarantor for the future peace and prosperity of our continent."[112]

The Union of European Federalists, and its youth organization, Young European Federalists, have been campaigning for a United States of Europe for over

[107] European Commission, Directorate-General for Communication, "Standard Eurobarometer 93 Summer 2020 Report," p. 12.
[108] European Commission, Directorate-General for Communication, "Standard Eurobarometer 93 Summer 2020 Report," p. 29.
[109] Pew Research Center, "Spring 2018 Global Attitudes Survey," Q42 a–f, Washington DC.
[110] Adam Bienkov, "Support for Brexit Is Collapsing as Poll Finds Big Majority of British People Want to Be in the EU," *Business Insider*, June 26, 2020, https://www.businessinsider.com/brexit-poll-most-british-people-want-to-rejoin-eu-2020-6?op=1 (accessed May 20, 2023).
[111] The Spinelli Group, "Our Members in the European Parliament," Union of European Federalists, 2020, https://www.federalists.eu/the-group-in-the-european-parliament (accessed December 8, 2020).
[112] The Spinelli Group, "Manifesto for the Future of Europe: A Shared Destiny," Union of European Federalists, 2018, https://www.federalists.eu/fileadmin/files_uef/Spinelli_Group_Page/2018_Manifesto_EN.pdf (accessed May 20, 2023).

seventy years. Carrying on the tradition of the European Movement, they argue against nationalism and intergovernmentalism for Europe, while pushing for the original goals of the movement. In calling for a federal Europe, they focus on raising awareness among the public, promoting federalism among politicians and political parties, appealing to national governments, lobbying for a federal approach to specific issue areas, and fighting back against nationalists and Euroskeptics.[113] They uphold both unity and diversity. They are also partnered with other federal organizations, such as the European Movement International and the World Federalist Movement. Ultimately, their successes over the past decades are clearly visible through the path Europe has taken toward more democracy, expanded membership, and more integration. Instead of being drawn to negative ideas about potentially rolling back integration, removing members, or stopping at economic reasoning, time and time again, the power of a highly ultrasocial idea—European federalism—has prevailed.

---

[113] The Spinelli Group, "What is UEF?," Union of European Federalists, 2022, https://www.federalists.eu/uef (accessed May 20, 2023).

Conclusion to Part II

The current so-called long peace—the absence of war among the forty-four most powerful actors in the international system since the Second World War—would not have been possible without developments in Europe. There is much debate over why countries in Europe after the Second World War were willing to bind their fates together, pooling their sovereignty for the explicit purpose of ending centuries of violence on the continent.

Through the knowledge that an ultrasocial landscape provides the underlying context for this story, it becomes apparent that looking for national self-interest as a motivation for the European project does not make sense. The power of possibility and idealistic aspiration[114] are an integral part, if not a driving force, of European integration over the decades. Without some sense of idealism, this unprecedented experiment at international cooperation would never have got off the ground. As the violence of the Second World War drew to a close, and Europe was in shambles with tens of millions dead, this was hardly cause for such idealistic dreams as a United States of Europe, but the people and the leaders that emerged to represent them pushed for it, nonetheless. And the call was strong.

As the institutions that would become central to today's European Union (EU) began to solidify, and as the Council of Europe went down a markedly different path, federalist ideas were discussed in social clubs, groups, and committees that comprised a vibrant, transnational society of individuals. Most historical research into the influence of federalism on European integration either argues that the idea experienced a brief window of popularity from 1949 to 1950, when the Council of Europe was new enough to keep the hope alive,[115] or that its influence was only significant until 1954, when the failure of the European Defence Community marked its final demise.[116] However, looking beyond the 1950s, different actors and members of society have been carriers of the federalist idea. And they have used various strategies to push for its influence.

---

[114] "Idealistic aspiration" was actually used in the 2016 Global Strategy to refer to the ways in which the EU still must continue to look beyond "principled pragmatism." European Union, "Shared Vision, Common Action: A Stronger Europe: A Global Strategy for the European Union's Foreign and Security Policy," June 2016, https://www.eeas.europa.eu/sites/default/files/eugs_review_web_0.pdf (accessed May 20, 2023).

[115] Martin K. Dedman, *The Origins and Development of the European Union 1945–95* (New York: Routledge, 1996).

[116] Walter Lipgens, *Sources for the History of European Integration 1945–55* (Leyden: Sijthoff, 1980); Walter Lipgens, *A History of European Integration 1945-47*, vol. 1 (Oxford: Clarendon Press, 1982).

The federalist idea, and the movement that supported it, clearly reflected an underlying ultrasocial drive and the power of possibility. Many Europeans had started to view political transformation, in the name of peace, as expected and desirable.[117] A new narrative about the problems with nationalism, and how to overcome them, was highly compelling. Barnett and Duvall argue that social relations and context "shape the capacities of actors to determine their circumstances and fate."[118] European leaders had come to believe that only through ceding national sovereignty to the supranational level would peace truly be possible. Ultimately, this initiative, originating in Europe, became the most advanced and successful experiment in transforming a region with centuries of violent conflict into one of enduring, and even permanent, peace. In the twenty-first century, the EU is recognized as a model for how to achieve peace through institutions and was awarded the Nobel Peace Prize in 2012.

A theme throughout these past seven decades is that ideas often percolate outside of the institutions they ultimately most influence. Indeed, the federalist idea has been remarkably enduring and influential, especially when it is advocated at the societal level. Even ideas that are not fully achieved can be crucial in setting the parameters for what is considered possible, broadening worldviews and setting the stage for the future. The EU is quasi-federal institution today, but if it continues its trajectory, there is nothing that rules out a federal EU tomorrow. The power of ideas holds the capacity for society to shape the European project in the face of future challenges.

---

[117] The power of possibility focuses on what the EU is able to accomplish (idealistic aspiration) rather than pessimistic assumptions that it has reached the end of the road or that it is only capable of transactional pragmatism.

[118] Michael Barnett and Robert Duvall (eds), *Power in Global Governance* (Cambridge: Cambridge University Press, 2005).

PART III

SPACE EXPLORATION

Outer space is often assumed to be the quintessential realm of great power competition. Since the launch of Sputnik in 1957 and the ensuing Space Race between the United States and the Soviet Union, most international relations experts have analyzed space as a classic realist security dilemma; that is, the more one country gains an advantage in space, the more all of the other countries feel less secure until they all find themselves in an escalating competition to prepare for the worst-case scenario. Even with the end of the Cold War, space has continued to be seen as a politically charged and increasingly militarized venue for conflict. In the twenty-first century, human use and exploration of space is now a global phenomenon, with seventy-two countries investing in their own space programs and a rapid increase in commercial activity, altogether contributing to an almost USD 450 billion economy that will likely reach over USD 1 trillion by the 2040s.[1] Many militaries, government leaders, and international relations realists describe this as an emerging, multi-polar arms race in space.[2] But is this an accurate portrayal?

In revisiting the case of space using the lens of ultrasociality, I bring together archival evidence from the John F. Kennedy Presidential Library (Boston), the National Aeronautics and Space Administration (NASA) Headquarters Archives (Washington DC), the European Space Agency archives (Florence, Italy), and Boeing archives, as well as observations at the 2018, 2019, and 2020 International Astronautical Congresses, the 2019 UN annual Space Security conference, and the 2018 and 2019 European Space Policy Institute annual conferences. As a result, I argue that space has actually been, and continues to be, a highly cooperative realm

---

[1] "The Space Report, "Economy," https://www.thespacereport.org/topics/economy/ (accessed July 3, 2023); Morgan Stanley, "The Space Economy's Next Giant Leap," https://www.morganstanley.com/Themes/global-space-economy (accessed July 3, 2023).

[2] Forrest E. Morgan, "Deterrence and First-Strike Stability in Space: A Preliminary Assessment," *RAND*, 2010 https://www.rand.org/pubs/monographs/MG916.html (accessed July 3, 2023); Michael Hansel, "The USA and Arms Control in Space: An IR Analysis," *Space Policy* 26, 2 (May 2010): 91–98, https://doi.org/10.1016/j.spacepol.2010.02.011; Baohui Zhang, "The Security Dilemma in the U.S.–China Military Space Relationship: The Prospects for Arms Control," *Asian Survey* 51, 2 (March/April 2011): 311–332, https://doi.org/10.1525/as.2011.51.2.311; Christian Davenport, "The Battlefield 22,000 Miles above Earth," *Wilson Quarterly*, Winter 2019, https://www.wilsonquarterly.com/quarterly/the-new-landscape-in-space/the-battlefield-22-000-miles-above-earth (accessed May 20, 2023).

for human interaction, and this dimension deserves more attention. Indeed, it has been an arena in which our ultrasocial predisposition has been particularly resonant because the idea of human space exploration inherently allows us to fulfill our ultrasocial drive. This is because, on a grand scale, space is a constant reminder of our common fragility as a single species traveling on a small planet in a vast universe.

Misunderstandings about the nature of the Space Race, however, have led most observers to ignore the highly cooperative trajectory of space exploration thus far. Cold War space historians were thought to have provided "definitive" accounts of the forces ostensibly driving the 1960s Space Race (military competition, the quest for dominance, and national self-interest), and this has heavily informed international relations and popular perceptions. But it has since been noted that many accounts were biased toward seeing things in a belligerent light,[3] so much so that British historian Rip Bulkeley argues that this bias in historical accounts of the early Space Race is what led to "hawkish attitudes" toward space, which then continued even after the Cold War. He argues that the "disinformation or misapprehensions of [. . .] early space writers" is significant.[4]

We need to revisit the historical record both in terms of how and why space as a peaceful domain emerged and in terms of the resilience over time of the original transformational idea behind human spaceflight. By starting with the origins of the idea, we can gain a more complete picture of the trajectory over time and of the window of opportunity it provided. Indeed, to the extent that there was an impetus in the early years (1920s–1950s, in particular) to explore space, it came from space enthusiasts, rocket societies, scientists, and the general public. This emerging space community was transnational and international in nature, and its members strongly believed that cooperation across borders was both necessary and ideal. They championed what I call the *Spaceflight Idea*, which was that space is for all, and exploration of it should be a fundamentally peaceful endeavor, belonging to no single country. This idea was the epitome of transcendent, aspirational, and optimistic thinking. It featured a new narrative that easily captured the public's imagination: humans could aspire to be a multiplanetary species, with all of the adventure and discovery that entailed.

The widespread belief in the Spaceflight Idea led to a transnational and international Spaceflight Movement. And as leaders emerged from the Spaceflight Movement, as scientists achieved breakthroughs in rocketry, and as space societies grew more robust, governments could no longer afford to ignore what had previously been thought to be a fringe movement. As governments took an interest in space, many officials saw it in more militarist and competitive terms, a perspective

---

[3] Rip Bulkeley, *The Sputniks Crisis and Early United States Space Policy* (London: Macmillan, 1991), p. 12.
[4] Bulkeley, *The Sputniks Crisis*, p. 15.

they ultimately pushed for in the wake of the Sputnik launch. However, it is important to recognize that this language was mainly just a surface-level gloss, covering a much different set of foundational attitudes and deeply held beliefs.

And this even applies directly to the launch of Sputnik itself. It is little understood in international relations that Sputnik was born out of the biggest international scientific sharing of knowledge that had ever happened to that point—the International Geophysical Year—and that the Moon landing was actually, at one point, conceived of as a cooperative mission shared between the United States and the Soviet Union, among other things. As I show in Chapters 8 and 9, public enthusiasm for the adventure of space and celebration of any milestone as a human accomplishment was very clear. The two biggest superpowers were even reluctant to come across as seeming to be unwilling to cooperate with the other when it came to space. At times, they actually competed to be seen as more cooperative than the other. To be sure, competition during the Space Race was certainly present, but a close look at the archival record shows that the main actors involved kept returning to the Spaceflight Idea. Even during the height of the Cold War, nearly every aspect of the activities leading to space exploration were cooperative in nature, even between the two rival superpowers themselves—once again, highlighting the crucial draw of ultrasociality.

As I discuss in Chapter 10, despite the broader conflict of the Cold War, and then subsequently what is known as Space Race 2.0 today, space has still largely been an arena for common aspirations and peaceful human achievement. The major crises of the First World War, the Second World War, and the Cold War helped to spur on the Spaceflight Idea—people craved the power of possibility after such misery and suffering. The spaceflight movement and its leaders strongly and consistently supported the Spaceflight Idea. Of course, the concrete expression of the Spaceflight Idea was not achieved all at once (it was too aspirational for that), but it clearly opened up pathways for progressive change. After the Space Race era, the cooperative nature of space exploration became even easier to see, culminating in the establishment of the International Space Station. As we look to the future, the dream of landing humans on Mars is rapidly reaching fruition, and ultrasociality is present at every turn.

8

The Spaceflight Idea and the Spaceflight Movement

The Spaceflight Idea Emerges: 1920s–1930s

For tens of thousands of years, humans have looked upward to the stars, using them for navigation, inspiration, and storytelling. The earliest known tale of people visiting the Moon dates back to AD 170 when Lucian of Samosata, a satirist from Roman Syria, wrote a fictional account of voyages to the Moon and Venus in his work, "A True Story." Much later, the more practical goal of exploring space started to blend seamlessly with astronomy and the invention of telescopes in the early 1600s. Once Isaac Newton discovered his laws of motion by the end of that century, the idea of putting something human-made into orbit became mathematically plausible. In the early twentieth century, the Wright brothers achieved another major jump toward the goal of escaping Earth's gravity with the invention of airplanes.

In the 1920s and 1930s, as actual spaceflight seemed increasingly within reach, the Spaceflight Movement was born. It was comprised of a diverse and international network of individuals interested in philosophy, technology, and rockets, galvanized by the shared goal of achieving the human capacity to travel to, and eventually settle on, other planets.[5] Members of the Spaceflight Movement espoused the *Spaceflight Idea*: space was for all of humankind and was a fundamentally peaceful domain for scientific and technological advancement and exploration.[6] They were well aware that the achievement of this goal would bring with it transcendent impact on human life. The underlying narrative they embraced was that, from the perspective of outer space, humans were no longer from any specific country; they were *one* people from planet Earth.[7] This very much resonated with human ultrasociality.

---

[5] Dimitrios Stroikos, "Engineering World Society? Scientists, Internationalism, and the Advent of the Space Age," *International Politics* 55, 1 (2018): 73–90, https://doi.org/10.1057/s41311-017-0070-8.

[6] Asif A. Siddiqi, "Making Spaceflight Modern: A Cultural History of the World's First Space Advocacy Group," in *Societal Impact of Spaceflight*, ed. Steven J. Dick and Roger D. Launius (Washington, DC: NASA Office of External Relations, 2007), pp. 513–537.

[7] This was also the precursor to the so-called "overview effect" that astronauts experience upon seeing Earth from outer space for the first time. Frank White, *The Overview Effect: Space Exploration and Human Evolution* (Reston, VA: American Institute of Aeronautics and Astronautics, 1998).

International Cooperation Against All Odds. Mai'a K. Davis Cross, Oxford University Press. © Mai'a K. Davis Cross (2024). DOI: 10.1093/oso/9780192873903.003.0009

Science fiction played an important role in putting spaceflight more squarely in the public's imagination and sparking the Spaceflight Idea. In particular, Jules Verne's 1865 novel *From the Earth to the Moon* and its sequel *Around the Moon* opened up future possibilities in people's minds.[8] H. G. Wells's 1897 book *The War of the Worlds* also offered inspiration to many who would eventually go on to actually making spaceflight possible. In Russia, Aleksei Tolstoi published his book *Aelita: Zakat Marsa (Aelita: Sunset of Mars)* in 1922, which tells the story of two men who travel to Mars to find an advanced civilization in the early stages of a capitalist society. All in all, the interwar period was a veritable "golden age of science fiction," and much of it focused on the possibility of space travel.[9]

At the same time as the regular public became increasingly invested in the Spaceflight Idea, scientists in different parts of the world worked in earnest on developing the rocketry that would make this a reality. These scientists became early leaders of the Spaceflight Movement and inspired others to join the effort. In 1909, Robert Hutchings Goddard, a professor at Clark College in Worcester, Massachusetts, began experimenting with rockets with the intention of being able to eventually launch one to the Moon. Crucially, he realized that the rockets would have to be liquid-fueled to achieve this feat. After facing strong ridicule in the media for suggesting that a rocket could even work in space, Goddard made a breakthrough and was able to launch the first ever liquid-fueled rocket on March 16, 1926.

A year later, on the other side of the Atlantic, Hermann Oberth became a key figure in Germany working with groups of scientists to develop a liquid-fueled rocket of their own. After all, Oberth's 1923 book *Die Rakete zu den Planeteraümen* (*The Rocket into Planetary Space*) had first demonstrated the calculations necessary to achieve it theoretically.[10] They had created an amateur rocket inventors club called the Society for Space Navigation to support this goal and had successfully launched one in 1931 near Berlin. Both Goddard and Oberth were inspired by Jules Verne's book, and Oberth was well aware of Goddard's earlier achievement, although the latter tended to work alone and in relative secrecy, while the former was bold and highly visible.[11] Oberth would ultimately go on to mentor Wernher von Braun, who eventually led the National Aeronautics and Space Administration's (NASA's) Apollo program, further demonstrating the interconnected and transnational nature of the movement.

---

[8] See Walter Sullivan, *Assault on the Unknown: The International Geophysical Year* (New York: McGraw Hill Book Company, 1961), p. 53: Douglas Brinkley, *American Moonshot: John F. Kennedy and the Great Space Race* (New York: HarperCollins, 2019), p. 3.

[9] Rip Bulkeley, *The Sputniks Crisis and Early United States Space Policy* (London: Macmillan, 1991), p. 45.

[10] Frank H. Winter, *Prelude to the Space Age: The Rocket Societies: 1924–1940* (Washington, DC: Smithsonian Institution Press, 1983), p. 13.

[11] Winter, *Prelude to the Space Age*, pp. 14, 21–22.

The Russians were also making advancements in rocketry around this time and were greatly impressed by both Goddard's and Oberth's discoveries. They formed their own rocket society, Group for the Study of Reactive Motion, known as GIRD. Konstantin Tsiolkovsky—a Russian schoolteacher and engineer, who would later be known as the father of astronautics in Russia—had been doing parallel work on space rockets. His first book on the subject had actually been published in 1903, pre-dating both Goddard's and Oberth's work but arriving at many of the same findings. When Tsiolkovsky published a novel in 1920 about an international team of space adventurers, he further sparked excitement among the Russian public about space travel. Indeed, in the 1920s, Goddard and Tsiolkovsky were spoken of among all walks of life in the Soviet Union as household names. They, in turn, inspired many others to work on aspects of space science and space-flight theorizing. In short, the movement, the scientists, and the writers were all well aware of each other and spurred each other on. Embodying the Spaceflight Idea and ultrasociality, they cared far more about their shared aspirations than their country of origin.

Thus, the interwar period featured the establishment of many amateur space-flight organizations, space activist groups, rocket clubs, and interplanetary orga-nizations, which shaped the more general public interest in space long before it was possible to actually go there. GIRD, the Society for the Study of Interplane-tary Communications, the Japanese Society of Aeronautics,[12] the German Rocket Society, the American Rocket Society, the British Interplanetary Society, and the All-Inventors' Vegetarian Club of Interplanetary Cosmopolitans, among many others, gained thousands of members seemingly overnight—mostly regular people who had become space enthusiasts. In the process, these space societies very much promoted the idea that space should be a peaceful domain for all of humankind. These societies quite simply lived and breathed the power of possibility.

To be sure, in these early days, cynics of the Spaceflight Idea at first saw this as a fringe movement, made up of crackpots. The *New York Times* even published a commentary in 1920 that mocked Goddard's efforts at rocketry and only pub-lished a retraction forty-nine years later when Apollo 11 landed on the Moon.[13] And yet, undeterred by the cynics, these space societies grew their memberships, became increasingly transnational, and did a significant amount of public out-reach. They wanted to further stoke popular interest in space exploration through a new narrative about the existence of a wider universe and the eventual colo-nization of other planets. In doing so, they tapped into the public's craving for something to believe in during what was otherwise a period of repeated crises.

[12] Founded in 1934, and restarted in 1953 after the war. Japan Society for Aeronautical and Space Sci-ences, "President's Message," 2022, https://www.jsass.or.jp/webe/society/57 (accessed November 26, 2020). Later other organizations emerged, such as the Brazilian Interplanetary Society and Argentine Association Interplanetary.

[13] Brinkley, *American Moonshot*, pp. 8–9.

The idea of space exploration as a shared endeavor fit the bill and tapped into an innate desire to belong to something bigger.

The public outreach worked. As Frank Winter writes, "For certain, the societies through their relentless, often romantic publicizing of space travel via newspaper and magazine articles, lectures, demonstrations, exhibits, radio talks, and films, influenced millions into accepting the possibility, and even the inevitability, of space travel."[14] Similarly, Dimitrios Stroikos argues, it "was largely a social and cultural phenomenon."[15] Importantly, these amateur groups were highly diverse and by no means confined to just a few countries. As the movement grew, the space societies together formed a strong transnational network with regular communication and exchange about everything from how to build spaceships to the day-to-day of how to live on other planets. The deep ties across these groups were so significant that, in 1931, members started to discuss the possibility of forming a common, supranational umbrella organization to bring them all together more formally.[16]

There were many reasons why the Spaceflight Idea in particular became so attractive and provided a groundswell of energy for the movement. Science fiction, rocketry, and the need for a source of optimism during an otherwise difficult period in global history were all important. In addition, the *substance* of the idea was key. As Stroikos writes, "the idea of science and technology as a unifier of humankind couched in the language of scientific cosmopolitanism and universalism" was undeniable.[17] Indeed, a kind of "scientific internationalism" had emerged in the 1920s, a type of supranational imagined community, led by both state and non-state actors.[18] Add to this the fact that humans have long had a pioneering spirit of discovery, and the story of human history has often involved expanding boundaries as a species. All of these motivations have in common a fundamentally *ultrasocial* underpinning; that is, those in the Spaceflight Movement, and the interested public more generally, could clearly think about humankind as a common civilization with space exploration as an intrinsically shared endeavor for the betterment of all.

The Spaceflight Idea Becomes Mainstream

Many of these spaceflight groups were forced into hiatus during the Second World War. However, despite the fact that the use of military rockets was a far cry from the peaceful and cooperative ideals at the core of the Spaceflight Idea, significant

---

[14] Winter, *Prelude to the Space Age*, p. 14.
[15] Stroikos, "Engineering World Society?," p. 81.
[16] Stroikos, "Engineering World Society?," p. 82.
[17] Stroikos, "Engineering World Society?," p. 87.
[18] Stroikos. "Engineering World Society?," p. 79.

advancements in rocketry during the war ironically helped to pave the way for a full-scale resumption of the movement after the war. Indeed, key spaceflight advocates in the movement, especially Von Braun in Germany, actually used the war as an opportunity to get more funding and support for the research that they knew would eventually lead to spaceflight. Indeed, while it is true that military efforts to develop missiles had significantly advanced rocketry technology, as in the past, space scientists' goals were still, first and foremost, to achieve peaceful spaceflight, international cooperation in space, and to build on the support of an enthusiastic public.

A silver lining of increased governmental attention to the war-fighting potential of rocketry after the war was that the Spaceflight Movement was no longer seen as a fringe group of crackpots.[19] Bainbridge writes, "As important parts of the Spaceflight Movement, they show the typical evolutionary pattern of successful social movements: born in obscurity as deviant outsider organizations, they grow and mature until they finally gain the status of conventional—more or less parts of the Establishment."[20] The notion that humans could go into outer space was no longer far-fetched and had become far more widely accepted. The public, especially in the wake of two devastating world wars, rallied around the idea. Space exploration offered them a sense of hope and optimism and something exciting to imagine that went beyond the crises of fighting wars on Earth. Still inspired by science fiction and even cartoons about space (Walt Disney himself had a long-standing relationship with NASA),[21] the American public had actually become even more "space-minded" than the US government in these years.[22]

Thus, as soon as the war ended, spaceflight enthusiasts picked up right where they had left off. Members of the movement had always shared the common goal of formally internationalizing their efforts, and they were able to achieve this in the post-Second World War period. On September 30, 1950, the first meeting of the International Astronautical Congress (IAC) took place in Paris. At this first meeting, around forty delegates from ten countries founded the International Astronautical Federation (IAF), bringing together fourteen rocket societies. They continued to push for the peaceful use of space from this elevated platform and advocated for more to be done to achieve the goals of human spaceflight. With a movement that included the public across many countries, the federation

[19] However, in the United States, engaging in space research was still considered highly risky career-wise. For example, it was looked down upon for a US Air Force pilot to declare his interest in working on human spaceflight. PBS Space Time, *American Experience: Space Men.*

[20] William Sims Bainbridge, *The Spaceflight Revolution: A Sociological Study* (Malabar, FL: Krieger Publishing Co., 1983), p. 125.

[21] Disney aired three episodes on space travel, entitled *Man in Space, Man and the Moon*, and *Mars and Beyond*, between 1955 and 1957. Wernher Von Braun served as technical advisor to help ensure their accuracy, and the episodes were tremendously popular. A subsequent comic book series was also published.

[22] Bulkeley, *The Sputniks Crisis*, p. 45.

empowered many transnational and international voices in support of the Spaceflight Idea. In the United States, for example, even in the early stages of government plans to place a satellite into orbit, the American Rocket Society lobbied from 1952 to 1954 to pursue this for purely scientific goals, not for national security.[23] The IAC and IAF, of course, would go on to become the flagship annual meeting and organization of the global space community, made up of thousands of members from scientists, to astronauts, to private companies and start-ups.

The impetus within the Spaceflight Movement, alongside support from the public at large, helped pave the way for space to be a major part of the next major step in scientific internationalism: the International Geophysical Year (IGY), which took place between July 1957 and December 1958. And this is important for while the standard historical narrative insists that the Soviets worked on their own and surprised the world with the launch of Sputnik, the goal of achieving this milestone was actually born out of the IGY. Indeed, the IGY could be a case study of ultrasociality in its own right, given its enormous flourishing of shared international scientific research and collaboration. With its key goal of putting the first satellite into orbit, the IGY was essentially the on-ramp to the Space Age.

The International Geophysical Year

Upon the arrival of British geophysicist Sydney Chapman in the United States on April 5, 1950, a small group of scientists and others from the US Research and Development Board (a group formed in 1947 to coordinate US and international scientific goals) gathered together.[24] It was over dinner at space scientist James Van Allen's house in Silver Spring, Maryland that the idea for the IGY was born.[25] Initially, the scientists thought this would be another International Polar Year, which had occurred twice before (it was slated to happen every fifty years), but it soon encompassed much more than that.

The group floated the IGY idea among US universities first, then expanded its outreach internationally. In 1952, an enhanced proposal arrived at the International Council of Scientific Unions (now the International Science Council) as a full-fledged agenda to include all major areas of scientific research.[26] It was accepted. The council led the planning for the IGY, and the timing of it was

---

[23] Bulkeley, *The Sputniks Crisis*, pp. 131–132.

[24] This board had already collaborated extensively internationally but notably without the Eastern bloc until the IGY. Fae L. Korsmo, "The Genesis of the International Geophysical Year," *Physics Today* 60, 7 (July 2007): 38–43, https://doi.org/10.1063/1.2761801.

[25] Korsmo, "The Genesis of the International Geophysical Year," p. 40.

[26] Harold Bullis, *The Political Legacy of the International Geophysical Year* (Ann Arbor, MI: University of Michigan Press, 1973); John Krige, Angelina Long Callahan, and Ashok Maharaj, *NASA in the World: Fifty Years of International Collaboration in Space* (Basingstoke: Palgrave, 2013). This was not entirely the first event of its kind as an International Polar Year was held in 1882–1883 and 1932–1933

designed to capitalize on a period of maximum solar activity, as well as recent advancements in rocketry and computing.[27]

At first, 26 countries were involved, but as momentum grew, the number climbed to 67, comprising over 60,000 scientists. Russian leaders took notice when, in October 1954, it became clear that the IGY would include plans to launch the first human-made satellites into orbit. The Soviet Union joined the IGY in 1955, and it quickly became the country's highest priority in terms of allocating money, personnel, and resources—possibly even a higher priority than in the United States.[28] Indeed, the Russians became so enthusiastic about the IGY that they offered a number of major initiatives and resources in nearly all areas of IGY preparations, including fifteen of the forty-eight ships for the oceanography section of the IGY.[29] The US government, for its part, consciously kept the IGY satellite program separate from its military program. Even though both the US and Soviet Union already had fledgling satellite programs at the national level,[30] the IGY clearly transformed the satellite goal into a peaceful, international endeavor for the benefit of shared scientific discovery.

The IGY is often described as "the largest and most complex international scientific undertaking ever attempted"[31] and "the single most significant peaceful activity of mankind since the Renaissance and the Copernican Revolution."[32] It is praised for its contributions "in overcoming ideological differences as a means of building bridges between science and diplomacy."[33] The cornerstone of the IGY was the "free movement of data."[34] In 1955, all participants in the IGY had agreed to a formal resolution that all data resulting from the endeavor would be freely and readily available to all. This was such a major part of the point of the IGY that many countries, including the United States and the Soviet Union, offered to support data centers to compile all of the discoveries in one place. Eventually, three World Data Centers were established for this purpose.[35] This was followed by the creation of literally thousands of stations filled with scientists from around

[27] NASA, "Sputnik and the Dawn of the Space Age," January 6, 2019, https://history.nasa.gov/sputnik.html (accessed July 3, 2023).

[28] Sullivan, *Assault on the Unknown*, p. 29.

[29] Korsmo, "The Genesis of the International Geophysical Year," p. 41.

[30] Stroikos, "Engineering World Society?," p. 84; Asif Siddiqi, "*Sputnik* 50 Years Later: New Evidence on Its Origins," *Acta Astronautica* 63, 1–4 (July-August 2008), https://doi.org/10.1016/j.actaastro.2007.12.042; Walter A. McDougall, *The Heavens and the Earth: A Political History of the Space Age* (New York: Basic Books, 1985), p. 118.

[31] Clement J. Zablocki, "Forward," in *The Political Legacy of the International Geophysical Year*, ed. Bullis.

[32] Hugh Odishaw, organizer of US IGY contributions, as quoted in Sullivan, *Assault on the Unknown*, p. 4.

[33] Zablocki, "Forward."

[34] Sullivan, *Assault on the Unknown*, pp. 34–35.

[35] World Data Center A was located in the United States, World Data Center B was in the Soviet Union (Moscow and Novosibirsk, Siberia), and World Data Center C was divided among Western Europe, Australia, and Japan. Each housed complete IGY scientific records so that nothing would be lost in the event that something happened to one of them. Sullivan, *Assault on the Unknown*, p. 35.

the world, working to advance knowledge in a multitude of areas, which was freely shared across the globe at the same time.

Participation was by no means limited to the world's scientific elite. Many regular members of the public participated, including teachers, students, and countless volunteers. The IGY was of so much interest at the societal level that the *New York Times* assigned a reporter to cover IGY activities full time.[36] Not only did it bring *humans* together, but it also affirmed that science could only truly advance through "experiments in concert," as Francis Bacon had put it in the seventeenth century, and that natural events on the planet itself were all interconnected.[37] The overarching message of the IGY was that the IGY offered an arena in which the barriers of the Cold War were no longer obstacles.[38] The IGY—and other events like it—provide true testimony to what can be achieved when humans work together for common goals, the energy this can generate, and how ultrasocial endeavors open up possibilities.

At the same time, IGY space science was not entirely lacking in tension at the level of governments. Notably, the Soviet government was initially quiet about plans involving space because Khrushchev had not endorsed the idea of sharing its satellite program with the international scientific community. After some efforts behind the scenes, in 1956, the Soviet Union opened up in this regard. US and Soviet representatives were able to agree to make their satellites compatible in terms of radio frequencies. However, the two governments had trouble formally agreeing to what specific satellite data would be shared. For example, they kept hidden details about rocket launch vehicles, as that had sensitive military implications, and were also more tight-lipped when it came to failures along the way.[39] Overall, however, the two countries shared much of their data with the world as they made steps toward the goal of putting a manmade satellite in orbit. As Korsmo writes, "The satellite launches of the IGY were among the most visible results of the participating countries' decisions to partially demilitarize science and participate in an open, civilian science program [. . .] the satellite programs were a huge step towards sharing scientific and technical information for peaceful purposes."[40]

To be sure, some of these tensions made for a few uncomfortable meetings of the IGY, but for the most part, the parties involved actually wanted to *continue* the cooperation they had launched even after the IGY was over. As evidence of this, both Soviet and US delegates found ways to convince their governments to extend cooperative programs, and a number of major international committees continued to exist, including the Committee on Space Research. In contrast to governments, the scientists involved, including members of the American Rocket

---

[36] Sullivan, *Assault on the Unknown*, Acknowledgements.
[37] Sullivan, *Assault on the Unknown*, pp. 4–5.
[38] Korsmo, "The Genesis of the International Geophysical Year."
[39] Bulkeley, *The Sputniks Crisis*, p. 109.
[40] Korsmo, "The Genesis of the International Geophysical Year," p. 42.

Society, clearly saw this as a peaceful endeavor, to the point where they convinced President Eisenhower of this approach, at least to a significant extent.[41] In short, the Spaceflight Idea was at the very core of the scientists' worldview during the IGY.

The number of advancements and discoveries that had occurred as a result of such widespread scientific cooperation are too numerous to count. The IGY made its mark in everything from atoms, to human health, to earth sciences, to Antarctica, to space. While the effort was clearly highly cooperative, the Cold War and the recent advent of nuclear weapons was certainly part of the context too. Governments continued to see the military implications in much of this even as civilian groups of scientists were looking at things in a different light. And yet, while there was obviously national interest to be gained through having access to so much data, it was all still undertaken in the name of mutual, collective benefit, even when it came to space. As Bulkeley argues, the conspiracy theory that the United States supported the IGY merely as some sort of foil for launching American satellites under the guise of scientific inquiry "must be rejected."[42]

Indeed, at the opening of the IGY, Eisenhower said, "the most important result of the International Geophysical Year is the demonstration of the ability of all nations to work together harmoniously for the common good."[43] Remarkably, despite a tense international climate, the very idea of advancing and sharing science, even in the domain of space, involved tens of thousands of people directly and captivated countless millions more, allowing a breath of fresh air to blow across the Iron Curtain. Participation was widespread and inspiration even stronger. For the Spaceflight Movement, the IGY championed the Spaceflight Idea in a visible and tangible way, ushering in an exciting first stage in the dream of sending humans into space on behalf of all mankind. The IGY played no small role in enabling the Spaceflight Idea to come to life, with its optimistic narrative that breaking the boundaries of gravity was an achievement for everyone. And crucially, contrary to conventional wisdom, it also helped set the tone for the very nature of the Space Race to come.

[41] Bulkeley, *The Sputniks Crisis*, pp. 12, 15–16, 98–99, 131.
[42] Bulkeley, *The Sputniks Crisis*, p. 131.
[43] Dwight D. Eisenhower, "Remarks in Connection with the Opening of the International Geophysical Year," DDE's Papers as President, Speech Series, Box 22, International Geophysical Year NAID # 16647171, June 30, 1957, as cited in Stroikos, "Engineering World Society?," p. 86.

9

International Cooperation
and the Space Race

Sputnik and Cooperation

The USSR launched Sputnik 1 and 2 in the fall of 1957, and the United States followed suit with Explorer 1 in 1958.[44] The Space Race had literally taken off. However, there are at least three common misconceptions about Sputnik and the nature of the Space Race that are important to dispel, especially when taking an ultrasocial approach to understanding international relations during this crucial period. These include that (1) Sputnik came out of nowhere, with little warning, (2) it immediately shocked the world, provoking fear and foreboding, and (3) it was a solo Russian success, with no cooperative dimension to it.[45] Correcting these misperceptions shows just how much the Space Race actually featured many cooperative efforts and initiatives, despite its notoriety as an ostensibly cutthroat competition between two superpowers constantly on the verge of war.

In terms of the first misperception, as discussed in Chapter 8, rather than the common assumption that Sputnik came out of nowhere, it was actually a central part of the International Geophysical Year (IGY). Sputnik's launch occurred during the IGY, meaning that the goal itself was a shared, international endeavor and the science needed to achieve it was being widely shared across countries. The USSR and United States themselves were, in fact, collaborators on satellite goals during the IGY. To be sure, there were differences in approach with regard to day-to-day activities. For their part, Russian scientists were open about saying that they would not announce when their attempted first launch would take place. They took the approach that it was inappropriate to brag about experimental breakthroughs unless they were actually successful.[46] By contrast, Americans were very open about each phase of their satellite plans. Thus, when the announcement was made that the Russians had been first to get a satellite into orbit, many scientists were surprised, but they had known very well that it would happen at some point

---

[44] Explorer 1 was actually only 6.4 inches in diameter.

[45] For more detail on this, see Mai'a K. Davis Cross, "The Social Construction of the Space Race," *International Affairs* 95, 6, (November 2019): 1403–1421, https://doi.org/10.1093/ia/iiz190.

[46] Walter Sullivan, *Assault on the Unknown: The International Geophysical Year* (New York: McGraw Hill Book Company, 1961), p. 66.

International Cooperation Against All Odds. Mai'a K. Davis Cross, Oxford University Press. © Mai'a K. Davis Cross (2024). DOI: 10.1093/oso/9780192873903.003.0010

relatively soon.[47] And again, the two countries were collaborating on many aspects of this, continually sharing scientific discoveries, along with all of the other countries involved in the IGY. Great Britain, Canada, Australia, and Japan were also operating in the satellite domain. Even at the political level, the Central Intelligence Agency (CIA) had actually gathered intelligence pointing to a USSR launch happening sometime soon and had informed President Eisenhower of this.[48]

Second, rather than creating immediate panic, Sputnik actually inspired the people of the United States and the world, many of whom were already drawn to the Spaceflight Idea. The usual story is that the launch of Sputnik 1 had an immediate and significant impact on American public opinion, sparking fear of a USSR ballistic missile attack and a grave loss of US power in the world. In reality, at the time, space had become, as one US general described it, "a glamorous and spectacular frontier" that had "generated worldwide public excitement."[49] Sputnik had put the issue of space squarely in the public eye. Instead of a predominant reaction of fear and desire to immediately compete with the USSR, the American public, from citizens to scientists, were immediately excited about the development. Their reaction across the board was very much in line with the Spaceflight Idea and an ultrasocial inclination. As Roger Launius writes,

> Most Americans seemed to recognize that the satellite did not pose a threat to the United States and instead congratulations ensued and many people seemed excited by the Soviet success [. . .] it seems a generation of Americans embraced the dawn of the space age as a symbol of progress and a better future both on Earth and beyond. Raised on visions of human colonies on the Moon and Mars, great starships plying galactic oceans, and prospects of a bright, limitless future.[50]

Five days after Sputnik 1 made it into orbit, President Eisenhower said:

> Every scientist that I have talked to since this occurred [. . .] has spoken in most congratulatory terms about the capabilities of the Russian scientists in putting this thing in the air. They expressed themselves as pleased, rather than chagrined, because at least the Soviets have proved the first part of it—that this thing will successfully orbit.[51]

---

[47] Sullivan, *Assault on the Unknown*, Acknowledgements.

[48] Sheng-Chih Wang, *Transatlantic Space Politics: Competition and Cooperation above the Clouds* (New York, Routledge, 2013), p. 41.

[49] Senate Committee on Aeronautical and Space Sciences, "Excerpts from General Schriver's Testimony before the Subcommittee on Governmental Organization for Space Activities," JFK Presidential Archives, Pre-Presidential Papers #2, Box 568, Folder 3, April 23, 1959.

[50] Roger D. Launius, "An Unintended Consequence of the IGY," *Acta Astronautica* 67, 1 (2010), pp. 257–258, https://doi.org/10.1016/j.actaastro.2009.10.019.

[51] As quoted in Sullivan, *Assault on the Unknown*, p. 77.

As the *New York Times* reported,

> American scientists at a Soviet Embassy reception, while disappointed that the Russians had beaten them into space, breathed a sigh of relief. "The pressure is off," they said. "Now we can concentrate on doing a good job."[52]

The *Chicago Daily News* wrote:

> The satellite project is a peaceful one. For that we can be thankful. Its primary purpose is to obtain knowledge that presumably will be pooled by all nations taking part in the International Geophysical Year. In that aspect we can in good faith congratulate the Russian technicians for a proud achievement.[53]

And Joseph Kaplan, chairman of the US program for the IGY described the development as nothing less than "fantastic."[54]

Numerous public opinion surveys were also conducted, asking Americans what they thought of space exploration before and after Sputnik. All of the surveys showed the same thing: there was no immediate fear or panic over the USSR achievement. For example, when social anthropologists Margaret Mead and Rhoda Metraux conducted a survey three days after the satellite launch, they discovered that the vast majority of people were not surprised by the launch, and neither were they alarmed that somehow the United States had lost something by not being first. Another survey, conducted by the government, found that only 13% "believed that we had fallen behind dangerously."[55]

After this initial reaction to Sputnik, however, those opposed to the Eisenhower administration sought to use the event as political strategy. Senator Lyndon Baines Johnson (LBJ) and other leaders from the Democratic Party constructed a sense of panic surrounding Sputnik that was not initially there. LBJ gave several speeches painting the satellite launch as a dangerous development for US security and reframed Sputnik as a much larger problem. Naturally, the media, which often thrives on covering crises, shifted tone as well. A *Washington Post* article on October 20, 1957 stated, for example, that "The United States could no longer proclaim the supremacy of its industrial machine or of the capitalist free system of economics" in reaction to Sputnik.[56] They essentially constructed an alarmist

[52] *New York Times*, October 5, 1957, 1: 6, as quoted in Martha Wheeler George, "The Impact of Sputnik I: Case-Study of American Public Opinion at the Break of the Space Age," NASA Historical Note No. 22, NASA HQ, Folder 6719, October 4, 1957.
[53] NASA HQ, "Russian 'Moon' Casts Big Shadow," *Chicago Daily News*, October 7, 1957. The article then goes on to address the "sinister" way this capacity could be used for missiles.
[54] New York Times, October 5, 1957, 1: 6 as quoted in Wheeler George, "The Impact of Sputnik I."
[55] As quoted in Launius, "An Unintended Consequence of the IGY," p. 258.
[56] Democratic Advisory Council, "Position Paper on Space Research: Prepared for Senator Kennedy," JFK Presidential Archives, Box 197 DNC 1960 Campaign, September 7, 1960.

narrative where none had existed before, stoking a kind of national tribalism and diminishing the initial narrative about common human achievement.

Ultimately, it was not difficult for them to pull this off considering that, of course, the IGY and Sputnik occurred in the broader context of a very tense time in geopolitics. Moreover, as explained in Chapter 2, humans are naturally credulous, and we often see more conflictual, tribal beliefs stemming from efforts on the part of politicians to pursue opportunism. As such, these efforts built over the next couple of years, and the subsequent US presidential debates focused heavily on the Soviet threat both in terms of a nuclear attack and of the Space Race. There was a clear assumption that, as John F. Kennedy put it in the debates, "If the Soviets control space they can control earth."[57] Eisenhower, for his part, did not do much to address the issue, neither did he respond to the growing sense that the United States was somehow behind because he quite simply saw this newer, panic-based narrative as overblown. Indeed, when looking back on this several years later, Eisenhower expressed surprise at just how "psychologically vulnerable" the American people were, given how readily they shifted to connect one achievement to everything else.[58] Of course, psychological vulnerability means nothing without someone trying to capitalize on it, and in this case, they were being influenced by leaders who sought to take political advantage of the situation.

With what some saw at the time as a leadership vacuum at the top in response to Sputnik, an epistemic coalition of a sort came together, comprised of "political opponents, scientists, military space advocates, space exploration enthusiasts, and leaders in the aerospace industry."[59] Many of them had actually been members of the Spaceflight Movement for some time, and they also saw Sputnik as an opening to craft a US response that was in line with their own goals: the Spaceflight Idea. It was their initiative and lobbying that ultimately pressured the US Congress and President Eisenhower to somewhat reluctantly create the National Aeronautics and Space Administration (NASA) in 1958. The agency ended up being much smaller than the epistemic coalition had initially wanted as it ultimately reflected Eisenhower's political preferences for small government. Nonetheless, they had managed to use the constructed controversy surrounding Sputnik to form NASA, whose formal remit was, nonetheless, to explore space for "peaceful purposes for the benefit of all mankind."[60] It also included US cooperation in space with other

---

[57] John F. Kennedy, "If the Soviets Control Space . . . They Can Control Earth," Missiles and Rockets, October 10, 1960, pp. 12–13 as cited in Edward Ezell and Linda Ezell (eds), *The Partnership: A History of the Apollo-Soyuz Test Project*, (Washington DC: NASA 1978) https://history.nasa.gov/SP-4209.pdf (accessed July 3, 2023).

[58] Dwight D. Eisenhower, *The White House Years: Waging Peace, 1956–1961* (New York: Doubleday & Co., 1965).

[59] Launius, "An Unintended Consequence of the IGY," p. 260.

[60] NASA, "National Aeronautics and Space Act of 1958 (unamended)," 1958, https://history.nasa.gov/spaceact.html (accessed November 21, 2020).

countries and with the International Committee on Space Research (COSPAR).[61] All of this was, of course, explicitly in line with the Spaceflight Idea that members of the Space Movement had long championed.

Public interest in space exploration, which itself had grown alongside the Spaceflight Movement, the IGY, and the excitement surrounding Sputnik, also gave the government the ability to increase spending in this area. NASA's existence meant that the use of rocketry technology for missiles and other military purposes could be kept distinct from space exploration.[62] The Department of Defense could pursue the use of these technologies for its own ends, while NASA could continue a focus on science, engineering, discovery, and exploration. In actuality, its creation involved literally taking some of the capacities and functions from the Department of Defense and transferring them to the civilian-controlled NASA,[63] all in all, a win for the Spaceflight Movement.

Thus, the notion that the public was immediately fearful of Sputnik is more an artifact of superficial political manipulation of public opinion after the fact than a true reflection of how people initially reacted. If anything, Sputnik showcased ultrasociality, sparked increased fascination in space, and strengthened social support of the Spaceflight Movement's goals. If alarm and fear had truly been taken as seriously as we are often led to believe, the creation of NASA, as a civilian organization with peaceful intent, would not really make sense.

The third misconception about Sputnik and the Space Race is that these events had no cooperative dimension to them to speak of. Again, the Space Race is often referenced as the archetype of pure nationalist competition. However, this simply was not true, both in terms of international cooperation and with regard to the USSR–US relationship. Time and time again, even the leaders of the two superpowers used the language of ultrasociality embodied in the Spaceflight Idea to express their aims in space.

Even as the alarmist narrative surrounding Sputnik shifted popular opinion toward apprehension, international cooperation on space actually intensified. During the IGY, countries had begun discussing how to cooperate on space at the UN, yet progress was piecemeal. They formed an ad hoc committee on space in 1958 but limited it to the context of disarmament.[64] Then, from late 1958 to late 1961, efforts turned toward more positive approaches to cooperation, specifically

---

[61] COSPAR was established in November 1958.

[62] Although there is always overlap to some degree, given the dual-use nature of the technology. Although the defense and civilian sides of space became more distinct, they also agreed to share information relevant to the other. Douglas Brinkley, *American Moonshot: John F. Kennedy and the Great Space Race* (New York: HarperCollins, 2019), p. 168.

[63] Brinkley, *American Moonshot*, p. 167.

[64] Yun Zhao, "The Role of Bilateral and Multilateral Agreements in International Space Cooperation," *Space Policy* 36 (2016): 12–18, https://doi.org/10.1016/j.spacepol.2016.02.007; UNGA (United Nations General Agreement), "Question of the Peaceful Use of Outer Space," UNGA Res. 1348 (XIII), December 13, 1958.

in terms of the peaceful use of outer space.[65] The United States made a proposal at the United Nations (UN) in 1958 that "the peaceful use of outer space be separated from disarmament."[66] In 1959, the ad hoc committee became permanent and was named the UN Committee on the Peaceful Uses of Outer Space (COPUOS).

The international sharing and collaboration that occurred in so many areas of science during the IGY also had lasting impact in the space arena, and it went far beyond UN discussions. American officials, in particular, took seriously the idea that "openness and cooperation go together."[67] NASA began to build a network of bilateral cooperative arrangements with other countries as well as multilateral cooperation involving American experimental communications and meteorological satellites.[68] Crucially, this even included cooperation with the USSR itself.

Indeed, Russian and American leaders continually and emphatically emphasized space exploration as a cooperative endeavor. In 1959, for example, the United States offered its own satellite services to the USSR. In a letter to the Academy of Sciences of the USSR, the specific proposal was "to extend the services of the U.S. satellite tracking network to the scientists of the USSR in the event that the USSR should at some time in the future desire to utilize them in connection with a manned space flight program."[69] The Soviet Academy of Sciences promptly accepted the offer.[70] The same was true for several other countries, who rapidly set up space programs in order to take advantage of new opportunities for cooperation.

During Kennedy's presidential campaign, even while he was overtly cultivating panic over Sputnik as a means to drum up political support, behind the scenes, NASA established an Office of International Programs. And this led to some real results once he became president. In 1961, scientists from ten countries, including the USSR, met in Vermont for four days to discuss international space cooperation and came up with a viable program involving the creation of a shared global system of weather and communication satellites, data exchange on space biology, and a common program of lunar and planetary space exploration.[71]

[65] Carl Kaysen, "Summary of Foreign Policy Aspects of the US Outer Space Program," JFK Presidential Archives, National Security Files, Box 377, June 5, 1962.

[66] Kaysen, "Summary of Foreign Policy Aspects of the US Outer Space Program."

[67] US Information Agency, "Potomac Cable No. 244—The US Lead in Space," JFK Presidential Archives, National Security Files, Box 377, October 10, 1962.

[68] Kaysen, "Summary of Foreign Policy Aspects of the US Outer Space Program."

[69] JFK Presidential Archives. "Letter from Richard W. Porter, US National Academy of Sciences, to Professor Federov, Academy of Sciences of the USSR," JFK Presidential Archives, National Security Files, Box 334, December 15, 1959.

[70] JFK Presidential Archives, "Letter from Professor Federov, Academy of Sciences of the USSR, to Richard W. Porter, US National Academy of Sciences," JFK Presidential Archives, National Security Files, Box 334, March 16, 1960.

[71] Edward Clinton Ezell and Linda Neuman Ezell, "Competition Versus Cooperation: 1959–1962," The Partnership, 2022, https://history.nasa.gov/SP-4225/documentation/competition/competition.htm (accessed November 26, 2022).

Demonstrating that his emphasis during the campaign had been motivated more by political opportunism than true belief, as soon as J. F. Kennedy actually moved into the White House, he dramatically toned down the pessimistic rhetoric about space and visibly shifted into a much more open attitude toward space cooperation with Soviet leaders. Indeed, when Russian cosmonaut Yuri Gagarin became the first human in space on April 12, 1961, Kennedy sent a telegram to Khrushchev stating that

The people of the United States share with the people of the Soviet Union their satisfaction for the safe flight of the astronaut in man's first venture into space. We congratulate you and the Soviet scientists and engineers who made this feat possible. It is my sincere desire that in the continuing quest for knowledge of outer space our nations work together to obtain the greatest benefit to mankind.[72]

Communication between NASA and the Soviet Academy commenced regularly in what became informally known as the "NASA–Soviet Academy channel."[73] And it wasn't just talk. The cooperation that ensued, while not always meeting all the deadlines, was nonetheless meaningful. As NASA Administrator James Webb put it, "In order to achieve real gains, we should push for substantive rather than token cooperation," echoing Kennedy's speech to the UN that "we should not put forward proposals merely for propaganda purposes."[74] In 1962, after two early meetings on space at the UN, a telegram from Geneva to the Secretary of State in Washington DC described the climate at the UN in a way that very much conveyed a clear embrace of the Spaceflight Idea:

It was now generally realized that international cooperation in the exploration and utilization of outer space would benefit all the nations of the world, irrespective of their size, political structure or industrial potential [. . .] one goal would undoubtedly be achieved: the nations of the world would come closer together and understand more clearly that they were members of one family—mankind.[75]

Similarly, on June 18, 1963 a secret paper—addressed to McGeorge Bundy, Special Assistant to the President for National Security Affairs and written by the

[72] John F. Kennedy, The White House, Office of the White House Press Secretary, "President's telegram to the chairman of the council of ministers, Union of Soviet Socialist Republics, N.S. Khrushchev," JFK Presidential Archives, National Security Files, Box 308, April 12, 1961.
[73] JFK Presidential Archives, "Letter from NASA Administrator James Webb to President Kennedy," JFK Presidential Archives, National Security Files, Box 342, September 1963.
[74] JFK Presidential Archives, "US–USSR Cooperation in Space Research Programs," JFK Presidential Archives, National Security Files, Box 342, 1963/64 (not specifically dated).
[75] Department of State, "Incoming Telegram from Geneva to Secretary State, Outer Space," JFK Presidential Archives, National Security Files, Box 308, May 31, 1962.

US Department of State's Policy Planning Council—was discussed in a special planning group on the "Implications of Outer Space in the 1970s."[76] This comprehensive paper again invoked the Spaceflight Idea, concluding that

> The nature of outer space activities themselves, and of the international context in which they develop, will necessarily lead to increased international interdependence in this field. International cooperation in space and space-related activities should be sought from the points of view both of the foreign support which the US program will need, and of the foreign policy objectives which can be served.[77]

The scientific community was especially enthusiastic about these prospects both for research and political reasons. After all, their predecessors had been pushing for the Spaceflight Idea since the 1920s, and they were pleased to see it gain traction. For example, Eugene Rabinowitch published an editorial in the *Bulletin of the Atomic Scientists* to that effect:

> In facing cosmic space, the quarrels and struggles between different factions of humanity appear petty and irrelevant [. . .] If space exploration could help bring together the two alienated parts of humanity and reduce, even slightly the danger of all-destroying nuclear war, that alone would make worthwhile investing in it many billions of dollars.[78]

This was certainly aided by separate talks in March 1962 between scientists from the USSR and the United States when discussions became noticeably more specific and technical.

These informal talks were held at the UN in New York between American and Soviet representatives—led by Hugh Dryden on the US side and Anatoli Blagonravov on the Russian side—on some of the specifics of these proposals, during which there was detailed agreement on the value of cooperation and the willingness to enter into it.[79] In a confidential summary of these events, a NASA representative described the talks as, "very relaxed in character, with an almost total absence of Cold War atmosphere."[80] In the process, the Spaceflight Idea was invoked time and time again. For example, a Russian cable, dated April 5, 1962, states:

[76] JFK Presidential Archives, "National Security Policy Planning Paper: Implications of Outer Space in the 1970's," JFK Presidential Archives, National Security Files, Box 308, May 31, 1963.
[77] JFK Presidential Archives, "National Security Policy Planning Paper: Implications of Outer Space in the 1970's."
[78] Eugene Rabinowitch, "Progress in Space Cooperation with USSR," *Bulletin of the Atomic Scientists*, NASA Archives File 15570, May 1963.
[79] Hugh Dryden, "US–Soviet Space Cooperation Talks," JFK Presidential Archives, National Security Files, Box 334, March 27, 28, 30, 1962.
[80] NASA, "Status of US/USSR Bilateral Space Talks," JFK Presidential Archives, National Security Files, Box 334, April 21, 1962.

all the data of our space research we publish in detail because we adhere to the principle that our achievements in space are the achievements of all of humanity, not simply of the Soviet people [. . .] we in the Soviet Union want very much to cooperate with the United States in space research.[81]

Even in the lead-up to the Cuban Missile Crisis in May–June 1962, they held a second round of talks in Geneva and reached the first formal agreement (known as the Dryden–Blagonravov agreement) on June 8, 1962, including how to work together with other countries beyond the United States and the USSR. Agreement was ultimately reached on three of the cooperative projects: weather data sharing and launching of meteorological satellites, magnetic field mapping of Earth, and experimental communication using the ECHO satellite and possible launching of future communications satellites.[82]

Later that year, even after the frightening events regarding Cuba had seemed to have brought the world to the brink of nuclear war, NASA Administrator Webb issued a formal response regarding the continued US–USSR agreements on space cooperation that was, while subdued, still very optimistic. In his words: "This is an important step toward cooperation among nations of the world to increase man's knowledge and use of his special environment."[83] And this optimism was shared as the USSR news agency wrote, at the same time, that "There is no doubt that this agreement will make a great contribution to the conquest of the universe and to the further advance of international cooperation between scientists."[84] The implementation of the Dryden–Blagonravov agreement began in January 1963.[85]

In short, the cooperative initiative spearheaded during the IGY had momentum and staying power when it came to space. Even though it continued to be a challenging area in which to overcome the barriers of the Cold War, the actors involved remained committed to it. They viewed space as categorically different from other areas of endeavor. Frequently invoked in letters, documents, and agendas at the time was the original Spaceflight Idea: that nations should vigorously pursue cooperation in space because it was an inherently peaceful domain with scientific potential for the benefit of everyone. And to the extent that the more conflictual public rhetoric surfaced from time to time, even this actually served as a useful political strategy to enable the United States, the USSR, and others to increase spending and efforts in space without fundamentally challenging their

[81] USSR International Affairs, "USSR Seeks Accord on Space with US," NASA Archives, File 15570, April 5, 1962,
[82] JFK Presidential Archives, "Memorandum for the President. 'Bilateral Talks Concerning US–USSR Cooperation in Outer Space Activities," JFK Presidential Archives, National Security Files, Box 334, July 5, 1962.
[83] NASA News Release 62-257, "US–USSR Join in Outer Space Program," December 5, 1962, as cited in Ezell and Ezell, *The Partnership*.
[84] Tass International Service, December 8, 1962, as cited in Ezell and Ezell, *The Partnership*.
[85] JFK Presidential Archives, "Letter from Hugh Dryden to Blagonravov," JFK Presidential Archives, National Security Files, Box 334, December 5, 1962.

shared lofty ideals. Indeed, in real terms, those involved kept coming back to an approach anchored in ultrasociality and one that perhaps reached its highest political expression through the joint Moon landing proposal.

A Proposal for a Joint Moon Landing

By September 1963, Kennedy was persuaded to push for US–USSR cooperation in programs related to going to the Moon.[86] This reached a high point when he delivered a speech at the United Nations on September 20, 1963 inviting the Russians to work with the United States on a joint Moon landing:

> Surely we should explore whether the scientists and astronauts of our two countries—indeed of all the world—cannot work together in the conquest of space, sending some day in this decade to the moon, not the representatives of a single nation, but the representatives of all of our countries.[87]

While there was general enthusiasm at the UN over this proposal,[88] there was also some debate over what motivated J. F. Kennedy's seeming intensification of his desire to achieve cooperation in space. After all, a year earlier, in his famous "Moon speech" at Rice University, Kennedy had described in detail what it would take for the United States to be first to land on the Moon before the end of the decade.[89] A RAND report at the time dismisses the notion that Kennedy was primarily motivated by pressure to achieve the Moon landing goal in time or overcome new budgeting constraints from Congress.[90] Instead, it seemed most likely that he genuinely wanted to pave the way for improvement in the relationship between the United States and the USSR. Members of the Spaceflight Movement, of course, had long supported this idea, and this breakthrough was significant because human spaceflight was a key omission in the various dimensions of space cooperation that had already been agreed.

Responding to Kennedy's call for a joint Moon landing, NASA proposed a range of projects involving unmanned dimensions of spaceflight that would support the manned landing, among other things. Many NASA scientists adhered to the

---

[86] John F. Kennedy, "National Security Action Memorandum No. 271," JFK Presidential Archives, National Security Files, Box 342, November 12, 1963.

[87] John F. Kennedy, "Speech to the United Nations," September 20, 1963, as quoted in Alton Frye, "The Proposal for a Joint Lunar Expedition: Background and Prospects," The RAND Corporation, NASA Archives, File 15570, January 1964.

[88] The Evening Star, "Moon-Trip Plan Stirs Enthusiastic Reaction," NASA Archives, File 15570, September 21, 1963.

[89] John F. Kennedy, Moon Speech—Rice Stadium, September 12, 1962.

[90] Alton Frye, "The Proposal for a Joint Lunar Expedition," Defense Technical Information Center, p. 6, https://apps.dtic.mil/sti/citations/ADA540204 (accessed May 20, 2023).

principles of the Spaceflight Movement. NASA Administrator James Webb argued that

> manned exploration of the moon constitutes the greatest single peaceful under-taking in the history of mankind. As a peaceful activity, it is appropriate to explore whether and to what extent those nations of the world interested in participating could band together in a cooperative effort. In such an exploration one might find some way or means of cooperation between the US and USSR on a plan for selecting a joint site for a lunar landing and base of exploration.[91]

In other words, ideally, a joint Moon landing would pave the way for cooperation, while avoiding any duplication of efforts.

The possibility of Russian scientists providing the booster while Americans provided the spacecraft was widely discussed within the US government. Joseph B. Weisner, the Chair of the Science Advisory Committee in the Kennedy administration, wrote to the president that the joint Moon landing proposal was now even more within reach, "in a way that will not only be in accord with U.S. objectives for peaceful cooperation if accepted by the USSR, but will also decisively dispel the doubts that have existed in the Congress and the press about the sincerity and feasibility of the proposal itself."[92] He went on to propose a division of labor in which the United States would do the mechanics of the Moon landing itself and the USSR would provide unmanned and logistical support. He wrote, "I believe such a program would utilize the combined resources of US and USSR in a technically practical manner, and might, in view of Premier Khrushchev's statement be politically attractive to him."[93]

In reaction to this proposal, Khrushchev accepted a joint Moon landing in principle,[94] and the leaders of the two space agencies signed an agreement to that effect. However, Khrushchev was also a bit circumspect about his concrete view on the matter. An internal US State Department intelligence memo put it this way:

> He appears to regard the President's suggestion as a vague one, to which he can appropriately respond in vaguely approving terms without undertaking negotiations or obligations. We believe that he would be more positive and definite in response to a more specific proposal for cooperation on some particular aspect

[91] "NASA, "NASA News Release: Address by James E. Webb, Administrator NASA," Annual Meeting Texas Mid-Continent Oil and Gas Association, Houston, Texas, JFK Presidential Archives, National Security Files, Box 308, September 25, 1963, p. 15.

[92] Jerome B. Wesiner, "Memorandum for the President: The US Proposal for a Joint US–USSR Lunar Program," JFK Presidential Archives, National Security Files, Box 308, Space Activities, October 29, 1963.

[93] Wesiner, "Memorandum for the President."

[94] JFK Presidential Archives, "Memorandum for Mr. McGeorge Bundy from the White House," JFK Presidential Archives, National Security Files, Box 308, Space Activities, November 7, 1963.

of a joint program which could be undertaken at an early time. We doubt, however, that he would be ready, for the sake of such a program, to make far-reaching commitments of Soviet resources or permit release of Soviet rocket technology at this time.[95]

Thus, there continued to be some ambiguity on what the joint Moon landing entailed in terms of specifics, although the overarching spirit of the proposal was being taken quite seriously. Unfortunately, the shocking and devastating assassination of President Kennedy occurred later that very same month.

It was, however, one thing to kill a man but something altogether different to kill an idea. After Kennedy's assassination, President Johnson continued the efforts at strong cooperation, even repeating the joint Moon landing proposal.[96] This admittedly ambitious endeavor ended up being too much for either side ultimately to embrace. As John Glenn put it, "Some misinterpretation of the President's intent with regard to space cooperation resulted in considerable criticism, with the House of Representatives voting to prohibit funds for joint ventures with the Russians."[97] As for the Soviets, their response to the proposal for a joint lunar landing was "that it had been so general and vague that [they] had nothing to go on."[98] Ultimately, the plan did not move forward, but the tone and tenor of the discussions between the two was very much about conveying a desire to cooperate and to explore space in a peaceful way, without weaponization of any kind. Even more remarkable was the fact that all of this happened at the political level. Clearly, the Spaceflight Movement and Spaceflight Idea had had a deep and abiding impact.

Not unlike what we have seen with the 1952 European Defense Community plan, I would argue that it is often the case that the power of possibility and idealistic aspiration paves the way for other goals, even if they fall short of the original. This bold call for a joint Moon landing made other cooperative breakthroughs—such as Apollo-Soyuz—much more within reach in the 1970s and beyond. Even the very thought of what could be possible had been percolating in the minds of scientists, engineers, and government officials for some time, and this was important for preparing the way. Just as the European federalist idea made European integration a realistic pursuit, the joint Moon landing proposal, among others, led to even broader discussions about cooperation in exploring the universe, especially sharing equipment and research on the lunar surface and working together

[95] Director of Intelligence and Research, Department of State, "Intelligence Note: Khrushchev's obscure and noncommittal statements about moon shots," to the Secretary from INR—Thomas L. Hughes, JFK Presidential Archives, National Security Files, Box 308, November 5, 1963.

[96] Frye, "The Proposal for a Joint Lunar Expedition," p. 15.

[97] NASA Manned Spacecraft Center, "Proposal Concerning Space Flight Information Negotiations with the Russians," memo from Lt Colonel John H. Glenn, Jr, to McGeorge Bundy, Special Assistant to the President, JFK Presidential Files, National Security Files, Box 308, November 4, 1963.

[98] NASA Manned Spacecraft Center, "Proposal Concerning Space Flight Information Negotiations with the Russians."

to go to Mars and Venus.[99] The joint Moon landing initiative is strong evidence of just how seriously the two countries took efforts to cooperate in space, even if good intentions ultimately encountered obstacles.

The demise of the joint Moon landing notwithstanding, through 1964 and 1965 various cooperative plans began to bear fruit, such as the Echo 2 satellite, a passive communications experiment that both Russian and American scientists worked on together. Again, some results fell short of the initial goals because of the sheer ambition of the ideas. But in 1965, things picked up again. American and Soviet officials agreed to engage in joint research on space biology and medicine, which resulted in a series of book publications. Significantly, 1965 also marks the year that the Soviet government made international cooperation in space an official policy. Of course, the IGY, as well as subsequent efforts through the UN and bilaterally with the United States, demonstrate that Soviet willingness to cooperate had certainly pre-dated this. But now, they had actually started to institutionalize this effort. In May 1966, the USSR formed the Council for the International Cooperation in Research and Use of Outer Space (later known as Intercosmos) under the Academy of Sciences. Along with this, numerous bilateral cooperative agreements with other countries besides the United States—including France, Sweden, and Austria, among others—took off. At the same time, the United States also supported the development of space programs in multiple countries and helped to launch their satellites into orbit.

It is important to note that all of this cooperative work took place during the period known as the Space Race and conventionally thought of as a time of exclusive rivalry, competition, and militaristic opposition. Indeed, if the main phase of the race had been triggered by Sputnik, the primary goal of the race was landing on the Moon. Yet, all indications show that the public and the government actually saw this as a peaceful, not conflictual endeavor, so much so that public opinion in the United States in 1962 revealed 47% in favor of cooperating directly with the Soviets on space, even despite strong political efforts during the previous presidential campaign to spark fear in Soviet space capabilities.[100]

As the Spaceflight Idea spread to more and more circles of society, the US government also amplified this cooperative drive in its outreach efforts. Its official objectives in 1963 were, in order, to (1) show "the peaceful intent of the United States program," (2) "emphasize the purpose of the program for exploration and research that will eventually benefit all nations," (3) "contribute to a sense of identification by other countries in the United States effort," (4) "emphasize contributions to science," (5) "emphasize excellent United States technology," (6) "contrast the closed Soviet program and the open United States program,"

[99] Howard Simons, "Vast US, Red Space Ventures behind JFK Bid," Washington Post, NASA Archives, File 15570, September 25, 1963.
[100] NASA Manned Spacecraft Center, "Proposal Concerning Space Flight Information Negotiations with the Russians."

(7) "provide a sense of continuing effort and interest in manned flight, and (8) "perpetuate and further the good will toward the United States manned space flight program."[101]

In short, it would be a significant misunderstanding to think of the Space Race as simply boiling down to geopolitical competition between two ideologically divergent superpowers. The lens of ultrasociality, with an emphasis on ideas and societal power, show the continuous importance of ultrasocial inclinations. The advancements in space technology that occurred during this period reflected unprecedented international cooperation on space exploration. Energized by the IGY, the Spaceflight Movement, and the pursuit of the Spaceflight Idea, space achievements were embedded in a global atmosphere of intense scientific collaboration. Looking beyond sending humans into space, cooperation between the United States, USSR, and any other interested countries, occurred in a range of new, space-related areas, such as weather detection satellites, geomagnetic mapping of Earth, space communications systems, and meteorology, among others. Subsequently, the UN formalized many aspects of the principles and norms behind international cooperation in space.[102] Most prominent were the 1963 UN Declaration of Legal Principles Governing the Activities of States in the Exploration and Use of Outer Space and the 1967 UN Outer Space Treaty.[103] What had started out as an unconventional fantasy among a few rocket enthusiasts and science-fiction writers had grown into a shared optimistic vision that resonated across borders and across political ideologies, the very embodiment of ultrasociality.

Arrival on the Moon

The Spaceflight Idea was strongly on display during the Moon landing itself. Even though Apollo 11 ultimately ended up being an American mission, when astronauts landed on the Moon in 1969, the spirit of the moment was neither tribal nor nationalistic.[104] Neil Armstrong, the first man on the Moon, captured this feeling with one of the most well-known quotes in history: "One small step for

---

[101] NASA Manned Spacecraft Center, "Proposal Concerning Space Flight Information Negotiations with the Russians."

[102] Zhao, "The Role of Bilateral and Multilateral Agreements in International Space Cooperation."

[103] Its full name is "Treaty on Principles Governing the Activities of States in the Exploration and Use of Outer Space, including the Moon and Other Celestial Bodies."

[104] Despite this success, it is important to note that the climate of the times made it impossible for American women to be astronauts—the Russians sent a female astronaut to space as early as 1963. William Randolph Lovelace II, the NASA official who chose the Mercury 7, simultaneously conducted tests on female aviators to see if they could also pass muster. Thirteen women qualified, perhaps most notably, Geraldyn "Jerrie" Cobb, who held world records in aviation for speed, distance, and altitude scored as well, and even better in some respects, than the men who were selected, including John Glenn and Alan Shepard. However, Congress determined that only military pilots could be candidates for going into space, and all women were barred from becoming astronauts for twenty more years.

a man, one giant leap for mankind." To add to that spirit, the plaque commemorating the Moon landing reads, "Here men from the planet Earth first set foot upon the Moon, July 1969, A.D. We came in peace for all mankind."[105] And this was accompanied by messages from seventy-three heads of state, an Apollo 1 mission patch, and medals from two Russian cosmonauts. In the immediate afterglow of the Moon landing, it became clear that this accomplishment was much more about human achievement than competition.

The whole world watched two men land on the Moon, and the world saw it as everyone's triumph. On a scientific level, Americans may have landed on the Moon alone, but their presence was international in a number of respects. The first video images of the first Moon walk were actually picked up by Australian antennae. The first of six experiments that Armstrong and Aldrin performed on the surface was funded and provided by the Swiss—a solar wind experiment that actually had to be launched even before they planted the US flag on the surface.[106] There was also US–USSR coordination when it came to ensuring that the Russian robotic probe, Luna 15, which was in lunar orbit at the time, would not interfere with the US lift-off from the Moon.[107] And at the conclusion of the mission, hundreds of pounds of Moon rocks were brought back to Earth and distributed all over the world for scientific study.

On a psychological level too, the Moon landing automatically inspired a sense of common humanity. Reflecting back on the experience, Command Module pilot Michael Collins of Apollo 11 described the astronauts' experience upon returning to Earth this way:

After the flight of Apollo 11, the three of us went on a round-the-world trip. Wherever we went people instead of saying "well, you Americans did it," everywhere they said, "We did it. We, humankind, we, the human race, we people did it." And I had never heard of people in different countries use this word, "We, we, we," as emphatically as we were hearing from Europeans, Asians, Africans, wherever we went. It was "we" finally did it. And I thought that was a wonderful thing.[108]

In more ways than one, the Apollo 11 landing was just as important in terms of looking back at Earth and realizing that we are all one civilization as was the

Martha Ackmann, "She Would Have Been the First American Woman in Space. Congress Held Her Back," *Washington Post*, April 25, 2019, https://www.washingtonpost.com/opinions/2019/04/25/she-would-have-been-first-american-woman-space-congress-held-her-back (accessed May 20, 2023).

[105] As cited in Alexander C. T. Geppert, "Space *Personae*: Cosmopolitan Networks of Peripheral Knowledge, 1927–1957," *Journal of Modern European History* 6, 2 (2008): 262, https://doi.org/10.17104/1611-8944.

[106] John Krige, Angelina Long Callahan, and Ashok Maharaj, *NASA in the World: Fifty Years of International Collaboration in Space* (Basingstoke: Palgrave Macmillan, 2013), pp. 3–4.

[107] Luna 15 ended up crashing into the Moon shortly before the US lift-off.

[108] MagellanTV, "In the Shadow of the Moon," directed by David McNab and Christopher Riley, 2007.

achievement itself. The so-called "overview effect" is a well-known, life-altering phenomenon among astronauts.[109] They describe it as a kind of overpowering ecstasy upon first seeing the Earth from space, and with it, the overwhelming realization that we are all one on planet Earth. Indeed, they describe spaceflight as a scientific, but also spiritual, experience.[110] In pre- and post-flight interviews, many of them actually undergo a significant change in values toward human universalism after spaceflight.[111] Similarly, when people on Earth saw the first images of Earthrise from the Moon, the overview effect spread more widely, even if not felt as powerfully as by the astronauts themselves.

Competition over Cooperation

In analyzing the trajectory from the IGY to the Moon landing, international cooperation underpinned competition in diverse and important ways. At the same time, the Spaceflight Idea was front and center in the minds of the key players and reflected the sentiments of society more generally. Interestingly, the idea was, at times, so strongly held that there was even a sense of competition over cooperation itself. Russian and American leaders actually jockeyed to see who could be stronger or lead the way in terms of international cooperation. Perhaps to the annoyance of some in the Kennedy administration, Khrushchev tended to take credit for originating the idea of US–USSR cooperation in space. For example, in a letter to Kennedy in March 1962, Khrushchev wrote that

As far back as the beginning of 1958 the Soviet Government proposed the conclusion of a broad international agreement on cooperation in the field of the study and peaceful use of outer space and took initiative in raising this question for examination by the United Nations. In 1961, immediately after the first space flight by man had been achieved in the Soviet Union, we reaffirmed our readiness to cooperate and unite our efforts with those of other countries, and most of all with your country [. . .] The Soviet Government considers and has always

[109] Frank White, *The Overview Effect: Space Exploration and Human Evolution*, 2nd edn (Reston, VA: American Institute of Aeronautics and Astronautics, 1998).

[110] Former French Astronaut Jean François Clervoy: "Even though you've seen the Earth through movies, pictures, when you look at the Earth with your own eyes changing very fast at the speed of eight kilometers per second, what you see is beautiful. You have tears in your eyes. Even if you are a tough person you can't avoid becoming a child again. And we wish all humankind could experience this view of Earth. You believe that Earth is a spaceship. You can't avoid the comparison between Earth looking as a finite object in front of your eyes, and your own spaceship which is closed with limited resources. All humankind being part of the same unique crew." The Royal Institution, "What does Earth look like from Space? An Astronaut's Perspective," December 8, 2015. https://www.youtube.com/watch?v=WzQSJXY7Zfk

[111] Peter Suedeld, Katya Legkaia, and Jelena Brcic, "Changes in the Hierarchy of Value References Associated with Flying in Space," *Journal of Personality* 78, 5 (October 2010): 1411–1436.

considered the successes of our country in the field of space exploration as achievements not only of the Soviet people but of all mankind.[112]

American officials also wanted to be seen as the first to initiate cooperation. They sometimes even expressed it behind the scenes in strategic terms: "It would be better if we made the offer first. If we made such an offer and it were rejected, and we then won the race, we would gain doubly."[113] So, some of the competitive drive with the USSR, ironically, was actually over who would hold the status of the better cooperator. This was, of course, alongside other motivations that sincerely aimed to reduce the tensions of the Cold War and instead to "open up possible routes of communication, association, and groundwork areas of cooperation which could eventually bear on world peace."[114]

Efforts at cooperation also inadvertently opened up new areas of competition, and there was a sense that cooperation itself might improve the chances of out-competing the other. An example of this seemingly contradictory logic is the 1958 "Preliminary US Policy on Outer Space." This policy stipulated that the United States should be open about providing information on its space programs specifi-cally because it believed that the USSR was in the lead.[115] As Ezell and Ezell put it, "On the one hand, Kennedy genuinely wanted to cooperate in this arena with the Soviets; on the other hand, military and technical superiority had to remain with the United States."[116] Not surprisingly, there was a complex relationship between competition and cooperation at the level of governments. In my analogy to the ultrasocial ecosystem, described in Chapter 4, this type of activity would still be within the bounds of the ultrasocial landscape but closer to the edges. It is also in the very nature of aspirational ideas that they cannot be achieved all at once but, if successful, open up new avenues for the future.

Beyond US–USSR Cooperation

In the context of the Cold War, the most significant breakthroughs in space coop-eration were certainly between the United States and the USSR. But there were

[112] JFK Presidential Archives, "Letter from Khrushchev to Kennedy," JFK Presidential Archives, National Security Files, Countries Series, USSR, Khrushchev Correspondence, Document 43, March 20, 1962. Also available here: https://history.state.gov/historicaldocuments/frus1961-63v06/d43 (accessed July 3, 2023)

[113] Office of the Historian, "381. National Security Planning Policy Paper, 'Implications of Outer Space in the 1970's," Foreign Relations of the United States, 1961–1963, Vol. XXV, Organization of Foreign Policy; Information Policy; United Nations; Scientific Matters, n.d., https://history.state.gov/historicaldocuments/frus1961-63v25/d381 (accessed November 21, 2020).

[114] NASA Manned Spacecraft Center, "Proposal Concerning Space Flight Information Negotiations with the Russians."

[115] Kaysen, "Summary of Foreign Policy Aspects of the US Outer Space Program."

[116] Ezell and Ezell, "Competition Versus Cooperation: 1959–1962."

also continual and robust efforts to bring in participation from a range of other countries. Not only did behind-the-scene discussions in both countries through the 1960s repeatedly mention this goal, but also various American political actors reiterated this loudly and repeatedly in public. For example, Senator Clinton Anderson said on January 15, 1963, "We can give validity to this nation's policy to internationalize space by asserting that the United States will accept offers of support from any nation which can contribute to the space program."[117] And as already mentioned, the 1958 National Aeronautics and Space Act had opened up the stage for NASA to cooperate with other countries. Starting with its creation, NASA quickly became the most committed space actor in the world, so it naturally also became a locus for cooperation.

By June 1962, there were three types of cooperative programs: (1) US launches of foreign payloads for the purposes of scientific experimentation, (2) research that involved both ground and space coordination, and (3) scientist exchanges for training.[118] The number of countries involved increased from there, and in all, around fifty-five countries were involved in these programs. The main stipulations for participation in these programs were that cooperating countries were responsible for the funding of their contributions, and the projects had to result in open dissemination of all data to the international community.[119]

The European Space Research Organization (ESRO) and European Launcher Development Organization (ELDO) were particularly interested in cooperation with the United States, and the latter actively encouraged those European countries involved to use US launchers to put their payloads into orbit for the sake of science.[120] Many European scientists and engineers were welcomed in the United States, where there was mutual sharing of new knowledge about launches and satellites. The Europeans returned home where this new space technology was shared further. The Americans, for their part, were open to technology transfer and signed a series of memorandums of understanding (MOUs) with ESRO to facilitate cooperation.[121]

The urgency of cooperating on a truly multinational level was also strong on the part of the Russians. In March 1962, Khrushchev wrote to Kennedy that

all peoples and all mankind are interested in achieving the object of exploration and peaceful use of outer space, and that the enormous scale of this task, as well

[117] JFK Presidential Archives, "US–USSR Cooperation in Space Research Programs."
[118] Kaysen, "Summary of Foreign Policy Aspects of the US Outer Space Program."
[119] Beyond the UN setting, there were, of course, other international regimes devoted to space—although not exploration—the World Meteorological Organization and the International Telecommunications Union.
[120] Kaysen, "Summary of Foreign Policy Aspects of the US Outer Space Program."
[121] European Space Agency archives; Eligar Sadeh, "Dynamics of International Space Cooperation: Evaluating Missions for Exploring Space and Protecting the Earth," PhD dissertation, Colorado State University, 1999.

as the enormous difficulties which must be overcome, urgently demand broad unification of the scientific, technical, and material capabilities and resources of nations [...] the greater the number of countries making their contribution to this truly complicated endeavor, which involves great expense, the more swiftly will the conquest of space in the interests of all humanity proceed. And this means that equal opportunities should be made available for all countries to participate in international cooperation in this field.[122]

The 1967 creation of Intercosmos, the Soviets' space agency for international cooperation, for example, brought together a number of Eastern European countries, plus Afghanistan, Cuba, Mongolia, Vietnam, India, Syria, France, and Austria to work together on satellite launches.[123] It was also under the direction of Intercosmos that Russian–US cooperation would eventually result in the highly successful Apollo-Soyuz program in the 1970s.

Through all of this discussion at the government level, non-state actors continued to press forward with the Spaceflight Idea, advocating that political leaders see this as a human, rather than nationalist, endeavor. The UN continued to be part of this backdrop. COPUOS had two subcommittees designed to oversee international cooperation in space.[124] And by 1966, the International Astronautical Federation, which had first brought all of the rocket societies together in 1950, had grown further, representing thirty-two countries and fifty rocket societies.[125] At this point, the Spaceflight Movement was no longer comprised mainly of amateur enthusiasts as in the 1920s and was taken more seriously than ever before. A culture of sharing space science across borders had solidified at the non-state level, helping to amplify the Spaceflight Idea and strengthening space diplomacy.

In 1968, not long before Apollo 11 and the Moon landing, specific discussion on the creation of an orbital space station took place at NASA. NASA scientists drafted detailed proposals outlining the necessity and benefit of having a permanent presence in orbit.[126] Chief among the rationales was the need to conduct experiments in space to assess the human capacity to be in space on longer missions. By 1969, international cooperation on the space station came into the picture. The concern was that in order to get it approved, it would have to be a "de-militarized" project and contribute to State Department goals of internationalizing space rather than under the aegis of the Defense Department, which did not find the space

[122] JFK Presidential Archives, "Letter from Khrushchev to Kennedy."
[123] Office of Technology Assessment, "International Cooperation and Competition in Civilian Space Activities" (Washington, DC: U.S. Congress, Office of Technology Assessment, OTA-ISC-239, July 1985) p. 42. https://ota.fas.org/reports/8513.pdf
[124] For more on the negotiations surrounding UN involvement in space, see Michael J. Peterson, International Regimes for the Final Frontier (New York: State University of New York Press, 2005).
[125] Geppert, "Space Personae," p. 282.
[126] NASA, "Post Apollo Earth Orbital Manned Space Flight Program Options to Post Apollo Advisory Group," NASA Archives, Folder 9164, Space Station 1968–1969, February 15, 1968.

station to be a high priority.[127] In November 1969, NASA Administrator T. O. Paine sent a letter to the president after a three-day trip to Germany, France, and the United Kingdom, as well as a conference held in Washington DC with forty-three representatives from Europe, expressing their strong interest in international cooperation on the space shuttle and space station programs. Paine also noted that he would be going to Canada, Australia, and Japan to extend similar offers of international participation.[128] The stage was set for the next major phase in international cooperation: a permanent presence in space. And once more, it tilted strongly toward the Spaceflight Idea in the face of military interest.

Despite the Cold War and the numerous points at which the USSR and the United States seemed to be at the brink of actual war, the superpowers treated space as a categorically different domain of activity. Cooperation was a serious aim, with space diplomacy persisting even during some of the toughest moments during these years. The period from 1957 to 1969 was the height of the Cold War, when tensions ran highest. As such, it was a hard test for the expression of ultrasociality and pursuit of international cooperation, especially between the United States and the USSR. To be sure, competition during the Space Race was certainly present. However, the main actors involved kept returning to the original Spaceflight Idea—that space should be a peaceful domain for all of humankind. At the end of the day, it was a productive kind of competition, and one that was grounded in cooperation. In addition, the Space Race both reflected and encouraged public interest in space, it justified unprecedented levels of government spending on space, and it created a kind of sportsmanship vis-à-vis space achievements. As a result, the various advancements in space technology were achieved in record time, and the end of the Space Race—the Moon landing itself—had an important impact in terms of politics, culture, and society. It brought people together across the entire planet, giving them a powerful sense of what it meant to truly be one species. The conflicts of the day paled in comparison, and the power of possibility soared.

[127] Alfred Eggers, "The Space Station and International Collaboration," NASA Archives, Folder 9164, Space Station 1968–1969, March 17, 1969.
[128] NASA Archives, "Letter from T. O. Paine to the President," NASA Archives, File 9165, Space Station 1968–1989, November 7, 1969.

10

A Permanent Presence in Space …
and Beyond

Space Cooperation Intensifies

Space diplomacy in the 1960s paved the way for a stronger expression of the Space-flight Idea at the policy, governmental, and scientific levels from the 1970s to the 1990s. American scientists had drafted detailed proposals outlining the necessity and benefit of having a permanent presence in orbit for some years, and by 1969, international discussions between US space experts and their German, French, British, Canadian, Japanese, and Australian counterparts were underway.[129] The explicit goal was to cooperate in building an international orbital space station.[130] This would allow for more scientific experiments and a better understanding of what it would take for humans to be able to travel much further than the Moon. Of course, all of this would eventually culminate in the establishment of the International Space Station (ISS).[131]

The question for the US government was how to justify building the orbital station in collaboration with other countries, given how far ahead the United States was in light of the Apollo program. The rationale National Aeronautics and Space Administration (NASA) personnel put forward was an explicit reiteration of the Spaceflight Idea: they emphasized the benefits of working together and seeing this as an endeavor for all of humankind. As NASA Assistant Administrator Alfred Eggers wrote in a memo,

> it is useful to note that the multi-man nature of the space station tends to make it uniquely suited to a multi-national operation. Indeed, it would be ideally suited to both the symbolic and actual pooling of resources on an international scale for forging ahead in space for the common good and inspiration of all men on earth. Apollo has dramatically demonstrated the degree to which "man on earth" enthusiastically relates to "man in space," and the Saturn V provides the capability for putting men of many nationalities in space.[132]

[129] Space Station and International Collaboration, "Memorandum from Dr. Alfred Eggers to Dr. Newell," NASA HQ, Folder 9164, March 17, 1969.
[130] NASA Archives, "Letter from T. O. Paine to the President," NASA Archives, File 9165, Space Station 1968–1989, November 7, 1969.
[131] NASA HQ, "Space Station Documentation (1968–69)," NASA HQ Archives, File 9164.
[132] Space Station and International Collaboration, "Memorandum from Dr. Alfred Eggers to Dr. Newell," p. 2.

International Cooperation Against All Odds. Mai'a K. Davis Cross, Oxford University Press. © Mai'a K. Davis Cross (2024).
DOI: 10.1093/oso/9780192873903.003.0011

After the success and impact of Apollo 11, the NASA Administrator really advo-cated for expanding the international dimension of the US space program. By 1970, Americans were openly discussing the desirability of making international cooperation the main approach to space, and by the mid-70s, were regularly in talks with other countries about formally making this a reality.[133] Each step of the way, from the 1970s to the 1990s, missions became increasingly multinational. And with each achievement, future opportunities emerged for more cooperative pro-grams, each more ambitious than the last, demonstrating the continued impact of the Spaceflight Movement.

First, there was *Spacelab*, a US–European project that started on September 24, 1973. Collaboration between the United States and Europe on space had begun with the 1964 establishment of the European Space Research Organiza-tion (ESRO), Europe's answer to NASA, but a deeper program for US–European cooperation in space was first proposed as part of Nixon's Space Task Group. The articulated goal was to create a reusable space transportation system that would attract "international involvement and participation on a broad basis."[134] While other countries were invited (Canada, Australia, and Japan), it ended up being a NASA–ESRO agreement. ESRO countries—West Germany, the United King-dom, France, Switzerland, the Netherlands, Belgium Italy, Denmark, and Spain—covered the cost of Spacelab ($300–400 million), while the United States provided the Space Shuttle. The hardware was structured in such a way that Spacelab was removable from the shuttle and could be composed in different ways, depend-ing on the experiments involved. After the end of the Apollo program, the United States ramped up its efforts to cooperate with European countries even further.[135]

Next, there was the July 1975 joint US–USSR *Apollo-Soyuz Test Project*, which achieved the capacity to perform space rescues with the creation of a compatible docking system. The two countries invested $150 billion in the project. In many respects, the USSR–US geopolitical relationship was at a low point in the early 1970s; however, space experts and space diplomats forged ahead to find new ways of performing joint ventures in space in spite of this. For the Apollo-Soyuz mission, the two countries were able to put aside differences and cooperate in a range of areas,[136] and this opened the door for broader sharing of information. Not slowing down, the momentum behind US–USSR cooperation continued with the planned Shuttle-Salyut mission to fly the US space shuttle to the Russian Salyut station, although this was ultimately shelved in favor of Shuttle-Mir, largely because, by that time, the USSR was in the midst of dissolution.

---

[133] NASA HQ, "Space Station Documentation (1968–69)."
[134] NASA, "Europe to Build Spacelab for U.S. Reusable Space Shuttle," NASA News Release No. 73-191, NASA HQ, Folder 8864, September 24, 1973.
[135] ESA (European Space Agency), "Cooperation between Europe and the United States in the Space Field," ESA Archives, File 8011, April 29, 1981.
[136] Hannah Kohler, "The Eagle and the Hare: U.S.–Chinese Relations, the Wolf Amendment, and the Future of International Cooperation in Space," *Georgetown Law Journal* 103, 4: 1148.

In the mid-1990s, the *Shuttle-Mir* project rested on such strong cooperation that it was hailed as a détente in space, solidifying the sense that the Space Race really was a thing of the past. It involved eleven missions of the US space shuttles docking on the Russian space station Mir for astronauts to learn from cosmonauts about long-duration expeditions in space. Even while this was playing out, there were ongoing discussions and planning for the eventual creation of a permanent international space station.

Formal discussions for the *International Space Station* itself began as far back as May 1977,[137] although the idea was floated even earlier, with an "eyes-only" memo circulated in June 1974.[138] Two months later, the NASA Administrator also brought it up in a staff meeting.[139] The eventual break-up of the USSR in the early 1990s made these space plans even easier, cooperation intensified, and the two countries worked together to launch the first stage of the ISS together in 1998. Since that year, humans have maintained a permanent presence in space, and it has been entirely under the umbrella of a truly international undertaking. While only five major space agencies—NASA (United States), Roscosmos (Russia), the Japan Aerospace Exploration Agency (JAXA), the European Space Agency (ESA), and the Canadian Space Agency (CSA)—technically "own" the ISS, more than 100 countries have benefitted from it through scientific experiments, and more than 240 astronauts or cosmonauts from 19 different countries have spent time on board.

Indeed, the ISS is acknowledged as "the largest civil cooperation programme in history,"[140] and its stated goal is very much in line with the Spaceflight Idea: a "merging of different cultures and techniques reinforcing human communication capabilities across borders and language barriers."[141] The activities, achievements, and operations of the International Space Station would not have been possible without a deep commitment to a common endeavor.[142] As Astronaut Alexander Gerst put it in a 2018 phone call from the ISS to the International Astronautical Congress (IAC),

I'm in the European module, but that is docked to an American module. Behind that is the Japanese module. Then there's another US module, and then there's

[137] NASA HQ, "U.S. and Russia Announce Talks on Operating Space Station in '80s," *New York Times*, May 5, 1977, NASA HQ Archives, p. A 15.
[138] NASA HQ, File 15523.
[139] David J. Shayler, "The Proposed USSR Salyut and US Shuttle Docking Mission Circa 1981," presented at the 6th Soviet Space Symposium, British Interplanetary Society, Headquarters, London, June 1, 1991, p. 7.
[140] European Space Agency Manned Space Programme, "Draft Programme Proposal on the European Participation in the ISSA," ES/PB-MS(94)60, Paris, ESA Archives, ESA File 18,499, December 22, 1994, p. 1.
[141] European Space Agency Manned Space Programme, "Draft Programme Proposal on the European Participation in the ISSA," p. 2.
[142] Kohler, "The Eagle and the Hare."

a Russia module, and so on. We live in this amazing machine that was built by around 100,000 people. So far, we have conducted around 3,000 experiments in the lifetime of the ISS, and experimenters from more than 100 different countries participated in scientific experiments up here. That means that more than 100 nations have benefitted from the ISS. And it is obvious that this is a machine— some say it's the most complex machine that humanity has ever built—no single nation could have done that alone. It would be next to impossible to do that. By putting our international discrepancies aside and focusing on what unites us, our common visions, putting that together, enabled us to put together this machine. And if you think about it, those modules that we stuck together in space they were never stuck together on earth. They were never stuck together on earth [...] Some said it was not possible. Well, here we are, and that is a sign of what international cooperation can do [...] International cooperation will be the key for getting further out into space.[143]

Indeed, the ISS may be one of the highest expressions of ultrasociality that humans have carried out, given the immense expense of the project, the unprecedented scientific challenge of it, the sheer scale of it, and the diverse range of countries involved.

Spacelab, Apollo-Soyuz, Shuttle-Mir, and the ISS are just some of the most high-profile missions. Other cooperative projects have been numerous, such as search-and-rescue agreements, the High Energy Astrophysics Observatory-3 (HEAO-3) (French–Danish–US), SMM Space Ltd (Dutch, German, UK, US), Landsat and satellite cooperation with China, seventeen areas of US–Japan cooperation, and regular exchanges of data with the USSR.[144] This cooperation has been facilitated to a significant extent by the Inter-Agency Consultative Group, which was founded in 1981 by the space agencies of Japan, Europe, the United States, and Russia with these common goals in mind. Altogether, these represent major investments and long-term loyalty to a common cause, one that otherwise might have taken a more conflictual and weaponized path but, instead, has been anchored in cooperation for the betterment of humankind.

At the same time, after the first Moon landing and the end of the so-called Space Race, public attention to space exploration had waned and the space-flight idea became mainly the purview of those working in this area. Not unlike the cases of European federalism and the non-use of nuclear weapons, when movements succeed in achieving their initial aspirational ideas through tangible changes in governmental policies or approaches, their overt efforts may fade from public attention (i.e., nuclear weapons) or go through more transactional period

[143] Participant observation, International Astronautical Congress, Bremen, Germany, October 2018.
[144] ESA, "Statement of Kenneth S. Pedersen, Director of International Affairs, NASA, before the Subcommittee on Science, Technology and Space of the Committee on Commerce, Science and Transportation, US Senate," ESA Archives, File 8011.

(i.e., European Union integration), especially in the absence of major crises. Having succeeded in pushing for the Spaceflight Idea, the movement itself lost some energy from the 1970s to the 2000s. International cooperation clearly continued in a more incremental way but without the achievement of some of the more transformational goals such as establishing a permanent presence on the Moon or landing humans on Mars. This is likely about to change, with a massive growth in the number of actors involved in space, including a full range of private actors and the highly anticipated return to the Moon.

Space Race 2.0?

Of the over seventy countries that now have active and growing space programs, fourteen have launch capabilities. Humans are going back to the moon and building a permanent Lunar Gateway. Infrastructure on or near the Moon will enable manned trips to Mars in a decade or so. All of this demonstrates humanity's strong commitment to space exploration. These are not simply governmental plans; the impetus comes from many areas of society, the scientific community, and the private sector. Indeed, the number of private space companies, working on a whole range of new technologies, far exceeds the handful of space tourism and rocket design companies that have become household names, such as Blue Origin, Virgin Galactic, and SpaceX. With the rapid growth in the size of the space economy, which will likely rise to over US$1 trillion by 2040,[145] space is becoming a new frontier for human activity.

Despite all of this, in the first two decades of the twenty-first century, there has been much talk of the start of a new Space Race (understood in a security dilemma sense), often referred to as Space Race 2.0. In this vein, China and India have tested their ability to explode satellites in space (in 2007 and 2018, respectively). And several countries—China, Russia, Japan, the United States, and possibly soon, India—have established special space forces within their national militaries. In 2018, US president Donald Trump went so far as to say that, "Space is a warfighting domain, just like the land, air, and sea."[146] American military officials during the Trump administration also publicly promoted the slogan, "Always the predator, never the prey" to justify the creation of the US Space Force as the newest branch of the military.[147] In 2019, Ambassador Li Song, Deputy PermRep of China to the United Nations (UN) in Geneva, said that "a superpower," by which he

[145] "The Space Report, "Economy," https://www.thespacereport.org/topics/economy/ (accessed July 3, 2023); Morgan Stanley, "The Space Economy's Next Giant Leap," https://www.morganstanley.com/Themes/global-space-economy (accessed July 3, 2023).

[146] Donald Trump, "Speech," Miramar Marine Corps Air Station, March 12, 2018.

[147] Theresa Hitchens, "Experts Warn Space Force Rhetoric Risks Backfiring," Breaking Defense, May 28, 2019, https://breakingdefense.com/2019/05/experts-warn-space-force-rhetoric-risks-backfiring (accessed May 20, 2023).

clearly meant the United States, had explicitly defined space as a war domain, and this constituted an imminent threat. Song argued that "if we still insist that there is no arms race, we are either selectively blind or lacking political will."[148] These actions and rhetoric have led some to argue that the Spaceflight Idea is on the decline and we are now on the cusp of Space Race 2.0.

I would argue that the legacy of the misperceptions surrounding the 1960s Space Race has had an impact on how political leaders understand it today. But if there is a lesson from examining the original Space Race with an ultrasocial approach, it is that aggressive rhetoric does not necessarily mean aggressive action. On the contrary, despite militarist and combative words regarding space in the 1960s, I have shown how the original Space Race actually featured strong efforts at cooperation alongside a widespread belief in space as a fundamentally peaceful domain for all of humankind. In the twenty-first century, despite occasional "space is the next battlefield" rhetoric, the international community of space experts still holds dearly the original Spaceflight Idea. As Stephen Hawking put it in 2016, "Space exploration has already been a great unifier, we seem able to cooperate between nations in space in a way we can only envy on Earth."[149] While we know that militaries around the world have long been using satellites to support their operations, space itself is still *not* weaponized. There is no arms race in space, no weapons in space that target Earth, no conflict between commercial actors, and no space-based missile interceptors.[150] This is significant in light of ongoing military attention to using space as a war domain. Despite this, no country or non-state actor has plans to build war-fighting spaceships or to immediately place weapons in space. Space Force experts, including some in the United States, largely view their creation as a logistical issue, a more efficient means of justifying a dedicated space budget should the need arise, not a step toward weaponizing space.[151]

Rather than Space Race 2.0, we should recognize that the 2020s is more accurately defined as the beginning of a new Space Age, very much in line with the hopes and dreams of those who carry on the legacy of the Spaceflight Movement today. The first phase of the movement brought the United States and USSR together, and the question is whether now—with so many new space actors on the scene—the Spaceflight Idea can continue to energize a truly global sphere of activity. Political leaders still lead the charge when it comes to space because of the sheer level of investment required, and it will take ongoing pressure from the Spaceflight Movement to ensure that they uphold the idea that space is for all of

---

[148] Participant observation, UN Space Security conference, 2019.

[149] Mark Wall, "Stephen Hawking Wants to Ride Virgin Galactic's New Passenger Spaceship," *Space.com*, February 20, 2016, https://www.space.com/31993-stephen-hawking-virgin-galactic-spaceshiptwo-unity.html (accessed May 21, 2023).

[150] Maïa K. Davis Cross, "The Social Construction of the Space Race: Then and Now," *International Affairs* 95, 6 (November 2019): 1403–1421, https://doi.org/10.1093/ia/iiz190.

[151] Participant observation, UN Space Security conference, 2019.

humankind. The pull of ultrasociality in the domain of space remains strong. At the 2018 and 2019 International Astronautical Congress, for example, every plenary speaker emphasized the indispensable nature of international cooperation and space as a peaceful realm of international activity, echoing the narrative from the rocket societies of a century ago.[152] The overarching message in the space community still is that international cooperation is indispensable to going further into space.[153] Sylvain Laporte, Canadian Space Agency President, said, "we all know how important it is to collaborate internationally in order to have success in space." And in the words of former NASA Administrator Jim Bridenstine,

> We can't do what we do without the support of our international partners [. . .] There are more space agencies on the planet today than ever before [. . .] that means we have been able to do more today that we have ever before [. . .] and collaboration and cooperation is the way to get it done.

The Indian Space Agency representative said, "Unless everyone comes together, [going further into space] won't be possible." The common belief, strongly shared by members of the space community, is that space exploration must be a *global* effort or there will be no effort at all. Some have even floated the more aspirational idea of a global space agency.

For its part, the UN Committee on the Peaceful Uses of Outer Space now has eighty-seven member states, and a growing number of non-governmental organizations (NGOs) and intergovernmental organizations (IGOs) as official observers, making it one of the biggest UN committees in existence. Over sixty countries or governmental organizations, as well as many private and scientific actors, have satellites in space.[154] Seventeen countries have official space programs. This amounts to around 1,700 active satellites in addition to tens of thousands of other manmade objects orbiting Earth. The effort to work together in space is very clearly present, and whether or not *all* spacefaring governments (Russia, India, the United States, and others) engage in common projects together, cooperation already includes a whole host of state and non-state, private, and multinational actors. At the same time, sometimes, the pull of ultrasociality is not enough to resolve political disagreements, as discussed in Chapter 4.

In this respect, a notable outlier in the landscape of international space cooperation is China. The country has engaged in space espionage, its scientists have stolen information from NASA repeatedly, and the country is responsible for a significant space debris field as a result of its 2007 anti-satellite test. China's behavior is the exception rather than the rule, and the country is clearly regarded as in

---

[152] Participant observation, IAC, 2018. Quotes in this paragraph are from this event.
[153] Participant observation, IAC, 2018 and 2019.
[154] Frank A. Rose, "Safeguarding the Heavens: The United States and the Future of Norms of Behavior in Outer Space," Brookings Policy Brief, June 2018.

violation of widely shared international norms. With the 2011 Wolf Amendment, the US Congress prohibited NASA from cooperating with China in any way that would result in the transfer of data related to military or economic technology or that would enable China to further violate human rights. The United States, under the Obama administration, made advancements in communicating and promising to cooperate more in space, but what little progress was made quickly unraveled under the Trump administration.

Nevertheless, even Chinese space experts still echo the Spaceflight Idea. Representatives of the Chinese space program at the IAC said that any UN member state or non-state actor (universities, research institutes, private companies) can apply to conduct experiments through the Chinese Space Station, which the country completed in 2023. Even with China's outsider status, there are many cross-cutting and multi-organizational cooperative initiatives that do involve China. For example, Israel cooperates with everyone, including China, as does the ESA. For now, having China as a full participant in the ultrasocial landscape of the new Space Age is still aspirational, but the fact that its space agency pursues a cooperative approach is a sign that more is possible.

Besides China, there are also some in society today who regard space exploration with scorn. They hold the misconception that the billions of dollars invested in space would be better spent on direct alleviation of poverty or curing diseases. However, even a slightly deeper look at the benefits of space, beyond the hope and inspiration it provides, shows very clearly that space benefits society on Earth directly and in countless ways, including the very realms of poverty alleviation and curing disease.[155] Space experts often cite the statistic that for every dollar spent on space, the return on investment is somewhere between 7 and 14 dollars.

In 2005, the ESA compiled dozens of responses from a diverse pool of people to reflect on the impact that human engagement with space has on society. The result of this compilation was the emergence of key understandings about space, all of which resonate with our ultrasocial nature as a species. First and foremost, the "one world perspective," which emerged when Apollo 8 took the first picture of the Earthrise, enables humans to see each other as coming from a single planet, from the whole Earth, rather than from small territories with boundaries. Second, space also provides the ability to dream about new frontiers, which, on a practical level, fuels science and careers. Third, it has developed new knowledge, especially with respect to technology, computers, and health. Fourth, satellites provide invaluable information on the Earth itself and have led to cooperation among nations and communication. In short, if anything, the space activities that have noticeably picked up in the twenty-first century point to a newly energized twenty-first-century Space Age rather than a Space Race 2.0.

---

[155] ESA (co-sponsored by the IAA), *The Impact of Space Activities upon Society* (Paris: ESA/IAA, 2005).

The Future and On to Mars

NASA's new Artemis program has garnered much attention as a herald of the new Space Age. It will take astronauts back to the Moon around 2025 as a first step. The Orion spacecraft will then be used for multiple launches to the Moon and beyond, creating the capacity for humans to stay on the Moon permanently, and establishing the movable Lunar Gateway in orbit around the Moon. In turn, the gateway will serve as a launching point for manned missions to other places, especially Mars. Even though NASA is leading the charge, Artemis has been explicitly international from the start. Most prominently, the ESA has provided Ariane, the heavy-lift launch vehicle, and will also contribute an aspect of the Gateway's habitation, lunar communications, and a means to refuel, all before 2030. Japan will contribute docking ports to the Gateway, and many other international collaborators are expected to follow. Moreover, the Gateway is open to all who want to contribute, with plans openly available so that others can build upon the same compatibilities.

NASA is building a coalition of dozens of allied countries from across the world through the Artemis Accords, which clearly echo the core values of the Spaceflight Idea. The goal behind the Artemis Accords is to continue to expand the signatories, and from there, agree upon shared, multinational understandings of best practices and standards in space exploration. If there is one message that the former NASA Administrator Jim Bridenstine, has conveyed at every opportunity at the IAC, it is that the United States cannot do anything in space without its international partners—which is a very different message than the one proponents of the new Space Force articulate with little to back up their assertions.[156]

Besides these near-term plans to return to the Moon, the future of space and human spaceflight is starting to lean more heavily toward non-governmental actors and space tourism, which is good news for those who would belong to the Spaceflight Movement today. Access to space is far more open than it once was, although the development of new technology is still necessary if it is going to be made affordable. Private companies began to develop independent space capabilities in the 1970s in the West, and in other countries in the 1980s and 1990s.[157] In the twenty-first century, these companies and new start-ups make up a significant portion of the global space economy. In 2019, 80% of the world's space economy was the result of commercial entities operating in space.[158] Many new

---

[156] Participant observation, IAC 2018 and 2019.
[157] M. J. Peterson, *International Regimes for the Final Frontier* (New York: State University of New York Press, 2005), p. 18.
[158] The Space Report, "Economy," https://www.thespacereport.org/topics/economy/ (accessed July 3, 2023).

and different types of space actors are entering the scene.[159] Lockheed, Boeing, SpaceX, Blue Origin, and Virgin Galactic are prominent among them, but there are literally hundreds of smaller start-ups that are producing everything from micro-satellites, to space debris removal solutions, to coffee makers that will work in space. They regularly receive government contracts, as SpaceX did for the Crew Dragon to take astronauts to the ISS, and they target private customers with a range of technologies and ways to access the benefits of space.

The increasing presence of non-state actors has proven to be helpful in terms of attracting funding for all sorts of ventures and re-engaging public interest in space. Even back in 1984, Erik Quistgaard, Director General of the ESA at the time, noticed that, "It has proved increasingly difficult to persuade govern-ments to finance space science when other apparently more immediate interests compete for limited monies."[160] Thus, the commercial side of space exploration is now crucial for its viability. Several of these non-state entities are working rapidly on developing various technologies that will enable regular travel to Mars and allow people to eventually settle there, a dream of the original Spaceflight Movement.

One of the key challenges for these non-state entities, and one they are deter-mined to overcome, is the problem of cost. While putting people on Mars for the long term seemed pretty far-fetched just a few years ago, it has rapidly entered the realm of possibility. Much of this has to do with the technological advancements achieved as space actors try to reduce the cost of space travel. Perhaps most promi-nently, in 2016, Elon Musk, the head of SpaceX, gave a speech at the annual IAC mapping out the precise steps required to make regular travel to Mars a reality. One solution to the cost problem was the creation of a reusable launch system, which he successfully created and used for the first time in March 2017. Both Blue Origin and SpaceX pursued this goal, and now, thanks to their work, the era of single-use rockets is over. The ability to land rockets back on Earth represents one of the greatest advancements in spaceflight in decades. In reaction to this, Ama-zon CEO Jeff Bezos, who is also the founder of Blue Origin, declared that we are entering a "golden age of space exploration."[161]

Leading experts in space have also long argued that settling on Mars will only be possible with long-term international cooperation. Despite being relative new-comers to space, private companies are no exception to the drive to work through international cooperation. As Mark Mulqueen, former space station program

[159] Alexander MacDonald, *The Long Space Age: The Economic Origins of Space Exploration from Colonial America to the Cold War* (New Haven, CT: Yale University Press, 2017).

[160] Norman Longdon and Duc Guyenne (eds), *Twenty Years of European Cooperation in Space: An ESA Report, '64–'84* (Paris: European Space Agency, 1984), p. 10.

[161] Calla Cofield, "Spaceflight Is Entering a New Golden Age, Says Blue Origin Founder Jeff Bezos," *Space.com*, November 25, 2015, https://www.space.com/31214-spaceflight-golden-age-jeff-bezos.html (accessed May 20, 2023).

manager at Boeing said at the IAC, "International cooperation [regarding] space goes back thousands of years," and as we look to the future, the Moon, and Mars, international cooperation will continue to be extremely important. Evgeny Mikrin, General Designer at the Russian company RSC Energia, praising the benefits of cooperation in the ISS, said:

> Being integrated, we have achieved a very synergistic effect. None of our part-
> ners would have been able to have made this achievement by themselves. This
> nice experience cannot be lost. We have to move together, working together. We
> consider and take into account the problems that arise when we work together.
> When we discuss future progress of deep space missions, we have already dealt
> with problems that have been solved on the ISS.

Private companies and space agencies alike also regularly emphasize the benefits to Earth from space research and exploration. For example, treatments for osteo-porosis, multiple sclerosis, and cancer, among others, and data for maximizing crop efficiency have all been studied in space. The ability to widen the benefits, understandings, and engagement with space among an increasingly diverse swath of society has really ignited renewed interest in space. In 2013, when Dutch busi-nessman Bas Lansdorp launched a call for volunteers to live on Mars through the British–Swiss organization Mars One, he quickly received over 200,000 applica-tions and much media coverage.[162] The hundred people finally selected to colonize Mars, after multiple rounds of review, were treated as minor celebrities. In 2019, beset with financial and technological difficulties, Mars One declared bankruptcy, but the fascination over the possibility of living on other planets, despite the risks, is still illustrative.[163]

Aspiration to achieve transformational goals, even if we do not yet have the capacity to reach them, is a mainstay of powerful, influential ideas. If such ideas also tap into our ultrasocial nature, they hold even more power to captivate and inspire. The main, shared space activity for over two decades has been the ISS, but it is reaching the end of its intended lifespan. Plans are not yet solidified on how to replace it, and this will be the next big test for the Spaceflight Idea in the near term. While the completion of the Chinese Space Station is impressive, although only around one-third the size of the ISS, Chinese officials still view it as primar-ily a national project. This has been met with skepticism and consternation in the space community, a sign that long-standing standards of behavior in space still

---

[162] Kate Andrews, "Over 200,000 People Apply to Live on Mars," *De Zeen*, September 11, 2003, https://www.dezeen.com/2013/09/11/over-200000-people-apply-to-live-on-mars (accessed May 20, 2023).

[163] Jonathan O'Callaghan, "Goodbye Mars One, The Fake Mission to Mars That Fooled the World," *Forbes*, February 11, 2019, https://www.forbes.com/sites/jonathanocallaghan/2019/02/11/goodbye-mars-one-the-fake-mission-to-mars-that-fooled-the-world/?sh=27c507022af5 (accessed May 20, 2023).

hold. If the ISS is retired without a replacement in 2030, it would be the first time in decades that humans have not had a continual presence in space. Whether there is a new version of the ISS or all efforts focus on the future Lunar Gateway, the spirit of the ISS as a truly international endeavor is incredibly important to the longevity of the Spaceflight Idea as we look to the future.

Conclusion to Part III

The Spaceflight Movement began in the 1920s and continues to exist today, held together for a hundred years by a shared idea in the power of possibility and the peaceful use of space for all of humankind. Even during the most tense international moments, key space actors have maintained communication and cooperation in a kind of ongoing space diplomacy.[164] Human engagement with outer space shows how the draw of an idea, grounded in the ultrasocial landscape, has pulled people and countries together, even during periods of international conflict. It demonstrates the staying power of a cooperative idea, especially one that taps into our collective imagination. The impact of the Spaceflight Idea emerged out of the actions of non-state actors, including the regular public, and at key moments, permeated into the highest levels of governments.

Despite the rush for American astronauts to get to the Moon before the end of the 1960s, the landing itself was far more of a collective human achievement than may have at first been anticipated. Moreover, the various and wide-ranging efforts at space diplomacy throughout the 1960s made possible the numerous tangible outcomes in the 1970s through to the 1990s. Some of the biggest projects included Spacelab, Apollo-Soyuz, Shuttle-Mir, and the International Space Station (ISS), but there were many more. Indeed, space historian John Krige estimates that since 1960, the National Aeronautics and Space Administration (NASA) has cooperated with other countries on around 4,000 different space projects.[165] The same could be said of the USSR, now Russia, with Russian scientists continually working with their counterparts from other countries and, more often than not, aiming for common goals in space. During this period, many other countries around the world formed fledgling space programs, oftentimes specifically to engage in exciting new initiatives in space cooperation.

Over the past hundred years, the Spaceflight Idea has been consistently important in influencing how humans have behaved vis-à-vis space. The idea of exploring and understanding space has clearly been a fundamentally human, rather than purely nationalistic, endeavor. Public enthusiasm for the adventure of space, and celebration of any milestone as a *human* accomplishment, has always been evident.

---

[164] Mai'a K. Davis Cross and Saadia Pekkanen (eds), "Space Diplomacy," *The Hague Journal of Diplomacy,* Special Issue, 18, 2-3 (2023). https://brill.com/view/journals/hjd/18/2-3/hjd.18.issue-2-3.xml (accessed July 4, 2023).

[165] John Krige, Angelina Long Callahan, and Ashok Maharaj, *NASA in the World: Fifty Years of International Collaboration in Space* (Basingstoke: Palgrove, 2013), p. 6.

Indeed, the psychological impact of seeing humans in outer space should not be discounted. Even as it has become far easier to send robots or probes into space, since the moon-landing images spread across the globe, society has especially valued *manned* exploration. In 1986, for example, just after the first space shuttle disaster, 80% of Americans polled still thought that the space program should be manned. And in 1988, 49% (versus just 15% opposed) thought that astronauts and cosmonauts should land on Mars together.[166]

Although non-state actors, including the public, were not always successful at getting states to prioritize the most ambitious of their cooperative goals, they have clearly been influential in promoting space exploration as a peaceful and cooperative endeavor. And as we head into the future of space exploration over the next decade or so, the most ambitious members of the original Spaceflight Movement may finally see their goal of colonizing other planets reach fruition in the 2030s. Resolving ongoing tensions between the United States, Russia, and China may ultimately not be possible, but this does not necessarily detract from ultrasociality. Russia and China are two countries that clearly exist outside of the ultrasocial landscape, with their human rights abuses and aggression toward neighbors. It will be up to them to prove that they can operate within the global space community without detracting from spaceflight's ultrasocial goals.

Standard international relations accounts gravitate toward theories of competition and conflict, and as a result, if space exploration is addressed at all, it is assumed to be simply part and parcel of the Cold War. Of course, there are numerous examples of competition and conflict that require a range of theories to understand them. However, by looking at these events and ideas through the lens of human ultrasociality, I seek to shine light on the underlying context present throughout this period. I have argued that space has been about the common identity of humans as a species and the fact that we are all traveling through space on planet Earth together, a "pale blue dot" in a vast universe.[167] While this may sound like an idealistic vision, it is this vision that has been behind much of the progress toward the achievements of new goals in space over the past hundred years. Indeed, it is precisely because of the idealism, aspiration, and optimism—the ability to fulfill our ultrasocial drive—that the Spaceflight Idea has been consistently championed all over the world. With a growing diversity of actors involved, and the immense unexplored depths of the cosmos, the resilience of the human Spaceflight Idea has anchored us all in the dream of scientific discovery, cooperation, and the power of possibility.

---

[166] NASA HQ, "Public Opinions and NASA 1969–1971," NASA HQ Archives, File 6717.
[167] Carl Sagan, "Pale Blue Dot," Speech, Cornell University, 1994.

PART IV
NUCLEAR WEAPONS

At the height of the nuclear arms race in 1986, the United States and the Soviet Union together had more than 60,000 nuclear weapons. Today, the global arsenal of nuclear weapons, now spread across 9 countries, is 13,000.[1] Despite these large numbers, the first and only time nuclear weapons have been used is when the United States bombed Hiroshima and Nagasaki at the end of the Second World War in August 1945. Given that many world leaders, at various junctures, have since supported the further development, stockpiling, and even potential use of nuclear weapons, this perfect track record of non-use for almost eighty years is puzzling. An ultrasocial lens, however, helps to uncover some of the major driving forces behind this.

Much has been written and debated about the role and consequences of nuclear weapons in our world. Zeroing in on the question of why these weapons have not been used since 1945, the dominant explanation amongst international relations scholars has been *deterrence*;[2] that is, building up a nuclear arsenal allows a state to threaten nuclear counterstrikes, thus dissuading other countries from attacking with nuclear weapons in the first place.[3] More recent literature has refined this

---

[1] These countries are Russia, the United States, China, France, the United Kingdom, Pakistan, India, Israel, and North Korea. At the height of the nuclear arms race, the USSR had more than 40,000 nuclear weapons and the United States had 23,000. World Population Review, "Nuclear Weapons by Country 2022," *World Population Review*, 2022, https://worldpopulationreview.com/country-rankings/nuclear-weapons-by-country (accessed November 29, 2022); Bulletin of the Atomic Scientists, "Nuclear Notebook," *Bulletin of the Atomic Scientists*, 2022, https://thebulletin.org/nuclear-notebook (accessed November 29, 2022).

[2] The earliest nuclear arms control theorists worked from the assumption that competition over nuclear weapons was purely about military strategy, and this tradition continued. See Jennifer Sims, "The Historiography of Arms Control," in *Icarus Restrained: An Intellectual History of Nuclear Arms Control, 1945–1960* (Boulder, CO: Westview Press, 1990), pp. 9–14.

[3] Robert Jervis, *The Meaning of the Nuclear Revolution* (Ithaca, NY: Cornell University Press, 1989); Charles L. Glaser, "Why Do Strategists Disagree about the Requirements of Strategic Nuclear Deterrence?," in *Nuclear Arguments: Understanding the Strategic Nuclear Arms and Arms Control Debates*, ed. Lynn Eden and Steven E. Miller (Ithaca: Cornell University Press, 1989), pp. 109–171; Michael Mandelbaum, *The Nuclear Revolution: International Politics before and after Hiroshima* (Cambridge: Cambridge University Press, 1981); James J. Wirtz, "How Does Nuclear Deterrence Differ from Conventional Deterrence?," *Strategic Studies Quarterly* 12, 4 (2018): 58–75; Kenneth N. Waltz, "Nuclear Myths and Political Realities," *American Political Science Review* 84, 3 (September 1990): 731–745, https://www.jstor.org/stable/1962764 (accessed May 21, 2023).

argument to focus on how nuclear deterrence is increasingly difficult to maintain. For example, advancements in technology, such as new remote sensing capability that can detect the location of nuclear arsenals and the increasing pin-point accuracy of these weapons, could make it possible to eliminate even expansive counterstrike capabilities.[4] Moreover, the risk of accident or human error is ever present, as in 1983, when there was a Soviet nuclear false alarm because of a radar malfunction, and one man's decision may have ultimately been what saved the world.[5]

Deterrence, however, does not necessarily prescribe non-use. The logic of deterrence is primarily about having the wherewithal to survive a first strike to be able to attack back.[6] However, the overwhelming power of nuclear weapons also brings the threat of mutually assured destruction (MAD) into the equation, providing a different motivation for deterrence beyond the scenario of waging a more limited nuclear war.[7] Indeed, rather than prompting a more limited approach to nuclear weapons, fear of mutually assured destruction also prompted several prominent scholars during the Cold War to advocate for the widescale *proliferation* of nuclear weapons around the world precisely to achieve a stalemate-type "nuclear peace."[8]

Ultimately, nuclear deterrence is an unsatisfying answer as to why nuclear weapons have not been used for so long as it infers a range of different motivations. It assumes that just because a nuclear power intends to deter, other countries will perceive it that way and, moreover, that possessing nuclear weapons as a deterrent will be 100% credible, which has historically been shown not to be the case.[9] Casting doubt on the argument that deterrence mainly works because it occurs between two nuclear powers, there have also been several instances in which a nuclear state did not use the bomb against a non-nuclear state (i.e., Vietnam, Afghanistan, and Korea), even when facing failure or stalemate on the battlefield.[10]

[4] Keir A. Lieber and Daryl G. Press, "The New Era of Counterforce: Technological Change and the Future of Nuclear Deterrence," *International Security* 41, 4 (2017): 9–49, https://doi.org/10.1162/ISEC_a_00273.

[5] Scott D. Sagan, *The Limits of Safety: Organizations, Accidents, and Nuclear Weapons* (Princeton, NJ: Princeton University Press, 1993); Pavel Aksenov, "Stanislav Petrov: The Man Who May Have Saved the World," *BBC.com*, 2013, https://www.bbc.com/news/world-europe-24280831 (accessed May 25, 2023).

[6] Lieber and Press, "The New Era of Counterforce."

[7] Aaron Friedberg, "A History of the US Strategic 'Doctrine'—1945–1980," *Journal of Strategic Studies* 3, 3 (1980): 37–71, https://doi.org/10.1080/01402398008437055.

[8] Kenneth Waltz is most associated with this argument. See: Kenneth Waltz, "The Spread of Nuclear Weapons: More May Be Better: Introduction," *The Adelphi Papers*, 21, 171 (1981): 1, https://doi.org/10.1080/05679328108457394; Scott Sagan and Kenneth Waltz, *The Spread of Nuclear Weapons: A Debate Renewed*, 2nd edn (New York: W. W. Norton, 2002).

[9] Nick Ritchie, "Deterrence Dogma? Challenging the Relevance of British Nuclear Weapons," *International Affairs* 85, 1 (2009):. 81–98, https://www.jstor.org/stable/27694921 (accessed May 20, 2023).

[10] T. V. Paul, "Taboo or Tradition? The Non-use of Nuclear Weapons in World Politics," *Review of International Studies* 36, 4 (2010): 853–863, https://www.jstor.org/stable/40961956 (accessed May 20, 2023).

The broader nuclear weapons debate also discredits realist theories of deterrence.[11] For example, from a more liberal perspective, scholars cite the decline of war amongst great powers more generally and the rise of international institutions that have dramatically increased trust and mutual understanding since the Second World War.[12] The argument is that if war in general is declining, then the non-use of nuclear weapons would naturally follow. The flipside of this argument, of course, brings us back to realism and deterrence: the existence of nuclear weapons has itself caused the decline of war because using them first would be imprudent.[13] This leaves us with a chicken-and-egg problem and the root causes of non-use still unknown.

Going beyond this, Nina Tannenwald—perhaps most associated with the so-called "nuclear taboo" in the field of international relations—has argued that we cannot fully understand the non-use of nuclear weapons without acknowledging the "normative stigma" or "moral opprobrium" that these weapons quickly acquired at the societal level after Hiroshima and Nagasaki.[14] Witnessing the effect these weapons had on Japanese civilians, many around the world developed a visceral aversion to anyone ever using them again. According to Tannenwald, a "taboo" is a kind of norm that is associated with revulsion and unthinkable danger.[15] However, she demurs from dismissing realist explanations, noting that her argument only supplements national interest calculations. In 2018, she joined the chorus of international relations scholars arguing that the nuclear taboo (if it ever existed[16]) is vanishing.

It is actually necessary to step outside of the field of international relations to find in-depth accounts that take the societal role in creating and maintaining the non-use norm seriously.[17] To date, the first and only highly comprehensive historical account of the world nuclear disarmament movement and its impact on international outcomes is Lawrence Wittner's trilogy, covering the period from

---

[11] Denise Garcia, *Common Good Governance in the Age of Artificial Intelligence* (Oxford: Oxford University Press, 2023), chapter 5.

[12] See e.g.,John Mueller, *Retreat from Doomsday: The Obsolescence of Major War* (New York: Basic Books, 1989).

[13] Joshua Goldstein, *Winning the War on War: The Decline of Armed Conflict Worldwide* (New York: Penguin, 2012); Tyler Bowen, Michael Goldfien, and Matthew Graham, "The Illusory Nuclear Taboo," Yale University, February 1, 2021, https://cpb-us-w2.wpmucdn.com/campuspress.yale.edu/dist/4/3650/files/2021/03/BowenGoldfienGraham_weaktaboo.pdf (accessed May 20, 2023).

[14] Nina Tannenwald, *The Nuclear Taboo: The United States and the Non-use of Nuclear Weapons since 1945* (Cambridge: Cambridge University Press, 2007), p. 2.

[15] Tannenwald, *The Nuclear Taboo*, pp. 10–14.

[16] Scott Sagan, "Realist Perspectives on Ethical Norms and Weapons of Mass Destruction," in *Ethics and Weapons of Mass Destruction: Religious and Secular Perspectives*, ed. Sohail Hashmi and Steven P. Lee (Cambridge: Cambridge University Press, 2004).

[17] Although as an exception, international relations research on feminist anti-nuclear activism does tend to take the role of society seriously too. For example, Catherine Eschle, "Feminism and Peace Movements: Engendering Anti-nuclear Activism," *Routledge Handbook of Feminist Peace Research*, ed. Tarja Väyrynen, Swati Parashar, Élise Féron, and Catia Cecilia Confortini (New York: Routledge, 2021), pp. 250–259.

1945 to 2009.[18] Bringing an impressive range and mountain of evidence to bear, Wittner demonstrates unambiguously that the anti-nuclear movement was powerful, persistent, and impossible to ignore. Members of this movement, and the larger global society that they influenced, crafted and amplified the non-use idea to such an extent that government leaders around the world capitulated. Indeed, governments have translated the movement's demands into various international agreements that allow for increased transparency, communication, limits, monitoring, and other guardrails designed to decrease the risk of nuclear war. Wittner's evidence that these leaders had to change their stance on nuclear weapons to align with global public opinion is incontrovertible. Subsequently, many historians have echoed Wittner's finding that the anti-nuclear movement played a key role in changing government policy.[19]

Drawing upon the wealth of historical evidence already brought to light, as well as select first-hand accounts from members of the antinuclear movement, I use an ultrasocial lens to further uncover the power of the *non-use idea*—the belief that, despite having nuclear weapons, one should never use them. I start with the origins of the idea, which emerged even before the weapons existed, and bring the analysis up to the present. After the United States dropped nuclear weapons on Hiroshima and Nagasaki, international society developed a strongly held belief that they should never be used again. How did this come to be? This book makes the case that humans as a species are inclined toward ideas that enable ultrasocial behavior. Building on this, certain ideas that reflect transcendent impact, optimism, and a new narrative are likely to matter more than others. I argue that the non-use idea is grounded in the ultrasocial landscape and that its proponents have fundamentally connected it to something greater than just revulsion or deterrence.[20] Rather, the non-use of nuclear weapons is situated within the larger

---

[18] The first volume was published in 1993.

[19] See, e.g., Dee Garrison, *Bracing for Armageddon: Why Civil Defense Never Worked* (Oxford: Oxford University Press, 2006); David Meyer, *A Winter of Discontent: The Nuclear Freeze and American Politics* (New York: Praeger, 1990), David S. Meyer and Robert Kleidman, "The Nuclear Freeze Movement in the United States," *International Social Movement Research* 3 (1991), pp. 231–262; Robert English, *Russia and the Idea of the West: Gorbachev, Intellectuals, and the End of the Cold War* (New York: Columbia University Press, 2000); T. V. Paul, *The Tradition of Non-use of Nuclear Weapons* (Stanford, CA: Stanford University Press, 2009).

[20] There are countless documents and first-hand accounts making the connection between the anti-nuclear aims of social movements and the general call for peace. See, e.g., "Earth Citizen Pledge," in *Waging Peace in the Nuclear Age: Ideas for Action*, ed. David Krieger and Frank Kelly (Santa Barbara, CA: Capra Press, 1988), p. 13; "Peace Pledge Union," as cited in Richard Taylor and Colin Pritchard (eds), *The Protest Makers: The British Nuclear Disarmament Movement of 1958–1965, Twenty Years On* (Oxford: Pergamon, 1980), p. 4; Edward Thompson and Vaclav Racek, *Human Rights and Disarmament: An Exchange of Letters between E. P. Thompson & Vaclav Racek* (Nottingham: Russell Press, 1981); Ruth Brandon, *The Burning Question: The Anti-nuclear Movement since 1945* (London: Heinemann, 1987).

quest for peace, itself reflective of the human predisposition to be other-oriented, empathic, and inclined to seek widescale cooperation.[21]

Part IV is organized as follows. Chapter 11 tracks how the non-use idea, with its ultrasocial resonance, emerged and gained widespread, societal support. Departing from studies of the nuclear taboo, I emphasize that the development of the non-use idea was not just a reaction *against* something but also a drive *for* something broader: a recognition of a common humanity and shared belief that peace is possible. Chapter 12 shows how this idea had the effect of radically transforming the conduct of war on the part of governments, even as some government and military leaders initially resisted it. The influence and visibility of the anti-nuclear movement came in waves, but the transcendent nature of the non-use idea, the optimism that accompanied it, and the new narrative surrounding it, made the idea resilient when it came under threat. Emergent ideas that tap into the power of possibility and resonate with our ultrasocial inclinations are often very persuasive, especially if they envision transcendent change. To be sure, these ideas still face competition and are regularly tested by norm violators and those who seek to undermine past ultrasocial consensus, but the underlying societal context—with its tendency toward peace and cooperation—should be an important part of our understanding.

Given a number of fresh and ongoing conflicts (North Korea, India–Pakistan, Russia, Iran), fading disarmament agreements, and the decline of membership and visibility of the anti-nuclear movement, there is debate over whether the nuclear taboo still exists.[22] In Chapter 13, I will argue that it does, albeit in a different form. While the international system today is one in which interstate war is largely considered a last resort and should only be embarked upon under legitimate circumstances (i.e., self-defense or a UN Security Council resolution), once war begins, I argue that the non-use idea is still a strong barrier in its conduct. An ultrasocial approach suggests that it is likely that the non-use idea has become more entrenched than both the taboo (unthinking, gut response) and the tradition (path-dependence) because it is intricately tied to norms against war and in favor of peace.

---

[21] It is important to note that being a proponent of peace is different from being a pacifist. Although there have been many grassroot, pacifist organizations, few would generally subscribe to the notion that there should be peace no matter what. This is because the context really matters, and in certain circumstances, the use of force may be necessary to uphold human dignity, values, and eventually, peace itself. The pursuit of peace is a widely regarded as desirable in that it relegates war to a last resort. It can also be more difficult to achieve than simply being a pacifist because it requires new agreements, policies, and governance.

[22] Nina Tannewald, "The Vanishing Nuclear Taboo?," *Foreign Affairs* 97, 6 (November/December 2018): 16–24.

11

The Non-use Idea and the Anti-nuclear Movement

Just as with the case of the European movement and the federalist idea, the strength of the anti-nuclear movement and the non-use idea came in waves from the 1940s to the 1980s. But even as protests waxed and waned, the non-use idea remained steadfast and widespread. Millions of ordinary citizens, activists, and scientists across dozens of countries were inspired to pursue the greater good, and they repeatedly refused to take no for an answer. Crucially, the anti-nuclear movement was embedded within the larger, pre-existing peace movement and its underlying ultrasocial principles. Specifically, I argue that the growth of the non-use idea was not just a reaction *against* a highly destructive weapon, as is often depicted, but also a renewed call *for* an ultrasocial response in its own right. The non-use idea, championed across the world, railed against nuclear weapons but also carried the optimistic narrative of transformation from a world of war to one of peace. Its appeal was that it resonated with a newly imagined reality. In this chapter, I describe the emergence of the non-use idea as a fundamental expression of human ultrasociality, carrying new possibilities for the achievement of peace.

The Origins of the Non-use Idea

For millennia, humans fought wars with little regard for restraint. Wars were thought to be glorious and necessary, and the point was to win. This started to change with the introduction of more explicit rules regarding the conduct of war. Early modern Dutch humanist Hugo Grotius's influential 1625 book, *De jure belli ac pacis* (*On the Law of War and Peace*) was the first to explicitly stipulate that war should only occur under agreed-upon rules that provided for its justification and that spelled out its conduct. His ideas were codified in the 1648 Peace of Westphalia. While these rules created a kind of restraint when it came to the decision to embark upon war, they also effectively ushered in an era that *enabled* war under certain broad conditions, such as to claim territory. Because of this, Grotius is often credited with "making the world safe for war."[23]

---

[23] Oona Hathaway and Scott Shapiro, *The Internationalists: How a Radical Plan to Outlaw War Remade the World* (New York: Simon and Schuster, 2017).

International Cooperation Against All Odds. Mai'a K. Davis Cross, Oxford University Press. © Mai'a K. Davis Cross (2024).
DOI: 10.1093/oso/9780192873903.003.0012

Some two centuries later, in the early nineteenth century, societal-level peace movements started to emerge that pushed for changes to the Grotian international order. Proponents of peace, especially in the United States and Europe, called for their governments to find alternatives to military build-up and to create policies that would prevent war whenever possible. As the world entered the twentieth century, more and more citizens joined these peace movements. Then, as often happens with major crises, the Second World War created space for the emergence of new ideas, and in particular, the notion that militarism should not be the way to resolve conflict.[24] Of course, these ideas also resonated with ultrasocial behavior, helping them to gain momentum. The leaders who could translate them into policy attracted attention. During the First World War, for example, Salmon Levinson, the lawyer who would eventually author the 1928 Kellogg–Briand Pact, argued, "We should have, not as now, laws of war, but laws against war; just as there are no laws of murder or of poisoning, but laws against them."[25] In 1918, Levinson published, "The Legal Status of War," seeking a new approach: the *outlawry* of war.[26] At the end of the First World War, he argued that the newly created League of Nations did not go far enough in achieving this. Indeed, among other things, the league further defined the ways in which war would be considered legal rather than actually trying to prevent it.

As Oona Hathaway and Scott Shapiro argue, the ideas that Levinson put forward in the Kellogg–Briand Pact played a key role in transforming the international system to emphasize the *illegality* of war. The pact stipulated that any land that had already changed hands up until 1928 was, from then on, regarded as legitimate, and any further modification of territory would be difficult to justify legally. The outlawry of war had widespread appeal. Hathaway and Shapiro write that it, "tapped into an already robust peace movement made up of hundreds of loosely coordinated groups [. . .] providing a nationwide network for events in support of outlawry."[27] Even though the Second World War broke out after the Kellogg–Briand Pact, the behavior of states was already different: far less territory changed from one state to another during the Second World War and later, especially when compared to the period from 1910 to 1928.[28]

It is in this context that nuclear weapons arrived on the scene. The nuclear non-use idea picked up where the outlawry of war left off and was a major development in the quest to fulfill ideas rooted in peace. While the 1899 and 1907 Hague conventions and the 1949 Geneva convention had served to limit certain types of conduct during war, nuclear weapons presented a new and pressing challenge for the peace

---

[24] Lawrence Wittner, *One World or None: A History of the World Nuclear Disarmament Movement through 1953* (Stanford, CA: Stanford University Press, 1993), p. 40.
[25] Hathaway and Shapiro, *The Internationalists*, p. 108.
[26] Hathaway and Shapiro, *The Internationalists*, pp. 105–110.
[27] Hathaway and Shapiro, *The Internationalists*, p. 114.
[28] Hathaway and Shapiro, *The Internationalists*.

movement. Before the advent of nuclear weapons, military strategists assumed that states at war would develop and use the most powerful munitions possible in order to win. For them, it was common sense: weapons technology was neutral and moral decisions only emerged in the circumstances of their use.[29] As Tannenwald writes, "a weapon once introduced inevitably comes to be widely accepted as legitimate."[30] After the advent of nuclear weapons, however, old assumptions became problematic because of their particular destructive potential. Dislodging the long-standing logic of war, however, required a forward-looking ultrasocial vision that engaged society's capacity for transcendence.

Paving the way for this was a small epistemic community of scientists and physicists, aware that atomic energy was within reach and adamant that experiments in nuclear fission had to be stopped before it was too late.[31] Even decades before the advent of nuclear weapons, many of these scientists had been strongly critical of pursuing such technology in the first place.[32] They represented the most significant early resistance to the bomb.[33] They did not see this weapon as just another advancement in weapons technology, as government leaders did; they saw it as so unusually devastating that it risked the imminent destruction of the Earth and humankind itself.

In the lead-up to the Second World War, many of these concerned scientists got drawn into working on nuclear weapons technology, most prominently in the Manhattan Project. However, their strong reservations remained. Some refused to work on this destructive technology altogether, while others felt compelled to do so out of fear that their German counterparts would develop the weapon first. Many still held tightly to the idea that these weapons should never actually be used and rationalized that having them would at least allow for deterrence. The University of Chicago's Met Lab—the first to create plutonium-producing nuclear reactors— repeatedly raised the alarm from 1944 to 1945, emphasizing that nuclear weapons needed to be carefully controlled as soon as possible.[34] In the 1950s, Chicago scientists shifted their main goal to preventing nuclear testing.[35] More generally, the

---

[29] Nina Tannenwald, "Stigmatizing the Bomb: Origins of the Nuclear Taboo," *International Security* 29 (2005): 11, https://www.jstor.org/stable/4137496 (accessed May 25, 2023).

[30] Tannenwald, "Stigmatizing the Bomb," p. 5.

[31] Emanuel Adler, "The Emergence of Cooperation: National Epistemic Communities and the International Evolution of the Idea of Nuclear Arms Control," *International Organization* 46, 1 (Winter 1992): 101–145, https://www.jstor.org/stable/2706953 (accessed May 25, 2023); Lawrence S. Wittner, *Confronting the Bomb: A Short History of the World Nuclear Disarmament Movement* (Stanford, CA: Stanford University Press, 2009), p. 2. For more on what constitutes epistemic communities, see Maïa K. Davis Cross, "Rethinking Epistemic Communities Twenty Years Later," *Review of International Studies* 39, 1 (2013): 137–160, https://doi.org/10.1017/S0260210512000034.

[32] Wittner, *Confronting the Bomb*, p. 1.

[33] Wittner, *Confronting the Bomb*, pp. 29–33, 43–44; Matthew Evangelista, *Unarmed Forces: The Transnational Movement to End the Cold War* (Ithaca, NY: Cornell University Press, 2002).

[34] Wittner, *Confronting the Bomb*, pp. 4–7. Jennifer Sims, *Icarus Restrained: An Intellectual History of Nuclear Arms Control, 1945–1960* (Boulder, CO: Westview Press, 1990), pp. 88–92.

[35] Evangelista, *Unarmed Forces*, p. 9.

scientists' efforts went far beyond the United States, where the bomb was being rapidly developed.[36] They formed a transnational network with other scientists, especially with those on the other side of the Iron Curtain.

Foreshadowing the anti-nuclear movement, these scientists also embedded their concerns about the bomb in a larger call for world peace. A prominent group threw their support behind the July 1955 Russell–Einstein Manifesto, which emphasized that the use of nuclear weapons would be an ongoing threat unless war itself was no longer a possibility. The reason for this, as stated in the manifesto, was that, "whatever agreements not to use H-bombs had been reached in time of peace, they would no longer be considered binding in time of war and both sides would set to work to manufacture H-bombs as soon as war broke out."[37] Invoking ultrasociality, Joseph Rotblat, who chaired the press conference where Bertrand Russell first publicly read the manifesto, describes how it, "managed to bring together scientists [. . .] who spoke on this occasion as members of the human species, rather than as representatives of individual camps."[38] Rotblat eventually won the Nobel Peace Prize for his steadfast stance against the bomb.

The manifesto strengthened the epistemic community of scientists through launching a series of conferences, starting in 1957, known as the Pugwash Movement.[39] Those who attended Pugwash unanimously agreed that nuclear testing must be stopped but differed somewhat in terms of how to achieve this. One group believed that general disarmament must be pursued, while another group, led by Leo Szilard, believed that it was politically impossible to get rid of the bomb, and thus their efforts should focus on controlling the bomb.[40]

Eventually, this scientific debate, based on genuine alarm, spread to broader society. As in the case of outer space exploration, H. G. Wells was an important early figure in influencing regular people to become passionately anti-nuclear. His 1914 book *The World Set Free* described an era of atomic weapons so destructive that those who were still alive in the aftermath felt compelled to create a world government, which ushered in a new period of peace and prosperity. The book again invoked the connection between the dangers of nuclear weapons and the opportunity to pursue peace. Wells was not alone in this. Many publications at the time championed the idea of world government as a solution to war. Wendell Willkie's best-seller *One World*, for example, sold millions of copies and appeared in

---

[36] See, e.g., Max Born, "Man, the Atom and the Renunciation of War," in *Voices from the Crowd: Against the H-Bomb*, ed. David Boulton (Wyomissing, PA: Dufour Editions; F edition, 1964), pp. 20–26.

[37] Joseph Rotblat, "Disarmament and World Security Issues at the Pugwash Conferences," in *A New Design for Nuclear Disarmament*, ed. William Epstein and Toyoda Toshiyuki (Nottingham: Pugwash Symposium, 1977), p. 29.

[38] Joseph Rotblat, "The Present Day Significance of the Russell–Einstein Manifesto," in *A New Design for Nuclear Disarmament*, ed. Epstein and Toshiyuki (1977), p. 23.

[39] Evangelista, *Unarmed Forces*.

[40] Rotblat, "Disarmament and World Security Issues at the Pugwash Conferences," p. 30.

installments across over a hundred American and Canadian newspapers. Emery Reves's *Anatomy of Peace* was also published in dozens of languages and quickly became a worldwide best-seller.[41]

After the United States used nuclear weapons against the Japanese cities of Hiroshima and Nagasaki in August 1945, a powerful and far-ranging anti-nuclear movement quickly emerged in protest, building on the long-standing world peace and world government precursors. Eventually, the non-aligned movement also disseminated the idea in many countries around the world that nuclear weapons should never be used.[42]

The Idea Grows into a Movement

There were three major waves in the anti-nuclear movement, each powerfully carrying forward the non-use idea. Although there was certainly the fear and horror of what the bomb could do, especially in a situation of mutually assured destruction, there was also a shared belief in the possibility of creating a better, more peaceful world. And it was not merely a Western phenomenon. The movement galvanized people across the globe and on every continent. Its worldwide reach and eventual impact on the behavior of states was a truly stunning example of the strength of ultrasociality, even in the context of a confrontational Cold War environment. Despite the fear of what "the enemy" might do, the non-use idea captured the minds of millions of people who were unwaveringly devoted to the achievement of peace. This non-use idea was widespread, enduring, and resulted in significant reversals in government policy everywhere.

First Wave

The first wave, from the 1940s to the early 1950s, emerged small but rapidly attracted a widespread following. Hundreds of societal-level peace movements around the world passionately and systematically championed the non-use idea, from the World Federalist Movement, to the Women's International League for Peace and Freedom, to the Bulletin of the Atomic Scientists, among many others. To the extent that there were transnational or international ties, the world federalists were most successful in establishing an international organization that solidified and spread anti-nuclear ideas, especially during the period from 1946 to 1949. The World Movement for World Federal Government, established in 1946, quickly drew a massive membership, bringing together thirty-seven organizations,

---

[41] Wittner, *Confronting the Bomb*, p. 10.
[42] Wittner, *One World or None*, pp. 39–54.

fifty-six groups, and citizens from seventy-eight countries.[43] Another powerful societal group advocating for peace and against the bomb was the *hibakusha*, led by the survivors of the Japanese bombings. In parallel, the USSR, its Eastern European satellites, and communist leaders across a range of countries also declared their stance against nuclear weapons as part of their communist version of a peace movement, for example, through the World Peace Council.[44] Although this communist peace movement lined up with many of the points that the democratic movements were pursuing, it was also distinctly anti-Western politically. In this sense, it appealed to the fast-growing embrace of the non-use idea but also had a tribal, rather than ultrasocial, underpinning.

Those who became members of these groups were so visible and effective at communicating their messages in the aftermath of Hiroshima and Nagasaki that there was an immense societal upswell in favor of world government, world federalism, and world peace. In the United States, for example, 67% of Americans surveyed wanted the United Nations strengthened in such a way as to make it impossible for all countries, including the United States, to make atomic weapons.[45] This sentiment was shared in Japan, Canada, Australia, and across Western Europe. Even in the Global South—Mexico, China, Argentina, India, Brazil, Turkey, Pakistan, the Philippines, and elsewhere—support for world federalism, world government, and anti-nuclear organizations also grew. As Wittner writes, "fear of the Bomb went hand-in-hand with the idea of world government."[46]

A new narrative that held the possibility of an optimistic future helped to capture the imagination of the public. The narrative was that the nationalist, militarist thinking of the past resulted in the advent and use of nuclear weapons but that the world could turn away from this through a global transformation toward peace and mutual respect for human rights.[47] Rather than coming only from a place of fear (the focus of much of the nuclear taboo literature), the anti-nuclear movement was also clearly rooted in ultrasociality, the sense that we are all one species deserving of empathy from one another. The peace, world government, and world federalism movements had all pursued goals in line with this, and the problem of nuclear weapons further energized their cause.

While scientists continued their efforts, including trying to bridge the East–West divide, these grassroots movements held meetings all over the world in

[43] Lawrence Wittner, "The Worldwide Movement against Nuclear Arms: Building an Effective Transnational Organization," *Peace Research* 31, 4 (1999): 19, https://www.jstor.org/stable/23607811 (accessed May 21, 2023).
[44] Wittner, *Confronting the Bomb*, pp. 25–27.
[45] Wittner, *Confronting the Bomb*, p. 15.
[46] Wittner, *Confronting the Bomb*, p. 15.
[47] See, e.g., Edward Thompson and Vaclav Racek, *Human Rights and Disarmament: An Exchange of Letters between E. P. Thompson & Vaclav Racek* (Nottingham: Russell Press, 1981); Ruth Brandon, *The Burning Question: The Anti-nuclear War Movement since 1945* (London: Heinemann, 1987).

support of disarmament and anti-militarism, organized largescale rallies, and issued statements, such as the prominent War Resisters' International's Declaration of Peace.[48] As Wittner describes it, "This movement argued that nations should end the traditional practice of securing their interests by marshaling superior military might—a practice that, with the advent of the Bomb, seemed fraught with new and terrible things."[49] All in all, the first wave saw anti-nuclear agendas crystalize across the globe, anchored in the belief that the Bomb was fundamentally wrong and that its eradication or non-use would herald more progress toward the quest for peace.

Second Wave

The first wave of the movement introduced the non-use idea and laid the groundwork for its pursuit over the subsequent decades. After experiencing some policy successes (see Chapter 12) and a sense of imminent threat, the movement subsided somewhat during the period 1950–1953.[50] In this lull, without strong popular pressure, several governments openly pursued the acquisition of more powerful nuclear weapons. Then, in 1954, the United States had its first successful hydrogen bomb test. This dangerous build-up, followed by technological breakthrough, and rollbacks in government disarmament policies, soon became too much to ignore. This was a call to action.

In 1954, the second wave of the movement started to regain steam and eventually reached its previous visibility. Regular citizens were not willing to accept a world armed to the hilt, and they became organized to amplify this message locally, transnationally, and internationally. Grassroots, national-level groups loosely coordinated their actions through the International Confederation for Disarmament and Peace.[51] The confederation brought together citizens of Western and non-aligned countries who were all galvanized toward the same goal of resolving conflict peacefully. Several policy setbacks further precipitated growing support for a test ban treaty. For example, the Soviet Union unilaterally resumed atmospheric testing of nuclear weapons in September 1961, and in March 1962, US President Kennedy announced his intention to do the same. Enough time had passed since the Second World War for even pacifist groups to experience a renaissance (they had scaled back in the face of Nazism). And perhaps, most importantly, the global, mass-level Ban-the-Bomb campaign took off.

---

[48] Wittner, *Confronting the Bomb*, p. 23.
[49] Wittner, *One World or None*, p. 39.
[50] Wittner, *Confronting the Bomb*, pp. 49–51.
[51] The formal goal of the International Confederation for Disarmament and Peace was "to promote the peaceful resolution of conflicts, human rights and civil liberties, liberation from colonial regimes, [and] economic equality between developing and developed countries." Wittner, "The Worldwide Movement against Nuclear Arms", pp. 18–25.

In the United Kingdom, for example, the Campaign for Nuclear Disarmament attracted a surge in membership, the inclusion of over 800 local groups, and a major protest in Trafalgar Square, with 60,000–100,000 people in attendance.[52] Similarly, in Canada, membership of Ban-the-Bomb organizations skyrocketed, and 200,000 people signed an anti-nuclear petition that included very prominent individuals.[53] Australia, New Zealand, and countries across Europe had similarly dramatic upswells in the movement. Many countries in Africa and the Middle East had mass demonstrations against the bomb, and various groups expressed their opposition to further testing.[54] In developing countries like India, China, Singapore, Brazil, Mexico, Venezuela, and Argentina, activism was not as visible as in the West, but strong majorities of the public supported the abolition of the bomb.[55] And despite the Soviet government's close control over any form of peace activism, international ties with peace groups and growing anti-nuclear sentiment meant that, even in the USSR, the movement grew.[56]

As a result of the widespread popularity of the non-use idea, there was a global governmental response, as discussed in more detail in Chapter 12. Many political leaders who had previously supported developing and amassing nuclear weapons could no longer bear the cost of global and domestic public opinion turning against them. The second wave culminated in the atmospheric test ban treaty of 1963.[57] With this hard-fought achievement, the anti-nuclear movement again retrenched somewhat, and societal attention on nuclear weapons waned. In this context, the Cold War arms race between the USSR and the United States persisted. But the non-use idea was so pervasive that any attempts of governments to backtrack on previous anti-nuclear promises resulted in an immediate societal response.

Third Wave

In the late 1970s, as nuclear rhetoric ratcheted up again, the threat of using these weapons crept back into the political discourse amongst great powers and ignited the third wave of the movement. As this final wave reached its height, it became, as Wittner describes, "the largest, most powerful reform movement of modern times."[58] Crucially, the all-important nuclear freeze campaign of the 1980s was about peace just as much as it was about disarmament.[59] Whereas in the 1940s and

---

[52] Wittner, *Confronting the Bomb*, pp. 82–83.
[53] Wittner, *Confronting the Bomb*, p. 85.
[54] Wittner, *Confronting the Bomb*, pp. 94–95.
[55] Wittner, *Confronting the Bomb*, p. 95.
[56] Wittner, *Confronting the Bomb*, pp. 95–99.
[57] Wittner, *Confronting the Bomb*, pp. 52–81; Wittner, *One World or None*, p. xi.
[58] Wittner, *One World or None*, p. xi.
[59] Pam Solo, *From Protest to Policy* (Cambridge: Ballinger Publishing Company, 1988), ; Thompson and Racek, *Human Rights and Disarmament*.

1950s, the emphasis was more on how the ongoing quest for peace and world government could also encompass a fight against nuclear weapons, in the late 1970s, the emphasis was reversed. It was nuclear weapons that gave the peace movement purpose.[60] As Pam Solo, one of the Nuclear Weapons Freeze Campaign's founders and organizers, writes,

> The Freeze movement was not just a reaction to the extreme rhetoric and overtly dangerous policies of the Reagan administration. It was a social movement intentionally and methodically organized by long-time peace organizations and activists. Those who organized the movement wanted to create a permanent public mobilization to freeze the nuclear arms race in place.[61]

Solo goes on to blame the assumptions embedded within bureaucracies, specifically the belief that violent conflict will always continue and that leaders must continually plan for the Third World War.[62] Indeed, these assumptions worked against ultrasociality and were conducive toward creating a self-fulfilling prophecy. Like the Freeze campaign, Solo situates nuclear weapons within a larger context: "we learn only half the lessons of history if we ignore the political, moral, economic, and social forces set in motion by the transformation of the international order into a war system."[63]

As in the previous two waves, the movement's goal was not only to convince national security leaders but also to educate the public. In this, they succeeded. The ultrasocial idea of freezing nuclear capacity as a means to achieve peace rallied societies together. For example, in 1983, 70% of Americans supported the idea of a freeze on nuclear weapons.[64] In 1988, 85% supported a test ban treaty and 71% were in favor of working with the USSR to get rid of nuclear weapons entirely.[65] Tens of thousands of Americans went to nuclear test sites and participated in nonviolent civil disobedience. 1.2 million signed a test ban petition and took it to the United Nations in Geneva. The movement was also strong across the globe, from Asia and the Pacific to Latin America, Africa, and the Middle East. Despite the risk of crackdown, it flourished in the USSR, where activists exhibited anti-militarist art in Red Square.[66] In 1986, 250,000 Australians protested at an anti-nuclear rally, while in New Zealand, 300 peace groups worked together to push the government

---

[60] Paul Wehr, "Nuclear Pacifism as Collective Action," *Journal of Peace Research* 23, 2 (1986): 104.
[61] Solo, *From Protest to Policy*, p. 19.
[62] Solo, *From Protest to Policy*, pp. 2–3. She writes, "Progress in disarmament will never be made until the fossilized tenets of cold war doctrine have been replaced with practical principles that face the world as it is but refuse to accept the permanence of violence."
[63] Solo, *From Protest to Policy*, p. 4.
[64] Jeremy Stone, "Introduction," in *Seeds of Promise: The First Real Hearings on the Nuclear Arms Freeze*, ed. Randall Forsberg and Alton Frye (Andover, MA: Brickhouse Publishing, 1983).
[65] Wittner, *Confronting the Bomb*, p. 178.
[66] Wittner, *Confronting the Bomb*, p. 179.

to ban nuclear warships.[67] Sixty thousand Brazilian scientists put their names on a statement to ban nuclear weapons, and Zimbabwe's activists held multiple demonstrations against the bomb. These are just a few examples of the grassroots efforts in the name of peace, shared humanity, and global transformation, now in its fourth decade.

The new, third-wave narrative surrounding Ban-the-Bomb elevated a sense of common moral reasoning and infused society with the firm belief that people and institutions could change for the better. The character of the movement itself shows how this dynamism reflected the human propensity to strive for ultrasociality. The nuclear taboo was fundamentally embedded in ideas that resonated with a sense of optimism for what was possible, transcendent change, and a new narrative that peace could be tied to non-use, and eventually eradication, of these weapons. The fact that the anti-nuclear movement grew out of the pre-existing world peace movement and world government movements was also significant. It meant that those involved had long experience with pushing for transformational change and efforts to dismantle boundaries. The advent of nuclear weapons represented an incontrovertible high-water mark in the human capacity for destruction, but the human reaction to this came with a clear purpose and a rallying cry for peace.

Chapter 12 turns to the combined impact of these globe-spanning grassroot movements and how it was central to the spread of the non-use idea. As Wittner writes, "opponents of the Bomb, by subjecting it to an onslaught of criticism, helped turn public sentiment against the weapon and thereby made it politically less acceptable as an instrument of war and diplomacy."[68] This eventually resulted in transformational change in government actions and, subsequently, new policies across the world.[69]

---

[67] Wittner, *Confronting the Bomb*, pp. 178–179.
[68] Wittner, *One World or None*, p. x.
[69] Richard Taylor and Colin Pritchard, *The Protest Makers: The British Nuclear Disarmament Movement of 1958–1965, Twenty Years On* (Oxford: Pergamon Press, 1980), p. 27.

12

The Nuclear Taboo and Disarmament

Global Policy Transformation

After the first successful atomic bomb test on July 18, 1945, Allied leaders—Harry Truman (United States), Winston Churchill (United Kingdom), and Joseph Stalin (USSR)—had no reservations whatsoever about using this powerful, new weapon. In fact, at no point did they even discuss whether its use was appropriate.[70] After the bomb detonated in Hiroshima, President Truman was initially triumphant, claiming that it was "the greatest thing in history."[71] Of course, all of this ultimately changed. With growing public opposition in the aftermath of the atomic explosions, it became increasingly difficult for governmental leaders around the world to support the further use of these weapons. Public pressure eventually led to an about-face in political rhetoric involving nuclear weapons and, subsequently, the signing of dozens of nuclear disarmament agreements. While efforts at disarmament certainly did not lead to the full eradication of nuclear weapons, there has been a perfect record of non-use of the bomb since Hiroshima and Nagasaki. While Chapter 11 explained the emergence and spread of the non-use idea in society, here, I focus on how this form of ultrasociality had a transformational impact on nuclear policy around the world.

Echoing Lawrence Wittner's research, Nina Tannenwald argues that societal moral indignation about the use of the bomb was a significant factor in a bottom-up push to persuade leaders to change their approach. In the first few years of the Cold War, the first wave of the anti-nuclear movement was just getting started and did not yet have the strength in numbers it would later have. But even in the weeks following the bombing of Hiroshima and Nagasaki, government leaders were forced to contend with a growing popular backlash to the use of these weapons. Then, in the subsequent months and years, they experienced strong pressure to sign nuclear arms control and disarmament agreements, even while they pursued a nuclear arms race in parallel.[72]

Of course, not all government leaders around the world started out in support of the bomb. Quite visibly, for example, India's prime minister, Jawaharlal Nehru,

---

[70] Lawrence Wittner, *Confronting the Bomb: A Short History of the World Nuclear Disarmament Movement* (Stanford, CA: Stanford University Press, 2009), p. 7.
[71] As cited in Wittner, *Confronting the Bomb*, p. 51.
[72] Wittner, *Confronting the Bomb*, p. 51.

International Cooperation Against All Odds. Mai'a K. Davis Cross, Oxford University Press. © Mai'a K. Davis Cross (2024).
DOI: 10.1093/oso/9780192873903.003.0013

was outspoken against it.[73] In the United Kingdom, several major political leaders also opposed the bomb, including Prime Minister Clement Attlee, who wrote to US President Truman, arguing for "a bold course [that] can save civilization."[74] Other leaders of developing countries and neutral countries such as Yugoslavia, Sweden, and Finland also expressed opposition.[75] But what is perhaps more significant are the many leaders who changed their positions in light of the public response. Truman, for example, was pressured from many sectors of society to begin a complete reversal of his earlier position on nuclear weapons. He finally caved in, and on October 3, 1945 (less than two months after Hiroshima and Nagasaki), he gave a speech to Congress stating that, "the hope of civilization lies in international arrangements looking, if possible, to the renunciation of the use and development of the atomic bomb."[76] In France and Canada, the public also pressured their governments to stand against nuclear weapons, and this worked to a degree. Several leaders made statements proclaiming nuclear restraint but did not go so far as to rule out the possibility of acquiring or using them.[77]

With the rise of the second wave of the movement, anti-nuclear public opinion had grown substantially. Whereas in the few years after Hiroshima and Nagasaki, general public opinion was still mixed, after the 1954 H-bomb test, there was a significant and decisive shift against nuclear weapons across the globe, and this heavily impacted government policies.[78] For example, Dwight D. Eisenhower had started off his presidency characterizing nuclear weapons as simply a more powerful battlefield option, but by 1957, in an internal meeting with top officials, he said, "we are [. . .] up against an extremely difficult world opinion situation."[79] In 1958, he publicly stated that the United States would stop nuclear testing and begin international negotiations on a nuclear test ban.[80]

The same transformative turn was also happening simultaneously in countries around the world, including the United Kingdom,[81] the USSR, Japan, Australia, New Zealand, various European countries, and especially non-aligned countries in Africa and Asia. In each instance, governments faced major pressure from below. For example, the Prime Minister of New Zealand told the British government, "Given the prevailing state of public opinion, I am sure you will understand why

---

[73] Jagdish P. Jain, *India and Disarmament: Nehru Era* (New Delhi: Radiant Publishers, 1974); Wittner, *Confronting the Bomb*, p. 48.

[74] As cited in Wittner, *Confronting the Bomb*, p. 37.

[75] Wittner, *Confronting the Bomb*, p. 47.

[76] As cited in Wittner, *Confronting the Bomb*, p. 30.

[77] Wittner, *Confronting the Bomb*, p. 45.

[78] Wittner, *Confronting the Bomb*, p. 52.

[79] Wittner, *Confronting the Bomb*, pp. 80–81.

[80] Wittner, *Confronting the Bomb*, pp. 80–81.

[81] Richard Taylor, *Against the Bomb: The British Peace Movement 1958–1965* (Oxford: Clarendon Press, 1988); Richard Taylor and Colin Pritchard, *The Protest Makers: The British Nuclear Disarmament Movement of 1958–1965, Twenty Years On* (Oxford: Pergamon Press, 1980); Edward P. Thompson, *The Defense of Britain* (London: European Nuclear Disarmament and Campaign for Nuclear Disarmament, 1983).

we regard the resumption of testing [...] as a matter of deprecation."[82] The leaders of Denmark, Norway, Iceland, and Canada followed suit, either going against the US request to have their missiles armed with American nuclear weapons, voting in favor of a UN disarmament resolution, or voting against nuclear testing. The United Kingdom also demurred, arguing in favor of a test ban treaty. The leaders of these countries cited sharp domestic and global public opinion against the bomb, making it impossible for them to align with a more pro-nuclear stance, even if the US government had requested it.[83]

To be sure, during this period of the Cold War, there were still a few instances in which leaders did put the use of nuclear weapons on the table again, albeit briefly.[84] Even though they dramatically changed their outward stance and rhetoric, they were still somewhat Janus-faced. Behind the scenes, for example, political or military leaders discussed the possibility of using the bomb during the Korean War against China, the 1954 Quemoy and Matsu crisis concerning Taiwan, the 1962 Cuban Missile Crisis, and the 1973 Yom Kippur War.[85] Military leaders even considered it in 1968, during the Vietnam War, despite President Johnson's assertion that he certainly did not want to resort to this option.[86] Despite these instances, the pressure from society was too strong to resist, especially from 1957 to 1963. One by one, leaders proclaimed their desire to rid the world of nuclear weapons (although outside of the public eye they often admitted that they were pressured into this position and, ultimately, had no choice).

In general, there are far more examples of nuclear countries making it clear that they do *not* intend to use the bomb than the reverse. For example, in 1961, Israel adopted a policy that it, "will not be the first country to introduce nuclear weapons into the Middle East."[87] While it is widely understood that Israel does possess nuclear weapons, its policy of "nuclear ambiguity," backed by the United States, signals that Israeli leaders neither want to ratchet up nuclear tensions nor use nuclear weapons.[88] And in 1991, India and Pakistan signed a Non-nuclear Aggression Agreement in which they promised not to attack each other's nuclear

[82] As cited in Wittner, *Confronting the Bomb*, p. 106.
[83] Wittner, *Confronting the Bomb*, p. 106.
[84] Nina Tannenwald, *The Nuclear Taboo: The United States and the Non-Use of Nuclear Weapons since 1945* (Cambridge: Cambridge University Press, 2007), p. 5.
[85] John Scherer, "Soviet and American Behavior during the Yom Kippur War," *World Affairs* 141, 1 (1978): 3–23; Yossi Melman, "Did Israel Ever Consider Using Nuclear Weapons?," *Haaretz*, October 7, 2010, https://www.haaretz.com/1.5122006 (accessed May 20, 2023).
[86] Theo Milonopoulos, "How Close Did the United States Actually Get to Using Nuclear Weapons in Vietnam in 1968?," *Texas National Security Review*, October 24, 2018, https://warontherocks.com/2018/10/how-close-did-the-united-states-actually-get-to-using-nuclear-weapons-in-vietnam-in-1968 (accessed May 20, 2023).
[87] Douglas Birch and R. Jeffrey Smith, "Israel's Worst-Kept Secret," *The Atlantic*, September 16, 2014, https://www.theatlantic.com/international/archive/2014/09/israel-nuclear-weapons-secret-united-states/380237 (accessed May 20, 2023).
[88] Melman, "Did Israel Ever Consider Using Nuclear Weapons?"

site locations, followed by India's explicit no-first-use policy adopted in 1998.[89] Beyond this, however, are the numerous regional and international treaties which go much further.

Anti-nuclear and Disarmament Treaties

The non-use idea permeated local, regional, and international dialogue, leading to well-defined goals of denuclearization, limitations on stockpiles, transparency, and disarmament. The Nuclear Freeze campaign, Ban the Bomb, and others like them galvanized society in nearly every corner of the globe around the power of possibility. Nuclear weapons were not difficult to condemn in terms of their destructive power, but their existence also provided an opening to pursue non-violence more generally. This ultimately resulted in some of the most significant and groundbreaking international treaties promoting peace and cooperation in history.

The very first international treaty to denuclearize and demilitarize a region was the 1959 Antarctic Treaty, although the arms control dimension was secondary to other goals. This first treaty was not so much the product of the anti-nuclear movement as it was of the International Geophysical Year (see Part III), but it did set an important precedent.[90] The 1963 Nuclear Test Ban Treaty was the first treaty that was a distinct product of the efforts of the anti-nuclear movement. It is worth noting that the Women's International League for Peace and Freedom (WILPF) played a key role in paving the way to the 1963 treaty.[91] The WILPF launched the World Truce campaign in 1953 and, four years later, collected and submitted 10,000 signatures against nuclear testing to the White House.

The Nuclear Test Ban Treaty was quickly followed by others, as summarized in Table 3. In 1967, the Outer Space Treaty prohibited placing nuclear weapons in space. The Treaty for the Prohibition of Nuclear Weapons in Latin America and the Caribbean (colloquially known as the Treaty of Tlatelolco) established Latin American and Caribbean countries as a nuclear-free zone.[92] That same year, several Southeast Asian nations founded the Association of Southeast Asian Nations (ASEAN), in part because they shared a belief in the non-use of nuclear

---

[89] Christopher Clary and Vipin Narang, "India's Counterforce Temptations," *International Security* 43, 3 (2018): 7–52, https://doi.org/10.1162/isec_a_00340; Nuclear Threat Initiative, "India–Pakistan Non-Attack Agreement," 2011, https://www.nti.org/education-center/treaties-and-regimes/india-pakistan-non-attack-agreement (accessed May 25, 2023).

[90] William Epstein and Toshiyuki Toyoda (eds), *A New Design for Nuclear Disarmament* (Nottingham: Pushwash Symposium, 1977), p. 3.

[91] WILPF, *"Generations of Courage: The Women's International League for Peace and Freedom from the 20th Century into the New Millennium,"* (Philadelphia, PA: WILPF), p. 9.

[92] Davis Robinson, "The Treaty of Tlatelolco and the United States: A Latin American Nuclear Free Zone," *American Journal of International Law* 64, 2 (1970): 282–309, https://doi.org/10.2307/2198666.

weapons.[93] The Nuclear Non-Proliferation Treaty (NPT), designed to stop the spread of nuclear weapons technology, was signed in 1968. It was particularly noteworthy, given that fifteen countries at the time were close to becoming nuclear powers (India, Pakistan, Israel, Egypt, South Africa,[94] Japan, Australia, Spain, Brazil, Argentina, Germany, Italy, the Netherlands, Belgium, and Switzerland).[95] The NPT was followed by the 1971 Sea-Bed Treaty, prohibiting nuclear weapons on the ocean floor. These major international treaties demonstrate the overarching success of the non-use movement and idea worldwide.

Arguably, some of the most important steps in nuclear disarmament were between the United States and the USSR as these were the two countries at the forefront of the nuclear arms race. The 1972 Strategic Arms Limitations Treaty (SALT) I, the 1972 Anti-Ballistic Missile (ABM) Treaty, the 1974 Vladivostok Agreement, and the 1979 SALT II agreements were key in this regard.[96] They set limits on the number of weapons that the United States and the USSR could amass in their arms race. In 1979, US President Carter proposed joint support of the nuclear freeze to President Brezhnev, directly echoing the calls of the movement.[97]

As described in Chapter 11, with so many international milestones achieved, the second wave of the anti-nuclear movement began to retrench. In this window of opportunity, governments once again started to escalate nuclear capabilities. However, as with the end of the first wave, government backsliding on commitments once again met with broad popular resistance. A third wave in the renewal of anti-nuclear mass mobilization brought into sharp focus the need to pursue peace instead of escalation, and subsequently, even more governments signed on to nuclear disarmament agreements. This popular pressure continued to have a major influence on international agreements at the regional level.

In 1985, the South Pacific became the next region to sign a nuclear-free agreement, with the Treaty of Rarotonga.[98] Western European governments, too, had moved firmly toward supporting major reductions in nuclear weapons by the mid-1980s. Already in place was the 1958 Treaty Establishing the European Atomic Energy Community (Euratom Treaty), which ensured that nuclear energy

[93] Amitav Acharya and Kenneth Boutin, "The Southeast Asia Nuclear-Weapon Free Zone," *Security Dialogue* 29, 2 (1988): 219–230, https://www.jstor.org/stable/44472123 (accessed May 19, 2023).

[94] Peter Lieberman, "The Rise and the Fall of the South African Bomb," *International Security* 26, 1 (2001): 45–86, https://www.jstor.org/stable/3092122 (accessed May 25, 2023); Helen Purkitt, Stephen Burgess, and Peter Lieberman, "South Africa's Nuclear Decisions," *International Security* 27, 1 (2002): 186–194, https://doi.org/10.1080/13523261003665618.

[95] Stockholm International Peace Research Institute, *The Near-Nuclear Countries and the NPT* (Stockholm: Almqvist & Wiksell, 1972).

[96] Michael Mazarr and Alexander Lennon (eds), *Toward a Nuclear Peace: The Future of Nuclear Weapons* (New York: St Martin's Press, 1991).

[97] Jeremy Stone, "Introduction," in *Seeds of Promise: The First Real Hearings on the Nuclear Arms Freeze*, ed. Randall Forsberg and Alton Frye. (Andover, MA: Brickhouse Publishing, 1983), p. vii.

[98] Arms and Disarmament Stockholm International Peace Research Institute (SIPRI) Findings, "The South Pacific Nuclear Free Zone," *Bulletin of Peace Proposals* 17, 3/4 (1986): 505–508.

Table 3 Main international and regional anti-nuclear policy agreements

Date signed	Name of treaty	Initial signatories
1 December 1959	Antarctic Treaty	Argentina, Australia, Belgium, Chile, France, Japan, New Zealand, Norway, South Africa, the USSR, United Kingdom, United States
5 August 1963	Treaty Banning Nuclear Weapon Tests in the Atmosphere in Outer Space and under Water (Partial Test Ban)	USSR, United Kingdom, United States
27 January 1967	Treaty on Principles Governing the Activities of States in the Exploration and Use of Outer Space, Including the Moon and Other Celestial Bodies (Outer Space Treaty)	USSR, United Kingdom, United States
14 February 1967	Treaty for the Prohibition of Nuclear Weapons in Latin America (Treaty of Tlatelolco)	Latin American countries
1 July 1968	Treaty on the Non-Proliferation of Nuclear Weapons (Non-Proliferation Treaty)	USSR, United Kingdom, United States
11 February 1971	Treaty on the Prohibition of Emplacement of Nuclear Weapons and Other Weapons of Mass Destruction on the Sea-Bed and the Ocean Floor and in the Subsoil Thereof (Sea-Bed Treaty)	USSR, United Kingdom, United States
26 May 1972	Strategic Arms Limitation Treaty (SALT 1)	USSR, United States
18 June 1979	Strategic Arms Limitation Treaty (SALT 2)	USSR, United States
6 August 1985	South Pacific Nuclear Free Zone Treaty (Treaty of Rarotonga)	South Pacific countries
15 December 1995	Treaty on the Southeast Asia Nuclear Weapon-Free Zone (Bangkok Treaty)	Southeast Asian countries
11 April 1996	African Nuclear-Weapon-Free-Zone Treaty (Pelindaba Treaty)	African countries
24 September 1996	Comprehensive Nuclear-Test-Ban Treaty	United Nations countries
8 September 2006	Central Asian Nuclear-Weapon-Free-Zone Treaty (Treaty of Semey)	Kazakhstan, Kyrgyzstan, Tajikistan, Turkmenistan, Uzbekistan
20 September 2017	Treaty on the Prohibition of Nuclear Weapons	United Nations countries

Source: United Nations. *Status of Multilateral Arms Regulation and Disarmament Agreements,* 3rd edn (New York: United Nations Publications, 1987).

technology would not be transformed into military use within the European Community (later European Union). Starting in the 1980s, in response to a concerted
European-wide movement called European Nuclear Disarmament, governments
committed further to the non-use idea. As Harald Müller writes, "This attitude was
expressed in no uncertain terms in the platform of the Western European Union of
autumn 1987."[99] There remained differences of emphasis (i.e., the extent to which
maintaining a minimum deterrent was needed), but progress on the non-use idea
in formal policy was unambiguous. In 1995 and 1996, respectively, the ten countries in the Southeast Asian region (the Bangkok Treaty)[100] and the African region
(Pelindaba Treaty) also formalized their commitments to be nuclear-free zones.[101]
Finally, in the 1990s, Brazil and Argentina agreed to a common nuclear policy
which intensified cooperation in Latin America and ensured that nuclear energy
would only be used for peaceful purposes.[102]

With regard to US–Russian efforts at disarmament, the two superpowers had
agreed to renew and intensify joint reductions in nuclear weapons. Mikhail Gorbachev's leadership, first as Soviet Communist Party secretary starting in 1985,
then as President of the Soviet Union in 1990, was crucial in this respect. Gorbachev had been thoroughly convinced of the importance of the anti-nuclear
movement and the non-use idea since his days in university, when scientists
released the Russell–Einstein Manifesto and sparked international attention.[103] As
a leader, Gorbachev admired anti-nuclear scientists and movement leaders. He
met with them regularly, and they clearly influenced him. In 1986, he announced
a Soviet plan to rid the world of nuclear weapons[104] and, in 1987, signed the
Intermediate-Range Nuclear Forces Treaty with US President Ronald Reagan.

The movement continued to have a strong influence even after the fall of
the USSR brought an end to Gorbachev's leadership. The 1994 Strategic Arms
Reduction Talks (START I) became the most significant and comprehensive arms
control treaty to have ever existed. With its final stage of implementation in 2001, it
resulted in the reduction of 80% of all strategic nuclear weapons in existence at the
time and included a range of verification and accountability mechanisms. Close on
the heels of START I was the 1996 Comprehensive Nuclear-Test-Ban Treaty. Continuing the track record of regional denuclearization, in 2006, Central Asia also

[99] Harald Müller (ed.), *A Survey of European Nuclear Policy, 1985–87* (Houndmills: Macmillan, 1989), p. 7.
[100] Acharya and Boutin, "The Southeast Asia Nuclear-Weapon Free Zone"; for later follow-up, see ASEAN, "Joint Statement of the 3rd ASEAN–U.S. Leaders' Meeting," 2011, https://asean.org/joint-statement-of-the-3rd-asean-u-s-leaders-meeting (accessed May 20, 2023).
[101] Sola Ogunbanwo, "The Treaty of Pelindaba: Africa is Nuclear-Weapon-Free," *Security Dialogue* 27, 2 (1996): 185–200, https://doi.org/10.1177/0967010696027002007.
[102] Jose Goldemberg, Carlos Feu Alvim, and Olga Mafra, "The Denuclearization in Argentina and Brazil," *Journal for Peace and Nuclear Disarmament* 1, 2 (2018): 383–403, https://www.tandfonline.com/doi/abs/10.1080/25751654.2018.1479129 (accessed May 25, 2023).
[103] Wittner, *Confronting the Bomb*, p. 183.
[104] Wittner, *Confronting the Bomb*, pp. 183–184.

joined the other regional nuclear-free zones,[105] and in 2010, New START replaced START I. Building on this, the most recent development—the 2017 Treaty on Prohibition of Nuclear Weapons—takes a human security approach, focusing on protecting potential victims of nuclear weapons use and environmental destruction.[106] For the first time, it also creates a path toward eliminating these weapons entirely.

While these various international treaties are probably the most straightforward way to see the overarching and substantial impact of the anti-nuclear movement, it is important to recognize that, alongside intense international negotiations, the biggest push for these leaders to align on nuclear weapons was global public opinion and domestic society. International negotiations were key to hashing out the details and maintaining transparency, but the political will to restrict nuclear weapons came from the strength of the non-use idea more generally. In effect, as T. V. Paul argues, leaders were willing to "self-deter"; they did not have to be pushed into restraint from their counterparts in other countries.[107] Indeed, some of the most groundbreaking cases of nuclear weapons reductions were unilateral actions on the part of the American (e.g., George H.W. Bush) and Russian (e.g., Mikhail Gorbachev) leaders.[108]

Thus, in response to the grassroots non-use idea, a veritable avalanche of new policies and agreements took hold, reflecting the acceptance by governments and political leaders of the movement's key principles. This is not to say that it was easy or straightforward for governments to act or sign agreements with each other. But it does show that beyond the nitty gritty of diplomacy, negotiations, persuasion, and bargaining, at the end of the day, the world transformed, and it did so in the name of powerful ultrasocial ideas. Just as with the story of European integration and that of international cooperation in space, some outcomes fell short of aspirational goals, but it was in the manifestation of this idealistic ambition that other policies became more acceptable.

In line with the notion that, as a species, we value ultrasocial leadership (those who inspire empathy and support the common good), it is telling that many of the key individuals and groups involved in promoting the non-use idea are Nobel Peace Prize laureates. To name a few, in 1975, Soviet Nuclear Physicist Andrei Sakharov, known as "the father of the Soviet hydrogen bomb," was awarded the

[105] Manasi Kakatkar and Miles Pomper, "Central Asian Nuclear-Weapon-Free Zone Formed," *Arms Control Today* 39, 1 (January/ February 2009): 42, https://www.jstor.org/stable/i23628264 (accessed May 20, 2023).

[106] Denise Garcia, "Attaining Human Security by Disarming," in *Edward Elgar Research Handbook on International Law and Human Security*, ed. Gerd Oberleitner (Northampton, MA: Edward Elgar Publishing, 2022).

[107] T. V. Paul, *The Tradition of Non-use of Nuclear Weapons* (Stanford, CA: Stanford University Press, 2009).

[108] Nina Tannenwald, "The Legacy of the Nuclear Taboo in the Twenty-First Century," in *The Age of Hiroshima*, ed. Michael Gordin and G. John Ikenberry (Princeton: Princeton University Press, 2020), p. 283.

prize. Despite designing the weapon originally, he spent most of the rest of his life speaking out against it, including openly criticizing the Soviet regime.[109] In 1982, Alva Myrdal and Alfonso Garcia Robles received the prize for their public advocacy and work to establish nuclear- and weapon-free zones.[110] In 1985, the International Physicians for the Prevention of Nuclear War received the Nobel Prize. The 1990 Nobel Peace Prize went to Mikhail Gorbachev, who was avidly against the bomb during his leadership of the USSR. 1995 was the year physicist Joseph Rotblat and the Pugwash Conferences were recognized, "for efforts to diminish the part played by nuclear arms in international affairs and, in the longer run, to eliminate such arms."[111] The 2005 prize recognized the International Atomic Energy Committee and Mohamed ElBaradei for working "to prevent nuclear energy from being used for military purposes."[112] In 2009, President Barack Obama was chosen in large part because of his early commitment to rid the world of nuclear weapons and pursue global peace through diplomacy. In 2017, the International Campaign to Abolish Nuclear Weapons was also recognized for the Nuclear Ban Treaty, which paves the way for the prohibition of these weapons entirely.

Of course, many more individuals and groups were involved in railing against the bomb and calling for peace than those chosen by the Nobel Peace Prize committee. However, it is important to emphasize that they would not have been nearly as successful without the general societal belief that non-use had to be the only path forward. To be sure, the non-use idea represented a radical reversal of previous military doctrine. The idea that you could develop a state-of-the-art weapon and then choose *not* to use it was anathema to strategic thinking up until that point. What started out as widespread public pressure, with millions taking to the streets over a period of decades, led to transformational change fueled by the power of possibility. Some leaders had to be forced into a corner before they would change their stance, but over time, the anti-nuclear movement, societal pressure, and the idea they championed became a source of inspiration for governmental leaders from Gorbachev to Obama.

As the twentieth century came to an end, mass protests opposing the bomb all but disappeared. With the end of the Cold War and the collapse of the USSR, the sense of immediate danger began to fade, even while public opinion against the bomb remained very strong.[113] Starting in the mid-1990s, as social pressure faded,

[109] The Nobel Prize, "Andrei Sakharov Facts," 2022, https://www.nobelprize.org/prizes/peace/1975/sakharov/facts (accessed November 30, 2022).

[110] The Nobel Prize, "Press Release," 2022, https://www.nobelprize.org/prizes/peace/1982/press-release (accessed November 30, 2023).

[111] The Nobel Prize, "The Nobel Peace Prize 1995," 2022, https://www.nobelprize.org/prizes/peace/1995/summary (accessed November 30, 2022).

[112] The Nobel Prize, "Mohamed Elbaradei," 2022, https://www.nobelprize.org/prizes/peace/2005/elbaradei/facts (accessed November 30, 2022).

[113] Wittner, *Confronting the Bomb*, p. 219.

governments started to relax efforts at disarmaments. In some cases, they disentangled themselves from previous anti-nuclear and disarmament agreements. For example, in 2002, US President George W. Bush withdrew the United States from the 1972 Anti-Ballistic Missile Treaty and broadened the parameters for the potential use of nuclear weapons (Obama subsequently reinforced nuclear non-use and disarmament, but Trump took the country backward again).[114] Russia and India made similar changes, lowering the threshold for use of the bomb in their nuclear doctrines. And Russian President Vladimir Putin suspended Russia from the Conventional Armed Forces Europe Treaty in 2007 as well as New START in 2023. These developments, among others, have led many experts to argue that the nuclear taboo has become a thing of the past. By contrast, I argue that this is not, in fact, the end of the story. Despite the dramatic weakening of the movement over the past thirty years, the non-use idea still holds when it comes to actual outcomes. Why is this so? I address this puzzle in Chapter 13.

---

[114] Tannenwald, "The Legacy of the Nuclear Taboo in the Twenty-First Century," pp. 284–286.

13

The Taboo and Its Rivals

The Twenty-First Century Nuclear Debate

As time passes and generations change, it is only natural that the more visceral reaction to the tragedy and horror of Hiroshima and Nagasaki would retreat from the public consciousness. And as even more time goes by, the "collective cultural awareness" that came with living under the constant nuclear threat of the Cold War would also fade, especially for the Western and Russian societies that felt it most.[115] But the direct memory of August 1945 and its aftermath was only the starting point for the emergence and persistence of the non-use idea and its implications for our species' tendency toward ultrasociality.

As I have argued, societal belief in a new narrative that connected non-use of nuclear weapons to the achievement of peace in general and the human capacity to create a better future was crucial. This new narrative was, of course, driven by the fear of mutually assured destruction, but it was also rooted in ultrasociality, the human inclination to feel empathy for one another, and the sense that we are all one species. The attraction of the non-use idea was so strong across the globe that it transformed national-security oriented governments and restricted what leaders could do over the course of decades. But with the sharp decline of the anti-nuclear movement by the end of the twentieth century, what has happened to the status of nuclear weapons in the twenty-first century? Is our ultrasocial world weakening?

Most international relations and policy experts contend that the nuclear taboo has significantly diminished since the beginning of this century, and as a result, we are now actually at the precipice of a very dangerous time in human history.[116] They point to several factors. First, they argue that the emergence of new nuclear

---

[115] Mary Sarotte, "I'm a Cold War Historian. We are in a Frightening New Era," *New York Times*, March 1, 2022.

[116] Magnus Loyold, "The Future of the Nuclear Taboo: Framing the Impact of the TPNW," *Journal for Peace and Nuclear Disarmament* 4, 1 (2021): 100–106, https://doi.org/10.1080/25751654.2021. 1940701; Tyler Bowen, Michael Goldfien, and Matthew Graham, "The Illusory Nuclear Taboo," Yale University, February 1, 2021, https://cpb-us-w2.wpmucdn.com/campuspress.yale.edu/dist/4/3650/ files/2021/03/BowenGoldfienGraham_weaktaboo.pdf (accessed May 20, 2023); Eryn MacDonald, "What Is the Nuclear Taboo and Is Putin About to Break It?," Union of Concerned Scientists, 2022, https://allthingsnuclear.org/emacdonald/what-is-the-nuclear-taboo-and-is-putin-about-to-break-it (accessed May 20, 2023); Scott Sagan and Benjamin Valentino, "Revisiting Hiroshima in Iran: What Americans Really Think about Using Nuclear Weapons and Killing Noncombatants," *International Security* 42, 1 (2017): 41–79, https://doi.org/10.1162/ISEC_a_00284; Michael Puttre, "The Taboo against Great Power War Is Gone," *Discourse*, May 16, 2022, https://www.discoursemagazine. com/politics/2022/05/16/the-taboo-against-great-power-war-is-gone (accessed May 20, 2023).

International Cooperation Against All Odds. Mai'a K. Davis Cross, Oxford University Press. © Mai'a K. Davis Cross (2024).
DOI: 10.1093/oso/9780192873903.003.0014

powers, such as Iran and North Korea, are an indication that nuclear proliferation is ongoing, and having the bomb is still regarded as a symbol of national prestige.[117] Second, they argue that the rhetoric around nuclear weapons use seems more cavalier instead of cautious.[118] Kim Jong Un, Donald Trump, and Vladimir Putin, in particular, have been guilty of nuclear saber rattling in recent years.

Third, they point to the fact that nuclear powers have invested large sums of money to upgrade and refine their nuclear arsenals.[119] Related to this, the United States and Russia have developed far more limited, precision-based nuclear weapons that are more tactical in nature, meaning that they have been scaled down to as little as 2% of the explosive force of the bombs used in Hiroshima and Nagasaki.[120] This has worried some leaders, including US President Joe Biden, that crossing the non-use redline and violating the taboo has become much easier to contemplate. Fourth, most international relations and policy experts contend that international nuclear and disarmament agreements in place now are few and far between compared with the Cold War period and that many of the guardrails that existed to de-escalate nuclear conflict have not been maintained.[121] Arguments like these have led many experts to conclude that the unthinkable is thinkable again. Just ten years after making the case that the remarkable strength of the nuclear taboo comes, in part, from society, Tannenwald herself suggests that the taboo is "vanishing."[122]

By contrast, for those who do believe the nuclear taboo holds, some contend that, with the passage of time, there has emerged a tradition (distinct from a taboo) of not resorting to nuclear weapons. The tradition stems from a track record of not using them, an acknowledgement that nuclear weapons are catastrophically destructive, and pointing to the reputational cost any leader would face by using

[117] Nina Tannenwald, "The Vanishing Nuclear Taboo? How Disarmament Fell Apart," *Foreign Affairs* 97, 6 (November/December 2018): 16–24; Erin Hahn and James Scouras, "Responding To North Korean Nuclear First Use: So Many Imperatives, So Little Time," Johns Hopkins Applied Physics Laboratory, 2020.
[118] Nina Tannenwald, "The Legacy of the Nuclear Taboo in the Twenty-First Century," in *The Age of Hiroshima*, ed. Michael Gordin and G. John Ikenberry (Princeton: Princeton University Press, 2020), p. 287; Jeffrey Leis, "'Night of Murder': On the Brink of Nuclear War in South Asia," The Nuclear Threat Initiative, 2019, https://www.nti.org/analysis/articles/night-murder-brink-nuclear-war-south-asia (accessed May 20, 2023); Ansar Abbasi, "Hope India Knows What NCA Means?," *News International*, February 27, 2019, https://www.thenews.com.pk/print/437316-hope-india-knows-what-nca-means (accessed May 19, 2023); Hans Kristensen and Matt Korda, "Pakistani Nuclear Weapons, 2021," *Bulletin of Atomic Scientists* 77, 5 (2021): 165–278; Ed Krayewsk, "Trump Admin Rhetoric Taking U.S.–North Korea Crisis to a Dangerous New Place, Says Kim Jong Il Biographer," *Reason.com*, April 14, 2017, https://reason.com/2017/04/14/trump-admin-rhetoric-taking-us-north-kor (accessed May 20, 2023).
[119] Tannenwald, "The Vanishing Nuclear Taboo?"
[120] William Broad, "The Smaller Bombs That Could Turn Ukraine into a Nuclear War Zone," *New York Times*, March 21, 2022, https://www.nytimes.com/2022/03/21/science/russia-nuclear-ukraine.html (accessed May 20, 2023).
[121] Sarotte, "I'm a Cold War Historian. We are in a Frightening New Era."
[122] Tannenwald, "The Vanishing Nuclear Taboo?"

them.[123] Others have connected non-use to the decline in war more generally over time.[124] If there are fewer wars, there is less need to resort to nuclear weapons in the first place. These two arguments hold some water but tend to discount human agency and do not necessarily tell us why the track record of non-use has been quite so consistent.

There is good reason to question the idea that the nuclear taboo is weakening in the first place. While the Cold War guardrails may have weakened, there is generally less use for nuclear weapons in the post-Cold War world, occasional instances of saber rattling notwithstanding. And since many regions of the world have already agreed to become nuclear-free zones, there is not much need for repeat agreements along these lines. To the extent that new agreements have been signed, they have continued to support previous ones, and they increasingly push back against the resistance that still exists (after all, there will likely always be some who seek to acquire or prepare to use nuclear weapons). Indeed, as Denise Garcia finds, the most recent international anti-nuclear agreement—the 2017 Treaty on the Prohibition of Nuclear Weapons—represents such a watershed in worldwide anti-nuclear policy that it codifies the obsolescence of nuclear deterrence as a viable strategy and grants the humanitarian dimension of the taboo legalized status.[125]

The Staying-Power of the Non-Use Idea

In this chapter, I argue that the power of the non-use idea remains strong, especially because it is connected to a deeper sense of common destiny, empathy for other human beings, and desire to live in a peaceful world—in a word, ultrasociality. At the same time, given that the debate over whether and when to use nuclear weapons is far more settled (it is nearly universally understood that they should not be used at all), I also argue that the non-use idea exerts influence in a different way than before. It is far less reliant on a societal-level movement actively championing it. In fact, the anti-nuclear movement's dissipation is actually a sign that their central idea is sufficiently engrained in our world. Transformational change that is grounded in ultrasociality has already been achieved. To be sure, the more aspirational idea of creating a nuclear-free world has not happened, but non-use has been completely successful for almost eighty years, and disarmament has occurred to a significant extent—from more than 60,000 weapons at the height of the Cold War to around 13,000 today. Building on what we know about the

---

[123] T. V. Paul, *The Tradition of Non-use of Nuclear Weapons* (Stanford, CA: Stanford University Press, 2009).

[124] John Mueller, "The Essential Irrelevance of Nuclear Weapons: Stability in the Postwar World," *International Security* 13, 2 (1988): 55–79, https://doi.org/10.2307/2538971.

[125] Denise Garcia, *Common Good Governance in the Age of Artificial Intelligence* (Oxford: Oxford University Press, 2023), Chapter 5.

nature of ultrasocial ideas, there are at least three reasons why the non-use idea is stronger than it may appear.

First, it is important to note that once an ultrasocial idea emerges and spreads, it is not unusual for it to experience periods of both relative strength and relative weakness. Just like in the cases of the European federalist idea and the Spaceflight Idea, it is not the case that the non-use idea was simply about the idealism of earlier years, which then gradually began to fade. Instead, once the idea captures society's imagination, the process by which it becomes engrained in our institutions and policies carries out over decades, at times more transformational and at others more incremental or transactional. These ups and downs reflect changes in leadership (e.g., from Bush, to Obama, to Trump, to Biden) as well as whether there is a context of crisis.[126] In analyzing the twentieth-century track record, each time a nuclear crisis took place—whether it was in terms of potential use or backsliding on governmental policies—worldwide calls to uphold the taboo grew *stronger*, not weaker. The first successful test of the H-bomb and the Cuban Missile Crisis are examples of crises that intensified the non-use idea. Both precipitated powerful responses from the anti-nuclear movement and the public at large. Moreover, even if the idea is less visible as a rallying point in society, it is not necessarily because it is weaker but, instead, that it is actually less challenged and more taken for granted. As a result, if a situation were to arise in which the non-use idea was truly put to the test, this would likely lead to a resurgence of popular calls to ban the bomb.

Second, and related to this, it is important to recognize that the *actual* non-use of nuclear weapons is distinct from the non-use *idea* but that the former rests on the latter. It will always be the case that one dictator or rogue actor could suddenly use nuclear weapons, defying any logic or common sense. While this would break the tradition of non-use, it would not fundamentally change the idea, neither would it change the prior transformation that has occurred in the international system because of this idea. Leadership responses in the midst of a crisis can be unpredictable and capricious, but entrenched societal norms of non-use are often effective in setting the broader parameters of nuclear policies and reinforcing non-use.

So, what do people think of nuclear weapons today? Public opinion around the world still stands in opposition to them. In 2017, when the United States was in a tense escalation with North Korea over nuclear weapons, 62% of Americans still opposed using the bomb against North Korea (26% supported it under certain circumstances).[127] A 2018 poll found that, "a staggering 85% of the Japanese population would not support US use of nuclear weapons against North Korea, even

---

[126] For examples of the differences between Trump and Biden, see Jack Detsch, "Biden Looks for a New, New START," *Foreign Policy*, 2021, https://foreignpolicy.com/2021/06/22/biden-putin-russia-arms-control-new-start (accessed May 22, 2023); Ellie Garenmayeh, "Iran, the US, and the Nuclear Deal: Biden's Chance to Remove Trump's Poison Pill," European Council on Foreign Relations, April 13, 2022, https://ecfr.eu/article/iran-the-us-and-the-nuclear-deal-bidens-chance-to-remove-trumps-poison-pill (accessed May 21, 2023).

[127] USA Today, "USA Today Poll: September 2017. Question 25: USSUFF.100517.R29," *USA Today*, Cornell University, Roper Center for Public Opinion Research, 2017.

if that country launched a nuclear strike on Japan."[128] In India, citizens responded, in 2015, that they are generally fine with having these weapons, but are highly opposed (around 90%) to "first use" of the bomb.[129] In European Union (EU) countries that host nuclear weapons, anti-nuclear sentiment in 2019 across these countries was consistently in favor of their country signing a nuclear ban treaty (64% in Belgium, 68% in Germany, 70% in Italy, and 62% in the Netherlands).[130]

Although somewhat different from non-use specifically, questions about the proliferation or acquisition of nuclear weapons also shed light on general societal attitudes toward the bomb. For example, around 94% of Americans think that an important foreign policy goal of the United States should be "preventing the spread of nuclear weapons" (only 4% said this was not important at all),[131] and 94% again think that cooperation with other countries on "dealing with the spread of nuclear weapons" is important (with 80% of them saying it is *very* important).[132] In November 2018, when Russians were asked, in a survey, about whether they should expand their country's nuclear arsenal, 57% said no, while 33% said yes.[133] This is particularly remarkable in a society that is continually fed highly nationalistic propaganda, but it is also testimony to the persistence of anti-nuclear ideas more generally. Iranians are in favor of having "a peaceful nuclear energy program" (90%) but are opposed to having nuclear weapons (59%).[134] 75% of Japanese citizens[135] and 74% of Canadians[136] support their countries joining the UN Treaty on the Prohibition of Nuclear Weapons. Going against long-held expert assumptions

[128] Jonathan Baron, Rebecca Davis Gibbons, and Stephen Herzog, "Japanese Public Opinion, Political Persuasion, and the Treaty on the Prohibition of Nuclear Weapons," *Journal for Peace and Nuclear Disarmament* 3, 2 (2020): 301, https://doi.org/10.1080/25751654.2020.1834961.
[129] Aditi Malhotra, "Assessing Indian Nuclear Attitudes," Stimson Center, 2016, p. 19, https://www.stimson.org/wp-content/files/file-attachments/Assessing%20Indian%20Nuclear%20Attitudes%20-%20Final.pdf (accessed May 20, 2023).
[130] ICAN (International Campaign to Abolish Nuclear Weapons), "Polls: Public Opinion in EU Host States Firmly Opposes Nuclear Weapons," International Campaign to Abolish Nuclear Weapons, April 24, 2019, https://www.icanw.org/polls_public_opinion_in_eu_host_states_firmly_opposes_nuclear_weapons (accessed May 21, 2023).
[131] The Chicago Council on Global Affairs, "Poll: 2018 Biannual Survey, Question 27 [31116769.00026]," The Chicago Council on Global Affairs, 2018, GfK Group, Cornell University, Roper Center for Public Opinion Research, 2018.
[132] Pew Global Attitudes Project, "Pew Global Attitudes Project Poll, Question 5 [31117305.00004]," *Pew Global Attitudes Project*, Abt Associates, Cornell University, Roper Center for Public Opinion Research, 2020.
[133] Anna Wagner, "Public Opinion on Nuclear Weapons and Arms Control in Russia," in *On the Horizon*, ed. Reja Younis (Washington DC: Center for Strategic and International Studies, 2021), pp. 168–169.
[134] Dina Smeltz and Amir Farmanesh, "Majority of Iranians Oppose Development of Nuclear Weapons," Chicago Council on Global Affairs, 2020, https://www.thechicagocouncil.org/research/public-opinion-survey/majority-iranians-oppose-development-nuclear-weapons (accessed May 20, 2023).
[135] Baron et al., "Japanese Public Opinion," p. 302.
[136] Nanos Research, "Poll: 74% of Canadians Support Joining the UN Treaty on the Prohibition of Nuclear Weapons," International Campaign to Abolish Nuclear Weapons, April 8, 2021, https://www.icanw.org/poll_74_of_canadians_support_joining_the_un_treaty_on_the_prohibition_of_nuclear_weapons (accessed May 20, 2023).

about nuclear deterrence, in 2015, only 38.46% of young EU citizens (aged 14–30) said that "nuclear weapons made them feel safe," and only 29.09% said that it would be "worse to live under [the Islamic State] than to die in an accidental nuclear explosion,"[137] meaning that a significant majority *really* doesn't want to be a victim of a nuclear attack.

Third, in many respects, the twenty-first century has been far safer than prior periods in terms of the potential of violating the nuclear taboo, despite seemingly weaker nuclear guardrails. Russia's unprovoked invasion of Ukraine on 24 February 2022, followed shortly after by Russian President Vladimir Putin's blatant threat to use nuclear weapons, is a case in point. These events led to much debate amongst Western observers about whether this war could escalate to a nuclear level. As the Russian army chalked up major losses and Western powers strongly rallied around Ukraine, Putin increasingly invoked his willingness to use nuclear weapons. However, this led the rest of the world, especially the West, to use every opportunity to *prevent* escalation to nuclear war. Even as the North Atlantic Treaty Organization (NATO) heavily re-armed in Eastern Europe, and the United States and the EU provided massive transfers of conventional weapons and supplies to Ukraine, leaders were also extremely careful to avoid any steps that could potentially provoke Putin to resort to nuclear war.

Ultimately, Putin did not resort to the use of nuclear weapons. Why is this? Given that more than one nuclear power was involved, some might argue that nuclear deterrence worked for Russia in the sense that Russia's war against Ukraine could be seen as a proxy war between nuclear powers—Russia and the West. Once Putin's attack on Ukraine began in 2022, all parties were very concerned that if NATO countries became directly involved in the conflict, this would constitute open war between nuclear powers, and the stakes would go up significantly. This argument, however, falls short as it fails to recognize that Putin did not actually see the invasion as a proxy war but as a "civilizational necessity" to unite Russian speakers and restore what he thought should rightfully be part of Russian territory.[138] Moreover, Putin's delusional thinking notwithstanding, for their part, Western powers had no formal obligation to protect Ukraine. They did so in the name of democracy and the liberal world order, cherished ideas that are intimately connected to the norm of use of force as a last resort. Each step of the way, NATO countries made significant efforts to avoid a larger war. Even Russia's own military doctrine of "escalate to de-escalate" means that the country seeks to get its enemies

---

[137] Benoit Pelopidas, "The Next Generation(S) of Europeans Facing Nuclear Weapons: Forgetful, Indifferent, But Supportive?" *Non-proliferation Papers* 56 (2017): 11.

[138] Benjamin Young, "Putin Has a Grimly Absolute Vision of the 'Western World'," *Foreign Policy*, March 6 2022, https://foreignpolicy.com/2022/03/06/russia-putin-civilization (accessed May 21, 2023).

to take a step backward and behave more cautiously.[139] The causes and conduct of the war were not based in nuclear deterrence but in the power of ideas.

Moreover, no one except Putin himself wanted the war in the first place, and the thought of nuclear war was highly undesirable to everyone else. Besides the tragic losses that the Ukrainians suffered, one of the most significant developments in the wake of Russia's invasion was that most of the world quickly stood together in support of Ukraine. Moreover, economically, militarily, and politically, the West spoke with one voice and threw its weight behind condemning Russia's invasion. Some compared Putin's behavior to nineteenth-century imperialism, arguing that the world has now moved beyond this type of behavior. In short, there was a silver lining to Russia's aggression: when put to the test, world leaders stood firmly against both unprovoked war and the use of nuclear weapons.

In the end, while the nuclear movement of the twentieth century did not carry over into the twenty-first, in many ways its decline is a product of its very success. The non-use idea holds, even when pushed to its limits. Human society is generally opposed to the spread, use, and threat of nuclear weapons. Nearly all leaders around the world take this for granted. When a rogue leader today threatens to break the nuclear taboo, this is met with widescale alarm and global condemnation. The most recent Nuclear Ban Treaty, which went into effect in 2021, is stronger than the treaties that came before and more reflective of our ultrasocial nature. It explicitly embeds the prohibition of nuclear weapons in the larger goals of peace and puts humanitarian concerns front and center. For the past two centuries, we, as a species, have increasingly sought to avoid war, and this is now reflected in national policies and global governance. We recognize that sometimes unprovoked aggression must be met with a response in order to uphold the order that exists today but that, even in these instances, the common goal is the maintenance of peace.

---

[139] Alexander Nazaryan, "How Serious Is Russia about Nuclear War?" *Yahoo News*, May 7, 2022, https://news.yahoo.com/how-serious-is-russia-about-nuclear-war-090015298.html (accessed May 20, 2023).

Conclusion to Part IV

Part IV of this book highlights the ultrasocial context underlying the emergence, solidification, and spread of the nuclear weapons taboo, which eventually led to significant policy transformation around the world. What started out as a dangerous game of nuclear one-upmanship, including the actual use of nuclear weapons at Hiroshima and Nagasaki, quickly developed into the widely held belief that these weapons should never be used. The non-use idea was not only a reaction *against* its consequences but also a parallel sense of *optimism* for what such opposition could mean for world order and peaceful co-existence.

In striving to explain a nearly eighty-year pattern of non-use, an ultrasocial approach draws attention to how a compelling idea, grounded in empathy and a sense of common humanity, led to the strongest societal movement in modern times. While much of the social movements literature focuses on campaigns to promote a particular political view or the self-interest of a particular identity-based group, an understanding of ultrasociality goes well beyond this to underscore the importance of inspiration, optimism, and transformational ideas in impacting the future of humankind and the potential for international cooperation.

In this context, the anti-nuclear movement played a key role in the achievement of a highly significant and transformational goal. Even though the outcome did not fulfill *all* of the movement's goals, such as ridding the world of nuclear weapons entirely or stopping the arms race between the United States and the USSR, its successes were striking.[140] Indeed, in 1945, the atomic scientists who heavily resisted and warned about the bomb would have been surprised that by the early 1980s, nuclear weapons had not been used again despite the ongoing Cold War. These scientists had also expected that far more countries—at least fifty—would have developed the bomb in this time, and even this did not come to pass.[141] Crucially, the movement succeeded in convincing many ordinary citizens in countries around the world that they had a right to have a voice when it came to national security, and they exercised this right.[142] This gave the idea and the movement its staying power, with dramatic results on the world stage.

---

[140] Jeremy Stone, "Introduction," in *Seeds of Promise: The First Real Hearings on the Nuclear Arms Freeze*, ed. Randall Forsberg and Alton Frye (Andover, MA: Brickhouse Publishing, 1983), p. vi. Also see, Noam Chomsky, *Internationalism or Extinction*, ed. Charles Derber, Suren Moodliar, and Paul Shannon (New York: Routledge, 2020), pp. 27–30.

[141] Stone, "Introduction," p. 7.

[142] Pam Solo, *From Protest to Policy* (Cambridge: Ballinger Publishing Company, 1988), p. 1.

Even though the international community today struggles to prevent countries like North Korea and Iran from developing their own nuclear weapons technology or Russia from threatening its use, the power of the ultrasocial world is now strongly felt, leading to widespread cooperation to condemn and prevent the use of nuclear weapons. Still, we should not be complacent. The case of nuclear weapons shows that societal values and beliefs do matter. Media headlines, even when seemingly alarmist, can sometimes help in recentering the importance of maintaining the taboo. Transformational change is possible based on a public desire to achieve it, and once transformed, the world tends to stay rooted in that area of the ultrasocial landscape. But as Pam Solo recognized at the height of the Cold War, "peace advocates will continue to fail or fall short of their goals unless they radically alter the terms of the debate and challenge the deep structures of militarism."[143] Railing against the bomb provided an opening for new ideas and opportunities, but these must also continue to be about the quest for peace more generally.

[143] Solo, *From Protest to Policy*, p. 3.

PART V

CLIMATE CHANGE

The climate crisis is the most pressing issue of the twenty-first century. Time to solve this crisis is running out, and even if we manage to achieve serious international cooperation, the effect of our efforts will not be felt immediately. Turning the tide on catastrophic climate change requires short-term dramatic transformation in human behavior, which will only have a tangible effect over the long term. But the survival of Earth itself as we know it is at stake. Some scholars have pointed out that the combination of aiming for long-term, intangible success with short-term significant sacrifice does not resonate well with human psychology.[1] And as discussed in Part I, we tend to be optimistic about the future. Given the overwhelmingly dire situation all living beings face, it can be tempting to assume that we will (because we must) find a way to deal with global warming before it's too late and that there will always be some avenue available that will save us.[2] But by that same token, it is also easy to succumb to a sense of hopelessness.

In contrast to the three previous cases discussed in this book, the climate crisis is far from settled and still very much a work in progress in terms of human efforts to grapple with it. While optimism may be warranted (after all, we have achieved great and unexpected things many times through the course of history), so far, climate change seems to be a story of doing too little, too late. Unlike the cases of European federalism and the Spaceflight Idea, achieving even a significant level of international cooperation may still be insufficient for the task at hand. As with the case of nuclear weapons, the fate of the planet is on the line. Carbon reductions must be meaningful enough to keep global warming to a limit of 1.5°C, or at most, 2°C. If we cross this threshold, then any amount of collective effort may ultimately be for nothing.

However, focusing only on the potential for failure and the ways in which cooperation has been insufficient runs the risk of ignoring how and why there actually

---

[1] George Hoberg, *The Resistance Dilemma: Place-Based Movements and the Climate Crisis* (Cambridge, MA: MIT University Press, 2021), p. 3.

[2] Jennie C. Stephens and Nils Markusson, "Technological Optimism in Climate Mitigation: The Case of Carbon Capture and Storage," in *Oxford Handbook of Energy and Society*, ed. Debra J. Davidson and Matthias Gross (Oxford: Oxford University Press, 2018).

has been significant progress in the quest to save the planet. Admittedly, the climate crisis entered the collective consciousness much more recently than European Union integration, space exploration, and nuclear weapons. It was not until the late 1980s and early 1990s that society started to become aware of an impending global-warming emergency. It was only in the mid-2000s that a societal upswell to address this started to take place. And the full-scale social impetus behind transforming our world and stopping climate change really only began in the mid-2010s. But progress since then has been real and significant, and we must understand the nature of what we *have* achieved—despite the obstacles and setbacks—in order to find the path forward. An ultrasocial approach is very helpful in this regard.

The transformational idea that arose as a rallying point for ultrasociality here was the concept of *net zero*, that is, the understanding that the emission of green-house gases must be reduced to such an extent planet-wide that it is possible to offset the remaining emissions entirely. There is a variety of ways to offset carbon, such as through carbon capture, methane capture, planting trees, and funding the reduction of synthetic fertilizer, among other things.[3] Climate data shows that net zero must be achieved by the middle of the twenty-first century to keep global warming to the now internationally agreed-upon target of 1.5°C. There is a small window of opportunity to prevent the worst, but it rests entirely in the hands of human beings and the governments that represent us.

There is a tendency to assume that because climate change is still a problem and countries have not yet committed to a level of emissions reduction that will save the planet, the net-zero idea has failed. However, it is still important to recognize the power and impact of the idea even as it has faced challenges and detractors. Since net zero's emergence, there has been a transformation in the way society and the climate movement have come together around the goal of climate action. In the lead-up to the 2015 Paris climate change agreement (COP21), as net zero moved from epistemic communities of climate scientists to the broader community of climate activists, businesses, economists, non-governmental organizations (NGOs), and citizens, the idea took on a broader and more forward-looking meaning. It started to develop the potential for transcendent impact, optimism, and a new narrative, qualities that can galvanize an ultrasocial response.

Each case in this book showcases the importance of starting with an ultrasocial ontology, but such an approach also reveals processes that might detract from ultrasociality. Part V shows how, when efforts to stop climate change become too bogged down with transactional identity-based claims and fragmentation of purpose, this sacrifices the power of possibility and the ability to inspire on a global scale. It takes a common, aspirational vision and wide-scale societal support to

---

[3] Renee Cho, "Net Zero Pledges: Can They Get Us Where We Need to Go?," Columbia Climate School, State of the Planet, December 16, 2021, https://news.climate.columbia.edu/2021/12/16/net-zero-pledges-can-they-get-us-where-we-need-to-go (accessed May 20, 2021).

provide momentum behind a broad-based movement that understands the planet as a single, shared home for us all. Climate activist Wen Stephenson, writing in 2015, describes the climate movement as, "less like environmentalism and more like the human-rights and social-justice struggles of the nineteenth and twentieth centuries. A movement for human solidarity."[4]

An ultrasocial approach sheds light on what has empowered and disempowered the growth of the net-zero idea, while still recognizing that, since the idea became part of the climate narrative, it has become unambiguously stronger. In contrast to the cases of European integration, human spaceflight, and nuclear weapons, those pioneers who worked toward mitigating climate change early on unintentionally helped to prevent a transformational idea from emerging and gaining traction at the societal level. Early leadership decisions and a tendency to disaggregate efforts in the climate movement played a role in undermining the idea's rise from within (beyond those who would actively work against it, such as deniers of climate science). A tendency for climate experts and those involved in international climate negotiations to become highly technical, create narrow goals, neglect an overarching narrative, and rely too heavily on localized, identity-based claims initially worked against unleashing what might have naturally reverberated through broader society as an ultrasocial endeavor.

Starting with the lead-up to the 2015 Paris climate change agreement, there has been palpable change. Diverse sectors of global civil society have come together and have been successful. They have amplified a new narrative that the net-zero idea goes hand-in-hand with economic growth and equitable development, that is, burden sharing—some countries will reach net zero faster, so developing countries can take more time.[5] In making this connection, they have created room for justified optimism and a narrative of a better future that is less about sacrifice than transformation. They have pursued a more ambitious, shared agenda of achieving net zero by the second half of the twenty-first century and have set a common goal of limiting climate change to 1.5°C. In just a few short years, the world went from having little understanding of climate change, and no concrete plan to reign it in, to a totally transformed international environment, where 136 countries—including the biggest emitters: China, the United States, and the European Union—have committed to reach net zero by mid-century.[6] While we cannot

[4] Wen Stephenson, *What We're Fighting For Now Is Each Other: Dispatches from the Front Lines of Climate Justice* (Boston, MA: Beacon Press, 2015), p. ix.

[5] Sam Fankhauser, Stephen M. Smith, Myles Allen, Kaya Axelsson, Thomas Hale, Cameron Hepburn, J. Michael Kendall, Radhika Khosla, Javier Lezaun, Eli Mitchell-Larson, Michael Obersteiner, Lavanya Rajamani, Rosalind Rickaby, Nathalie Seddon, and Thom Wetzer, "The Meaning of Net Zero and How to Get It Right," *Nature Climate Change* 12 (2022): p. 18, https://doi.org/10.1038/s41558-021-01245-w.

[6] Fankhauser et al., "The Meaning of Net Zero and How to Get It Right," p. 16; Energy and Climate Intelligence Unit, "Net Zero Scoreboard," 2022, https://eciu.net/netzerotracker (accessed May 22, 2023); Renee Cho, "Net Zero Pledges."

yet know the extent to which they will actually abide by this, there has clearly been significant progress. In short, the net-zero idea that started out as aspirational in 2013 had become mainstream by 2021.[7]

To be sure, not enough has been done yet to avoid crossing the threshold. If we stay on the path charted at the 2021 UN Climate Summit in Glasgow (COP26), scientists estimate that temperatures will rise 2.4°C above pre-industrial levels by the end of the twenty-first century. This is not good enough. It would result in mass extinction, water shortages, and significant agricultural land loss.[8] However, without any efforts at international cooperation, temperatures would have risen 4–6°C by the end of the twenty-first century.[9] The Paris Agreement brought this down to 3–5°C, COP24 in 2018 achieved 3°C, followed by that 2.4°C level at COP26 in Glasgow. International cooperation in successive phases—as long as there is follow-through—has clearly made a difference, and there is no reason to assume that efforts cannot become more ambitious still.

If we manage to keep warming at, or below, the goal of 1.5°C since pre-industrial times, the world may yet find ways to adapt and avoid environmental catastrophe. But the first step is to understand what has worked so far in the short period of time that has elapsed since awareness of climate change became widespread. After each United Nations climate summit, there is typically an avalanche of criticism and little recognition of achievement, but this can be counterproductive. Many scholars have pointed to the hopelessness of our situation because of the self-interest of individual countries,[10] but this sort of obstacle has actually been surmountable in the past. An ultrasocial approach recognizes shortcomings but also underlines the power of possibility, revealing more about where we actually stand and what is imaginable in our progress to stop climate change.

Chapter 14 examines the period from the late 1980s when decision makers and environmental leaders initially made choices that worked against the flourishing of ultrasociality. Chapter 15 describes the emergence of the net-zero idea and the early development of the climate movement. Drawing upon my own participant observation at the 2015 UN Paris climate summit (COP21), I shed light on the lead-up to COP21 and the Paris Agreement itself to explain how and why the climate movement became galvanized around the idea of net zero. The net-zero idea became so powerful that various facets of civil society set aside differences to work

---

[7] Michael Jacobs, "High Pressure for Low Emissions: How Civil Society Created the Paris Climate Agreement," *Juncture* 22, 4 (2016): 314–323, https://doi.org/10.1111/j.2050-5876.2016.00881.x.

[8] Michael Jacobs, "Reflections on COP26: International Diplomacy, Global Justice and the Greening of Capitalism," *Political Quarterly* 93, 2 (April–June 2022): 272, https://doi.org/10.1111/1467-923X.13083.

[9] Jacobs, "Reflections on COP26," p. 273.

[10] Eugene Nulman, *Climate Change and Social Movements: Civil Society and the Development of National Climate Change Policy* (Basingstoke: Palgrave Macmillan, 2015); Matthew Paterson, "IR Theory: Neo-realism, Neo-institutionalism and the Climate Convention," in *The Environment and International Relations*, ed. John Vogler and Mark Imber (Oxfordshire: Taylor & Francis, 1995), pp. 59–77.

toward a common goal. Local and regional initiatives to tackle climate change also blossomed. Throughout Part V, we can see how an ultrasocial approach shows that the climate movement has been most effective at inspiring change when it frames the net-zero idea as a transformational opportunity to address the climate crisis in a broad and inclusive way. When climate efforts become too bogged down in technical details or specific special interests, it falters.

14

The Climate Movement

The so-called Great Acceleration began around 1950: carbon concentration levels in the atmosphere started to rise far more quickly than at any point in the current geological epoch, eventually surpassing safe levels in the 2010s.[11] Of course, in the mid-twentieth century, most people were unaware that their activities would grow into a twenty-first-century climate crisis.[12] It wasn't until almost four decades later, in 1988, that the National Aeronautics and Space Administration (NASA) scientist James Hansen testified to the US Senate that climate change was already happening and that the science behind it gave him "99% confidence" in this.[13] To be sure, scientists had started to document a persistent rise in global temperatures by the 1970s, but Hansen's testimony was a major juncture at which the American public started to become aware of global warming. In 1989, TIME Magazine's cover named Earth the "Planet of the Year," with an issue devoted to climate change, and Bill McKibben published *The End of Nature*, the first book on climate change aimed at informing the public.[14] In his book, McKibben vividly describes how humans have changed the very composition of the atmosphere and lays out what the near future on a warming planet will look like.[15]

Over the subsequent decades, a significant climate movement emerged, spreading the knowledge that human-caused global warming threatens life on Earth and that governments therefore must make radical changes in policy to avert global catastrophe.[16] The public became increasingly informed of this planetary threat

---

[11] Michael Mann, Raymond Bradley, and Malcolm Hughes, "Global-Scale Temperature Patterns and Climate Forcing over the Past Six Centuries," *Nature* 392, 6678 (1998): 779–787, https://doi.org/10.1038/33859; Noam Chomsky, *Internationalism or Extinction*, ed. Charles Derber, Suren Moodliar, and Paul Shannon (New York: Routledge, 2020), pp. 7–8. Up to 350 parts per million (ppm) is safe; the world exceeded 400 ppm in 2016. See UC San Diego, "The Keeling Curve," 2022, https://keelingcurve.ucsd.edu (accessed May 25, 2023) for the latest carbon dioxide reading and the Keeling Curve, which depicts the Great Acceleration.

[12] In the late 1950s, atmospheric carbon dioxide rise was observed for the first time at the Oak Ridge National Laboratory, but widespread knowledge of this took decades to become mainstream. Oak Ridge National Laboratory, "Cumulative Global Fossil-Fuel CO2 Emissions," chart, 2008. Brian Tokar, "Democracy, Localism, and the Future of the Climate Movement," *World Futures* 71, 3–4 (2015): 65–75, https://doi.org/10.1080/02604027.2015.1092785.

[13] United States, Congress, Senate, Committee on Energy and Natural Resources, *Greenhouse Effect and Global Climate Change, Before the U.S. Senate Committee on Energy and Natural Resources* (Washington, DC: U.S. Government Printing Office, 1988), p. 39.

[14] Kelsey Dunn, "Currents of Change: Tracing the History of the U.S. Climate Movement," Honors thesis, Wellesley College, June 2021, p. 15.

[15] Bill McKibben, *The End of Nature* (New York: Random House, 1989).

[16] Matthias Dietz and Heiko Garrelts (eds), *Routledge Handbook of the Climate Change Movement* (London and New York: Routledge, 2014), p. 1.

International Cooperation Against All Odds. Mai'a K. Davis Cross, Oxford University Press. © Mai'a K. Davis Cross (2024).
DOI: 10.1093/oso/9780192873903.003.0015

and threw their support behind working together to find a solution. Then, as the effects of climate change actually began to be felt, with rising temperatures, extreme weather patterns, and wildfires, the problem attracted even more attention. In 2006, TIME Magazine published another famous cover: "Be Worried, Be Very Worried," with an iconic image of a polar bear on vanishing ice. As heartbreaking as this image was, and what it represented for all life on Earth, these galvanizing moments also heralded eventual progress in human efforts to start to solve this emergency. International consensus solidified around an understanding that a 2°C limit needed to be set on global warming.[17] Then world leaders reduced this to a more ambitious 1.5°C limit.

This chapter describes the emergence of the early climate movement before the rise of the transformational idea of net zero. In the 1980s and 1990s, the climate movement, initially rooted in the earlier environmental movement, at first struggled to have an impact, both on society and on governments. However, understanding precisely why this happened is valuable in highlighting the ways in which leaders and strategies can sometimes undermine what would otherwise be an area of human interaction that not only taps into but also requires ultrasociality. Eventually, as we will see in Chapter 15, the emergence of the transformational idea of net zero—how to eliminate net carbon emissions by the mid-twenty-first century—would pull the climate movement together to be a powerful human force on a global scale.

Climate Activists and Society

Ecological awareness amongst humans can be traced back to at least 5,000 years ago. Several of the earliest known stories from across culture, time, and place expressed the importance of existing in harmony with nature and limiting human action to protect the sacred and precious wilderness.[18] From the Mesopotamian Epic of Gilgamesh, to the Indus civilization of Mohenjo Darro, to Ancient Greek mythology, there is evidence of a concern for the environment. The ideational origins of modern environmental protectionism can be found in the eighteenth century. Several major figures produced works explicitly advocating for ecological conservation, including Jeremy Bentham, Thomas Malthus, and Joseph Fourier. The first environmental activists are thought to be the Bishnoi Hindus of Khejarli, who gave their lives in 1720 trying to protect a forest that was subsequently

---

[17] Jim Yong Kim, "Transforming the Economy to Achieve Zero Net Emissions," Council on Foreign Relations, 2014, https://www.worldbank.org/en/news/speech/2014/12/08/transforming-the-economy-to-achieve-zero-net-emissions (accessed July 4, 2023).

[18] Rex Weyler, "A Brief History of Environmentalism," Greenpeace, January 5, 2018, https://www.greenpeace.org/international/story/11658/a-brief-history-of-environmentalism (accessed May 21, 2023).

THE CLIMATE MOVEMENT 219

demolished for the Maharaja of Jodhpur's palace.[19] These early efforts, and the many that followed, paved the way to the twenty-first-century climate movement and the power of the net-zero idea.

While the science of climate change was already clear in the 1970s, the movement initially got off to a slow start, particularly in the United States. The goal was to reduce carbon emissions, and in pursing this, early activists encountered several obstacles. Early leadership decisions inadvertently worked against ultrasociality. Just as during certain periods of the European integration project, efforts to mitigate climate change started off in a more transactional, rather than transformational, way. This led to a delay in broader awareness of the climate crisis both in the United States—home to many of the most influential international environmental organizations—and around the world.

To be sure, although scientists knew that humans were causing climate change, they had not yet arrived at the specific concept of net zero in the first two decades of climate action. Scientists and environmentalists certainly pursued the goal that carbon emissions had to be reduced, and this had to be done quickly through an all-out global effort. This knowledge was enough to allow environmental activists to get to work right away. As they began to push for reductions in carbon emissions, climate science got more and more precise, and the power of international scientific consensus, especially communicated through the Intergovernmental Panel on Climate Change (IPCC), was increasingly solidified. In this sense, the climate case is distinct from the others in this book: the movement got underway without necessarily having solidified the transformational idea that they would have later.

At the same time, the environmental movement was no stranger to the power of possibility and the galvanizing momentum of ultrasocial ideas. One prominent example is Earth Day, which first occurred in the United States on April 22, 1970. With more than 20 million people participating, including many who had not been part of environmental initiatives in the past, such as the United Auto Workers and the peace movement, it is still the largest protest to occur on a single day in history. Among other things, it was inspired by Rachel Carson's 1962 *Silent Spring*, which was one of the first major works to alert Americans to the problems with pesticides and pollution. It was also inspired by the famous 1968 NASA photo of the Earth-rise as seen from the Moon. The strength of Earth Day, which has been celebrated annually ever since, led to a whole range of groundbreaking environmental legislation in the United States that had not previously existed, such as the Clean Air Act and the Clean Water Act. Then, in 1990, on its twentieth anniversary, Earth Day went global, resulting in a large range of events and gatherings in 141 countries. It eventually grew to include over a billion people from 193 countries. Underlining its historic prominence, the Paris climate change agreement was signed by over 120 countries on Earth Day in 2016.

[19] Welyer, "A Brief History of Environmentalism."

Importantly, major environmental initiatives like Earth Day not only demonstrate the inherent ultrasocial capacity of people around the world when it comes to the environment but also provide precursors to what the net-zero idea would become. Earth Day activists realized that even though pollution and environmental destruction disproportionately impacted poor communities, it was important to elevate environmental issues to a broader level so that those in the middle class would also see it as an issue that impacted all of society, not just the poor. Like many environmental problems, the climate movement's eventually agreed-upon net-zero idea relies on ultrasociality—the whole world must work together to bring it about and see it as a *human* concern and a *human* opportunity.

Just as the anti-nuclear movement grew out of the peace movement, the climate movement grew out of the environmental movement. And just as atomic scientists were first involved in raising the alarm about nuclear weapons, environmental scientists did the same for global warming. In both cases, these experts started to warn government officials. For climate, this effort began in the 1970s.[20] However, climate experts were not able to make much headway until the realities of global warming began to gain the attention of major environmental groups in the late 1980s. Various mainstream groups in the United States and Europe (see Table 4), such as the World Wildlife Fund, the Environmental Defense Fund, and Greenpeace International, began to get organized and formed the first international network, the Climate Action Network (CAN) in 1989. CAN quickly grew to encompass sixty-three non-governmental organizations (NGOs) based in twenty-two countries,[21] and a big part of this expansion was the inclusion of those in developing countries.[22] In 2022, CAN's membership comprised 1,800 NGOs from more than 130 countries.[23]

In the early stages, however, these mainstream environmental groups still had difficulty building a ground-up climate change movement of the sort that would tap into the power of possibility and human ultrasociality. Instead, they focused more narrowly on the science behind climate change and pushed for governments to change their policies.[24] As such, they were up against entrenched fossil-fuel lobbies,[25] and they, in turn, had to lobby politicians for specific carbon reduction targets, among other things. Accustomed to earlier environmental

---

[20] Dietz and Garrelts, *Routledge Handbook of the Climate Change Movement*), p. 5.

[21] Eugene Nulman, *Climate Change and Social Movements: Civil Society and the Development of Climate Change Policy* (Basingstoke: Palgrave MacMillan, 2015), p. 12.

[22] Ian McGregor, "Organising to Influence the Global Politics of Climate Change," School of Management, UTS, Sydney, p. 5, https://opus.lib.uts.edu.au/bitstream/10453/11492/1/2008000811OK.pdf (accessed May 20, 2023).

[23] Climate Network Action International, "Tackling the Climate Crisis," 2022, https://climatenetwork.org (accessed May 20, 2023).

[24] Dunn, "Currents of Change."

[25] Peter Newell, *Climate for Change: Non-state Actors and the Global Politics of the Greenhouse* (Cambridge: Cambridge University Press, 2000), pp. 96–122.

strategies and campaigns, they focused on small successes in the hopes that being able to claim incremental victories would keep the momentum of the campaign going.[26]

Unfortunately, during this initial period, environmental groups were rarely able to secure even small achievements, although they did manage to play a role in kicking off the first United Nations General Assembly to establish the Intergovernmental Negotiating Committee for a Framework Convention on Climate Change, which resulted in the UN Framework Convention on Climate Change (UNFCCC) signed at the 1992 Earth Summit in Rio de Janeiro.[27] This first major attempt at international agreement on climate, however, ended up without specific targets and only a non-binding aim to keep emissions at 1990 levels by the year 2000. Nonetheless, the Earth Summit was still a major milestone, and it paved the way for the 1997 Kyoto Protocol, which was legally binding.[28]

The annual UN Conference of the Parties (COP), established as the supreme decision-making body of the UNFCC, first convened in 1995 in Berlin. It quickly became the main opportunity for governments to negotiate their coordinated response to climate change. From the very first UNFCC meeting, governments agreed that civil society's participation was important and invited civil society groups to be involved. However, after Kyoto, many civil society groups, including the Climate Action Network, participated at UN international negotiations with a strategy of pushing for small and gradual reductions in emissions.[29] COP meetings ceased to be a venue for the types of arguments, grounded in the common good, that the fledgling climate movement needed to make in order to create real momentum.[30] Before Kyoto, although still not oriented toward broader international society, the discussions were still bigger picture and more political than technical.[31] So, even though climate activists were able to participate at these major international forums, they did so in a way that did not foster broader public awareness and participation. Any kind of ultrasocial breakthrough was stymied.

---

[26] Nulman, *Climate Change and Social Movements*, p. xiii.

[27] United Nations Conference, "United Nations Conference on Environment and Development," Rio de Janeiro, Brazil, June 3–14, 1992, https://www.un.org/en/conferences/environment/rio1992 (accessed May 21, 2023).

[28] Nulman, *Climate Change and Social Movements*, p. 15.

[29] Patrick Bond, *The Politics of Climate Justice: Paralysis Above, Movement Below* (Scottsville, KY: University of KwaZulu–Natal Press, 2012), pp. 185–186.

[30] Simone Pulver, "Power in the Public Sphere: The Battles between Oil Companies and Environmental Groups in the United Nations Climate Change Negotiations 1991–2003," PhD thesis, University of California Berkeley, 2004, p. 278.

[31] Christian Holz, "The Public Spheres of Climate Change Advocacy Networks: An Ethnography of Climate Action Network International within the United Nations Framework Convention on Climate Change (UNFCC)," PhD thesis, University of Glasgow, 2012, p. 80.

The US Case

It is worth focusing on the US side of these developments because of the central role the United States has played both as a major carbon emitter and a significant leader in international negotiations. Just like early efforts to foster a bottom-up climate movement, the American story of addressing climate change has also been one of early setbacks. In the late 1980s and the 1990s, mainstream environmental groups, such as the Sierra Club, National Resources Defense Council, Friends of the Earth, and Environmental Action largely framed tackling climate change in an individualist, consumerist way.[32] Their public outreach emphasized how individuals should buy the "right" cars, conserve energy, recycle, and personally lobby their representatives to call attention to the problem. Michael Maniates points to a range of reasons for this approach, including, "the historic baggage of mainstream environmentalism, the core tenets of liberalism, the dynamic ability of capitalism to commodify dissent, and the relatively recent rise of *global* environmental threats to human prosperity."[33] However, shifting the emphasis and responsibility from governance and society to individuals made it difficult to galvanize a common cause around climate change that would resonate with our ultrasocial inclinations.

In addition, these US-based environmental groups at first set very limited and technical goals, explicitly shying away from bolder demands. They chose an insider-politics strategy, focusing their efforts on lobbying Congress. In particular, they concentrated on achieving energy efficiency and had specifically zeroed in on automobile fuel efficiency. As Kelsey Dunn argues, by focusing on these insider strategies, the environmental groups were playing a game in which the auto industry could also participate on its own terms.[34] This made it a difficult game to win.

Beyond these initially narrow aims, environmental groups in the United States also tended to compromise on goals very quickly. In his study comparing national-level environmental organizations to grassroots groups, Douglas Bevington finds that whenever the former sought political compromise instead of what was really necessary from an environmental perspective, they inevitably failed. He writes:

> The climate crisis is an unprecedented threat. Stopping global warming will require large-scale social change. To achieve that level of social change, we will need environmental groups that are bold and unconstrained, that do not fear controversy or conflict, and that advocate for what is ecologically necessary rather than what is narrowly seen as politically realistic.[35]

---

[32] Dunn, "Currents of Change," pp. 28–29.

[33] Michael Maniates, "Individualization: Plant a Tree, Buy a Bike, Save the World?" *Global Environmental Politics* 1, 3 (2001): 33, https://doi.org/10.1162/152638001316881395.

[34] Dunn, "Currents of Change," p. 26.

[35] Douglas Bevington, *The Rebirth of Environmentalism: Grassroots Activism from the Spotted Owl to the Polar Bear* (Washington, DC: Island Press, 2009), p. 237.

Table 4 Examples of mainstream environmental organizations

Organization	Year founded/location	Membership	Goals
Sierra Club	1892 San Francisco	3.8 million supporters, 750,000 of which are members	To educate and empower citizens to protect and responsibly enjoy the Earth's natural resources, decrease atmospheric pollution, and prevent a warming climate.
National Wildlife Federation	1936 Washington DC	6 million	To advance wildlife conservation efforts through advocacy and strategic action plans aimed at defending public lands, protecting at-risk wildlife, and restoring natural habitats.
National Resources Defense Council	1970 New York	Over 3 million	To ensure universal access to the Earth's natural resources, tackle the climate crisis, and build resilient communities through the support of transnational advocacy and expert networks.
Environmental Defense Fund	1967 New York	1.5 million	To bring together scientists and other experts to solve environmental challenges facing the climate, oceans, ecosystems, and health.
Greenpeace	1971 Vancouver	250,000 (US) 2.8 million (worldwide)	To support a global network that takes creative action to protect the environment and push for peace through non-violent means.
Friends of the Earth International	1969 San Francisco	Seventy-five national organizations	To promote a healthy climate and social justice through awareness, grassroots advocacy, and the empowerment of all people to participate in public decision making.
Rainforest Action Network	1985 San Francisco	10,000	To protect forests, the climate, and human rights by confronting corporate power and injustice through impactful partnerships and action plans.
World Wildlife Fund	1961 Morges, Switzerland	5 million members	To focus on climate resilience, food security, and conservation to reduce humanity's environmental footprint.

Sources: Environmental Defense Fund, "About Building a Better Future Together," 2022, http://edf.org/about (accessed December 1, 2022); Friends of the Earth International, "Who We Are," 2022, https://www.foei.org/who-are-friends-of-the-earth/ (accessed July 11, 2023); Greenpeace, "About Us," 2022, http://greenpeace.org/international/tag/about-us (accessed December 1, 2022); National Resources Defense Council, "About NRDC," 2022, http://nrdc.org/about (accessed December 1, 2022); National Wildlife Federation, "Our Mission," 2022, http://nwf.org/About-Us/Our-Mission (accessed December 1, 2022); Rainforest Action Network, "Mission and Values," 2022, http://ran.org/mission-and-values (accessed December 1, 2022); Sierra Club, "About the Sierra Club," 2022, http://sierraclub.org/about-sierra-club (accessed December 1, 2022); World Wildlife Fund, "Our Values," 2022, http://worldwildlife.org/pages/our-values (accessed December 1, 2022).

For example, originally the Sierra Club had *avoided* the "zero-cut" goal when it came to protecting forest biodiversity. As a result, its successes in this area were very limited. However, in the late 1980s and 1990s, when the club switched to endorse the more maximalist goal of zero cut, they were suddenly able to achieve much more in terms of tangible successes. Indeed, in the early 2000s, the Sierra Club and grassroots proponents of zero cut played a significant role in reducing national forest logging to levels not seen since the 1930s. Pushing for the bold, aspirational idea was actually far more effective than settling for a moderate position.[36] This lesson needed to be applied to climate as well.

But instead, as climate science became more precise, environmental groups narrowed their focus to the impact on localities rather than engaging with the public and fostering a greater vision for the future and the planet.[37] From an ultrasociality perspective, these US, national-level environmental groups missed the mark entirely in terms of how society is captured by the power of possibility and transformative change. This was all the more difficult alongside the still abstract and intangible nature of climate change in the 1990s.

Technical, lobbying-oriented, and individualistic approaches started to change when Bill McKibben launched Step It Up in 2007 with a group of students from Middlebury College. Instead of relying on the legacy of pre-existing, mainstream environmental organizations, this was a true climate change organization in the making (see Table 5). It was explicitly motivated by the desire to spark a mass movement that was more than simply about individuals doing their part as consumers, or as they put it, instead of "change out lightbulbs," it would be "the first nationwide do-it-yourself mass protest."[38] The organization started a grassroots online sign-up initiative which eventually brought people together around hosting local actions of various types in 1,400 locations to raise awareness and demand that Congress mandate a significant reduction in carbon emissions—80% by 2050.

Internationalization of the Environmental Movement

While the United States' ability to be strongly committed to climate action has always been crucial to worldwide capacity to succeed, the climate movement was growing all over the world, and major Western-based environmental groups, such as the Climate Action Network, Friends of the Earth, Greenpeace, and others, started to unambiguously internationalize their efforts. The more traditional environmental groups stopped being the primary engine behind the net-zero idea as

---

[36] Bevington, *The Rebirth of Environmentalism*, pp. 225–226.
[37] Dunn, "Currents of Change," pp. 31–32.
[38] Danielle Endres, Leah Sprain, and Tarla Rai Peterson (eds), *Social Movement to Address Climate Change: Local Steps for Global Action* (Amherst, MA: Cambria Press, 2009), p. 1.

Table 5 Examples of climate change organizations in the United States

Organization	Year founded/location	Member numbers	Goals
Step It Up	2007 Middlebury, VT	1,400 communities across 50 states	To pressure the US government to commit to reducing carbon emissions 80% by 2050 through local actions.
Future Coalition	2018 United States	Coalition of 100 youth-led activist organizations	To organize young people and take action on issues, including gun control, climate change, and racial justice.
Sunrise Movement	2017 Washington DC	13,000	To empower youth to stop climate change, end corrupt influence over fossil-fuel resources, and elect leaders who advocate for the health and well-being of all.
The Climate Mobilization	2014 New York	Comprising thirty-eight decentralized, local network member groups	To nurture a movement of people dedicated to reversing global warming and rehabilitating the climate.
People's Climate Movement	2014 New York	Close to one million people have participated in events	To demand action on climate change through mass mobilization and movement alignment.
Climate Justice Alliance	2013 Detroit, MI	Alliance of seventy urban and rural front-line communities, organizations, and supporting networks	To mobilize communities on the front lines of climate change and inspire them to challenge the extractive economic structures that oppress them.
Action for the Climate Emergency	2008 Boulder, CO	25 million high schoolers engaged in the program	To educate young people and support them to confront social injustice, climate change, and eliminate the spread of misinformation.

Sources: Action for the Climate Emergency, "About Us," 2022, http://acespace.org/about-us (accessed December 1, 2022); Climate Justice Alliance, "About Climate Justice Alliance," 2022, http://climatejusticealliance.org/about (accessed December 1, 2022); The Climate Mobilization, "About the Climate Mobilization," 2022, http://theclimatemobilization.org/about (accessed December 1, 2022); Future Coalition, "Our Mission," 2022, http://futurecoalition.org/mission (accessed December 1, 2022); People's Climate Movement, "To Change Everything, We Need Everyone," 2022, http://peoplesclimate.org/our-movement (accessed December 1, 2022); Sunrise Movement, "Who We Are," 2022, http://sunrisemovement.org/about (accessed December 1, 2022).

other dimensions of civil society stepped forward.[39] Climate activists formed organizations devoted specifically to address climate change, and they developed new strategies.

Every region of the world developed climate change organizations that increasingly brought people together under the goal of stopping climate change and fostering regional and international cooperation at the same time. This had a significant impact on how the climate change crisis was communicated to the public. In some cases, new organizations emerged, and in other cases, pre-existing environmental organizations shifted their focus to climate change. Tables 6, 7, and 8 provide some examples of this internationalization. The climate movement was beginning to stand on its own two feet, shifting the tide toward an ultrasocial response.

Starting in Europe, the European Union (EU) and nearly all countries on the continent have long been the strongest supporters of environmentalism and combatting climate change. Since the 1980s, the EU has brought member states' environmental goals together under one umbrella, making the EU one of the most vocal advocates of the Kyoto Protocol. Since the early 1990s, membership in environmental organizations has been the largest "social movement industry" in Europe, with more than two-thirds of members in the most well-known environmental organizations residing in the EU.[40] Of all the environmental issues that concern Europeans, climate change has long been at the top of the list, and EU citizens indicate very strong support for providing assistance to non-EU countries in this regard.[41]

Countries in Asia and the Pacific Islands also developed a robust track record of advocating to save the climate, holding numerous rallies and pushing governments to pass climate-friendly policies. Numerous grassroots organizations, such as the Asian Pacific Environmental Network, Pacific Climate Warriors, and Under2 Coalition, have created and launched local initiatives as well as taking their activism to the international level.[42] As a result of these grassroots societal efforts, Hawai'i became the first US state to declare a climate emergency, and Chungnam, South Korea was the first East Asian local government to do the same. In Southeast Asia, a growing and organized youth movement has been fighting to stop climate change.[43] The exception to these grassroots efforts has been China, where, thanks

[39] Dietz and Garrelts, *Routledge Handbook of the Climate Change Movement*, p. 3.

[40] Hein-Anton van der Heijden, *Social Movements, Public Spheres and the European Politics of the Environment: Green Power Europe?* (Basingstoke: Palgrave Macmillan, 2020), p. 9.

[41] Van der Heijden, *Social Movements, Public Spheres and the European Politics of the Environment*, p. 8.

[42] The Climate Group, "Asian and Pacific Islands Are Leading the Environmental Movement," May 27, 2021, https://www.theclimategroup.org/our-work/news/asian-and-pacific-islands-are-leading-environmental-movement (accessed May 20, 2023).

[43] Preeti Jha, "The Young Activists Fighting Southeast Asia's Climate Crisis," *The Diplomat*, October 11, 2019, https://thediplomat.com/2019/10/the-young-activists-fighting-southeast-asias-climate-crisis (accessed May 20, 2023).

Table 6 Examples of regional climate change organizations

Regional organization	Year founded/location	Member numbers	Goals
Africa Civil Society Network on Water and Sanitation	1961 Kenya	Fifty civil society organizations across twenty-six countries	To support civil society groups in Africa in their pursuit to develop water sanitation plans and to strengthen civil society influence over public policy.
Asia-Pacific Network on Food Sovereignty	2002 Bali	Several organizations, non-governmental organizations (NGOs), and social movements in seven Asia-Pacific countries	To ensure food security in the Asian-Pacific region by confronting agricultural and climate policies that undermine food self-sufficiency.
Asian-Regional Exchange for New Alternatives	1983 Hong Kong	Decentralized network of academics and activists in eighteen countries	To connect Asian scholars in their investigations on social change, the improvement of the well-being of the underprivileged, and on ways to nurture ecological consciousness.
Climate Action Network Latin America	2009 Buenos Aires	1,500+ civil society organizations in 130+ countries	To support civil society organizations to fight the climate crisis and pressure governments to adopt policies to reduce fossil fuel dependency and improve the well-being of underserved communities.
European Environmental Bureau	1974 Brussels	180+ environmental organizations across 38 European countries	To impact EU decision making and support deals that focus on sustainable development and fighting the climate crisis.
Ecopeace Middle East	1994 Taba, Egypt	Unspecified	To protect water resources in Israel, Palestine, and Jordan and to support sustainable development and regional integration in the Middle East.

Sources: Africa Civil Society Network on Water and Sanitation, "ANEW Overview," 2022, http://anew.africa/overview/#:~:text=The%20African%20Civil%20Society%20Network,%20and%20sanitation%20across%20the%20continent (accessed July 11, 2022); Asia-Pacific Network on Food Sovereignty, "About Us," 2022, http://apnfs.info/about (accessed December 1, 2022); Asian-Regional Exchange for New Alternatives, "About ARENA," 2022, http://arena-council.org/arenac/en (accessed December 1, 2022); Climate Action Network Latin America, "Overview," 2022, http://climatenetwork.org/overview (accessed December 1, 2022); Ecopeace Middle East, "Our Mission," 2022, http://ecopeaceme.org/about (accessed December 1, 2022); European Environmental Bureau, "About EEB," 2022, http://eeb.org/homepage/about (accessed December 1, 2022).

Table 7 Examples of national climate change organizations

National organization	Year founded/location	Member numbers	Goals
Australian Youth Climate Coalition	2006 Melbourne	150,000	To mobilize young people across Australia to lead campaigns that support a safe climate and a reduction of fossil fuel consumption.
Egyptian National Competitiveness Council	2005 Cairo	National network of businesses, academia, and civil society organizations throughout Egypt	To enhance competitiveness and inclusive growth of the Egyptian economy by promoting and challenging policies affecting the labor market and natural resources.
India Climate Collaborative	Preparation began 2018, launched 2020 Mumbai	Individual philanthropists and several partner institutions	To create scalable solutions in energy and natural resources and to take action to mitigate the climate crisis.
Japan Climate Initiative	2018 Japan	Over 700 Japanese companies, local governments, research institutions and NGOs	To deliver the goals of the Paris Agreement on climate change and decarbonize Japan by 2050.
Wildlife and Environment Society of South Africa	1926 Durban, South Africa	Five education centers, several partnerships/ collaborations	To launch high-impact projects that support the health of the environment and climate and foster public participation for the caring of the Earth.

Sources: Australian Youth Climate Coalition, "About AYCC," 2022, http://aycc.org.au/about (accessed December 1, 2022); Egyptian National Competitiveness Council, "About Us," 2022, http://encc.org.eg/about/default.aspx (accessed December 1, 2022); India Climate Collaborative, "Our Vision," 2022, http://indiaclimatecollaborative. org/about (accessed December 1, 2022); Japan Climate Initiative, "Japan Climate Initiative," 2022, http://japanclimate.org/english (accessed December 1, 2022); Wildlife and Environmental Society of South Africa, "Our Story, Overview," 2022, http://wessa.org.za/our-story/overview (accessed December 1, 2022).

Table 8 Examples of international climate change organizations

International organizations	Year founded/location	Member numbers	Goals
350.org	2007 Vermont	750,000 globally	To eliminate fossil-fuel dependency, build a system that supports access to renewable energy for all, and addresses economic injustice through coalition building and advocacy for pro-environmental and climate policies.
Fridays for Future (youth)	2018 Stockholm	13 million (worldwide) Presence in over 7,500 cities	To overcome the climate crisis and build a world where people live in harmony with nature by staging coordinated "Strikes for Climate" protests on Fridays.
Alliance of Small Island Nations	1990 New York City	Thirty-five member states and five observers	To negotiate on behalf of the member states to secure deals that promote sustainability and progress on international climate-change issues.
Avaaz	2007 United States	69 million	To empower people to take action on pressing international issues, including poverty and climate change, through coordinated, online efforts.
GCCA (Global Campaign for Climate Action)	2009 Copenhagen	Unspecified, partners with religious, environmental, and other organizations	To help shape the 2009 UN climate talks in Copenhagen and, more broadly, to influence environmental issues with the signature "tck tck tck" campaign.
Stop Climate Chaos!	2005 Dublin	Thirty-six nonprofit organizations	To encourage and support civil society organizations in Ireland to tackle causes of climate change and work for solutions.
Youth Climate Movement	2009 Durban, South Africa	200 youth NGOs and 5,500+ individuals	To coordinate international youth-led movements to confront climate change issues within the United Nations Framework Convention on Climate Change.

Sources: 350.org, "About 350," 2022, http://350.org/about (accessed December 1, 2022); Alliance of Small Island Nations, "About Us," 2022, http://aosis.org/about/chair-of-aosis (accessed December 1, 2022); Avaaz, "About Us," 2022, http://secure.avaaz.org/page/en/about (accessed December 1, 2022); Fridays for Future, "What We Do," 2022, http://fridaysforfuture.org/what-we-do (accessed December 1, 2022); GCCA (Global Campaign for Climate Action), "75 Years of Care," 2022, http://ghf-ge.org/tcktcktck.php (accessed December 1, 2022); Stop Climate Chaos!, "The Stop Climate Chaos Coalition," 2022, http://stopclimatechaos.ie/about (accessed December 1, 2022); Youth Climate Movement, "About Us," 2022, https://youngoclimate.org/about-us/.

to its authoritarian government and intolerance for free speech, climate activists have been silenced, and the public is largely unaware of the severity of climate change.[44] Nonetheless, the Chinese government has gradually agreed to do more to stop climate change as a result of international pressure.

Africa has done little to contribute to climate change itself, but it is in many ways the region most vulnerable to it. Not surprisingly, the movement emerged in Africa as well. In the 1990s, for example, the Nigerian Ogoni people protested and then prevented Shell from extracting oil in the Niger Delta after Shell's operations had led to burning off huge quantities of gas and poisoning their land.[45] Through Rise Up, the African Climate Alliance, and Fridays for Future, among others, many young people got involved. More recently, like Greta Thunberg in Europe, Vanessa Nakate has helped to raise even more awareness and momentum across society in Africa.

In Latin America and the Caribbean, the stakes are high as well, and the region has a long history of popular protest. Young people from indigenous and peasant communities have joined the climate movement, coming together in organizations such as Minga Indígena for the Climate.[46] In some countries in Latin America, such as Guatemala, Honduras, Brazil, Columbia, and Nicaragua, it has been dangerous to speak freely about the need for climate action because it conflicts with the interests of those who control natural resources, such as organized crime.[47] Nonetheless, climate activists have pushed forward, calling loudly for net zero, and from 2010 to 2018, they worked on a treaty that protects the right of environmentalists to speak freely.

Finally, in the Middle East, young people have formed civil society groups such as the Arab Youth Climate Movement and Youth Non-Governmental Organizations and Environment Association from the Arab region (YOUNGO).[48] In the face of authoritarianism, it has been difficult to organize on-the-ground climate protests, but on December 1, 2012, Middle Eastern youth were able to hold a climate march in Doha, Qatar with around 800 in attendance.

---

[44] Helen Davidson, "'You Follow the Government's Agenda': China's Climate Activists Walk a Tightrope," *The Guardian*, August 16, 2021, https://www.theguardian.com/world/2021/aug/16/you-follow-the-governments-agenda-chinas-climate-activists-walk-a-tightrope (accessed May.

[45] John Vidal, "Shell Settlement with Ogoni People Stops Short of Full Justice," *The Guardian*, June 10, 2009, https://www.theguardian.com/environment/cif-green/2009/jun/09/saro-wiwa-shell (accessed May 21, 2023).

[46] Juan Wahren, "Youth Activism and Climate Change in Latin America," Global Campus Latin American–Caribbean, Global Campus of Human Rights, http://doi.org/20.500.11825/2334; Guy Edwards and Timmons Roberts, *A Fragmented Continent: Latin America and the Global Politics of Climate Change* (Cambridge, MA: The MIT Press, 2015).

[47] Ysabelle Kempe, "It's Dangerous to Be a Climate Activist in Latin America," *Grist*, April 22, 2021, https://grist.org/regulation/its-dangerous-to-be-an-environmental-activist-in-latin-america-a-new-treaty-is-trying-to-change-that (accessed May 20, 2023).

[48] Neeshad Shafi, "Young People Are Leading Climate Activism in the Middle East," *Cairo Review of Global Affairs*, Fall 2021, https://www.thecairoreview.com/essays/young-people-are-leading-climate-activism-in-the-middle-east (accessed May 20, 2023).

Around the world, the climate movement had arrived on the scene. Overcoming early leadership missteps and a somewhat slow start, regular people from all walks of life woke up to the fact that something major had to happen to save the planet, and it would require that everyone pull together to achieve it. They were still missing their galvanizing, ultrasocial idea, but the stage was being set.

The Rise of Climate Justice and the Radical Wing

In light of internationalization and the increasing involvement of young people, the climate movement also developed a more radical wing focused explicitly on climate *justice*. In a nutshell, proponents of climate justice underscored strongly that the developed world caused climate change and therefore it should pay to fix it. They emphasized inequality in the North–South relationship, as well as how indigenous peoples, the poor, and those disadvantaged by discrimination, low-quality housing, and immigration experience disproportionately more severe impacts from climate change. The climate movement first started to incorporate these issues of climate justice in the late 1990s, and then it became a major focus throughout the 2000s.[49]

The first climate justice summit took place in 2000 in the Hague as a radical alternative to COP6, which was taking place at the same time in the same city. Organized by the grassroots group Radical Tide, activists at the parallel summit were explicitly protesting the lack of developing world representatives at COP6. In the mid-2000s, climate justice activists started to connect climate change to broader issues of gender, human rights, race, anti-war efforts, and labor, among other things. Across the world, civil society groups already working on these other issues formed linkages with climate change groups to combine forces and lobby together. For example, in 2008, several climate justice organizations set up Mobilization for Climate Justice to connect US efforts to international ones in the lead-up to the 2009 UN Copenhagen summit. Climate Justice Now! also brought together over 200 groups across the world, including many in the Global South, to empower broader participation and coordinated efforts in climate justice campaigns worldwide. Table 9 lists just some of these groups.

It is now common wisdom in the climate movement more broadly that those who have contributed the least to climate change (i.e., poor populations, indigenous communities, people of color, and those in the Global South) have, and will, suffer the most from its effects. However, the radical wing differed in its approach in terms of how to redress this problem. Instead of drawing directly from efforts in the climate movement, such as net zero or differentiated responsibilities, the

---

[49] Thomas Dietz, Rachel Shwon, and Cameron Whitley, "Climate Change and Society," *Annual Review of Sociology* 46 (2020): 144.

radical wing often imported other policy road maps from the outside. Indeed, climate justice proponents often positioned themselves in *opposition* to the mainstream climate movement in this respect. Because of this, for a time, the radical wing played a role in actually fragmenting the broader movement and detracting from a more cohesive, ultrasocial momentum.

Perhaps most visibly, by invoking climate *justice*, they called for the end of the international capitalist system and major changes to the human way of life.[50] Rather than transforming capitalism and development to be compatible with environmentalism, the radical wing sought the complete destruction of the capitalist global economy—a goal that had already existed in circles unrelated to climate change.[51] They were also more interested in direct action on the ground, even if it sometimes rose to the level of civil disobedience or illegal action. In turning against existing climate change organizations, the radicals accused these groups of working *within* the very system that allowed environmental degradation in the first place, an approach that the radical wing felt was doomed to fail.[52] They argued that climate change organizations were mainly focused on raising public awareness and exerting pressure on leaders but not actually achieving anything tangible. The more radical wing of the climate movement became particularly visible and more outspoken after the failure of the 2009 Copenhagen summit.

At the same time, it was quite challenging to create linkages from climate change to such a broad and diverse range of social justice issue areas. In 2008 and 2009, there was a big influx of social NGOs seeking to strategically connect their own causes to climate. As Jen Allan argues, they had jumped on the "climate bandwagon" to further their own organizations' social goals.[53] However, Allan finds that only some of these connections to social justice issues made it into the dialogue around climate when it came to the 2015 Paris Agreement (e.g., labor, gender, and justice), while others remained more at the fringes of the climate movement (such as human rights and health). For their part, mainstream climate movement activists were also hesitant to open up their cause to the more tangentially related issues because they did not want to lose track of what was really at stake for everyone.[54] In this new arena of activity, many NGOs did not effectively convince others that their issues were actually of key importance to climate.[55] For those

[50] Donatella della Porta and Louisa Parks, "Framing Processes in the Climate Movement," in *Routledge Handbook of the Climate Change Movement*, ed. Dietz and Garrelts, p. 23.

[51] For instance, Naomi Klein's numerous works have strongly influenced the radical wing's argument for the destruction of capitalism, but Klein was making this argument long before becoming a climate activist. See, e.g., Naomi Klein, *No Logo: Taking Aim at the Brand Bullies* (New York: Picador, 1999); Matthias Dietz, "Activist Profile—Naomi Klein," in *Routledge Handbook of the Climate Change Movement*, ed. Dietz and Garrelts, pp. 224–225.

[52] Della Porta and Parks, "Framing Processes in the Climate Movement," p. 24.

[53] Jen Iris Allan, *The New Climate Activism: NGO Authority and Participation in Climate Change Governance* (Toronto: University of Toronto Press, 2020), p. 6.

[54] Allan, *The New Climate Activism*.

[55] Allan, *The New Climate Activism*, p. 11.

that did manage to bandwagon onto the climate movement, they introduced much more fragmentation of purpose within discussions that had been intended to be primarily focused on climate change.[56]

Some of the specific strategies of the more radical wing also had unintended consequences that detracted from an overarching, shared approach. In North America, for example, the climate movement specifically adopted a place-based strategy in the face of what activists saw as a serious lack of progress at the national and international levels. They aligned themselves with specific local groups, especially indigenous people, to stop local anti-environmental developments such as the opening of new coal plants, fracking, and building new oil pipelines.[57] By focusing attention on these local, place-based issues, they were able to attract significant media coverage and some victories—notably with the Keystone XL pipeline, the Northern Gateway, and the Trans Mountain Expansion Project. However, there was also an important sense in which this backfired. As George Hoberg finds, by activating place-based resistance and the notion of "keep it in the ground," the North American climate movement also had the unintended consequence of cultivating local groups' resistance to solar, wind, and nuclear power infrastructure.[58] Hoberg writes that, ultimately, "the impact of the strategic choice by climate activists to shift from lobbying for policy reform to blocking fossil fuel infrastructure" had the effect of also making it difficult to secure alternative forms of energy.[59]

To be sure, scientists and members of the climate movement saw climate justice—redressing the disproportionate impact of climate change on poorer sectors of society—as intrinsic to their goals. The idea of standing up for those who are marginalized and ensuring that their cause is part and parcel of broader goals is fundamentally ultrasocial in its inclusivity. However, they did not want attempts to strategically link other social issues to climate goals to detract from the momentum of the broader movement. To succeed, the climate movement had to be fully energized with common purpose, not mired in fragmentation.

All in all, despite some setbacks and obstacles, early efforts to deal with the climate crisis did ultimately lead to the creation of a significant and effective movement, as will be discussed in Chapter 15. While the science to support the idea of net zero had not yet come into focus during the 1990s and early 2000s, the more general goal—that carbon emissions had to be reduced to save the planet—clearly provided a rallying point for these efforts. What started as mainly a domestic-level and Western-based environmental movement quickly grew into a transnational

[56] Bond, *Politics of Climate Justice*.

[57] George Hoberg, *The Resistance Dilemma: Place-Based Movements and the Climate Crisis* (Cambridge, MA: MIT Press, 2021).

[58] Hoberg, *The Resistance Dilemma*, p. 5.

[59] Hoberg, *The Resistance Dilemma*, p. 10.

Table 9 Examples of climate justice groups

Organization	Year founded/location	Membership	Goals
Rising Tide North America	2000 The Hague	Fifty plus chapters across North America	To promote community-based solutions to climate change through grassroots organization.
The Climate Camps (Klimacamp bei Wien)	2016 Vienna	Seventy-person team that hosts workshops and camps	To connect people and stimulate productive discussions on sustainability and climate and social justice, as well as coordinate collective action on these issues.
Camp for Climate Action	2006 Stirling	Global network	To carry out climate change research and advocacy aimed at building a more equitable, democratic, and sustainable world.
Extinction Rebellion	2018 London	Thousands of local, regional, national, and special-interest groups	To carry out direct action and civil disobedience to fight the climate crisis, biodiversity loss, and rising greenhouse gas emissions through decentralized, political, non-partisan movements.
Indigenous Environmental Network	1990 United States	Unspecified	To represent indigenous communities in the United States in their fight to secure the rights for their sacred sites, natural resources, and their path to grow sustainable communities.
Global Justice Ecology Project	2003 United States	Unspecified	To bring awareness to the intertwining relationship between social injustice, ecological destruction, and economic domination.
Climate Justice Now!	2007 Bali	Thirty-eight affiliated environmental organizations	To coordinate a global movement to take action on social, climate change, and gender justice issues.
Climate Justice Action	2009 Copenhagen	Eighty-four affiliated communities, organizations, and networks	To achieve climate justice by supporting affected communities in the Global South, spreading awareness, contesting market-based climate "solutions," and fostering a global network of activists.

Sources: Bib van der Zee, "Climate Camp Disbanded," *The Guardian*, March 2, 2011. https://www.theguardian.com/environment/2011/mar/02/climate-camp-disbanded (accessed July 11, 2023); The Climate Camps, "Our Vision," 2022 http://klimacamp.at/our-vision/?lang=en (accessed December 1, 2022); Climate Justice Action, "About Climate Justice Alliance," 2022, http://climatejusticealliance.org/about (accessed December 1, 2022); Climate Justice Now!, "Climate Justice Now!," 2022, http://climate-justice-now.org (accessed December 1, 2022); Extinction Rebellion, "About Us," 2022, http://rebellion.global/about-us (accessed December 1, 2022); Global Justice Ecology Project, "About," 2022, http://globaljusticeecology.org/about (accessed December 1, 2022); Indigenous Environmental Network, "Our History," 2022, http://ienearth.org/about (accessed December 1, 2022); Rising Tide North America, "Rising Tide North America," 2022, http://actionnetwork.org/groups/rising-tide-north-america (accessed December 1, 2022).

and international movement, with highly activated organizations in nearly every country across the world.

As illustrated here, there were ways in which early efforts unintentionally worked against the emergence of a stronger ultrasocial impulse. First, early on, starting with the Kyoto Protocol, international negotiations went from being about mainly pursuing the common good to focusing on small, highly technical areas of policy change. Second, environmental agencies and domestic institutions also set for themselves relatively narrow goals.[60] Third, to the extent that international organizations like the UN Environmental Program existed, they struggled to bring global climate goals under a coherent and energizing narrative.[61] Fourth, with the pivot toward climate justice in the twenty-first century, new efforts sometimes focused heavily on specific identity and place-based demands,[62] which, while important, had the unintended consequence of moving away from a common, global approach. They also stoked opposition from these identity groups to clean energy alternatives. The result is that the overarching narrative tended to get diluted and technical, which made it harder to mobilize widespread aspiration to tackle climate change as a common endeavor. However, this was about to change in the lead-up to the 2015 Paris Agreement.

---

[60] Maria Ivanova, "At 50, the UN Environment Programme Must Lead Again," *Nature*, February 16, 2021, https://www.nature.com/articles/d41586-021-00393-5 (accessed May 20, 2023).

[61] Ivanova, "At 50, the UN Environment Programme Must Lead Again."

[62] Bond, *Politics of Climate Justice*.

15

The Net Zero Idea and the Race to Save the Earth

The first two decades of the climate movement accompanied growing societal awareness of the climate emergency, increasing scientific consensus to back this up, and the formation of a broad transnational and international network of activists. While the net-zero idea was still percolating amongst epistemic communities of climate scientists, the overarching goal of reducing carbon emissions had clearly brought people together in a context of ultrasociality. This chapter explains how, in the lead-up to the 2015 Paris Agreement, the climate movement overcame early impasses, paving the way for an ultrasocial breakthrough around the idea of net zero.

To be sure, the ultrasocial underpinnings of the movement had been getting stronger over time. During the negotiations leading to the 1997 Kyoto Protocol, for example, civil-society organizations and non-governmental organizations (NGOs) lacked access to the plenaries and deliberations, even though decision makers recognized them as the voice of the people.[63] To the extent that they did have influence, it was minimal, and their efforts to secure a stronger agreement failed. As civil society climate proponents sought more influence, they shifted their appeals from science to climate justice, especially in the lead-up to the 2009 United Nations climate summit in Copenhagen.[64] And yet, even the forceful efforts of climate justice's radical wing ultimately did not result in the transformation that activists sought. Copenhagen came and went with little attention to the calls of the climate movement.[65]

The failures at Copenhagen did, however, precipitate a sense of urgency. And this coincided with new scientific findings indicating that achievement of net zero had to occur by around 2050 to avoid a climate catastrophe. As a result, the climate movement was able to turn net zero into something much greater than a scientific

---

[63] Elisabeth Corell and Michelle Betsill, "A Comparative Look at NGO Influence in International Environmental Negotiations: Desertification and Climate Change," *Global Environmental Politics* 1, 4 (2021): 95, https://doi.org/10.1162/152638001317146381.

[64] Jen Allen and Jennifer Haden, "Exploring the Framing Power of NGOs in Global Climate Politics," *Environmental Politics* 26, 4 (2017): 600–620, https://doi.org/10.1080/09644016.2017.1319017; Stuart Rosewarne, James Goodman, and Rebecca Pearse, *Climate Action Upsurge: The Ethnography of Climate Movement Politics* (London and New York: Routledge, 2013), Preface.

[65] Katharina Rietig, "The Power of Strategy: Environmental NGO Influence in International Climate Negotiations," *Global Governance* 22, 2 (2016): 269–288, https://www.jstor.org/stable/44861077 (accessed May 20, 2023).

International Cooperation Against All Odds. Mai'a K. Davis Cross, Oxford University Press. © Mai'a K. Davis Cross (2024).
DOI: 10.1093/oso/9780192873903.003.0016

benchmark, making it into a truly transformational idea that captured the imagination of international society and allowed the movement to put forward a positive narrative of how to achieve it. Indeed, the lead-up to the 2015 Paris climate change summit was very different to the previous rounds and featured a diverse range of different actors coming together in an unprecedented way. At last, the power of ultrasociality tipped the scales against the transactionalism of the previous decades and toward transcendent impact.

The Origins of the Net Zero Idea

The net-zero idea still has a relatively short history. Scientists only started to converge on net zero during 2009–2013 as the data around climate change became ever more sophisticated.[66] Specifically, they now began to argue that there was a need to pay attention to *cumulative* carbon emissions. After all, since they had discovered that the accumulation of carbon in the atmosphere remains for decades, if not centuries, the deadline for achieving net zero had to take into account what had already been emitted into the atmosphere since the beginning of the Industrial Revolution. As a result, they calculated that by around 2050, the overall amount of carbon released into the atmosphere had to drop to zero, and stay there indefinitely, to avoid catastrophic climate change. This could be achieved either by extracting carbon from the atmosphere or by using only non-emitting, renewable forms of energy, that is, powered by wind, solar, and water. Moving beyond the previous goals of stabilized emissions or specific reduction targets, net zero is the correct scientific formulation to keep global temperature rise under control. Solidifying this consensus, in 2013, the scientists in the Intergovernmental Panel on Climate Change (IPCC) formally confirmed that the only way to keep global warming at 1.5°C would be to achieve net zero by 2050.[67]

As the idea spread through policy circles and broader swaths of society, it took on significantly more meaning than the scientific requirement. As Sam Fankhauser et al. argue, it became a "frame of reference through which global action against climate change can be (and is increasingly) structured and understood."[68] In other words, getting to net zero emissions is a straightforward requirement in scientific

---

[66] John Lang, "Net Zero: A Short History," Energy and Climate Intelligence Unit, 2022, https://eciu.net/analysis/infographics/net-zero-history (accessed May 20, 2023).

[67] See, e.g., Rajendra K. Pachauri and Leo Meyer (eds), "Climate Change 2014: Synthesis Report," Intergovernmental Panel on Climate Change, 2014, https://www.ipcc.ch/site/assets/uploads/2018/05/SYR_AR5_FINAL_full_wcover.pdf (accessed May 22, 2034); Lang, "Net Zero."

[68] Sam Fankhauser, Stephen M. Smith, Myles Allen, Kaya Axelsson, Thomas Hale, Cameron Hepburn, J. Michael Kendall, Radhika Khosla, Javier Lezaun, Eli Mitchell-Larson, Michael Obersteiner, Lavanya Rajamani, Rosalind Rickaby, Nathalie Seddon, and Thom Wetzer, "The Meaning of Net Zero and How to Get It Right," *Nature Climate Change* 12 (2022): 16, https://doi.org/10.1038/s41558-021-01245-w; Energy and Climate Intelligence Unit, "Net Zero Scoreboard," 2022, p. 15, https://eciu.net/netzerotracker (accessed May 22, 2023).

terms, but the myriad of social, economic, and political actions needed to achieve it are as complex as they are challenging.

The climate movement picked up this challenge, eventually embedding net zero in a broader transformational vision that called for changing the nature of capitalism itself and addressing calls for social justice, both of which were fundamentally ultrasocial visions for the future of humanity. Changing the nature of capitalism meant moving away from a more unfettered version to a more social and environmental one that embeds economic growth within the boundaries that protect the integrity of the planet. Similarly, addressing calls for social justice meant moving away from agreements that seek equality across global society to those that achieve equity by transferring environmental resources and knowledge from richer regions to poorer regions.

In effect, now that the climate movement had come together as a distinct initiative from the environmental movement, this effort helped to shape the net-zero idea. As awareness of climate change spread, net zero became much more than a scientific concept and took on a far broader societal meaning. As I argue in Chapter 4, based on what we know about human ultrasociality, at least three specific qualities of ideas make their success more likely: transcendent impact, optimism, and a new narrative. In the case of net zero, a transcendent and optimistic narrative emerged around achieving it: there is hope for the future if we transform the way countries develop (i.e., net zero and economic growth are compatible) and if wealthier countries take on more of the burden to help poorer countries through transfers of resources and technology, as well as allowing a slower transition time. The creation of this narrative of possibility allowed those involved to envision a positive future of clean energy, economic development, and international cooperation.

Lead-Up to the 2015 Paris Climate Change Agreement

After years of allowing fragmentation, working at cross-purposes, and focusing on relatively narrow, technical issues, a diverse range of civil society actors converged in the lead-up to the Paris climate negotiations at the United Nations (UN) Climate Change Conference 2015 (COP21). These various groups, from scientists, to businesses, to NGOs, set aside enough of their differences to pursue the overarching idea of net zero and the goal of limiting global warming to 1.5°C. In 2014, the Global Commission on the Economy and Climate produced a groundbreaking report entitled *Better Growth, Better Climate*, arguing that net zero actually could be achieved through climate-friendly policies and economic growth.[69] The

---

[69] Global Commission on the Climate and Economy, "Better Growth, Better Climate: The New Climate Economy Report," 2014, https://newclimateeconomy.report/2014/wp-content/uploads/sites/2/2014/08/NCE-Global-Report_web.pdf (accessed May 20, 2023).

report argues that humans can make the climate and the economy work together in a virtuous cycle such that economic growth supports green policies rather than undermining them. As Michael Jacobs, lead author and director of strategy for the Global Commission's report, writes, "Cutting emissions was not just compatible with economic growth: it could generate *better* growth, with lower air pollution, more livable and economically efficient cities, more sustainable use of land and greater energy security."[70] This quickly became the dominant narrative of the climate movement in the 2010s.[71]

When the head of the Global Commission, former Mexican president Felipe Calderón, presented the report three months after its release, it was met with a standing ovation. As Jacobs describes it, this transformation in thinking had the effect of lining up several diverse groups: economic actors, scientists, businesses, and NGOs. For the first time since the start of the climate crisis, special interests gave way just enough to see net zero as compelling. The major components conducive to the flourishing of ultrasociality had fallen into place: a transformational idea (net zero), a positive narrative (climate aims and economic growth go hand-in-hand), and a sense of optimism for the future (1.5°C was still within reach and something that all major players could support). Various groups embraced it.

First, the leaders of the world's major economic organizations, including the heads of the International Monetary Fund, the Organisation for Economic Co-operation and Development (OECD), and the World Bank, strongly amplified the message that any future growth had to be low-carbon in nature. Along with them, the world's largest shareholder institutions realized that their investments were at risk if companies did not start paying attention to climate change and the fact that they could no longer count on using greenhouse-gas-emitting sources of energy.

Second, the scientists through the fifth IPCC Assessment Report (2013–2014) provided the data that there was *no choice* but to reach net zero by the second half of the twenty-first century and that if the world continued to extract carbon from the Earth and release it into the atmosphere, this amount could not exceed 800 billion metric tons since the start of the Industrial Revolution. Armed with this data, they fought hard and lobbied to pressure governments to act. In this sense, science crystallized an existential crisis, which often creates an opening beneficial for ultrasociality, as discussed in Chapter 4.

Third, high-profile global corporations and businesses started to make it known that they would no longer stand opposed to climate policy as they had done in the past. They understood that if climate change were to continue, unfettered supply chains, water, food, and energy were all under threat, and this was certainly bad for business. Since at least 2006, several major companies had made it

---

[70] Michael Jacobs, "High Pressure for Low Emissions: How Civil Society Created the Paris Climate Agreement," *Juncture* 22, 4 (2016): 316.
[71] Jacobs, "High Pressure for Low Emissions," p. 316.

clear that they needed, and wanted, governments to embrace carbon neutrality so that they could respond and prepare for this expectation,[72] but in the lead-up to Paris, they ramped up a collective effort dramatically. Companies such as Unilever, Nike, Bank of America, and IKEA together formed a transnational network called We Mean Business, founded in 2014, which quickly grew in size and drew upon corporate resources to push governments to adopt new climate policies and take international cooperation on climate change seriously.[73]

Finally, NGO efforts became far more global, membership in them grew, and many new climate organizations emerged, such as 350.org, Youth Climate Movement, and Global Campaign for Climate Action. Avaaz, a major online climate organization, amassed one million new members per month until it had brought together 42 million paying members as the Paris climate change conference got underway.[74]

Not only did these disparate sectors of civil society agree in unprecedented ways, but also the number of new sectors of civil society that had become activated in support of the net-zero idea grew dramatically. This happened to such a degree that it constituted a new kind of climate activism.[75] With this momentum, 350.org and Avaaz were able to organize the People's Climate March in New York City in 2014 with 400,000 participating, in addition to hundreds of sister marches around the world. This became the climate movement's largest protest to date and the largest environmental march since Earth Day.[76]

Importantly, there was also a key climate justice dimension, although not so much of the radical variety. The second narrative connected to the achievement of net zero—after the message that carbon reduction and economic growth go hand in hand—was that richer countries would strive to reach net zero faster to let poorer countries continue to develop. A multitude of efforts from public and government officials focused on how to help the Global South become integrated into a new world centered on net zero. For example, working alongside this cooperative momentum from civil society was the European Union's Green Diplomacy Network. It focused on how European countries could assist developing countries in preparing their own national contributions to the Paris Agreement.[77] The European Union (EU) provided funding to NGOs to support local governments and cities in emerging economies to develop low-emissions approaches and provide technical know-how "to improve institutional capacity to plan, act and monitor"

---

[72] Kurt Kleiner, "The Corporate Race to Cut Carbon," *Nature Climate Change* 1 (2007): 40–43, https://doi.org/10.1038/climate.2007.31.

[73] Jacobs, "High Pressure for Low Emissions," p. 317.

[74] Jacobs, "High Pressure for Low Emissions," p. 319.

[75] Jen Iris Allan, *The New Climate Activism: NGO Authority and Participation in Climate Change Governance* (Toronto: University of Toronto Press, 2020).

[76] Jacobs, "High Pressure for Low Emissions," p. 319.

[77] Maïa K. Davis Cross, "Partners at Paris? Climate Negotiations and Transatlantic Relations," *Journal of European Integration* 40, 5 (2018): 571–586, https://doi.org/10.1080/07036337.2018.1487962.

and to ensure that "the local and national contexts are considered when developing tailor-made approaches."[78]

One initiative of the Green Diplomacy Network was to support UN-Habitat and Local Governments for Sustainability, which received €6,700,000 for the period March 1, 2012 to August 31, 2015 to pursue low-emissions development. This EU-funded project involved a focus on helping "model cities" in India, South Africa, Indonesia, and Brazil that would adopt these new policies with the help of practitioners and experts, based on both European experiences and local conditions. They also designated "satellite cities" nearby that would further seek to implement these policies based on the model cities. Effectively, this created a South–South–North network of cities that would contribute to the achievement of nationally determined contributions to climate mitigation of these countries overall.[79]

Thus, in the lead-up to Paris, there was a palpable change in human efforts to grapple with the climate crisis. The transformational idea of net zero had created room for ultrasociality to emerge, fragmentation had diminished, and there was strong support for those most impacted by climate change, creating a broadly inclusive approach.

The Breakthrough: The Paris Climate Agreement

The Paris Agreement, which was adopted on December 12, 2015 and entered into force on November 4, 2016, aims to achieve carbon neutrality by mid-century. The agreement is binding and is the first to bring all countries in the world together under a common and ambitious effort to fight climate change. Each of the 196 parties to the agreement pledge to reduce greenhouse gas emissions as quickly as possible. They also recognize that to achieve net zero by mid-century, they must embark on significant economic and social transformation, including measures to adapt to a warmer world. Every five years, countries are committed to present to the rest of the international community newly ambitious national determined contributions (NDCs) toward the goal of net zero.[80]

In line with calls from social groups, as well as concerted efforts on the part of NGOs, the Paris Agreement is the first to include issues such as human rights, gender, indigenous perspectives, and labor. Along these lines, the agreement recognizes the need for an equitable transition to net zero that encourages differentiated responsibilities: richer countries must reach net zero faster than poorer

---

[78] Urban Low Emission Development Strategies, "Urban-LEDS: Cities in Action 2012–2016: Final Report Low Emission Development in Brazil, India, Indonesia and South Africa," 2016, https://e-lib. iclei.org/wp-content/uploads/2016/05/Urban-LEDS-Final-Report-finalbook-web.pdf (accessed July 4, 2023).
[79] Urban Low Emission Development Strategies, "Urban-LEDS: Cities in Action 2012–2016."
[80] United Nations, "The Paris Agreement," 2015, https://unfccc.int/process-and-meetings/the-paris-agreement/the-paris-agreement (accessed May 20, 2023).

countries so that the latter can continue to develop. And richer countries must provide technology, know-how, and resources to help developing countries adapt. In short, the climate justice component of the agreement includes affirmations that richer countries have a responsibility to poorer countries, fulfilling the broader meaning of the net-zero idea.

The level of achievement at Paris had by no means been a foregone conclusion. In particular, the especially ambitious aim of keeping warming to 1.5°C, instead of 2°C, among other major components of the agreement, were only achieved during the final days of the summit.[81] The EU—whose diplomats were, in fact, the backbone of the negotiations—brought together what became known on the ground as the "high-ambition coalition." This coalition included the EU (and its twenty-eight member states) as well as seventy-nine African, Caribbean, and Pacific countries. These countries publicly announced their commitment to having:

- a legally binding and fair agreement;
- long-term ambition that responds to science;
- a review mechanism to examine progress every five years;
- transparency and accountability in following through with carbon reduction commitment.

And EU Commissioner Miguel Arias Cañete made a remarkably ultrasocial statement to justify this new ambition in the final days:

> These negotiations are not about "them" and "us." These negotiations are about all of us, both developed and developing countries, finding common ground and solutions together. This is why the EU and the African, Caribbean, and Pacific countries have agreed to join forces for an ambitious outcome here in Paris. We urge other countries to join us. Together we can do it. The EU stands shoulder to shoulder with its long-term partners in the African, Caribbean, and Pacific regions.[82]

This inspiring expression of ultrasociality had the intended effect. Two days after the high-ambition coalition made its announcement, the United States was persuaded to join, along with Norway, Mexico, Columbia, and many others. Very quickly, well over a hundred countries added their names to the list. This watershed initiative, which depended on skillful EU leadership and diplomacy in the moment, was years in the making. As Jacobs writes, "By orchestrating the narratives of science and economics to demand strong climate action, and organizing

---

[81] Carbon Brief, "Two Degrees: The History of Climate Change's Speed Limit," Carbon Brief, December 8, 2014, https://www.carbonbrief.org/two-degrees-the-history-of-climate-changes-speed-limit (accessed May 21, 2023).

[82] Participant observation, COP21.

the business community, NGOs and many others in support of a strong agreement, it was civil society that pressured governments into the positions that made the final negotiations possible."[83] The fact that disparate interests, a wide range of countries, and the growing voices of the climate movement had started to rally around the net-zero idea and prepare the groundwork for its implementation mattered. Ultimately, as celebrations over the first universal climate agreement broke out, a majority of countries had agreed (though unofficially) to limit global warming to 1.5°C instead of the original 2°C.

Follow-Through

Paris, of course, is not the end of the net-zero story but just the beginning. In the years after COP21, the narrative of net zero proved to be very attractive to a whole range of actors, from countries, to subnational actors, to individual organizations and private companies. In 2019, the United Kingdom became the first country to introduce domestic legislation that would lead to achieving net zero by 2050. Of course, as the first country to do this, it is counting on the rapid developing of a new market for greenhouse gas removal.[84] By COP26 in Glasgow in 2021, 136 countries—including the biggest emitters: China, the United States, and the EU—had formally committed to reaching net zero by mid-century.[85] And eleven countries—Surinam, Bhutan, Benin, Gabon, Guinea-Bissau, Guyana, Cambodia, Liberia, Madagascar, Cambodia, and Mali—had actually already achieved net zero, or even carbon negative, status.[86] Since Paris, there have been watershed advancements in climate technology, new markets in low and zero carbon solutions, transformations in private businesses, and a major growth in cities and localities pledging and acting on their own net-zero targets. In evaluating this progress, Sam Fankhauser et al. write that the net-zero narrative has had "unifying and galvanizing power."[87]

The commitment to combat climate change at the city and local levels grew significantly during the Trump presidency, when that administration began the

[83] Jacobs, "High Pressure for Low Emissions," p. 322.

[84] Mark Workman, Devon Platt, Uday Reddivari, Bianca Valmarana, Steve Hall, and Rob Ganpatsingh, "Establishing a Large-Scale Greenhouse Gas Removal Sector in the United Kingdom by 2030: First Mover Dilemmas," *Energy Research & Social Science* 88 (2022), https://doi.org/10.1016/j.erss.2022.102512.

[85] Fankhauser et al., "The Meaning of Net Zero and How to Get It Right," p. 16; Renee Cho, "Net Zero Pledges: Can They Get Us Where We Need to Go?," Columbia Climate School, State of the Planet, December 16, 2021, https://news.climate.columbia.edu/2021/12/16/net-zero-pledges-can-they-get-us-where-we-need-to-go (accessed May 20, 2023).

[86] Cho, "Net Zero Pledges."

[87] Fankhauser et al., "The Meaning of Net Zero and How to Get It Right," p. 17.

process of withdrawing the United States from the Paris Agreement.[88] And yet, the withdrawal itself didn't end up lasting long as it took effect on November 4, 2020, the day after Trump lost his bid for re-election, so the United States rejoined the agreement just two-and-half months later, on January 20, 2021, which was President Biden's first day in office. In the EU, the Covenant of Mayors had already been in place since 2008, and it became the largest movement in the world in support of local climate action, with the common pledge of reaching climate neutrality by 2050.[89] US mayors launched a similar initiative, Climate Mayors, in 2014, which eventually grew to include 470 mayors across 48 states, representing 47 million Americans.[90] As an umbrella organization, the Global Covenant of Mayors for Climate & Energy brings together over 11,500 cities and local governments across 142 countries, representing over 1 billion people, all working toward the goals of the Paris climate agreement.[91] Following the success of the 2014 People's Climate March came the 2017 Global Climate March and the climate strikes in September 2019.

In terms of the private sector, hundreds of companies have signed on to achieve the net-zero goal by 2040.[92] Indeed, one-third of companies in the Forbes Global 2,000 list have set for themselves a net-zero aim.[93] Demand from private companies to have well-designed climate rules has been strong because they can then plan and invest with a clear structure in place.[94] Together, they have focused on transforming energy, industry, the built environment, transportation, and finance, among other areas. Moreover, the We Mean Business coalition has brought over 10,000 highly influential global businesses together to devise business-oriented climate action strategies. Their goal has been to catalyze the private sector to halve emissions by 2030, build a net-zero economy, and keep warming to the 1.5°C goal.[95] And they regularly seek advice from climate non-profit groups.

Indeed, since the Paris Agreement, We Mean Business has taken major steps to fulfill its mission. For example, in 2015, it launched the 100% renewable (RE100) campaign to reach net zero in line with the Paris Agreement. RE100 explicitly

[88] Brian Tokar, "Democracy, Localism, and The Future of The Climate Movement," *World Futures* 71, 3–4 (2015): 65–75.

[89] Nives Dolsak and Aseem Prakash, "Join the Club: How the Domestic NGO Sector Induces Participation in the Covenant of Mayors Program," *International Interactions* 43, 1 (2017): 26–47, https://doi.org/10.1080/03050629.2017.1226668.

[90] Climate Mayors, "Who We Are," 2022, https://climatemayors.org/who-we-are (accessed May 21, 2023).

[91] Global Covenant of Mayors, "Who We Are," 2022, https://www.globalcovenantofmayors.org/who-we-are (accessed May 21, 2023).

[92] The Climate Pledge, "Signatories," 2022, https://www.theclimatepledge.com/us/en/Signatories (accessed May 20, 2023); Cho, "Net Zero Pledges."

[93] Net Zero Tracker, "Data Explorer," June 2022, https://zerotracker.net/# (accessed July 4, 2023).

[94] Joel Makower, "A Powerhouse Corporate Climate Coalition Says, 'We Mean Business," *Greenbiz*, 2014, https://www.greenbiz.com/article/powerhouse-corporate-climate-coalition-says-we-mean-business (accessed May 20, 2023).

[95] We Mean Business Coalition, "We Are in the Decisive Decade. It's Time to Accelerate Climate Action," 2022, https://www.wemeanbusinesscoalition.org (accessed December 1, 2022).

seeks to avoid being labeled as simply "green-washing," so it has built in transparent standards and open-source inspections.[96] The UN has recognized RE100 as one of the most important climate initiatives in the world. By 2020, RE100 had grown to over 100 countries and then quickly surpassed this to reach over 4,000 companies, including most prominently, Facebook, Google, J. P. Morgan Chase, Walmart, General Motors, and many others that are in the Global 500.[97] Companies from China, India, Mexico, the Middle East, and Africa have also joined the initiative. The main criterion to join is that companies must be "a recognized brand, member of the Fortune 1000, or have a significant power footprint that exceeds 100 [gigawatt hours]."[98] Then, those who join must adopt a renewable energy strategy with clear deadlines that achieve, at minimum, carbon reductions of 30% by 2020, 60% by 2030, 90% by 2040, and 100% by 2050. Remarkably, these ambitious standards are both rigorous and voluntary and are all inspired by the net-zero idea.

The Way Forward for Net Zero

The climate movement, their transformational idea of net zero, and worrying real-world climate-induced changes have made this an impossible issue for governments to ignore. Climate Action Network (CAN)—the first transnational network to bring environmental networks together in the name of climate change—is now the largest international climate network in the world, with over 1,900 civil society organizations across more than 130 countries.[99] The climate movement exists in every continent on Earth but is particularly strong in Western societies, such as the Americas, Europe, and Australia.[100] The movement is most spotlighted internationally during annual UN COP meetings, when the media covers its activities, including pressure on governments to adopt specific goals and large-scale protests.[101] However, this is also just the tip of the iceberg in terms of how we, as humans, are coming together everywhere to save the planet. At all levels of society

---

[96] Aaron Teater, "Putting Their Money Where Their Mouth Is: The We Mean Business Coalition and the Role of Corporate Governance within the International Climate Regime," *Cornell International Affairs Review* XIII (2019): 72, https://doi.org/10.37513/ciar.v13i1.546; Aki Kachi, Silke Mooldijk, and Carsten Warnecke, "How to Distinguish between Climate Leadership and Greenwashing," New Climate Institute, 2020, http://admin.indiaenvironmentportal.org.in/reports-documents/climate-neutrality-claims-how-distinguish-between-climate-leadership-and (accessed May 20, 2023).

[97] We Mean Business Coalition, "RE100: Renewable Electricity Demand Initiative Growing In Reach And Impact," February 3, 2023, https://www.wemeanbusinesscoalition.org/blog/re100-renewable-electricity-demand-initiative-growing-in-reach-and-impact/ (accessed July 4, 2023).

[98] Teater, "Putting Their Money Where Their Mouth Is," p. 59.

[99] Climate Action Network International, "About CAN," 2023, https://climatenetwork.org/overview (accessed July 4, 2023).

[100] Dietz and Garrelts (eds), *Routledge Handbook of the Climate Change Movement*, p. 12.

[101] Dietz and Garrelts (eds), *Routledge Handbook of the Climate Change Movement*, p. 1.

and across the world, there is climate action, and net zero is increasingly invoked as the main idea driving it.

Naturally, controversy still exists. The optimistic net-zero narrative that 1.5°C is still within reach and that the economy can benefit from new, green approaches does not sit well with everyone. Young people, with much at stake, have stepped up to carry forward the climate movement and to intensify it. For example, Extinction Rebellion has ratcheted up a full-throated attack on government leaders and companies that are not doing enough and has criticized the net zero idea. They often echo the arguments of Naomi Klein and others, who say that the economic system of capitalism itself must go.[102] Understandably, the tone of their protest has become that of outrage and anger, and they regularly engage in non-violent civil disobedience. It has also been firmly on the more radical wing of the climate justice side of the movement. In this vein, in 2019, Greta Thunberg led a march of half a million people in Madrid, and many groups with social issues and rights as their primary concern—indigenous interests, queer rights, racial justice groups, health advocates, peace supporters, and so on—were a part of this march. Even though key stakeholders came together in the lead-up to the Paris Agreement and beyond, continuing lines of fragmentation within the climate movement still remain. On the one hand, if the more radical activists' primary concern is social justice rather than the environment, their aims may not always sit well with that of the climate movement and may end up being counterproductive. On the other hand, for those who prioritize climate change, this agitation can be helpful in holding the decision makers to account.

While groups like Extinction Rebellion and leaders like Greta Thunberg may sometimes detract from the net-zero idea in their efforts to argue that it does not go far enough, they do so because their pessimism is all-encompassing. In this respect, they do have a point. Government follow-through with the idea is not as strong as it could be,[103] and even if all countries reach their net zero target dates, the most optimistic scenarios still forecast 1.8°C global warming compared to pre-industrial levels by 2100 (a 2023 Intergovernmental Panel on Climate Change report estimates 1.5°C warming before 2035[104]). In addition, right-wing populists who are far more swayed by tribalism, and who would seek to work against ultrasociality, either claim that climate change is a hoax or that the net-zero idea is an

---

[102] Matthias Schmelzer, Aaron Vansintjan, and Andrea Vetter, *The Future Is Degrowth: A Guide to a World beyond Capitalism* (New York: Verso, 2022).

[103] Climate Action Tracker, "Glasgow's 2030 Credibility Gap: Net Zero's Lip Service to Climate Action," November 9, 2021, https://climateactiontracker.org/publications/glasgows-2030-credibility-gap-net-zeros-lip-service-to-climate-action (accessed May 26, 2023).

[104] Intergovernmental Panel on Climate Change, "Climate Change 2023: Synthesis Report," A Report of the Intergovernmental Panel on Climate Change," Geneva, Switzerland, 2023. https://www.ipcc.ch/report/ar6/syr/ (accessed July 4, 2023).

undemocratic ultimatum imposed from above.[105] They continue to look at efforts to tackle climate change in terms of self-interest and short-term gain, as many factions within the United States and China do. There is also a global power shift underway. In the past, industrialized countries accounted for the lion's share of carbon emissions. Now, countries in the Global South have rapidly increased their energy consumption.[106]

These developments, among others, contribute to an understandable sense of despair and frustration, especially among young activists. And yet, the passion that they bring to the table in terms of holding governments to account, condemning global efforts as insufficient, and attracting others to join the movement has garnered much attention for the climate emergency. Since 2018, Fridays for Future, for example, has organized tens of thousands of coordinated school strikes across well over 100 countries, with millions of young people participating several times every year. While some have criticized this effort, especially when it means skipping school, for the most part, these young environmentalists have received strong support from scientists, academics, public figures, and politicians.

With time running out, an unrelenting youth movement that continually pushes everyone to do more is ultimately a good thing. In just a few short years, they will be the people working in local governments, NGOs, international organizations, private companies, and climate science labs, productively contributing to the social, economic, and political transformations needed to accelerate the achievement of the net-zero idea. Nevertheless, as an ultrasocial approach demonstrates, it will be necessary for the youth of today to see that there is hope for the future and to recognize the level of progress that has already been achieved and why. As Al Gore said in 2016,

When any great moral challenge is ultimately resolved into a binary choice between what is right and what is wrong the outcome is foreordained because of who we are as human beings, 99% of us. That is where we are now, and it is why we are going to win this.[107]

It is time for all of us to take net zero even further, to celebrate successes, vow to overcome failures, and aspire to do more.

[105] Ed Atkins, "Bigger than Brexit': Exploring Right-Wing Populism and Net-Zero Policies in the United Kingdom," *Energy Research and Social Science* 90 (2022), https://doi.org/10.1016/j.erss.2022.102681.
[106] Dietz and Garrelts (eds), *Routledge Handbook of the Climate Change Movement*, p. 5.
[107] Al Gore, "Ted Talk," February 2016, https://www.ted.com/talks/al_gore_the_case_for_optimism_on_climate_change?language=en (accessed May 26, 2023).

Conclusion to Part V

Over the course of human evolution, our capacity for empathy has grown to encompass more and more living things. And yet, as Jeremy Rifkin laments, it is "a grand paradox to human history"[108] that, just as we start to have "biosphere consciousness," we find ourselves on the brink of extinction.[109] For the most part, people really do care about the planet, recognize its beauty, seek to protect all living things, and understand its fragility. The human tendency to gravitate toward ultrasociality has made a strong mark on efforts to stop climate change through a worldwide, unrelenting movement that relies on both voluntary and required transformation. It is often hard to see this progress because the tenuous fate of the planet tends to eclipse it. Moreover, after each major climate summit, the media, pundits, and experts, disappointed by the result, tend to deride any agreement as a failure, sometimes before the negotiations have even ended. However, as Jacobs argues, "If you cannot recognise victory when it comes, how can your supporters ever feel that campaigning is worth it?"[110]

The net-zero idea is fundamentally ultrasocial in nature—it can only be achieved with a planet-wide coordinated effort, and climate change can only be understood in the first place through "social channels of communication."[111] As is the case with any push for transformational change, there are lines of differentiation behind how to actually achieve it. On the one hand, some in the climate movement believe that only by redesigning existing institutions and dismantling the global system of capitalism will the Earth be saved.[112] On the other hand, others believe that we can build on existing institutions to modernize technology and create green jobs to solve the climate crisis.[113] While the former view seeks to amplify a negative outcry against the failures of capitalism, the latter embraces the narrative that environmentalism and economic prosperity are actually compatible and

---

[108] Jeremy Rifkin, *The Empathic Civilization: The Race to Global Consciousness in a World in Crisis* (New York: TarcherPerigee, 2009), p. 21.

[109] Rifkin, *The Empathic Civilization*, p. 26.

[110] Michael Jacobs, "High Pressure for Low Emissions: How Civil Society Created the Paris Climate Agreement," *Juncture* 22, 4 (2016): 322.

[111] Peter Newell, *Climate for Change: Non-state Actors and the Global Politics of the Greenhouse* (Cambridge: Cambridge University Press, 2000), p. 69.

[112] Naomi Klein, *This Changes Everything: Capitalism vs the Climate* (New York: Simon & Schuster, 2014).

[113] Matthias Dietz and Heiko Garrelts (eds), *Routledge Handbook of the Climate Change Movement* (London and New York: Routledge, 2014), p. 2.

even enable *better* growth.[114] Even though there are these distinctions and debates over the best approach to achieve net zero, the general goal of stopping climate change is shared. In that sense, the climate movement and the broader societal push to solve climate change has an overarching belief holding everyone together in pursuit of transformation and a better future.

The outcome of this case may not be known until at least the 2030s. If, by then, countries have not stayed on track or accelerated their carbon emission reductions promises, then it is unlikely that net zero will be achievable by mid-century. It is unrealistic to expect the overthrow of global capitalism itself (much less its world-wide replacement by an even more efficient, better-functioning system) as a way to end the climate emergency in time. But most of the technology already exists today to decarbonize dramatically and dematerialize our way of life. There is no reason to expect that we cannot make more breakthroughs that will, for example, capture and store carbon, decarbonize industries, create electrical smart grids out of renewables, and invent liquid biofuels for heavy emitters like airplanes and trucks.[115] Many policy instruments also exist for governments to manage, regulate, and limit capitalism so that it works for the good of the planet rather than against it. Breakthroughs in international relations always require governments to undergo change and to work together, even when it is difficult. It is in the power of societies to rally around ultrasocial ideas to enable this change to happen.

[114] Global Commission on the Economy and Climate, "Better Growth, Better Climate," 2014, http://newclimateeconomy.report/2014 (accessed May 20, 2023).

[115] Steven Pinker, *Enlightenment Now: The Case of Reason, Science, Humanism, and Progress* (New York: Viking, 2018), pp. 145–155; Ines Azevedo, Michael Davidson, Jesse Jenkins, Valerie Karplus, and David Victor, "The Paths to Net Zero: How Technology Can Save the Planet," *Foreign Affairs*, May/June 2020, p. 18.

Conclusion

We live in an ultrasocial world. On September 11, 2001, people around the world watched in horror as the twin towers of the World Trade Center fell and collectively expressed their strong support for the United States. When the 2004 tsunami hit fourteen countries across Southeast Asia, killing over 280,000 people, the international community raised tens of billions of dollars in aid almost overnight. In 2014, when Boko Haram kidnapped more than 270 Nigerian girls from Chibok Government Secondary School, social media was ablaze with the #bringbackourgirls campaign. In 2019, as Notre Dame cathedral burned, people expressed their sadness from all corners of the Earth, not just at the destruction of a French monument but for a part of *human* history. The Olympic games, the United Nations, global transportation, the Montreal Protocol, the Women's March, Black Lives Matter are just a few examples of how we come together as a species. Ultrasociality does not mean we live in a utopia, but it does mean that there is an underlying structure to our shared humanity—with important implications.

As described in Part I, we are pre-wired (enabled), hard-wired (compelled), and soft-wired (pre-disposed) to be empathic, cooperative, and socially oriented.[1] A broad range of disciplines, including social neuroscience, evolutionary biology, anthropology, cognitive psychology, and ecology have arrived at conclusions to support this. The question for this book has been: what does this mean for international relations? I have illustrated how unexpected instances of international cooperation are rooted in the ultrasocial landscape and have been made tangible through transformational ideas. Humans are drawn to finding ways to express mutual empathy, to feel a sense of societal belonging, and to pursue a common, cooperative endeavor. In the face of existential crises, when much is at stake, we tend to gravitate toward ultrasocial solutions, particularly when they provide optimism, transcendence, and a new narrative.

The four cases discussed in this book are illustrative of how an ultrasocial approach can offer new and important insights into understanding and recognizing breakthroughs in international cooperation. They show that transformational ideas that resonate with ultrasociality—European federalism, spaceflight, non-use of nuclear weapons, and net-zero carbon emissions—have had significant and

---

[1] Nicholas A. Christakis, *Blueprint: The Evolutionary Origins of a Good Society* (New York: Little, Brown Spark, 2019); Jeremy Rifkin, *The Empathic Civilization: The Race to Global Consciousness in a World in Crisis* (New York: TarcherPerigee, 2009).

International Cooperation Against All Odds. Mai'a K. Davis Cross, Oxford University Press. © Mai'a K. Davis Cross (2024). DOI: 10.1093/oso/9780192873903.003.0017

enduring impact. Altogether, this supports the notion that we have changed the nature of the international system for the better as a result of ideas that support empathy, altruism, and pursuit of the common good. Each case shows how society became galvanized around an idea of transformational change, how this led to the formation of societal-level movements and then moved governments to taking radically different approaches. Without an effort to work toward federalism in Europe, to explore space as a peaceful domain for all humankind, to commit to the non-use of nuclear weapons, and to progressively achieve net-zero carbon emissions, the world today would be a very different place.

This is a hopeful story of human capacity but not a naïve one. Our individual agency means that there are many pathways leading away from our socially oriented nature and toward a world outside of the ultrasocial landscape. Corrupt leaders can manipulate followers toward tribalism. A natural desire to feel part of a group can become warped into an us-versus-them dynamic. Deep-seated political disagreement, a sense of in-group disaffection, a lack of good leadership, or a focus on transactionalism can work against ultrasocial ideas. Of course, we still need to understand more fine-grained processes of conflict, diplomacy, negotiation, governance, socialization, and persuasion, among many others, to shed light on the detailed substance of cooperation, why cooperation sometimes becomes elusive, or how our actions can lead to unintended consequences. But given new and important discoveries about the nature of human interaction and behavior, I have argued that the complexity and nuance of all politics should be examined *within* a context of ultrasociality. For example, instead of asking "Why did we overcome self-interest?" we should be asking, "Why did we deviate from ultrasociality?"

Explanations of outcomes in international relations need not just rely on an ideational approach, as I have taken in the four cases examined here. Indeed, an ultrasocial lens should actually *open up* the field and practice of international relations rather than limit it, as has happened in the past with other approaches. Ultrasociality offers a new starting point for international relations that is grounded in science, at the same time as recognizing the demonstrated human capacity to pursue the power of possibility together.

The Wrong Tangent

How is it that we came to misjudge international relations, and indeed to act upon this misunderstanding, in the first place? The answer is necessarily US-focused. While some of the first steps were taken in the United Kingdom, much of international relations field, as we know it today, originated in the United States before spreading overseas. Most of the highest-ranking universities with international relations programs, as well as most academic journals devoted to the field, are American. Moreover, whether desirable or not, the United States has long been the most powerful actor in the international system, meaning that its foreign policy actions impact other countries disproportionately. As such, the US approach, which is still dominated by realism, has set the tone, and this is where we must turn.

First, the field of international relations has been heavily shaped by its false origins. International relations as a discipline emerged right after the First World War,[2] and in the early years, it was synonymous with the study of race, with heavy racist undertones. Indeed, the flagship international relations journal *Foreign Affairs* started out as the *Journal of Race Development*. As the study of international relations grew in the interwar period, scholars devoted much of their work to explaining the existence of international anarchy and the meaning of sovereignty.[3] After the Second World War, these ideas solidified more concretely into realism. The realist school of thought was born with thinkers like George Kennan and Henry Kissinger prominently expressing its major tenets. However, part of the success of this effort stemmed from a quiet process of "retrospectively constructed traditions," as Brian Schmidt puts it;[4] that is, realism was falsely presented as having an epic and unassailable tradition that could be traced back to ancient times, especially classical Greece. As Schmidt notes, suddenly Thucydides, Machiavelli, and Hobbes were labeled as the "founding fathers" of a discipline that was actually very new and, in the process, claiming a sense of theoretical weight and progress. This quickly became the conventional wisdom of the history of the study of international relations, giving priority and legitimacy to certain approaches over others. Realism easily achieved dominance, given that scholars in this vein of thinking could claim such major, historical philosophers. There was no need to justify their assumptions beyond invoking this intellectual tradition, despite the fact that there has never existed a clear line between this past and the new discipline of international relations, neither had there been any serious reflection on the distortions this bias introduced. These early international relations scholars invoked one version of history to justify their present-day goals.

Second, and relatedly, international relations in the United States has been crafted in reaction to foreign policy justifications, which have also influenced research funding. As Ann Tickner notes, the emphasis on so-called "scientific" method and rationalism was a reaction to the totalitarian ideologies that had grown during the Second World War and the Cold War.[5] It developed in this way to justify US foreign policy. In the 1970s, the so-called behavioralist revolution for the first time sought

---

[2] Ann Tickner, "Gendering a Discipline: Some Feminist Methodological Contributions to International Relations," *Signs: Journal of Women in Culture and Society* 30, 4 (2005): 2174, https://doi.org/10.1086/428416.

[3] Brian C. Schmidt, "On the History and Historiography of International Relations," in *Handbook of International Relations*, ed. Walter Carlsnaes, Thomas Risse, and Beth A. Simmons (London: Sage Publications Ltd, 2013) pp. 3–22.

[4] Schmidt, "On the History and Historiography of International Relations," p. 9.

[5] Tickner, "Gendering a Discipline."

to use methods from the natural sciences in international relations. They also borrowed methods from economics, believing it to be rigorous and "scientific." In so doing, it became more and more popular to rely on rationalist game theory and modeling to predict behavior that would be in the best self-interest of states, with the assumption that maximizing power over others is the goal of all. The Cold War further reaffirmed the realist approach, instead of more socially oriented or ideational alternatives. It became common to assume that all states are unitary, rational actors, whose main goal is to maximize survival in an anarchic international system—drives that cohered with US interests. As such, National Science Foundation (NSF) funding for political science in the United States has a hard orientation toward protecting national security or economic interests.[6] Rationalism and realism helped to justify US foreign policy during the Cold War, and this has continued in the decades that have followed. A case in point is when, in 2013, congressional Republicans deemed the discipline not sufficiently related to national defense, they went so far as to gut NSF support for political science entirely.

Third, there has been a kind of long-standing denial of anything to do with human nature. As biologist Edward O. Wilson writes, "The very existence of human nature was denied during the last century by most social scientists. They clung to the dogma, in spite of mounting evidence, that all social behavior is learned, and all culture is the product of history passed from one generation to the next."[7] Psychologist Daniel Kahneman writes:

> Social scientists [...] rely on a view of human nature that provides the background of most discussions of specific behaviors but is rarely questioned. Social scientists in the 1970s broadly accepted two ideas about human nature. First, people are generally rational, and their thinking is normally sound. Second, emotions such as fear, affection, and hatred explain most of the occasions on which people depart from rationality.[8]

Humans are either assumed to be self-interested and conflict-prone (rationalism and/or realism) or to be empty vessels that are then socialized into cooperating and learning from each other (constructivism). Understandably, there has been a strong reluctance in the social sciences and humanities to invoke human nature because of the dangers these arguments have posed in the past, that is, eugenics, "scientific" racism, and so on.

---

[6] Derek Reinbold, "In Defense of Political Science Spending," *The Key Reporter*, October 2, 2013.
[7] Edward O. Wilson, *The Social Conquest of Earth* (New York: W. W. Norton & Company, 2012), p. 191.
[8] Daniel Kahneman, *Thinking, Fast and Slow* (New York: Farrar, Straus and Giroux, 2011), p. 8. Kahneman and his co-author, Amos Tversky, in their 1974 article, go on to argue that people are not rational because of their "machinery of cognition" rather than emotion. Amos Tversky and Daniel Kahneman, "Judgement under Uncertainty: Heuristics and Biases," *Science* 185: 1124-1131, https://doi.org/10.1126/science.185.4157.1124.

To a large extent, however, human nature is already part of the discussion; it just tends to be implicit rather than explicit. If our studies implicitly bring in human nature, we should know precisely how this is done and, moreover, consider how best to do it. Continual mischaracterizations of how humans behave together, and what is possible in terms of cooperation, can lead to self-fulfilling prophecies of conflict and doomed efforts.[9] If most experts say that cooperation is highly unlikely because power competition dominates, why would anyone ever embark upon something like the European Union or the United Nations in the future?

To be sure, many scholars outside of the United States have actually turned away from these realist, intellectual origins. However, much of this critical scholarship has not permeated into policy debates. At least to some degree, this is because they are more oriented toward pointing out flaws in dominant assumptions rather than focusing on offering a solid alternative, or they have continually held themselves up against realism as the natural "default." Governments still frequently talk about, and act on, foreign policy in competitive, power-based terms. Given the dominant influence that the United States still has on most issues in international relations, both in academia and in world politics, this is problematic. How can we change this?

A Road Map

If humans have an ultrasocial predisposition, we should be able to not only recognize it but also capitalize on it. A willingness to engage in empathy, altruism, and cooperation as a species is an opportunity that continually sits in waiting. This potential requires recognizing its existence, practicing its attributes, and requiring socially intelligent leadership. Many times, as described in this book, a societal upswell overcomes opposition to ultrasocial behavior such that cooperation is achieved seemingly against all odds. But we can also create an environment more conducive to empathic cooperation. This requires going back to ultrasociality's building blocks because policy prescription involves going from a more species-level understanding to the level of societies, groups, and individuals. In this respect, it is important to remember that cultivating a global sense of empathy requires acknowledging both our common humanity *and* the fact that each of us possesses a unique individuality.[10]

At the broadest, most grassroots level, ultrasociality can be more embedded in educational and social institutions, especially through the liberal arts.

---

[9] By self-fulfilling prophecy, I refer to the idea that when people's expectations of a certain outcome are so strong, they may actually act in ways that make that outcome happen, even though other outcomes were possible and even more likely. The logic of self-fulfilling prophecy is inherently tautological or circular, thus taking human agency out of the process.

[10] Rifkin, *Empathic Civilization*, p. 575.

Encouraging broad questions and big-picture answers, rather than narrow, procedural and technical questions, leads to inclusivity and creativity.[11] And since achieving a more ultrasocial world often requires breakthrough ideas, cultivating true curiosity is important. Children are born curious, but curiosity diminishes as they grow into adults and is often replaced with pragmatism. And yet, curiosity is necessary for deep thinking, individuality, and open-mindedness. If our institutions, products, and society specifically encourage curiosity as a valued quality, it can balance out the pragmaticism, procedures, and repetition of the working world and the daily grind. The liberal arts excel in this area because they put curiosity at the center of education, rather than technical skills. People can always learn and relearn skills, especially on the job, but curiosity is what enables leadership and engagement in issues broader than oneself.

In addition, social neuroscientist Matthew Lieberman argues that educational institutions should capitalize much more on the *social* brain.[12] For example, rather than teaching history as a series of outcomes, largely based on power, teachers should satisfy the cravings of the social brain by focusing on the social context that informed leaders' decisions. This would have the added value of exposing people to the contribution of ultrasociality in explaining historical outcomes as well. Similarly, in English classes, rather than devoting large portions of the class to grammatical rules and spelling, Lieberman argues that teachers could focus on communication and emphasize that good writing is primarily about being able to explain things to others better, a far more socially oriented approach to learning.

At the societal level, political institutions and political leadership can purposefully incorporate the knowledge of ultrasociality as part of a path to positive and progressive outcomes. After all, ultrasociality resides in our collective minds. Our political institutions can use this to cultivate an engaged citizenry. Somewhat cynically, Noam Chomsky has said that "we surely cannot expect systems of organized power, state, or private systems to take appropriate actions [. . .] unless they are compelled to do so by constant dedicated popular mobilization and activism."[13] He advocates for education, organization, and action precisely because popular mobilization has been highly effective many times—and the four cases in this book certainly support this notion. But at the same time, we should not have to assume that ultrasocial initiatives cannot come from governments and institutions too. Indeed, the European Union is a good example of institutions carrying forward the ideas that popular mobilization had previously championed, even during more

[11] Spencer Harrison and Jon Cohen, "Curiosity is Your Super Power, TEDxLosGatos," *Youtube.com*, 2018, https://www.youtube.com/watch?%20v=xZJwMYeE9Ak&feature=emb (accessed May 20, 2023).
[12] Matthew D. Lieberman, *Social: Why Our Brains Are Wired to Connect* (New York: Crown, 2013), pp. 285–288.
[13] Noam Chomsky, *Internationalism or Extinction*, ed. Charles Derber, Suren Moodliar, and Paul Shannon (New York: Routledge, 2020), p. 39.

transactional periods. The early European Movement, in effect, infused EU governing institutions with the momentum toward more and more integration, and this is now infused in the very nature, initiatives, and operating procedures of these institutions themselves.

Socially intelligent political leaders can help an engaged citizenry identify when our shared humanity is at stake and when policy solutions can be found through a common approach. While crises often create space for new ideas to emerge, in the heat of the moment, leaders sometimes too hastily set aside empathy and fall back on self-interest, competition, violence, and in-group survival. This only serves to reinforce anti-social thinking and tribalism, qualities that all too easily spill over into other areas of governance and ultimately erode democracy. Leaders must model the behavior they expect from their citizenry, understanding that tolerance, inclusivity, open debate, and mutual respect not only achieve more democratic outcomes but are also in our very nature as humans. The official EU motto, "united in diversity," exemplifies the goal of intelligent leadership that builds on our ultrasocial inclinations.

We will never rid the world of tribalistic groups, but we should not be discouraged by them. Indeed, extreme tribalism is often met with an ultrasocial backlash. For example, in reaction to a president who cared little about women's rights, the internationalization of the US Women's March in 2017 represented a widespread ultrasocial backlash. The same could be said of the Black Lives Matter Movement, which internationalized after the murder of George Floyd on May 25, 2020. Tribalism itself can be a crisis catalyst for major policy initiatives at a global scale that reflect ultrasociality. It is not that *all* of society needs to believe a transformational idea for it to succeed. A sufficient number of people must believe and care enough to make their voices heard. These ultrasocial moments should be recognized and amplified more than the failures that precipitated them. They can be framed as positive efforts of hope, carrying with them the power of possibility.

At the global level, certain areas of cooperation have come to be increasingly taken for granted. For instance, there is not only a taboo against the use of nuclear weapons but also against inter-state conquest more broadly. Declarations supporting universal human rights and economic development of all peoples are now commonplace. Shared norms of international travel, communication, and trade are widely accepted and followed. A whole host of treaties and agreements bind countries and people together in a multitude of ways. But there is still much work to be done, and it is important to not be complacent. Constant reflection on how the ultrasocial world holds together is still necessary. How does the core human trait of empathy manifest itself in practices like diplomatic negotiations, international summits, transnational social movements, foreign policy, elections, public opinion, and so on? How can existing practices evolve to consciously incorporate the capacity of ultrasociality to flourish? For example, meetings amongst professional diplomats and summits of political leaders have long focused on preparing the proper protocol. What if this protocol also included time to acknowl-edge the individuality and social context of those present and the larger, human implications of the negotiations?

Ronald Inglehart discovered in his World Values Survey of post-materialist val-ues that, "individual security increases empathy."[14] Communications technology and high-speed travel may also contribute to this, and by extension, to ultrasocial-ity. At the same time, there is no denying that these advancements and a sense of security are more available to people in the more developed regions of the world and also tend to be reliant on the exploitation of Earth's natural resources.[15] Many of the scholars cited in this book—Rifkin, Wilson, Lieberman, and so on—warn that the factors that support ultrasociality are neither completely reliable nor nec-essarily sustainable. What can be done then to involve more marginalized peoples and the least developed areas of the world?

Going back to the building blocks, we know that empathy and ultrasociality require being able to imagine how others experience their world. Holding more summits and conferences in developing countries could go a long way toward putting ourselves in the shoes of others. Training diplomats not only in the skills of *démarches*, foreign cultures, and negotiation but also in the ability to think socially and empathically could further cultivate ultrasocial approaches. From the field of outer space exploration, the experience of the overview effect—seeing the fragility and beauty of Earth from space—has left astronauts with a sense of awe and a visceral understanding that political borders and international conflict are not actually central to our lives.[16] We share one home and one unique planet. As the new Space Age further evolves, if more leaders and would-be leaders could have the experience of the overview effect, this would undoubtedly benefit the ultrasocial world.

The Future

In the 1970 book *Future Shock*, Alvin Toffler imagines a world of such acceler-ated technological and social change that it would precipitate a widespread sense of becoming unrooted from society.[17] Everything in his imagined future is tem-porary, and it leaves many people behind, overwhelmed by stress, "information-overload," and a feeling of disorientation. Futurists and science-fiction writers have long played an important role in warning us of how dramatically things on Earth could go wrong. Rather than a sudden apocalypse, Toffler cautions against the

---

[14] Quoting Inglehart in Rifkin, *The Empathic Civilization*, p. 451.

[15] Rifkin, *The Empathic Civilization*, p. 452.

[16] Frank White, *The Overview Effect: Space Exploration and Human Evolution, Second Edition* (Reston, VA: American Institute of Aeronautics and Astronautics, 1998).

[17] Alvin Toffler, *Future Shock* (New York: Random House, 1970).

dangers of a "super-industrial society" that humans create but can no longer reign in.

In 2022, in the pages of *The New York Times*, David Brooks described our present world in a way that, in many respects, echoes Toffler's imagined future.[18] Democracy is no longer on the rise. Globalization (political, economic, and social) is decelerating or reversing. Convergence around the universal values of freedom, democracy, equality, open debate, human rights, and dignity—is giving way to divergence. Brooks laments that the very human qualities that lead us to crave belonging, respect, and being seen by others are breaking down into resentment, nationalism, and aggression. Authoritarian leaders around the world have strategically put the liberal values of free speech, pluralism, tolerance, and self-determination into the same basket as "the West" so that they can disavow all of it to pursue their own power machinations.

An ultrasocial approach should allow us to see through some of this to realize that things are not as hopeless as they might seem on the surface. We do actually have a kind of moral grounding that should have universal resonance despite how authoritarians attempt to manipulate it. We share so-called human universals that provide a basis for mutual understanding. The sheer attractive power of human ingenuity, imagination, and forward thinking can, and has, resulted in large-scale breakthroughs in international cooperation. Conflicts of the moment receive disproportionate attention. Sometimes, new progress requires tireless effort on the part of global society, and at other times, unexpected crises accelerate the push and pull of ultrasociality.

There are no quick ways to become more deeply rooted in the ultrasocial world, but awareness and a willingness to entertain the idea is the first step. If the alternative is succumbing to conflict, culture wars, democratic erosion, authoritarianism, declining globalization, trade wars, social inequality, nationalism, and apathy, among other ills, then it is certainly worth the effort. Although the scientific basis of ultrasociality is relatively new, the intuition of its existence has long been in place. We just need to work for it instead of against it.

---

[18] David Brooks, "Globalization Is Over. The Global Culture Wars Have Begun," *New York Times*, April 8, 2022, https://www.nytimes.com/2022/04/08/opinion/globalization-global-culture-war.html (accessed May 20, 2023).

Bibliography

350.org, "About 350," 2022, http://350.org/about (accessed December 1, 2022).

Abbasi, Ansar. "Hope India Knows What NCA Means?," *News International*, February 27, 2019, https://www.thenews.com.pk/print/437316-hope-india-knows-what-nca-means (accessed May 19, 2023).

Acharya, Amitav and Kenneth Boutin, "The Southeast Asia Nuclear-Weapon Free Zone," *Security Dialogue* 29, 2 (1988): 219–230, https://www.jstor.org/stable/44472123 (accessed May 19, 2023).

Action Committee for the United States of Europe, "Note, 1970," accessible at Jean Monnet Fondation, Lausanne, Paris, record code AMK 1/2/11.

Action for the Climate Emergency, "About Us," 2022, http://acespace.org/about-us (accessed December 1, 2022).

Adler, Emanuel, "The Emergence of Cooperation: National Epistemic Communities and the International Evolution of the Idea of Nuclear Arms Control," *International Organization* 46 1 (Winter 1992): 101–145.

Africa Civil Society Network on Water and Sanitation, "ANEW Overview," 2022, http://anew.africa/overview/#:~:text=The%20African%20Civil%20Society%20Network,and %20sanitation%20across%20the%20continent (accessed December 1, 2022).

Aksenov, Pavel, "Stanislav Petrov: The Man Who May Have Saved the World,'" *BBC.com*, 2013, https://www.bbc.com/news/world-europe-24280831 (accessed May 25, 2023).

Albright, Madeleine K., "Interview on NBC-TV 'The Today Show' with Matt Lauer,'" Columbus, OH, February 19, 1998, as released by the Office of the Spokesman, US Department of State, https://1997-2001.state.gov/statements/1998/980219a.html#:~: text=It%20is%20the%20threat%20of,here%20to%20all%20of%20us (accessed May 23, 2023). https://obamawhitehouse.archives.gov/realitycheck/the-press-office/remarks-president-uschina-strategic-and-economic-dialogue (accessed May 23, 2023).

Alford, John R. and John R. Hibbing, "The Origin of Politics: An Evolutionary Theory of Political Behavior," *Perspectives on Politics* 2, 4 (2004): 707–723, https://www.jstor.org/ stable/3688539 (accessed May 19, 2023).

Allan, Jen Iris, *The New Climate Activism: NGO Authority and Participation in Climate Change Governance* (Toronto: University of Toronto Press, 2020).

Allen, Jen and Jennifer Haden, "Exploring the Framing Power of NGOs in Global Climate Politics," *Environmental Politics* 26, 4 (2017): 600–620, https://doi.org/10.1080/ 09644016.2017.1319017.

Alliance of Small Island Nations, "About Us," 2022, http://aosis.org/about/chair-of-aosis (accessed December 1, 2022).

Andrews, Kate, "Over 200,000 People Apply to Live on Mars," *De Zeen*, September 11, 2003, https://www.dezeen.com/2013/09/11/over-200000-people-apply-to-live-on-mars (accessed May 20, 2023).

Annan, Kofi, "Interview Kofi Annan: 'Sometimes You Don't Have to Pick a Fight to Get Your Way,'" *The Guardian*, September 30, 2012, https://www.theguardian.com/world/ 2012/sep/30/kofi-annan-dont-pick-fight#:~:text=But%20what%20governments%20and

%20people,country%20won%20independence%20from%20Britain (accessed May 23, 2023).

Applebaum, Anne, "History Will Judge the Complicit," *The Atlantic*, June 1, 2020, p. 5. https://www.anneapplebaum.com/2020/06/01/history-will-judge-the-complicit (accessed May 23, 2023).

Aquinas, Thomas, *St. Thomas Aquinas on Politics and Ethics: A New Translation, Backgrounds, Interpretations*, ed. Paul E. Sigmund (New York: Norton, 1988).

Arafat, Yasser, "Israel's Worst-Kept Secret," *The Times*, August 5, 1980.

Aristotle, *Politics*, Book I, trans. Carnes Lord, (Chicago: University of Chicago Press, 1984).

Aristotle, *Politics*, Book II, trans. Carnes Lord, (Chicago: University of Chicago Press, 1984).

Arms and Disarmament Stockholm International Peace Research Institute (SIPRI) Findings, "The South Pacific Nuclear Free Zone," *Bulletin of Peace Proposals* 17, 3/4 (1986): 505–508.

ASEAN (Association of Southeast Asian Nations), "Joint Statement of the 3rd ASEAN–U.S. Leaders' Meeting," 2011, https://asean.org/joint-statement-of-the-3rd-asean-u-s-leaders-meeting (accessed May 20, 2023).

Asian-Regional Exchange for New Alternatives, "About ARENA," 2022, http://arena-council.org/arenac/en (accessed December 1, 2022).

Asia-Pacific Network on Food Sovereignty, "About Us," 2022, http://apnfs.info/about (accessed December 1, 2022).

Atkins, Ed, "'Bigger Than Brexit': Exploring Right-Wing Populism and Net-Zero Policies in the United Kingdom," *Energy Research and Social Science* 90 (2022), https://doi.org/10.1016/j.erss.2022.102681.

Australian Youth Climate Coalition, "About AYCC," 2022, http://aycc.org.au/about (accessed December 1, 2022).

Avaaz, "About Us," 2022, http://secure.avaaz.org/page/en/about (accessed December 1, 2022).

Axelrod, Robert, *The Evolution of Cooperation*, 2nd edn (New York: Basic Books, 2006).

Axelrod, Robert A. and William D. Hamilton, "The Evolution of Cooperation," *Science* 211, 4489 (1981): 1390–1396, https://doi.org/10.1126/science.7466396.

Azevedo, Ines, Michael Davidson, Jesse Jenkins, Valerie Karplus, and David Victor, "The Paths to Net Zero: How Technology can Save the Planet," *Foreign Affairs*, May/June 2020, p. 18.

Bainbridge, William Sims, *The Spaceflight Revolution: A Sociological Study* (Malabar, FL: Krieger Publishing Co., 1983).

Bardoux, Jacques (France), "Official Report of the Fifteenth Sitting," Council of Europe documents, September 5, 1949, p. 483.

Barnett, Michael and Robert Duvall (eds), *Power in Global Governance* (Cambridge: Cambridge University Press, 2005).

Baron, Jonathan, Rebecca Davis Gibbons, and Stephen Herzog, "Japanese Public Opinion, Political Persuasion, and the Treaty on the Prohibition of Nuclear Weapons," *Journal for Peace and Nuclear Disarmament* 3, 2 (2020): 301. https://doi.org/10.1080/25751654.2020.1834961.

Baron-Cohen, Simon, *The Science of Evil: On Empathy and the Origins of Cruelty* (New York: Basic Books, 2011).

Bell, Adrian V., Peter J. Richerson, and Richard McElreath, "Culture Rather Than Genes Provides Greater Scope for the Evolution of Large-Scale Human Prosociality,"

Proceedings of the National Academy of Sciences of the United States of America 106, 42 (2009): 17671–17674, https://www.jstor.org/stable/i25592873 (accessed May 20, 2023).

Bevington, Douglas, *The Rebirth of Environmentalism: Grassroots Activism from the Spotted Owl to the Polar Bear* (Washington, DC: Island Press, 2009).

Bienkov, Adam, "Support for Brexit Is Collapsing as Poll Finds Big Majority of British People Want to Be in the EU," *Business Insider*, June 26, 2020, https://www.businessinsider.com/brexit-poll-most-british-people-want-to-rejoin-eu-2020-6?op=1 (accessed May 20, 2023).

Bingham, Colin, *Australian Financial Review*, February 2, 1961.

Birch, Douglas and R. Jeffrey Smith, "Israel's Worst-Kept Secret," *The Atlantic*, September 16, 2014, https://www.theatlantic.com/international/archive/2014/09/israel-nuclear-weapons-secret-united-states/380237 (accessed May 20, 2023).

Bird, Michael and Blaz Zgaga, "US Billionaires Funding EU Culture War," *EUObserver*, August 22, 2019, https://euobserver.com/eu-political/14568 (accessed May 20, 2023).

Blainey, Geoffrey, *Causes of War*, 3rd edn (New York: Free Press, 1988).

Bloom, Paul, *Against Empathy: The Case for Rational Compassion* (New York: Harper Collins, 2016).

Boardman, Jason D, "Gene–Environment Interplay for the Study of Political Behaviors," in *Man is by Nature a Political Animal*, ed. Peter K. Hatemi and Rose McDermott (Chicago, IL: University of Chicago Press, 2011).

Bond, Patrick, *The Politics of Climate Justice: Paralysis Above, Movement Below* (Scottsville, KY: University of KwaZulu—Natal Press, 2012).

Bonnefous, Édouard (France), "Official Report of the Fifteenth Sitting," Council of Europe documents, September 5, 1949, p. 495.

Max Born, "Man, the Atom and the Renunciation of War," in *Voices from the Crowd: Against the H-Bomb*, ed. David Boulton (Wyomissing, PA: Dufour Editions; F edition, 1964), pp. 20–26.

Bowen, Tyler, Michael Goldfien and Matthew Graham, "The Illusory Nuclear Taboo," Yale University, February 1, 2021, https://cpb-us-w2.wpmucdn.com/campuspress.yale.edu/dist/4/3650/files/2021/03/BowenGoldfienGraham_weaktaboo.pdf (accessed May 20, 2023).

Boyd, Robert and Peter Richerson, *Culture and the Evolutionary Process* (Chicago, IL: University of Chicago Press, 1985).

Boyd, Robert and Peter J. Richerson, "Culture and the Evolution of Human Cooperation," *Philosophical Transactions of the Royal Society* B364 (2009): 3281–3288, https://doi.org/10.1098/rstb.2009.0134.

Brandon, Ruth, *The Burning Question: The Anti-nuclear Movement since 1945* (London: Heinemann, 1987).

Bregman, Rutger, "People Are Basically Good," Youtube, 2020, https://www.youtube.com/watch?v=tZ_unq8rDzU&feature=share&fbclid=IwAR0ZHeqdNfpSzBdV0oVpExbzwR2h-N32bqv0CatkCu5NO0nkZ-q3Svx_Uaw (accessed May 20, 2023).

Brinkley, Douglas, *American Moonshot: John F. Kennedy and the Great Space Race* (New York: HarperCollins, 2019).

Broad, William, "The Smaller Bombs That Could Turn Ukraine into a Nuclear War Zone," *New York Times*, March 21, 2022, https://www.nytimes.com/2022/03/21/science/russia-nuclear-ukraine.html (accessed May 20, 2023).

Brooks, David, "Globalization Is Over. The Global Culture Wars Have Begun," *New York Times*, April 8, 2022, https://www.nytimes.com/2022/04/08/opinion/globalization-global-culture-war.html (accessed May 20, 2023).

Brown, Donald E., *Human Universals* (New York: McGraw Hill, 1991).

Brugmans, Henri, "The Vital Question," Congress of Europe speech, folder ME 424, EUI Historical Archives, May 7, 1948.

Brzezinski, Zbigniew, "Discussing Democracy," *The Hill*, March 4, 2021, https://thehill. news/opinion/the-eu-cant-stand-for-democracy-until-it-stops-sitting-for-china-and-russia (accessed May 23, 2023).

Bulkeley, Rip, *The Sputniks Crisis and Early United States Space Policy* (London: Macmillan, 1991).

Bullis, Harold, *The Political Legacy of the International Geophysical Year* (Ann Arbor, MI: University of Michigan Press, 1973).

Burgess, Michael, *Federalism and European Union: The Building of Europe, 1950–2000* (Oxfordshire: Routledge, 2000).

Cadwalladr, Carole, "Robert Mercer: The Big Data Billionaire Waging War on Mainstream Media," *The Guardian*, February 26, 2019, https://www.theguardian.com/politics/2017/ feb/26/robert-mercer-breitbart-war-on-media-steve-bannon-donald-trump-nigel-farage (accessed May 20, 2023).

Çalkıvik, Aslı, "Poststructuralism and Postmodernism in International Relations," in eds Joyce Neu and Louis Kriesberg *Oxford Research Encyclopedia of International Studies* (Oxford: Oxford University Press, 2017). https://oxfordre.com/internationalstudies/ display/10.1093/acrefore/9780190846626.001.0001/acrefore-9780190846626-e-102 (accessed July 4, 2023).

Camp for Climate Action, "Camp for Climate Action," 2022, http://tni.org/en/profile/ camp-for-climate-action (accessed December 1, 2022).

Campbell, Donald T., "Legal and Primary-Group Social Controls," in *Law, Biology and Culture: The Evolution of Law*, eds. Margeret Gruter and Paul Bohannan (Santa Barbara, CA: Ross Erikson, 1982), pp. 159–170.

Campbell, Donald T., "Rationality and Utility from the Standpoint of Evolutionary Biology," *Journal of Business* 59, 4 (1986): S355–S364, https://www.jstor.org/stable/2352766 (accessed May 20, 2023).

Cappi, Giuseppe, "Official Report of the Fifth Sitting," Council of Europe documents, August 16, 1949, p. 82.

Carbon Brief, "Two Degrees: The History of Climate Change's Speed Limit," December 8, 2014, https://www.carbonbrief.org/two-degrees-the-history-of-climate-changes-speed-limit (accessed May 21, 2023).

Checkel, Jeffrey T., "Why Comply? Social Learning and European Identity Change," *International Organization* 55, 3 (2001): 553–588, https://www.jstor.org/stable/3078657 (accessed May 20, 2023).

Checkel, Jeffrey T., "International Institutions and Socialization in Europe: Introduction and Framework," *International Organization* 59, 04 (2005): 801–826, https://www.jstor. org/stable/3877829 (accessed May 20, 2023).

Chiappe, Dan, Adam Brown, and Marisela Rodriquez, "Remembering the Faces of Potential Cheaters and Cooperators in Social Contract Situations," paper presented at the annual meeting of the Human Behavior and Evolution Society, New Brunswick, NJ, June 8, 2002.

Chicago Council on Global Affairs, "Poll: 2018 Biannual Survey, Question 27 [31116769.00026]," Chicago Council on Global Affairs, GfK Group, Cornell University, Roper Center for Public Opinion Research, 2018.

Cho, Renee, "Net Zero Pledges: Can They Get Us Where We Need to Go?," Columbia Climate School, State of the Planet, December 16, 2021, https://news.climate.columbia.

edu/2021/12/16/net-zero-pledges-can-they-get-us-where-we-need-to-go (accessed May 20, 2023).

Chomsky, Noam, *Internationalism or Extinction*, ed. Charles Derber, Suren Moodliar, and Paul Shannon (New York: Routledge, 2020), pp. 7–8.

Christakis, Nicholas, *Blueprint: The Evolutionary Origins of a Good Society* (New York: Little Brown, 2019).

Churchill, Winston, "Masters of Our Fate," speech to Joint Session of the US Congress delivered on December 26, 1941.

Cicero, *The Republic and the Laws*, trans. Niall Rudd (Oxford: Oxford University Press, 2009).

Clary, Christopher and Vipin Narang, "India's Counterforce Temptations," *International Security* 43, 3 (2018): 7–52, https://doi.org/10.1162/isec_a_00340.

Climate Action Network Latin America, "Overview," 2022, http://climatenetwork.org/overview (accessed December 1, 2022).

Climate Action Network International, "About CAN," 2022, https://climatenetwork.org/overview (accessed December 1, 2022).

The Climate Camps, "Our Vision," 2022, http://klimacamp.at/our-vision/?lang=en (accessed December 1, 2022).

Climate Action Tracker, "Glasgow's 2030 Credibility Gap: Net Zero's Lip Service to Climate Action," 2021, https://climateactiontracker.org/publications/glasgows-2030-credibility-gap-net-zeros-lip-service-to-climate-action (accessed May 26, 2023).

The Climate Group, "Asian and Pacific Islands Are Leading the Environmental Movement," May 27, 2021, https://www.theclimategroup.org/our-work/news/asian-and-pacific-islands-are-leading-environmental-movement (accessed May 20, 2023).

Climate Justice Action, "About Climate Justice Alliance," 2022, http://climatejusticealliance.org/about (accessed December 1, 2022).

Climate Justice Now!, "Climate Justice Now!," 2022, http://climate-justice-now.org (accessed May 20, 2023).

Climate Mayors, "Who We are," 2022, https://climatemayors.org/who-we-are (accessed May 21, 2023).

The Climate Mobilization, "About the Climate Mobilization," 2022, http://theclimatemobilization.org/about (accessed December 1, 2022).

Climate Network Action International, "Tackling the Climate Crisis," 2022, https://climatenetwork.org (accessed May 20, 2023).

The Climate Pledge, "Signatories," 2022, https://www.theclimatepledge.com/us/en/Signatories (accessed May 20, 2023).

Cofield, Calla, "Spaceflight Is Entering a New Golden Age, Says Blue Origin Founder Jeff Bezos," *Space.com*, November 25, 2015, https://www.space.com/31214-spaceflight-golden-age-jeff-bezos.html (accessed May 20, 2023).

Congress of Europe, "Message of Mr. Winston Churchill," May 1948, ME 424, Historical Archives of the European University Institute.

Corell, Elisabeth and Michelle Betsill, "A Comparative Look at NGO Influence in International Environmental Negotiations: Desertification and Climate Change," *Global Environmental Politics* 1, 4 (2021): 95, https://doi.org/10.1162/152638001317146381.

Coudenhove-Kalergi, Richard von, "Letter to Mr. James Frederick Wiseman," in response to his letter in support of the work of Count Coudenhove-Kalergi's advocacy for European unity as chairman of the Pan-European Union, July 11, 1958.

Council of Europe, Founding documents and transcripts of discussions in the early Council of Europe, Nobel Peace Institute Library and Archive, Oslo.

Council of Europe Consultative Assembly, "Seventh Ordinary Session (First Part), Official Report, Third Sitting," National Archives and Records Administration (NARA), Wednesday July 6, 1955.

Council of Europe Consultative Assembly, "Seventh Ordinary Session, Speech Made by M. Paul-Henri Spaak, Minister for Foreign Affairs of Belgium at the Twenty-First Sitting of the Consultative Assembly," NARA, Friday October 21, 1955, pp. 3–4.

Council of Europe Secretariat-General, "European Unity: Achievement and Prospects," SG (58) I Part II (Nobel Peace Archive), Strasbourg, April 25, 1958, pp. 11, 13, 24, 27–28.

Council on Foreign Relations, "Council of Councils Twelfth Regional Conference Report," January 30, 2020, https://www.cfr.org/report/council-councils-twelfth-regional-conference (accessed May 20, 2023).

Count Coudenhove-Kalergi, speech given at the University of Heidelberg, NARA, January 26, 1956.

Cross, Mai'aK. Davis, *Security Integration in Europe: How Knowledge-Based Networks Are Transforming the European Union* (Ann Arbor, MI: University of Michigan Press, 2011).

Cross, Mai'a K. Davis, "Rethinking Epistemic Communities Twenty Years Later," *Review of International Studies* 39, 1 (2013): 137–160, https://doi.org/10.1017/S0260210512000034.

Cross, Mai'a K. Davis, *The Politics of Crisis in Europe* (New York: Cambridge University Press, 2017).

Cross, Mai'a K. Davis, "Partners at Paris? Climate Negotiations and Transatlantic Relations," *Journal of European Integration* 40, 5 (2018): 571–586, https://doi.org/10.1080/07036337.2018.1487962.

Mai'a K. Davis Cross and Saadia Pekkanen (eds), "Space Diplomacy," *The Hague Journal of Diplomacy*, Special Issue, 18, 2–3 (2023). https://brill.com/view/journals/hjd/18/2-3/hjd.18.issue-2-3.xml (accessed July 4, 2023).

Cross, Mai'a K. Davis, "The Social Construction of the Space Race: Then and Now," *International Affairs* 95, 6 (November 2019): 1403–1421. https://doi.org/10.1093/ia/iiz190.

Cross, Mai'a K. Davis and Xinru Ma, "EU Crises and Integrational Panic: The Role of the Media," *Journal of European Public Policy* 22, 8 (2015): 1053–1070, https://doi.org/10.1080/13501763.2014.984748.

Currin, Grant, "Why are Humans So Curious?," *LiveScience*, July 19, 2020, https://www.livescience.com/why-are-humans-curious.html (accessed May 20, 2023).

Davenport, Christian, "The Battlefield 22,000 Miles above Earth," *Wilson Quarterly*, Winter 2019, https://www.wilsonquarterly.com/quarterly/the-new-landscape-in-space/the-battlefield-22-000-miles-above-earth (accessed May 20, 2023).

David Pakman Show, "Rutger Bregman: People Are Basically Good," Youtube, 2020, https://www.youtube.com/watch?v=tZ_unq8rDzU (accessed May 20, 2023).

Davidson, Helen, "'You Follow the Government's Agenda': China's Climate Activists Walk a Tightrope," *The Guardian*, August 16, 2021, https://www.theguardian.com/world/2021/aug/16/you-follow-the-governments-agenda-chinas-climate-activists-walk-a-tightrope (accessed May 20, 2023).

Dawkins, Richard, *The Selfish Gene* (Oxford: Oxford University Press, 1976).

de Montesquieu, Charles, *Spirit of the Laws* (New York: Prometheus Books, 2002 [1748]).

De Valera, Éamon (Ireland), "Official Report of the Sixth Sitting," Council of Europe documents, August 17, 1949, p. 141.

de Vries, Gijs, "Cultural Freedom in European Foreign Policy," *Institut für Auslandsbeziehungen (IFA) Edition Culture and Foreign Policy* 2019, p. 27, https://www.cultureinexternalrelations.eu/2019/05/17/31490/ (accessed July 4, 2023).

Dedman, Martin, *The Origins and Development of the European Union: 1945–95* (New York: Routledge, 1996).

Dedman, Martin, *The Origins and Development of the European Union: 1945–2008* (Oxfordshire: Routledge, 2009), p. 15.

della Porta, Donatella and Louisa Parks, "Framing Processes in the Climate Movement," in *Routledge Handbook of the Climate Change Movement*, ed. Matthias Dietz and Heiko Garrelts (London and New York: Routledge, 2014), pp. 19–30.

Democratic Advisory Council, "Position Paper on Space Research: Prepared for Senator Kennedy," JFK Presidential Archives, Box 197 DNC 1960 Campaign, September 7, 1960.

Department of State, "Incoming Telegram from Geneva to Secretary State, Outer Space," JFK Presidential Archives, National Security Files, Box 308, May 31, 1962.

Dietz, Matthias, "Activist Profile—Naomi Klein," in *Routledge Handbook of the Climate Change Movement*, ed. Matthias Dietz and Heiko Garrelts (London and New York: Routledge, 2014), p. 224.

Dietz, Matthias and Heiko Garrelts (eds), *Routledge Handbook of the Climate Change Movement* (London and New York: Routledge, 2014).

Dietz, Thomas, Rachel Shwon, and Cameron Whitley, "Climate Change and Society," *Annual Review of Sociology* 46 (2020): 135–158.

Dinan, Desmond, *Ever Closer Union: An Introduction to European Integration* (Basingstoke: Palgrave MacMillan, 1999), p. 12.

Dinan, Desmond, *Europe Recast: A History of European Union* (Basingstoke: Palgrave, 2004), p. 25.

Dinan, Desmond, *Ever Closer Union: An Introduction to European Integration* (London: Lynne Reiner, 2010).

Director of Intelligence and Research, Department of State, "Intelligence Note: Khrushchev's Obscure and Noncommittal Statements about Moon Shots," to the Secretary from INR—Thomas L. Hughes, JFK Presidential Archives, National Security Files, Box 308, November 5, 1963.

Dolsak, Nives and Aseem Prakash, "Join the Club: How the Domestic NGO Sector Induces Participation in the Covenant of Mayors Program," *International Interactions* 43, 1 (2017): 26–47. https://doi.org/10.1080/03050629.2017.1226668.

Dryden, Hugh, "US–Soviet Space Cooperation Talks," JFK Presidential Archives, National Security Files, Box 334, March 27, 28, 30, 1962.

Dunn, Kelsey, "Currents of Change: Tracing the History of the U.S. Climate Movement," Honors thesis, Wellesley College. June 2021.

Düsünsel, Feridun (Turkey), "Official Report of the Sixth Sitting," Council of Europe documents, August 17, 1949, p. 143.

Econlib (Library of Economics and Liberty), "Paul Bloom on Empathy," February 27, 2017, https://www.econtalk.org/paul-bloom-on-empathy (accessed May 20, 2023).

Ecopeace Middle East, "Our Mission," 2022, http://ecopeaceme.org/about (accessed December 1, 2022).

Edwards, Guy and Timmons Roberts, *A Fragmented Continent: Latin America and the Global Politics of Climate Change* (Cambridge, MA: MIT Press, 2015).

Eggers, Alfred, "The Space Station and International Collaboration," National Aeronautics and Space Administration (NASA) Archives, Folder 9164, Space Station 1968–1969, March 17, 1969.

Egyptian National Competitiveness Council, "About Us," 2022, http://encc.org.eg/about/default.aspx (accessed December 1, 2022).

Eisenhower, Dwight D., "Remarks in Connection with the Opening of the International Geophysical Year," DDE's Papers as President, Speech Series, Box 22, International Geophysical Year NAID # 16647171, June 30, 1957, as cited in Dimitrios Stroikos, "Engineering World Society? Scientists, Internationalism, and the Advent of the Space Age." *International Politics* 55, 1 (2018): 73–90, https://doi.org/10.1057/s41311-017-0070-8.

Eisenhower, Dwight D., *The White House Years: Waging Peace, 1956–1961* (New York: Doubleday & Co., 1965).

Endres, Danielle, Leah Sprain, and Tarla Rai Peterson (eds), *Social Movement to Address Climate Change: Local Steps for Global Action* (Amherst, MA: Cambria Press, 2009).

English, Robert, *Russia and the Idea of the West: Gorbachev, Intellectuals, and the End of the Cold War* (New York: Columbia University Press, 2000).

Environmental Defense Fund, "About Building a Better Future Together," 2022, http://edf.org/about (accessed December 1, 2022).

Epstein, William and Toshiyuki Toyoda (eds), *A New Design for Nuclear Disarmament* (Nottingham: Pushwash Symposium, 1977).

Erritzoe, David, Leor Roseman, Matthew M. Nour, Katherine MacLean, Mendel Kaelen, David J. Nutt, and Robin L. Carhart-Harris, "Effects of Psilocybin Therapy on Personality Structure," *Acta Psychiatrica Scandinavica* 138, 5 (2018): 368–378, https://doi.org/10.1111/acps.12904.

ESA (European Space Agency), "Statement of Kenneth S. Pedersen, Director of International Affairs, NASA, before the Subcommittee on Science, Technology and Space of the Committee on Commerce, Science and Transportation, US Senate," ESA Archives, File 8011, February 25, 1980.

ESA, "Cooperation between Europe and the United States in the Space Field," April 29, 1981, ESA Archives, File 8011.

ESA (co-sponsored by the International Academy of Astronautics), *The Impact of Space Activities upon Society* (Paris: European Space Agency/International Academy of Astronautics, 2005).

Eschle, Catherine, "Feminism and Peace Movements: Engendering Anti-nuclear Activism," in eds. Väyrynen, Tarja, Swati Parashar, Élise Féron, and Catia Cecilia. Confortini, *Routledge Handbook of Feminist Peace Research* (New York: Routledge, 2021), pp. 250–259.

European Commission, Directorate-General for Communication, "Standard Eurobarometer 93 Summer 2020 Report: European Citizenship, Fieldwork: July–August 2020," 2020, https://doi.org/10.2775/581547.

European Environmental Bureau, "About EEB," 2022, http://eeb.org/homepage/about (accessed December 1, 2022).

European Space Agency Manned Space Programme, "Draft Programme Proposal on the European Participation in the ISSA," ES/PB-MS(94)60, Paris, European Space Agency (ESA) Archives, ESA File 18,499, December 22, 1994. p. 1.

European Union, "Shared Vision, Common Action: A Stronger Europe: A Global Strategy for the European Union's Foreign and Security Policy," June 2016, https://www.eeas.europa.eu/sites/default/files/eugsreviewweb0.pdf (accessed May 20, 2023).

Evangelista, Matthew, *Unarmed Forces: The Transnational Movement to End the Cold War* (Ithaca, NY: Cornell University Press, 2002).

The Evening Star, "Moon-Trip Plan Stirs Enthusiastic Reaction," NASA Archives, File 15570, September 21, 1963.

Extinction Rebellion, "About Us," 2022, http://rebellion.global/about-us (accessed December 1, 2022).

Ezell, Edward Clinton and Linda Neuman Ezell, "Competition Versus Cooperation: 1959–1962," *The Partnership*, 2022, https://history.nasa.gov/SP-4225/documentation/competition/competition.htm (accessed November 26, 2022).

Fankhauser, Sam, Stephen M. Smith, Myles Allen, Kaya Axelsson, Thomas Hale, Cameron Hepburn, J. Michael Kendall, Radhika Khosla, Javier Lezaun, Eli Mitchell-Larson, Michael Obersteiner, Lavanya Rajamani, Rosalind Rickaby, Nathalie Seddon, and Thom Wetzer, "The Meaning of Net Zero and How to Get it Right," *Nature Climate Change* 12 (2022): 18, https://doi.org/10.1038/s41558-021-01245-w.

Feldman Barrett, Lisa, *How Emotions are Made: The Secret Life of the Brain* (New York: Mariner Books, 2017).

Fishel, Ruth, *Peace in Our Hearts, Peace in the World: Meditations of Hope and Healing* (New York: Sterling Publishing Co. Inc., 2008).

Foreign Service, "Despatch No. 504 from Anthony Clinton Swezey, First Secretary of Embassy to the Department of State Washington," NARA, RG 59, Box 3101, Folder 740.00/1-555, January 18, 1955.

Foreign Service, "Despatch No. 62 from William D. Wolle, American Consul in Manchester to the Department of State Washington," NARA, RG 59, Box 3101, Folder 740.00/2–855, February 8, 1955.

Foreign Service, "Despatch No. 1567 from Elim O'Shaughnessy, Counselor of Embassy, American embassy Bonn to the Department of State, Washington," NARA, RG 59, Box 3103, Folder 740.00/1–1056, January 30, 1956.

Foreign Service, "Despatch No. 654 from J. Harold Shullaw, First Secretary of Embassy, American Embassy in the Hague to the Department of State Washington," NARA, RG 59, Box 3103, Folder 740.00/1–1056, February 3, 1956.

Foreign Service, "Despatch No. 918 from Sheldon B. Vance, Second Secretary of Embassy, American Embassy in Brussels to the Department of State Washington," NARA, RG 59, Box 3103, Folder 740.00/1–1056, February 21, 1956.

Franco–British St. Malo Declaration (December 4, 1998). https://www.cvce.eu/obj/franco_british_st_malo_declaration_4_december_1998-en-f3cd16fb-fc37-4d52-936f-c8e9bc80f24f.html (accessed July 3, 2023)

Friends of the Earth International, "Who We are," 2022, https://www.foei.org/who-are-friends-of-the-earth/ (accessed July 4, 2023).

Fridays for Future, "What We Do," 2022, http://fridaysforfuture.org/what-we-do (accessed December 1, 2023).

Friedberg, Aaron, "A History of the US Strategic 'Doctrine'—1945–1980," *Journal of Strategic Studies* 3, 3 (1980): 37–71. https://doi.org/10.1080/01402398008437055.

Frye, Alton, "The Proposal for a Joint Lunar Expedition," Defense Technical Information Center, p. 6, https://apps.dtic.mil/sti/citations/ADA540204 (accessed May 20, 2023).

Fuentes, Agustín, *Why We Believe: Evolution and the Human Way of Being* (New Haven, CT: Yale University Press, 2019).

Future Coalition, "Our Mission," 2022, http://futurecoalition.org/mission (accessed December 1, 2022).

Garcia, Denise, "Attaining Human Security by Disarming," in *Edward Elgar Research Handbook on International Law and Human Security*, ed. Gerd Oberleitner (Northampton, MA: Edward Elgar Publishing, 2022).

Garcia, Denise, *Common Good Governance in the Age of Artificial Intelligence* (Oxford: Oxford University Press, 2023), Chapter 5.

GCCA (Global Campaign for Climate Action), "75 Years of Care," 2022, http://ghf-ge.org/tcktcktck.php (accessed December 1, 2022).

George, Martha Wheeler, "The Impact of Sputnik I: Case-Study of American Public Opinion at the Break of the Space Age," NASA Historical Note No. 22, NASA HQ, Folder 6719, October 4, 1957.

Geppert, Alexander C. T., "Space *Personae*: Cosmopolitan Networks of Peripheral Knowledge, 1927–1957," *Journal of Modern European History* 6, 2 (2008): 262, https://doi.org/10.17104/1611-8944.

Giugni, Marco, *Social Protest and Policy Change: Ecology, Antinuclear, and Peace Movements in Comparative Perspective* (Oxford: Roman & Littlefield, 2004), pp. 8–9.

Glaser, Charles L., "Why Do Strategists Disagree about the Requirements of Strategic Nuclear Deterrence?," in *Nuclear Arguments: Understanding the Strategic Nuclear Arms and Arms Control Debates*, ed. Lynn Eden and Steven E. Miller (Ithaca: Cornell University Press, 1989), pp. 109–171.

Global Commission on the Climate and Economy, "Better Growth, Better Climate: The New Climate Economy Report," 2014, https://newclimateeconomy.report/2014/wp-content/uploads/sites/2/2014/08/NCE-Global-Report_web.pdf (accessed May 20, 2023).

Global Covenant of Mayors, "Who We Are," 2022, https://www.globalcovenantofmayors.org/who-we-are (accessed May 21, 2023).

Global Justice Ecology Project, "About," 2022, http://globaljusticeecology.org/about (accessed December 1, 2022).

Goldemberg, Jose, Carols Feu Alvim, and Olga Mafra, "The Denuclearization in Argentina and Brazil," *Journal for Peace and Nuclear Disarmament* 1, 2 (2018), https://www.tandfonline.com/doi/abs/10.1080/25751654.2018.1479129 (accessed May 25, 2023).

Goldstein, Joshua, *Winning the War on War: The Decline of Armed Conflict Worldwide* (New York: Penguin, 2012).

Goldstein, Judith and Robert Keohane (eds), *Ideas and Foreign Policy: Beliefs, Institutions, and Political Change.* (New York: Cornell University Press, 1993), pp. 7–8.

Goodwin, Jeff and James Jasper (eds), *The Social Movements Reader: Cases and Concepts*, 3rd edn (Oxford: Wiley Blackwell, 2015).

Gore, Al, "Ted Talk," February 2016, https://www.ted.com/talks/al_gore_the_case_for_optimism_on_climate_change?language=en (accessed May 26, 2023).

Gowdy, John and Lisi Krall, "The Ultrasocial Origin of the Anthropocene," *Ecological Economics* 95 (November 2013), https://doi.org/10.1016/j.ecolecon.2013.08.006.

Granovetter, Mark, "The Strength of Weak Ties," *American Journal of Sociology* 78, 6 (May 1973): 1360–1380, https://www.jstor.org/stable/2776392 (accessed May 20, 2023).

Greenpeace, "About Us," 2022, http://greenpeace.org/international/tag/about-us (accessed December 1, 2022).

Grin, Gilles, "The Community Method: From Jean Monnet to Current Challenges," *EuroAtlantic Union Review* 2, 2 (2015): 15–29, https://www.ecb.europa.eu/press/key/date/2017/html/ecb.sp170504.en.html (accessed May 20, 2023).

Gupta, Sujata, "Social Distancing Comes with Psychological Fallout," *Science News*, March 29, 2020, https://www.sciencenews.org/article/coronavirus-covid-19-social-distancing-psychological-fallout (accessed May 20, 2023).

Gurven, Michael, "Reciprocal Altruism and Food Sharing Decisions among Hiki and Ache Hunter-Gatherers," *Behavioral Ecology and Sociobiology* 56, 4 (2004): 366–380, https://doi.org/10.1007/s00265-004-0793-6.

Haas, Ernst B., *Beyond the Nation State: Functionalism and International Organization* (Colchester: ECPR Press, 2008).

Habermas, Jürgen, *Communication and the Evolution of Society* (Toronto: Beacon Press, 1979).

Habermas, Jürgen, *The Theory of Communicative Action* (Toronto: Beacon Press, 1981).

Hahn, Erin and James Scouras, "Responding to North Korean Nuclear First Use: So Many Imperatives, So Little Time," Johns Hopkins Applied Physics Laboratory, 2020.

Halloran, Neil, "The Fallen of WWII," documentary, 2015, http://www.fallen.io/ww2 (accessed May 20, 2023).

Hallstein, Walter, "The European Economic Community," speech, Jean Monnet Fondation, Lausanne, Paris, January 23, 1961.

Hallstein, Walter, "Economic Integration and Political Unity in Europe," speech before the joint meeting of Harvard University and the Massachusetts Institute of Technology, Jean Monnet Fondation, Lausanne, Paris, May 23, 1961, p. 9.

Hallstein, Walter, "The EEC and the Community of the Free World," speech in Zurich to the Schweizerische Europa-Union, Jean Monnet Fondation, Lausanne, Paris, November 24, 1961, p. 2.

Harari, Yuval Noah, *Sapiens: A Brief History of Humankind* (New York: Harper Collins Books, 2015), pp. 20–22.

Hansel, Michael, "The USA and Arms Control in Space: An IR Analysis," *Space Policy* 26, 2 (May 2010): 91–98, https://doi.org/10.1016/j.spacepol.2010.02.011.

Harrison, Spencer and Jon Cohen, "Curiosity is Your Super Power," TEDxLosGatos, Youtube.com, 2018, https://www.youtube.com/watch?v=xZJwMYeE9Ak&feature=emb (accessed May 20, 2023).

Hatemi, Peter and Rose McDermott (eds), *Man Is by Nature a Political Animal: Evolution, Biology, and Politics* (Chicago, IL: University of Chicago Press, 2011).

Hathaway, Oona and Scott Shapiro, *The Internationalists: How a Radical Plan to Outlaw War Remade the World* (New York: Simon & Schuster, 2017).

Helliwell, John F. and Robert D. Putnam, "The Social Context of Well-Being," *Philosophical Transactions Biological Sciences* 359, 1449 (2004): 1435–446, https://doi.org/10.1098/rstb.2004.1522.

Hitchens, Theresa, "Experts Warn Space Force Rhetoric Risks Backfiring," *Breaking Defense*, May 28, 2019, https://breakingdefense.com/2019/05/experts-warn-space-force-rhetoric-risks-backfiring (accessed May 20, 2023).

Hobbes, Thomas, *Leviathan* (Oxford: Oxford University Press, 1929 [1651]).

Hoberg, George, *The Resistance Dilemma: Place-Based Movements and the Climate Crisis* (Cambridge, MA: MIT Press, 2021), p. 3.

Hoffmann, Stanley, "Obstinate or Obsolete? The Fate of the Nation-State and the Case of Western Europe," *Daedalus* (1966): 862–915, https://www.jstor.org/stable/20027004 (accessed May 20, 2023).

Holt-Lunstad, Julianne, Timothy B. Smith, Mark Baker, Tyler Harris, and David Stephenson, "Loneliness and Social Isolation as Risk Factors for Mortality: A Meta-analytic Review," *Perspectives on Psychological Science* 10, 2 (2015): 227–237, https://doi.org/10.1177/1745691614568352.

Holz, Christian, "The Public Spheres of Climate Change Advocacy Networks: An Ethnography of Climate Action Network International within the United Nations Framework Convention on Climate Change (UNFCC)," PhD thesis, University of Glasgow. 2012, p. 80.

Hooghe, Liesbet, *Cohesion Policy and European Integration: Building Multi-level Governance* (Oxford: Oxford University Press, 1996).

Hooghe, Liesbet and Gary Marks, *Multi-level Governance and European Integration* (Lanham, MD: Rowman & Littlefield, 2001).

Howorth, Jolyon, "Discourse, Ideas, and Epistemic Communities in European Security and Defence Policy," *West European Politics* 27, 2 (2004): 211–234.

ICAN (International Campaign to Abolish Nuclear Weapons), "Polls: Public Opinion in EU Host States Firmly Opposes Nuclear Weapons," International Campaign to Abolish Nuclear Weapons, 2019, https://www.icanw.org/polls_public_opinion_in_eu_host_states_firmly_opposes_nuclear_weapons (accessed May 21, 2023).

India Climate Collaborative, "Our Vision," 2022, http://indiaclimatecollaborative.org/about (accessed December 1, 2022).

Indigenous Environmental Network, "Our History," 2022, http://ienearth.org/about (accessed December 1, 2022).

Intergovernmental Panel on Climate Change, "Climate Change 2023: Synthesis Report," A Report of the Intergovernmental Panel on Climate Change," Geneva, Switzerland, 2023. https://www.ipcc.ch/report/ar6/syr/ (accessed July 4, 2023)

Ivanova, Maria, "At 50, the UN Environment Programme Must Lead Again," *Nature.* February 16, 2021, http://doi.org/10.1038/d41586-021-00393-5 (accessed July 4, 2023).

Jabko, Nicolas, *Playing the Market: A Political Strategy for Uniting Europe, 1985–2005* (Ithaca, NY: Cornell University Press, 2006).

Jacobs, Michael, "High Pressure for Low Emissions: How Civil Society Created the Paris Climate Agreement," *Juncture* 22, 4 (2016): 314–323.

Jacobs, Michael, "Reflections on COP26: International Diplomacy, Global Justice and the Greening of Capitalism," *Political Quarterly* 93, 2 (April–June 2022): 272, https://doi.org/10.1111/1467-923X.13083.

Jain, Jagdish P., *India and Disarmament: Nehru Era* (New Delhi: Radiant Publishers, 1974).

Japan Climate Initiative, "Japan Climate Initiative," 2022, http://japanclimate.org/english (accessed December 1, 2023).

Jefferson, Thomas, "The Declaration of Independence," Miscellaneous Papers of the Continental Congress, 1774-1789; Records of the Continental and Confederation Congresses and the Constitutional Convention, 1774–1789, Record Group 360; National Archives.

Jervis, Robert, "Cooperation under the Security Dilemma," *World Politics* 30, 2 (1978): 167–214.

Jervis, Robert, *The Meaning of the Nuclear Revolution* (Ithaca, NY: Cornell University Press, 1989).

JFK Presidential Archives, "Letter from Richard W. Porter, US National Academy of Sciences, to Professor Federov. Academy of Sciences of the USSR," JFK Presidential Archives, National Security Files, Box 334, December 15, 1959.

JFK Presidential Archives, "Letter from Professor Federov, Academy of Sciences of the USSR, to Richard W. Porter. US National Academy of Sciences," JFK Presidential Archives, National Security Files, Box 334, March 16, 1960.

JFK Presidential Archives, "Letter from Khrushchev to Kennedy," JFK Presidential Archives, National Security Files, Countries Series, USSR, Khrushchev Correspondence, Document 43, March 20, 1962. Also available here: https://history.state.gov/historicaldocuments/frus1961-63v06/d43 (accessed July 3, 2023)

JFK Presidential Archives, "Memorandum for the President. 'Bilateral Talks Concerning US–USSR Cooperation in Outer Space Activities,'" JFK Presidential Archives, National Security Files, Box 334, July 5, 1962.

JFK Presidential Archives, "Letter from Hugh Dryden to Blagonravov," JFK Presidential Archives, National Security Files, Box 334, December 5, 1962.

JFK Presidential Archives, "National Security Policy Planning Paper: Implications of Outer Space in the 1970's," JFK Presidential Archives, National Security Files, Box 308, May 31, 1963.

JFK Presidential Archives, "Letter from NASA Administrator James Webb to President Kennedy," JFK Presidential Archives, National Security Files, Box 342, September 1963.

JFK Presidential Archives, "Memo from John Glenn to McGeorge Bundy, "Proposal Concerning Space Flight Information Negotiations with the Russians," JFK Presidential Archives, National Security Files, Box 308, November 4, 1963.

JFK Presidential Archives, "Memorandum for Mr. McGeorge Bundy from the White House," JFK Presidential Archives, National Security Files, Box 308, Space Activities, November 7, 1963.

JFK Presidential Archives, "US–USSR Cooperation in Space Research Programs," JFK Presidential Archives, National Security Files, Box 342, 1963/64 (not specifically dated).

Jha, Preeti, "The Young Activists Fighting Southeast Asia's Climate Crisis," *The Diplomat*, October 11, 2019, https://thediplomat.com/2019/10/the-young-activists-fighting-southeast-asias-climate-crisis (accessed May 20, 2023).

Jones, Shirley (ed.), *Simply Living: The Spirit of the Indigenous People* (Novato, CA: New World Library, 1999).

Kachi, Aki, Silke Mooldijk, and Carsten Warnecke, "How to Distinguish between Climate Leadership and Greenwashing," New Climate Institute, 2020, http://admin.indiaenvironmentportal.org.in/reports-documents/climate-neutrality-claims-how-distinguish-between-climate-leadership-and-greenwashing (accessed May 20, 2023).

Kahneman, Daniel, *Thinking Fast and Slow* (New York: Farrar, Straus and Giroux, 2013).

Kakatkar, Manasi and Miles Pomper, "Central Asian Nuclear-Weapon-Free Zone Formed," *Arms Control Today* 39, 1 (January/February 2009): 42, https://www.jstor.org/stable/i23628264 (accessed May 20, 2023).

Kaysen, Carl, "Summary of Foreign Policy Aspects of the US Outer Space Program," JFK Presidential Archives, National Security Files, Box 377, June 5, 1962.

Kempe, Ysabelle, "It's Dangerous to be a Climate Activist in Latin America," *Grist*, April 22, 2021, https://grist.org/regulation/its-dangerous-to-be-an-environmental-activist-in-latin-america-a-new-treaty-is-trying-to-change-that (accessed May 20, 2023).

Kennedy, John F., "If the Soviets Control Space .. . They Can Control Earth," *Missiles and Rockets*, October 10, 1960, pp. 12–13, as cited in Edward Ezell and Linda Ezell (eds), *The Partnership: A History of the Apollo-Soyuz Test Project*, (Washington DC: NASA, 1978) https://history.nasa.gov/SP-4209.pdf (accessed July 3, 2023).

Kennedy, John F., "Moon Speech—Rice Stadium," September 12, 1962.

Kennedy, John F., "Speech to the United Nations," September 20, 1963, as quoted in Alton Frye, "The Proposal for a Joint Lunar Expedition: Background and Prospects," The RAND Corporation. NASA Archives, File 15570, January 1964.

Kennedy, John F., "National Security Action Memorandum No. 271," JFK Presidential Archives, National Security Files, Box 342, November 12, 1963.

Keohane, Robert O., "International Institutions: Two Approaches," *International Studies Quarterly* 32, 4 (December 1988): 379–396.

Keohane, Robert O. and Stanley Hoffmann, *Institutional Change in Europe in the 1980s* (London: Macmillan Education, 1994).

Kennedy, John F. Kennedy, The White House, Office of the White House Press Secretary, "President's telegram to the chairman of the council of ministers, Union of Soviet Socialist Republics, N.S. Khrushchev," JFK Presidential Archives, National Security Files, Box 308, April 12, 1961

Kidd, Celeste and Benjamin Hayden, "The Psychology and Neuroscience of Curiosity," *Neuron* 88 (November 2015): 449–460, https://doi.org/10.1016/j.neuron.2015.09.010.

Kim, Jim Yong, "Transforming the Economy to Achieve Zero Net Emissions," Council on Foreign Relations, 2014, https://www.worldbank.org/en/news/speech/2014/12/08/transforming-the-economy-to-achieve-zero-net-emissions (accessed July 4, 2023).

Kimmel, Michael, *Angry White Men: American Masculinity at the End of an Era* (New York: Nation Books, 2013), as cited in Elizabeth Mika, "Who Goes Trump: Tyranny as a Triumph of Narcissism," in *The Dangerous Case of Donald Trump*, ed. Bandy Lee (New York: St Martin's Press, 2019): 297.

Kissinger, Henry, *The White House Years* (Boston, MA: Little Brown an Company, 1979).

Klein, Naomi. *No Logo: Taking Aim at the Brand Bullies* (New York: Picador, 1999).

Klein, Naomi. *This Changes Everything: Capitalism vs the Climate* (New York: Simon & Schuster, 2014).

Kleiner, Kurt. "The Corporate Race to Cut Carbon," *Nature Climate Change* 1 (2007): 40–43, https://doi.org/10.1038/climate.2007.31.

Kohler, Hannah. "The Eagle and the Hare: U.S.–Chinese Relations, the Wolf Amendment, and the Future of International Cooperation in Space," *Georgetown Law Journal* 103, 4: 1148.

Korsmo, Fae L. "The Genesis of the International Geophysical Year," *Physics Today* 60, 7 (July 2007): 38–43, https://doi.org/10.1063/1.2761801.

Krayewsk, Ed, "Trump Admin Rhetoric Taking U.S.–North Korea Crisis to a Dangerous New Place, Says Kim Jong Il Biographer," April 14, *Reason.com*, 2017, https://reason.com/2017/04/14/trump-admin-rhetoric-taking-us-north-kor (accessed May 20, 2023).

Krige, John, Angelina Long Callahan, and Ashok Maharaj, *NASA in the World: Fifty Years of International Collaboration in Space* (Basingstoke: Palgrave, 2013).

Kristensen, Hans and Matt Korda, "Pakistani Nuclear Weapons, 2021," *Bulletin of Atomic Scientists* 77, 5 (2021): 165–278.

Kristensen, Hans M. and Robert S. Norris, "Nuclear Notebook," *Bulletin of the Atomic Scientists*, 2022, https://thebulletin.org/nuclear-notebook (accessed November 29, 2022).

Kurzban, Robert and X. Athena Aktipis, "Modularity and the Social Mind: Are Psychologists Too Self-ish?," *Personality and Social Psychology Review* 11, 2 (May 2007): 131–149, https://doi.org/10.1177/1088868306294906.

Lahti, David C. and Bret S. Weinstein, "The Better Angels of Our Nature: Group Stability and the Evolution of Moral Tension," *Evolution and Human Behavior* 26, 1 (2005): 47–63, https://doi.org/10.1016/j.evolhumbehav.2004.09.004.

Lake, David and Robert Powell (eds), *Strategic Choice and International Relations* (Princeton, NJ: Princeton University Press, 1999).

Lang, John, "Net Zero: A Short History," Energy and Climate Intelligence Unit, 2022, https://eciu.net/analysis/infographics/net-zero-history (accessed May 20, 2023).

Launius, Roger D., "An Unintended Consequence of the IGY," *Acta Astronautica* 67, 1 (2010): 257–258, https://doi.org/10.1016/j.actaastro.2009.10.019.

Le Bail, Jean (France), "Official Report of the Sixth Sitting," Council of Europe documents, August 17, 1949, p. 119.

Legro, Jeffrey, "The Transformation of Policy Ideas," *American Journal of Political Science* 44, 3 (2002): 419–432, https://doi.org/10.2307/2669256.

Leis, Jeffrey, "'Night of Murder': On the Brink of Nuclear War in South Asia," The Nuclear Threat Initiative, 2019, https://www.nti.org/analysis/articles/night-murder-brink-nuclear-war-south-asia (accessed May 20, 2023).

Leslie, Ian, "Why Your 'Weak-Tie' Friendships May Mean More Than You Think," *The Life Project*, July 2, 2020.

Lieber, Keir A. and Daryl G. Press, "The New Era of Counterforce: Technological Change and the Future of Nuclear Deterrence," *International Security* 41, 4 (2017): 9–49, https://doi.org/10.1162/ISEC_a_00273.

Lieberman, Matthew, *Social: Why Our Brains are Wired to Connect* (New York: Crown Publishing Group, 2013).

Lieberman, Peter. "The Rise and Fall of the South African Bomb," *International Security* 26, 1 (2001): 45–86, https://www.jstor.org/stable/3092122 (accessed May 25, 2023).

Lindley-French, Julian, *A Chronology of European Security and Defence Policy, 1945–2007* (New York: Oxford University Press, 2007).

Lindseth, Peter L., "Democratic Legitimacy and the Administrative Character of Supra-nationalism: The Example of the European Community," *Columbia Law Review* 99, 3 (1999): 628–738, https://doi.org/10.2307/1123519.

Lipgens, Walter (ed.), *Sources for the History of European Integration 1945–55* (Leyden: Sijthoff, 1980).

Lipgens, Walter (ed.), *Documents on the History of European Integration*, Series B, Vol. 1 (Berlin: Walter de Gruyter, 1985).

Lipgens, Walter (ed.), "General Introduction," in *Documents on the History of European Integration*, Series B, Vol. 2 (Berlin: Walter de Gruyter, 1985), p. 4.

Locke, John, "An Essay Concerning Human Understanding," Liberty Fund, 1689, https://oll.libertyfund.org/title/locke-the-works-vol-1-an-essay-concerning-human-understanding-part–1 (accessed May 20, 2023).

Locke, John, "Second Treatise of Government, Chapter 2," in *The Project Gutenberg eBook of Second Treatise of Government*, April 22, 2003, https://www.gutenberg.org/files/7370/7370-h/7370-h.htm (accessed May 20, 2023).

Longdon, Normam and Duc Guyenne (eds), *Twenty Years of European Cooperation in Space: An ESA Report, '64–'84* (Paris: European Space Agency, 1984), p. 10.

Maathai, Wangari, *The Challenge for Africa* (New York: Pantheon, 2009).

MacDonald, Alexander, *The Long Space Age: The Economic Origins of Space Exploration from Colonial America to the Cold War* (New Haven, CT: Yale University Press, 2017).

MacDonald, Eryn, "What Is the Nuclear Taboo and Is Putin About to Break It?," Union of Concerned Scientists, 2022, https://allthingsnuclear.org/emacdonald/what-is-the-nuclear-taboo-and-is-putin-about-to-break-it (accessed May 20, 2023).

Machiavelli, Niccolo, *The Discourses*, trans. Leslie Walker (New York: Penguin Classics, 1983).

Macmillan, Harold, "Official Report of the Sixth Sitting," Council of Europe documents, August 17, 1949, p. 125.

Madison, James, *Federalist Papers* No. 51 in ed. Clinton Rossiter, *The Federalist Papers* (New York: Penguin, 1961).

MagellanTV, "In the Shadow of the Moon," directed by David McNab and Christopher Riley, 2007.

Magnus, Loyold, "The Future of the Nuclear Taboo: Framing the Impact of the TPNW," *Journal for Peace and Nuclear Disarmament* 4, 1 (2021): 100–106, https://doi.org/10.1080/25751654.2021.1940701.

Makower, Joel, "A Powerhouse Corporate Climate Coalition Says, 'We Mean Business,'" *Greenbiz*, 2014, https://www.greenbiz.com/article/powerhouse-corporate-climate-coalition-says-we-mean-business (accessed May 20, 2023).

Malhotra, Aditi, "Assessing Indian Nuclear Attitudes," Stimson Center, 2016, https://www.stimson.org/wp-content/files/file-attachments/Assessing%20Indian%20Nuclear%20Attitudes%20-%20Final.pdf (accessed May 20, 2023).

Mandelbaum, Michael, *The Nuclear Revolution: International Politics before and after Hiroshima* (Cambridge: Cambridge University Press, 1981).

Maniates, Michael, "Individualization: Plant a Tree, Buy a Bike, Save the World?," *Global Environmental Politics* 1, 3 (2001): 33, https://doi.org/10.1162/152638001316881395.

Mann, Michael, Raymond Bradley, and Malcolm Hughes, "Global-Scale Temperature Patterns and Climate Forcing over the Past Six Centuries," *Nature* 392, 6678 (1998): 779–787, https://doi.org/10.1038/33859.

Martin, Lisa and Beth A. Simmons, "Theories and Empirical Studies of International Institutions," *International Organization* 52, 4 (1998): 729–757, https://doi.org/10.1162/002081898550734.

Mathew, Sarah, "Evolution of Human Cooperation," in *International Encyclopedia of the Social & Behavioral Sciences*, 2nd edn, Vol. 11., ed. James D. Wright (Oxford: Elsevier, 2015), pp. 259–266.

Mayne, Richard and John Pinder, *Federal Union: The Pioneers* (New York: St Martin's Press, 1990), Chapter 1.

Mazarr, Michael and Alexander Lennon (eds), *Toward a Nuclear Peace: The Future of Nuclear Weapons* (New York: St Martin's Press, 1991).

Mazower, Mark, *Governing the World: The History of an Idea, 1815 to the Present* (London: Penguin, 2012).

McCormick, John, *The European Superpower* (Basingstoke: Palgrave Macmillan, 2007).

McDougall, Walter A., *The Heavens and the Earth: A political History of the Space Age* (New York: Basic Books, 1985).

McGregor, Ian, "Organising to Influence the Global Politics of Climate Change," School of Management, UTS, Sydney, p. 5, https://opus.lib.uts.edu.au/bitstream/10453/11492/1/2008000811OK.pdf (accessed May 20, 2023).

McKibben, Bill, *The End of Nature* (New York: Random House, 1989).

McNamara, Kathleen R., *The Currency of Ideas: Monetary Politics in the European Union* (Ithaca, NY: Cornell University Press, 1998).

Mearsheimer, John, *The Tragedy of Great Power Politics* (New York: W. W. Norton & Company, 2001).

Melman, Yossi, "Did Israel Ever Consider Using Nuclear Weapons?," *Haaretz*, October 7, 2010, https://www.haaretz.com/1.5122006 (accessed May 20, 2023).

Mérand, Frédéric, "Social Representations in the European Security and Defense Policy," *Cooperation and Conflict* 41, 2 (2006): 131–152.

Meyer, David, *A Winter of Discontent: The Nuclear Freeze and American Politics* (New York: Praeger, 1990).

Meyer, David S. and Robert Kleidman, "The Nuclear Freeze Movement in the United States," *International Social Movement Research* 3 (1991), pp. 231–262.

Mika, Elizabeth, "Who Goes Trump: Tyranny as a Triumph of Narcissism," in *The Dangerous Case of Donald Trump*, ed. Bandy Lee (New York: St Martin's Press, 2019), p. 305.

Milonopoulos, Theo, "How Close Did The United States Actually Get to Using Nuclear Weapons in Vietnam in 1968?," *Texas National Security Review*, 2018, https://

warontherocks.com/2018/10/how-close-did-the-united-states-actually-get-to-using-nuclear-weapons-in-vietnam-in-1968/ (accessed July 4, 2023).

Miłosz, Czesław, "The Captive Mind," 1951, as cited in Anne Applebaum, "History Will Judge the Complicit," June 1, 2020, https://www.anneapplebaum.com/2020/06/01/history-will-judge-the-complicit (accessed May 20, 2023).

Monnet, Jean, *Memoirs*, trans. Richard Mayne (Garden City: Doubleday & Company, Inc. 1978), pp. 273, 281.

Mooney, Chris, *The Republican Brain: The Science of Why They Deny Science—and Reality* (New York: Wiley, 2012).

Moravcsik, Andrew, "Preferences and Power in the European Community: A Liberal Inter-governmentalist Approach," *Journal of Common Market Studies* 31, 4 (1993): 473–524, https://doi.org/10.1111/j.1468-5965.1993.tb00477.x.

Moravcsik, Andrew, "Europe: The Quiet Superpower," *French Politics* 7, 3 (2009): 403–422.

Morgan, Forrest E., "Deterrence and First-Strike Stability in Space: A Preliminary Assessment," *RAND*, 2010. https://www.rand.org/pubs/monographs/MG916.html (accessed July 3, 2023)

Morgenthau, Hans, *Politics among Nations: The Struggle for Power and Peace* (New York: McGraw Hill, 1985).

Mullan, Terrence, "The Corrosion of World Order in the Age of Donald Trump," Council on Foreign Relations, February 13, 2020, https://www.cfr.org/blog/corrosion-world-order-age-donald-trump (accessed May 20, 2023).

Mueller, John, "The Essential Irrelevance of Nuclear Weapons: Stability in the Postwar World," *International Security* 13, 2 (1988): 55–79, https://doi.org/10.2307/2538971.

Mueller, John, *Retreat from Doomsday: The Obsolescence of Major War* (New York: Basic Books, 1989).

Müller, Harald (ed.), *A Survey of European Nuclear Policy, 1985–87* (Houndmills: Macmillan, 1989), p. 7.

Nanos Research, "Poll: 74% of Canadians Support Joining the UN Treaty on the Prohibition of Nuclear Weapons," International Campaign to Abolish Nuclear Weapons, April 8, 2021, https://www.icanw.org/poll_74_of_canadians_support_joining_the_un_treaty_on_the_prohibition_of_nuclear_weapons (accessed May 20, 2023).

NARA, "Speech to the Council of Ministers," September 8, 1952.

NARA, "Speech to the Common Assembly," June 16, 1953.

NARA, "Speech to the Common Assembly," Strasbourg, June 19, 1953.

NARA, "Statement before 'Randall Committee' Investigating United States Foreign Trade Policy," Paris, November 11, 1953.

NASA, "National Aeronautics and Space Act of 1958 (unamended)," 1958, https://history.nasa.gov/spaceact.html (accessed November 21, 2020).

NASA, "Status of US/USSR Bilateral Space Talks," JFK Presidential Archives, National Security Files, Box 334, April 21, 1962.

NASA, "US–USSR Join in Outer Space Program," News Release 62–257, December 5, 1962, as cited in Edward Ezell and Linda Ezell (eds), *The Partnership: A History of the Apollo–Soyuz Test Project*, NASA Special Publication-4209 in the NASA History Series (NASA, 1978), https://history.nasa.gov/SP-4209.pdf (accessed July 4, 2023).

NASA, "NASA News Release: Address by James E. Webb, Administrator NASA," Annual Meeting Texas Mid-Continent Oil and Gas Association. Houston, Texas, JFK Presidential Archives, National Security Files, Box 308, September 25, 1963, p. 15.

NASA, "Post Apollo Earth Orbital Manned Space Flight Program Options to Post Apollo Advisory Group," NASA Archives, Folder 9164, Space Station 1968–1969, February 15, 1968.

NASA Archives, "Letter from T. O. Paine to the President," NASA Archives, File 9165, Space Station 1968–1989, November 7, 1969.

NASA, "Europe to Build Spacelab for U.S. Reusable Space Shuttle," NASA News Release No. 73–191, NASA HQ, Folder 8864, September 24, 1973.

NASA, "Sputnik and the Dawn of the Space Age," January 6, 2019, https://history.nasa.gov/sputnik.html (accessed July 3, 2023).

NASA HQ, "Public Opinions and NASA 1969–1971," NASA HQ Archives, File 6717, 1969–1971.

NASA HQ, "International Space Station US/USSR 1974–1997," File 15523, 1974–1997.

NASA HQ, "Space Station Documentation (1968–69)," NASA HQ Archives, File 9164, 1968–1969.

NASA HQ, "Russian 'Moon' Casts Big Shadow," *Chicago Daily News*, October 7, 1957, NASA HQ Archives File 6737, Public Opinion on Sputnik.

NASA HQ, "U.S. and Russia Announce Talks on Operating Space Station in '80s,'" *New York Times*, May 5, 1977. NASA HQ Archives, p. A 15.

National Resources Defense Council, "About NRDC," 2022, http://nrdc.org/about (accessed December 1, 2022).

National Wildlife Federation, "Our Mission," 2022, http://nwf.org/About-Us/Our-Mission (accessed December 1, 2022).

Nazaryan, Alexander, "How Serious is Russia about Nuclear War?," *Yahoo News*, May 7, 2022, https://news.yahoo.com/how-serious-is-russia-about-nuclear-war-090015298.html (accessed May 20, 2023).

Newsweek, "Federated Europe: A Bold, New Plan," accessible at Jean Monnet Fondation, Lausanne, Paris, record code AMK 4–15, January 30, 1956.

Newell, Peter, *Climate for Change: Non-state Actors and the Global Politics of the Greenhouse* (Cambridge: Cambridge University Press, 2000), pp. 96–122.

The Nobel Prize, "Andrei Sakharov Facts," 2022, https://www.nobelprize.org/prizes/peace/1975/sakharov/facts (accessed November 30, 2022).

The Nobel Prize, "Mohamed Elbaradei," 2022, https://www.nobelprize.org/prizes/peace/2005/elbaradei/facts (accessed November 30, 2022).

The Nobel Prize, "The Nobel Peace Prize 1995," 2022, https://www.nobelprize.org/prizes/peace/1995/summary (accessed May 20, 2023).

The Nobel Prize, "Press Release," 2022, https://www.nobelprize.org/prizes/peace/1982/press-release (accessed November 30, 2022).

"Note sur l'histoire du comite," Jean Monnet Fondation, Lausanne, Paris, record code AMK 1/1/4.

Nowak, Martin A., "Five Rules for the Evolution of Cooperation," *Science* 314, 5805 (2006): 1560–1563, https://doi.org/10.1126/science.1133755.

NPR (National Public Radio), "Lui Xiaobo: 'No Enemies, No Hatred,' Only Courage," *NPR*, February 16, 2012, https://www.npr.org/2012/02/16/146988012/liu-xiaobo-no-enemies-no-hatred-only-courage (accessed May 20, 2023).

Nuclear Threat Initiative, "India–Pakistan Non-Attack Agreement," 2011, https://www.nti.org/education-center/treaties-and-regimes/india-pakistan-non-attack-agreement (accessed May 20, 2023).

Nulman, Eugene, *Climate Change and Social Movements: Civil Society and the Development of National Climate Change Policy* (Basingstoke: Palgrave Macmillan, 2015).

Nye Jr, Joseph S., *Powers to Lead* (Oxford: Oxford University Press, 2010).

Oak Ridge National Laboratory, "Cumulative Global Fossil-Fuel CO_2 Emissions," chart, 2008.

Obama, Barack, "Remarks by the President at the U.S./China Strategic and Economic Dialogue,'" The White House, Office of the Press Secretary, July 7, 2009, https://obamawhitehouse.archives.gov/realitycheck/the-press-office/remarks-president-uschina-strategic-and-economic-dialogue (accessed May 23, 2023).

O'Callaghan, Jonathan, "Goodbye Mars One, The Fake Mission to Mars That Fooled the World," *Forbes*, February 11, 2019, https://www.forbes.com/sites/jonathanocallaghan/2019/02/11/goodbye-mars-one-the-fake-mission-to-mars-that-fooled-the-world/?sh=27c507022af5 (accessed May 20, 2023).

Office of the Historian, "381. National Security Planning Policy Paper, 'Implications of Outer Space in the 1970's,'" Foreign Relations of the United States, 1961–1963, Vol. XXV, Organization of Foreign Policy; Information Policy; United Nations; Scientific Matters, n.d., https://history.state.gov/historicaldocuments/frus1961-63v25/d381 (accessed November 21, 2020).

Office of Technology Assessment, "International Cooperation and Competition in Civilian Space Activities" (Washington, DC: U.S. Congress, Office of Technology Assessment, OTA-ISC-239, July 1985).p. 42. https://ota.fas.org/reports/8513.pdf

Ogunbanwo, Sola, "The Treaty of Pelindaba: Africa Is Nuclear-Weapon-Free," *Security Dialogue* 27, 2 (1996): 185–200, https://doi.org/10.1177/0967010696027002007.

Olsen, Mancur, *The Logic of Collective Action: Public Goods and the Theory of Groups* (Cambridge, MA: Harvard University Press, 1971).

Ord, Toby, *Precipice: Existential Risk and the Future of Humanity* (New York: Hachette Books, 2020).

Parri, Ferrucio (Italy), "Official Report of the Fifteenth Sitting," Council of Europe documents, September 5, 1949, p. 481.

Parsons, Craig, "Showing Ideas as Causes: The Origins of the European Union," *International Organization* 56, 1 (2002): 47–84, p. 51, https://www.jstor.org/stable/3078670 (accessed May 20, 2023).

Paterson, Matthew, "IR Theory: Neo-realism, Neo-institutionalism and the Climate Convention," in *The Environment and International Relations*, ed. John Vogler and Mark Imber (Oxfordshire: Taylor & Francis, 1995), pp. 59–77.

Paul, T. V., *The Tradition of Non-use of Nuclear Weapons* (Stanford, CA: Stanford University Press, 2009).

Paul, T. V., "Taboo or Tradition? The Non-use of Nuclear Weapons in World Politics," *Review of International Studies* 36, 4 (October 2010): 853–863, https://www.jstor.org/stable/40961956 (accessed May 20, 2023).

PBS Space Time, *American Experience*: Space Men, Aired July 9, 2019.

"Peace Pledge Union," as cited in Richard Taylor and Colin Pritchard (PBS Space Time), *The Protest Makers: The British Nuclear Disarmament Movement of 1958–1965, Twenty Years On* (Amsterdam: Elsevier, 1980).

Pelopidas, Benoit, "The Next Generation(S) of Europeans Facing Nuclear Weapons: Forgetful, Indifferent, But Supportive?," *Non-proliferation Papers* 56 (2017): 11.

People's Climate Movement, "To Change Everything, We Need Everyone," 2022, http://peoplesclimate.org/our-movement (accessed December 1, 2022).

Pew Global Attitudes Project, "Pew Global Attitudes Project Poll, Question 5 [31117305.00004]," *Pew Global Attitudes Project*, Abt Associates, Cornell University, Roper Center for Public Opinion Research, 2020.

Pew Research Center, "Spring 2018 Global Attitudes Survey," 2018, Q42 a–f, Washington DC.

Philip, André (France), "Official Report of the Fifth Sitting," Council of Europe documents, August 16ʹ 1949, p. 78.

Pinker, Steven, *The Blank Slate: The Modern Denial of Human Nature* (New York: Penguin Books, 2002), pp. 112–113, 122.

Pinker, Steven, *The Better Angels of Our Nature: Why Violence Has Declined* (New York: Penguin Books, 2011).

Pinker, Steven, "The False Allure of Group Selection," *The Edge*, June 18, 2012, https://www.edge.org/conversation/steven_pinker-the-false-allure-of-group-selection (accessed May 20, 2023).

Pinker, Steven, *Enlightenment Now: The Case of Reason, Science, Humanism, and Progress* (New York: Viking, 2018), pp. 145–155.

Post, Jerrold, "The Charismatic Leader–Follower Relationship," in *The Dangerous Case of Donald Trump*, ed. Bandy Lee (New York: St Martin's Press, 2019), pp. 389–90.

Proctor, Darby and Sarah Brosnan, "Political Primates: What Other Primates Can Tell Us About the Evolutionary Roots of Our Own Political Behavior," in *Man Is by Nature a Political Animal*, ed. Peter K. Hatemi and Rose McDermott (Chicago, IL: University of Chicago Press, 2011), pp. 47–71.

Purkitt, Helen, Stephen Burgess, and Peter Lieberman, "South Africa's Nuclear Decisions," *International Security* 27, 1 (2002): 186–194, https://doi.org/10.1080/13523261003665618.

Pulver, Simone, "Power in the Public Sphere: The Battles between Oil Companies and Environmental Groups in the United Nations Climate Change Negotiations 1991–2003," PhD thesis, University of California Berkeley. 2004, p. 278.

Puttre, Michael, "The Taboo against Great Power War Is Gone," *Discourse*, May 16, 2022, https://www.discoursemagazine.com/politics/2022/05/16/the-taboo-against-great-power-war-is-gone (accessed May 20, 2023).

Rabinowitch, Eugene, "Progress in Space Cooperation with USSR," *Bulletin of the Atomic Scientists*, NASA Archives, File 15570, May 1963.

Rainforest Action Network, "Mission and Values," 2022, http://ran.org/mission-and-values (accessed December 1, 2022).

Rankin, Jennifer, "EU Takes Hungary to ECJ over Crackdown 'Aimed at George Soros,'" *The Guardian*, December 7, 2017, https://www.theguardian.com/world/2017/dec/07/eu-hungary-court-crackdown-george-soros (accessed May 20, 2023).

Reason Podcast, "The Reason Interview with Nicholas Christakis," April, 2019, https://reason.com/podcast/2019/04/05/the-yale-professor-attacked-by-angry-stu (accessed May 23, 2023).

Reinbold, Derek, "In Defense of Political Science Spending," *The Key Reporter*, October 2, 2013, http://www.keyreporter.org/PbkNews/PbkNews/Details/747.html (accessed May 20, 2023).

Rhodes, Ben, *After the Fall: Being American in the World We've Made* (New York: Random House, 2021).

Rietig, Katharina, "The Power of Strategy: Environmental NGO Influence in International Climate Negotiations," *Global Governance* 22, 2 (2016): 269–288, https://www.jstor.org/stable/44861077 (accessed May 20, 2023).

Rifkin, Jeremy, *The Empathic Civilization: The Race to Global Consciousness in a World in Crisis* (New York: TarcherPerigee, 2009).

Rising Tide North America, "Rising Tide North America," 2022, http://actionnetwork.org/groups/rising-tide-north-america (accessed July 4, 2023).

Ritchie, Nick, "Deterrence Dogma? Challenging the Relevance of British Nuclear Weapons," *International Affairs* 85, 1 (2009): 81–98, https://www.jstor.org/stable/27694921 (accessed May 20, 2023).

Robinson, Davis, "The Treaty of Tlatelolco and the United States: A Latin American Nuclear Free Zone," *American Journal of International Law* 64, 2 (1970): 282–309, https://doi.org/10.2307/2198666.

Rose, Frank A., "Safeguarding the Heavens: The United States and the Future of Norms of Behavior in Outer Space," Brookings Policy Brief, June 2018.

Rosewarne, Stuart, James Goodman, and Rebecca Pearse, *Climate Action Upsurge: The Ethnography of Climate Movement Politics* (London and New York: Routledge, 2013), Preface.

Rotblat, Joseph, "Disarmament and World Security Issues at the Pugwash Conferences," in *A New Design for Nuclear Disarmament*, ed. William Epstein and Toyoda Toshiyuki (Nottingham: Pushwash Symposium, 1977), p. 29.

Rotblat, Joseph, "The Present Day Significance of the Russell-Einstein Manifesto," in *A New Design for Nuclear Disarmament*, ed. William Epstein and Toyoda Toshiyuki (Nottingham: Pushwash Symposium, 1977), p. 23.

Rousseau, Jean-Jacques, *The Social Contract*, trans. with an historical and critical introduction and notes by Henry John Tozer (London: Swan Sonnenschein & Co., 1895).

Sadeh, Eligar, "Dynamics of International Space Cooperation: Evaluating Missions for Exploring Space and Protecting the Earth," PhD dissertation, Colorado State University, 1999.

Sagan, Carl, "Pale Blue Dot," speech, Cornell University, 1994.

Sagan, Scott, "Realist Perspectives on Ethical Norms and Weapons of Mass Destruction," in *Ethics and Weapons of Mass Destruction: Religious and Secular Perspectives*, ed. Sohail Hashmi and Steven P. Lee (New York: Cambridge University Press, 2004), pp. 73–95.

Sagan, Scott and Benjamin Valentino. "Revisiting Hiroshima in Iran: What Americans Really Think about Using Nuclear Weapons and Killing Noncombatants," *International Security* 42, 1 (2017): 41–79.

Sagan, Scott D., *The Limits of Safety: Organizations, Accidents, and Nuclear Weapons* (Princeton, NJ: Princeton University Press, 1993).

Sapolsky, Robert, *Behave: The Biology of Humans at Our Best and Worst* (New York: Penguin Press, 2017).

Sapolsky, Robert, "The Biology of Our Best and Worst Selves," Ted conference, 2017, https://www.ted.com/talks/robert_sapolsky_the_biology_of_our_best_and_worst_selves?utm_source=newsletter_weekly_2017-05-14&utm_campaign=newsletter_weekly&utm_medium=email&utm_content=talk_of_the_week_image#t-913951 (accessed May 20, 2023).

Sarotte, Mary, "I'm a Cold War Historian. We Are in a Frightening New Era," *New York Times*, March 1, 2022.

Schelling, Thomas, *The Strategy of Conflict* (Cambridge, MA: Harvard University Press, 1981).

Scherer, John, "Soviet and American Behavior during the Yom Kippur War," *World Affairs* 141, 1 (1978): 3–23.

Schmelzer, Matthias, Aaron Vansintjan, and Andrea Vetter, *The Future is Degrowth: A Guide to a World beyond Capitalism* (New York: Verso, 2022).

Schmidt, Brian C., "On the History and Historiography of International Relations," in *Handbook of International Relations*, ed. Walter Carlsnaes, Thomas Risse, and Beth A. Simmons (London: Sage Publications Ltd, 2013), pp. 3–22.

Schmidt, Vivien, "Discursive Institutionalism: The Explanatory Power of Ideas and Discourse," *Annual Review of Political Science* 11 (2008): 303–326, https://doi.org/10.1146/annurev.polisci.11.060606.135342.

Schreiber, Darren, "Red Brain, Blue Brain: Republicans and Democrats Process Risk Differently, Research Finds," *Science Daily*, February 13, 2013, https://www.sciencedaily.com/releases/2013/02/130213173131.htm (accessed May 20, 2023).

Schwartz, Barry, *The Paradox of Choice: Why More is Less* (New York: Ecco, 2004).

Senate Committee on Aeronautical and Space Sciences, "Excerpts from General Schriver's Testimony before the Subcommittee on Governmental Organization for Space Activities," JFK Presidential Archives. Pre-Presidential Papers #2, Box 568, Folder 3, April 23, 1959.

Serrarens, Jos (Netherlands), "Official Report of the Fifth Sitting," Council of Europe documents (Nobel Peace Archive), August 16, 1949, p. 103.

Shafi, Neeshad, "Young People Are Leading Climate Activism in the Middle East," *Cairo Review of Global Affairs*, Fall 2021, https://www.thecairoreview.com/essays/young-people-are-leading-climate-activism-in-the-middle-east (accessed May 20, 2023).

Sharot, Tali, *The Optimism Bias: A Tour of the Irrationally Positive Brain* (New York: Vintage, 2012).

Sharot, Tali, "The Optimism Bias," TED conference, 2012, https://www.ted.com/talks/tali_sharot_the_optimism_bias#t–648688 (accessed May 20, 2023).

Shayler, David J., "The Proposed USSR Salyut and US Shuttle Docking Mission Circa 1981," presented at the 6th Soviet Space Symposium, British Interplanetary Society, Headquarters, London, June 1, 1991, p. 7.

Siddiqi, Asif A., "Making Spaceflight Modern: A Cultural History of the World's First Space Advocacy Group," in *Societal Impact of Spaceflight*, ed. Steven J. Dick and Roger D. Launius (Washington, DC: NASA Office of External Relations, 2007), pp. 513–537.

Siddiqi, Asif A., "*Sputnik* 50 Years Later: New Evidence on Its Origins," *Acta Astronautica* 63, 1–4 (July–August 2008), https://doi.org/10.1016/j.actaastro.2007.12.042.

Sierra Club, "About the Sierra Club," 2022, http://sierraclub.org/about-sierra-club (accessed December 1, 2022).

Simons, Howard, "Vast US, Red Space Ventures behind JFK Bid," *Washington Post*, NASA Archives, File 15570, September 25, 1963.

Sims, Jennifer, *Icarus Restrained: An Intellectual History of Nuclear Arms Control, 1945–1960* (Boulder, CO: Westview Press, 1990).

Singer, Thomas, "Trump and the American Psyche," in *The Dangerous Case of Donald Trump*, ed. Bandy Lee (New York: St Martin's Press, 2019). p. 278.

Smeltz, Dina and Amir Farmanesh, "Majority of Iranians Oppose Development of Nuclear Weapons," Chicago Council on Global Affairs, 2020, https://www.thechicagocouncil.org/research/public-opinion-survey/majority-iranians-oppose-development-nuclear-weapons (accessed May 20, 2023).

Smith, Sarah, "Feminism," in *International Relations Theory*, ed. Stephen McGlinchey, Rosie Walters, and Christian Scheinpflug (Bristol: E-International Relations Publishing, 2017), pp. 62–68.

Solo, Pam, *From Protest to Policy* (Cambridge: Ballinger Publishing Company, 1988).

Soto, Christopher J., Oliver P. John, Samuel D. Gosling, and Jeff Potter, "Age Differences in Personality Traits from 10 to 65: Big Five Domains and Facets in a Large Cross-Sectional Sample," *Journal of Personality and Social Psychology* 100, 2 (2011), pp. 330–348, https://doi.org/10.1037/a0021717.

Space Foundation, "Space Foundation Updates Appropriations Information," October 2, 2011, https://www.spacefoundation.org/2011/10/02/space-foundation-updates-appropriations-information (accessed May 20, 2023).

Space Foundation, *National Geographic*, July 2019, p. 91.

The Space Report, "Economy," https://www.thespacereport.org/topics/economy/ (accessed July 3, 2023).

Space Station and International Collaboration, "Memorandum from Dr. Alfred Eggers to Dr. Newell," Space Station and International Collaboration, NASA HQ, Folder 9164, March 17, 1969.

The Spinelli Group, "Manifesto for the Future of Europe: A Shared Destiny," Union of European Federalists, 2018, https://www.federalists.eu/fileadmin/files_uef/Spinelli_Group_Page/2018_Manifesto_EN.pdf (accessed May 20, 2023).

The Spinelli Group, "Our Members in the European Parliament," Union of European Federalists, 2020, https://www.federalists.eu/the-group-in-the-european-parliament (accessed December 8, 2020).

The Spinelli Group, "What Is UEF?," Union of European Federalists, 2022, https://www.federalists.eu/uef (accessed May 20, 2023).

Spinney, Laura, "Karma of the Crowd," *National Geographic*, February 2014, pp. 123–135.

Stanley, Morgan, "The Space Economy's Next Giant Leap," https://www.morganstanley.com/Themes/global-space-economy (accessed July 3, 2023).

Stephens, Jennie C. and Nils Markusson, "Technological Optimism in Climate Mitigation: The Case of Carbon Capture and Storage," in *Oxford Handbook of Energy and Society*, ed. Debra J. Davidson, and Matthias Gross (Oxford: Oxford University Press, 2018) pp. 503–518.

Stephenson, Wen, *What We're Fighting For Now Is Each Other: Dispatches from the Front Lines of Climate Justice* (Boston, MA: Beacon Press, 2015), p. ix.

Stockholm International Peace Research Institute, *The Near-Nuclear Countries and the NPT* (Stockholm: Almqvist & Wiksell, 1972).

Stone, Jeremy, "Introduction," in *Seeds of Promise: The First Real Hearings on the Nuclear Arms Freeze*, ed. Randall Forsberg and Alton Frye (Andover, MA: Brickhouse Publishing, 1983), p. vii.

Stone Sweet, Alec and Wayne Sandholtz (eds), "Integration, Supranational Governance, and the Institutionalization of the European Polity," *European Integration and Supranational Governance* 1 (1998), https://doi.org/10.1093/0198294646.001.0001.

Stop Climate Chaos!, "The Stop Climate Chaos Coalition," 2022, http://stopclimatechaos.ie/about (accessed December 1, 2022).

Stroikos, Dimitrios, "Engineering World Society? Scientists, Internationalism, and the Advent of the Space Age," *International Politics* 55, 1 (2018): 73–90, https://doi.org/10.1057/s41311-017-0070-8.

Strub, Harry, "The Theory of Panoptical Control: Bentham's Panopticon and Orwell's Nineteen Eighty-Four," *Journal of the History of the Behavioral Sciences* 25 (1989): 40–59, https://doi.org/10.1002/1520-6696(198901)25:1<40::AID-JHBS2300250104>3.0.CO;2-W.

Suedeld, Peter, Katya Legkaia, and Jelena Brcic, "Changes in the Hierarchy of Value References Associated with Flying in Space," *Journal of Personality* 78, 5 (October 2010): 1411–1436.

Sullivan, Frank, *Assault on the Unknown: The International Geophysical Year* (New York: McGraw Hill Book Company, 1961).

Sunrise Movement, "Who We are," 2022, http://sunrisemovement.org/about (accessed December 1, 2022).

Tajfel, Henri and John C. Turner, "The Social Identity Theory of Intergroup Behavior," *Psychology of Intergroup Relations* 2 (1986): 7–24, https://doi.org/10.4324/9780203505984-16.

Tannenwald, Nina, "Ideas and Explanation: Advancing the Theoretical Agenda," *Journal of Cold War Studies* 7, 2 (Spring 2005): 13–42, https://www.jstor.org/stable/26925808 (accessed May 20, 2023).

Tannenwald, Nina, "Stigmatizing the Bomb: Origins of the Nuclear Taboo," *International Security* 29 (2005): 11, https://www.jstor.org/stable/4137496 (accessed May 25, 2023).

Tannenwald, Nina, *The Nuclear Taboo: The United States and the Non-use of Nuclear Weapons since 1945* (Cambridge: Cambridge University Press, 2007).

Tannenwald, Nina, "The Vanishing Nuclear Taboo? How Disarmament Fell Apart," *Foreign Affairs* 97, 6 (November/December 2018): 16–24.

Tannenwald, Nina, "The Legacy of the Nuclear Taboo in the Twenty-First Century," in *The Age of Hiroshima*, ed. Michael Gordin and G. John Ikenberry (Princeton: Princeton University Press, 2020).

Tass International Service, December 8, 1962, as cited in Edward Ezell and Linda Ezell (eds), *The Partnership: A History of the Apollo-Soyuz Test Project*, NASA Special Publication-4209 in the NASA History Series (NASA, 1978), https://history.nasa.gov/SP-4209.pdf (accessed July 3, 2023).

Taylor, Richard, *Against the Bomb: The British Peace Movement 1958–1965* (Oxford: Clarendon Press, 1988).

Taylor, Richard and Colin Pritchard, *The Protest Makers: The British Nuclear Disarmament Movement of 1958–1965, Twenty Years On* (Oxford: Pergamon Press, 1980).

Teater, Aaron, "Putting Their Money Where Their Mouth Is: The We Mean Business Coalition and the Role of Corporate Governance within the International Climate Regime," *Cornell International Affairs Review* XIII (2019): 72, https://doi.org/10.37513/ciar.v13i1.546.

Theil, Markus, "LGBT Politics, Queer Theory, and International Relations," *E-International Relations*, October 31, 2014, https://www.e-ir.info/2014/10/31/lgbt-politics-queer-theory-and-international-relations (accessed May 20, 2023).

Theriault, Jordan E., Liane Young, and Lisa Feldman Barrett, "The Sense of Should: A Biologically-Based Framework for Modeling Social Pressure," *Physics of Life Reviews* 36 (2021), https://doi.org/10.1016/j.plrev.2020.01.004.

Thompson, Edward and Vaclav Racek, *Human Rights and Disarmament: An Exchange of Letters between E. P. Thompson & Vaclav Racek* (Nottingham: Russell Press, 1981).

Thompson, Edward P., *The Defense of Britain* (London: European Nuclear Disarmament and Campaign for Nuclear Disarmament, 1983).

Thucydides, *The Peloponnesian War*, trans by Martin Hammond, (Oxford: Oxford World's Classics, 2009).

Tickner, Ann, "Gendering a Discipline: Some Feminist Methodological Contributions to International Relations," *Signs: Journal of Women in Culture and Society* 30, 4 (2005): 2174, https://doi.org/10.1086/428416.

Tickner, J. Ann, "You May Never Understand: Prospects for Feminist Futures in International Relations," *Australian Feminist Law Journal* 32, 1 (2010): 9–20.

Tilly, Charles, "Reflections on the History of European State-Making," in *The Formation of National States in Western Europe*, ed. Charles Tilly (Princeton, NJ: Princeton University Press, 2020).

Tilly, Charles, "Social Movements as Historically Specific Clusters of Political Performances," *Berkeley Journal of Sociology* 38 (1993): 1–30, https://www.jstor.org/stable/41035464 (accessed May 20, 2023).

Tilly, Charles and Lesley Wood, *Social Movements 1768–2012*, 3rd edn (New York: Routledge, 2012).

Toffler, Alvin, *Future Shock* (New York: Bantam, 1984).

Toje, Asle, *The European Union as a Small Power: After the Post-Cold War* (Basingstoke: Palgrave Macmillan, 2011).

Tokar, Brian, "Democracy, Localism, and the Future of the Climate Movement," *World Futures* 71, 3–4 (2015): 65–75, https://doi.org/10.1080/02604027.2015.1092785.

Touraine, Alain, "An Introduction to the Study of Social Movements," *Social Research* 52, 4 (1985): 749–787, https://www.jstor.org/stable/40970397 (accessed May 21, 2023).

Touraine, Alain, *Le Mouvement de Mai oule communism utopique* (Paris: Seuil, 1968), as cited in Charles Tilly and Lesley J. Wood, *Social Movements 1768–2012*, 3rd edn (London: Paradigm Publishers, 2013).

Tsebelis, George and Geoffrey Garrett, "The Institutional Foundations of Intergovernmentalism and Supranationalism in the European Union," *International Organization* 55, 2 (2001): 357–390, https://www.jstor.org/stable/3078635 (accessed May 21, 2023).

Trump, Donald, "Speech," Miramar Marine Corps Air Station, March 12, 2018.

Turchin, Peter, *Ultrasociety: How 10,000 Years of War Made Humans the Greatest Cooperators on Earth* (Chaplin, CT: Beresta Books, 2015).

Tversky, Amos and Daniel Kahneman, "Judgement under Uncertainty: Heuristics and Biases," Science 185: 1124–1131, as cited in Steven Pinker, *Enlightenment Now: The Case for Reason, Science, Humanism, and Progress* (New York: Viking Press, 2018), pp. 41–42.

Tversky, Amos and Daniel Kahneman, "Judgement under Uncertainty: Heuristics and Biases," Science 185: 1124–1131, https://doi.org/10.1126/science.185.4157.1124.

UC San Diego, "The Keeling Curve," 2022, https://keelingcurve.ucsd.edu (accessed May 25, 2023).

UNGA (United Nations General Agreement), "Question of the Peaceful Use of Outer Space," UNGA Res. 1348 (XIII), December 13, 1958.

United Nations, "The Paris Agreement," 2015, https://unfccc.int/process-and-meetings/the-paris-agreement/the-paris-agreement (accessed May 20, 2023).

United Nations Conference, "United Nations Conference on Environment and Development," Rio de Janeiro, June 3–14, 1992, https://www.un.org/en/conferences/environment/rio1992 (accessed May 21, 2023).

United Nations, *Status of Multilateral Arms Regulation and Disarmament Agreements*, 3rd edn (New York: United Nations Publications, 1987).

University of Oxford News, "Seven Moral Rules Found All Around the World," February 11, 2019, https://www.ox.ac.uk/news/2019-02-11-seven-moral-rules-found-all-around-world#:~:text=The%20rules%3A%20help%20your%20family,from%20all%20around%20the%20world (accessed May 20, 2023).

University of Toronto, "Personality Predicts Political Preferences," *ScienceDaily*, June 10, 2012, https://www.sciencedaily.com/releases/2010/06/100609111312.htm (accessed May 20, 2023).

Urban Low Emission Development Strategies, "Urban-LEDS: Cities in Action 2012–2016: Final Report Low Emission Development in Brazil, India, Indonesia and South

Africa," 2016, https://e-lib.iclei.org/wp-content/uploads/2016/05/Urban-LEDS-Final-Report-finalbook-web.pdf (accessed July 4, 2023).

USA Today, "USA Today Poll: September 2017. Question 25: USSUFF.100517.R29," *USA Today*, Cornell University, Roper Center for Public Opinion Research, 2017.

US Information Agency, "Potomac Cable No. 244—the US Lead in Space," JFK Presidential Archives, National Security Files, Box 377, October 10, 1962.

USSR International Affairs, "USSR Seeks Accord on Space with US," NASA Archives, File 15570, April 5, 1962.

van der Heijden, Hein-Anton, *Social Movements, Public Spheres and the European Politics of the Environment: Green Power Europe?* (Basingstoke: Palgrave Macmillan, 2020).

V-Dem, "Autocratization Surges—Resistance Grows," Democracy Report, University of Gothenburg, 2020, https://www.v-dem.net/media/filer_public/de/39/de39af54-0bc5-4421-89ae-fb20dcc53dba/democracyreport.pdf (accessed 13 November, 2020).

Vidal, John, "Shell Settlement with Ogoni People Stops Short of Full Justice," *The Guardian*, June 10, 2009, https://www.theguardian.com/environment/cif-green/2009/jun/09/saro-wiwa-shell (accessed May 21, 2023).

von Rucht, Dieter, *Modernisierung und neue soziale Bewegungen* (Frankfurt: Campus, 1994), pp. 76–77, as cited and translated in Matthias Dietz and Heiko Garrelts (eds), *Routledge Handbook of the Climate Change Movement* (London and New York: Routledge, 2014), p. 6.

Wagner, Anna, "Public Opinion on Nuclear Weapons and Arms Control in Russia," in *On the Horizon* (Washington, DC: Center for Strategic and International Studies, 2021), pp. 168–169.

Wahren, Juan, "Youth Activism and Climate Change in Latin America," Global Campus Latin American–Caribbean, Global Campus of Human Rights, 2021, http://doi.org/20.500.11825/2334.

Wall, Mark, "Stephen Hawking Wants to Ride Virgin Galactic's New Passenger Spaceship," *Space.com*, February 20, 2016, https://www.space.com/31993-stephen-hawking-virgin-galactic-spaceshiptwo-unity.html (accessed May 21, 2023).

Wallace, William, "Europe as a Confederation: The Community and the Nation-State," *Journal of Common Market Studies* 21, 1 (1982): pp. 57–68, https://doi.org/10.1111/j.1468-5965.1982.tb00639.x.

Walt, Stephen, *The Origins of Alliances* (Ithaca, NY: Cornell University Press, 1990).

Waltz, Kenneth, *Theory of International Politics* (Long Grove, IL: Waveland Press, 1979).

Waltz, Kenneth N., "Nuclear Myths and Political Realities," *American Political Science Review*, 84, 3 (September 1990): 731–745, https://www.jstor.org/stable/1962764 (accessed May 21, 2023).

Wang, Sheng-Chih, *Transatlantic Space Politics: Competition and Cooperation above the Clouds* (New York, Routledge, 2013), p. 41.

We Mean Business Coalition, "RE100: Renewable Electricity Demand Initiative Growing in Reach And Impact," February 3, 2023, https://www.wemeanbusinesscoalition.org/blog/re100-renewable-electricity-demand-initiative-growing-in-reach-and-impact/ (accessed July 4, 2023)

We Mean Business Coalition, "We are in the Decisive Decade. It's Time to Accelerate Climate Action," 2022, https://www.wemeanbusinesscoalition.org (accessed December 1, 2023).

Wehr, Paul, "Nuclear Pacifism as Collective Action," *Journal of Peace Research* 23, 2 (1986).

Weiss, Thomas G., "What Happened to the Idea of World Government?," *International Studies Quarterly* 53, 2 (2009): 259.

Welyer, Rex, "A Brief History of Environmentalism," Greenpeace, January 5, 2018, https://www.greenpeace.org/international/story/11658/a-brief-history-of-environmentalism (accessed May 21, 2023).

Wesiner, Jerome B., "Memorandum for the President: The US Proposal for a Joint US–USSR Lunar Program," JFK Presidential Archives, National Security Files, Box 308, Space Activities, October 29, 1963.

White, Frank, *The Overview Effect: Space Exploration and Human Evolution, Second Edition* (Reston, V: American Institute of Aeronautics and Astronautics, 1998).

Wildlife and Environmental Society of South Africa, "Our Story, Overview," 2022, http://wessa.org.za/our-story/overview (accessed December 1, 2022).

WILPF (Women's International League for Peace and Freedom), "Generations of Courage: The Women's International League for Peace and Freedom from the 20th Century into the New Millennium," (Philadelphia, PA: WILPF), p. 9.

Wilson, Edward O., *Consilience: The Unity of Knowledge* (New York: Vintage, 1998).

Wilson, Edward O., *The Social Conquest of Earth* (New York: Liveright, 2013), p. 243.

Winter, Frank H., *Prelude to the Space Age: The Rocket Societies: 1924–1940* (Washington, DC: Smithsonian Institution Press, 1983), p. 13.

Wirtz, James J., "How Does Nuclear Deterrence Differ from Conventional Deterrence?," *Strategic Studies Quarterly* 12, 4 (2018): 58–75.

Wittner, Lawrence, *One World or None: A History of the World Nuclear Disarmament Movement through 1953* (Stanford, CA: Stanford University Press, 1993).

Wittner, Lawrence, "The Worldwide Movement against Nuclear Arms: Building an Effective Transnational Organization," *Peace Research* 31, 4 (1999): 19, https://www.jstor.org/stable/23607811 (accessed May 21, 2023).

Wittner, Lawrence S., *Confronting the Bomb: A Short History of the World Nuclear Disarmament Movement* (Stanford, CA: Stanford University Press, 2009).

Workman, Mark, Devon Platt, Uday Reddivari, Bianca Valmarana, Steve Hall, and Rob Ganpatsingh, "Establishing a Large-Scale Greenhouse Gas Removal Sector in the United Kingdom by 2030: First Mover Dilemmas," *Energy Research & Social Science* 88 (2022), https://doi.org/10.1016/j.erss.2022.102512.

World Bank, "Poverty Headcount Ratio at $2.15 a Day (2017 PPP) (% of Population)," n.d., https://data.worldbank.org/indicator/SI.POV.DDAY?end=2018&start=1960&view=map&year=2018 (accessed May 20, 2023).

World Wildlife Fund, "Our Values," 2022, http://worldwildlife.org/pages/our-values (accessed December 1, 2022).

World Population Review, "Nuclear Weapons by Country 2022," *World Population Review*, 2022, https://worldpopulationreview.com/country-rankings/nuclear-weapons-by-country (accessed November 29, 2022).

Wrangham, Richard, *The Goodness Paradox: The Strange Relationship between Virtue and Violence in Human Evolution* (New York: Vintage Books, 2019), p. 9.

Wrangham, Richard and Amy Parish, "Evolution: Why Sex?," WGBH Educational Foundation. Clear Blue Skies Productions (video), 2001, https://www.pbs.org/wgbh/evolution/library/01/5/quicktime/l_015_01.html (accessed May 21, 2023).

Yondorf, Walter, "Monnet and the Action Committee: The Formative Period of the European Communities," *International Organization* 19, 4 (1965): 885–912. https://www.jstor.org/stable/2705648 (accessed May 21, 2023).

Young, Benjamin, "Putin Has a Grimly Absolute Vision of the 'Western World,'" *Foreign Policy*, March 6, 2022, https://foreignpolicy.com/2022/03/06/russia-putin-civilization (accessed May 21, 2023).

Young, Oran R., "International Regimes: Problems of Concept Formation," *World Politics* 32, 3 (1980): 331–356.

Youth Climate Movement, "About Us," 2022, https://youngoclimate.org/about-us/ (accessed July 4, 2023).

Zablocki, Clement J., "Forward," in *The Political Legacy of the International Geophysical Year,* ed. Harold Bullis (Washington, DC: US Government Printing Office, 1973).

Zakaria, Fareed, *The Post-American World* (New York: W. W. Norton & Company, 2008), p. 224.

Zaki, Jamil, *The War for Kindness: Building Empathy in Fractured World* (New York: Broadway Books, 2019), p. 6.

Zaki, Jamil, "We Volunteer to Help Others, But Research Shows How Much It Helps Us, Too," *Washington Post,* January 13, 2020, https://www.washingtonpost.com/health/ we-volunteer-to-help-others-but-research-shows-how-much-it-helps-us-too/2020/01/ 10/7b365ee2-331b-11ea-9313-6cba89bfb_story.html?utm_campaign=wp_main&utm_ medium=social&utm_source=facebook (accessed May 21, 2023).

Zhang, Baohui, "The Security Dilemma in the U.S.–China Military Space Relationship: The Prospects for Arms Control," *Asian Survey* 51, 2 (March/April 2011): 311–332, https:// doi.org/10.1525/as.2011.51.2.311.

Zhao, Yun, "The Role of Bilateral and Multilateral Agreements in International Space Cooperation," *Space Policy* 36 (2016): 12–18, https://doi.org/10.1016/j.spacepol.2016. 02.007.

Further Reading

Acharya, Amitav, "After Liberal Hegemony: The Advent of a Multiplex World Order," *Ethics & International Affairs* 31, 3 (2017): 271–285, https://doi.org/10.1017/ S089267941700020X.

Ackmann, Martha, "She Would Have Been the First American Woman in Space. Congress Held Her Back," *Washington Post,* April 25, 2019, https://www.washingtonpost.com/ opinions/2019/04/25/she-would-have-been-first-american-woman-space-congress- held-her-back (accessed May 22, 2023).

Alford, John R. and John R. Hibbing, "The Origin of Politics: An Evolutionary Theory of Political Behavior," *Perspectives on Politics* 2, 4 (2004): 712, https://www.jstor.org/stable/ 3688539 (accessed May 22, 2023).

Bulletin of the Atomic Scientists, "The Doomsday Clock: A Timeline of Conflict, Cul- ture, and Change," *Bulletin of the Atomic Scientists,* n.d., http://thebulletin.org/timeline (accessed May 22, 2023).

Caplan, Bryan, *Selfish Reasons to Have More Kids: Why Being a Great Parent Is Less Work and More Fun Than You Think* (New York: Basic Books, 2012).

Christakis, Nicholas, *Blueprint: The Evolutionary Origins of a Good Society* (New York: Little Brown, 2019).

Christakis, Nicholas, "Blueprint: Evolutionary Origins of a Good Society," lecture delivered for the Beckman Institute, October 7, 2021.

Cross, Mai'a K Davis, "The Social Construction of the Space Race," *International Affairs* 95, 6 (November 2019): 1403–1421, https://doi.org/10.1093/ia/iiz190.

Cross, Mai'a K. Davis and Saadia Pekkanen (eds), "Space Diplomacy," The Hague Journal of Diplomacy, Special Issue, 18, 2–3 (2023). https://brill.com/view/journals/hjd/18/2-3/ hjd.18.issue-2-3.xml

Detsch, Jack, "Biden Looks for a New, New START," *Foreign Policy*, 2021, https://foreignpolicy.com/2021/06/22/biden-putin-russia-arms-control-new-start (accessed May 22, 2023).

"Earth Citizen Pledge," in *Waging Peace in the Nuclear Age: Ideas for Action*, ed. David Krieger and Frank Kelly (Santa Barbara, CA: Capra Press, 1988)

Energy and Climate Intelligence Unit, "Net Zero Scoreboard," 2022, p. 15, https://eciu.net/netzerotracker (accessed May 22, 2023).

Garenmayeh, Ellie, "Iran, the US, and the Nuclear Deal: Biden's Chance to Remove Trump's Poison Pill," European Council on Foreign Relations, 2022, https://ecfr.eu/article/iran-the-us-and-the-nuclear-deal-bidens-chance-to-remove-trumps-poison-pill (accessed May 21, 2023).

Garrison, Dee, *Bracing for Armageddon: Why Civil Defense Never Worked* (Oxford: Oxford University Press, 2006).

Japan Society for Aeronautical and Space Sciences, "President's Message," 2020, https://www.jsass.or.jp/webe/society/57 (accessed November 26, 2020).

Kagan, Robert, "The Twilight of the Liberal World Order," The Brookings Institution, January 24, 2017, https://www.brookings.edu/research/the-twilight-of-the-liberal-world-order (accessed May 21, 2023).

Pachauri, Rajendra and Leo Meyer (eds), "Climate Change 2014: Synthesis Report," The Intergovernmental Panel on Climate Change, 2014, https://www.ipcc.ch/site/assets/uploads/2018/05/SYR_AR5_FINAL_full_wcover.pdf (accessed May 22, 2023).

Peterson, Michael J., *International Regimes for the Final Frontier* (New York: State University of New York Press, 2005).

Rifkin, Jeremy, *The Empathic Civilization: The Race to Global Consciousness in a World in Crisis* (New York: TarcherPerigee, 2009).

Sagan, Scott and Kenneth Waltz, *The Spread of Nuclear Weapons: A Debate Renewed*, 2nd edn (New York: W. W. Norton, 2002).

Simpson, Emile, "This is How the Liberal World Order Ends," *Foreign Policy*, February 19, 2016, https://foreignpolicy.com/2016/02/19/this-is-how-the-liberal-world-order-ends (accessed May 22, 2023).

Sullivan, Frank, *Assault on the Unknown: The International Geophysical Year* (New York: McGraw Hill Book Company, 1961).

Turchin, Peter, *Ultra-Society: How 10,000 Years of War Made Humans the Greatest Cooperators on Earth* (Chaplin, CT: Beresta Books, 2016).

Walt, Stephen M., "The Collapse of the Liberal World Order," *Foreign Policy*, June 26, 2016, https://foreignpolicy.com/2016/06/26/the-collapse-of-the-liberal-world-order-european-union-brexit-donald-trump (accessed May 22, 2023).

Waltz, Kenneth, "The Spread of Nuclear Weapons: More May Be Better: Introduction," *The Adelphi Papers* 21, 171 (1981): 1, https://doi.org/10.1080/05679328108457394.

White, Frank, *The Overview Effect: Space Exploration and Human Evolution* (Reston, VA: American Institute of Aeronautics and Astronautics, 1988).

Wittner, Lawrence, *Confronting the Bomb: A Short History of the World Nuclear Disarmament Movement* (Stanford, CA: Stanford University Press, 2009), p. 10.

Index

Tables are indicated by an italic *t* following the page number.